The Internationalization of the
Japanese Economy, Second Edition

THE INTERNATIONALIZATION OF THE JAPANESE ECONOMY
Second Edition

CHIKARA HIGASHI
Member, House of Representatives, Tokyo
Chairman of the Board and
President, Temple University, Japan

G. PETER LAUTER
School of Government and Business Administration
The George Washington University
Washington, D.C. 20052
USA

KLUWER ACADEMIC PUBLISHERS
Boston/Dordrecht/London

Distributors for North America:
Kluwer Academic Publishers
101 Philip Drive
Assinippi Park
Norwell, Massachusetts 02061 USA

Distributors for all other countries:
Kluwer Academic Publishers Group
Distribution Centre
Post Office Box 322
3300 AH Dordrecht, THE NETHERLANDS

Library of Congress Cataloging-in-Publication Data

Higashi, Chikara.
    The internationalization of the Japanese economy/Chikara
  Higashi, G. Peter Lauter. — [2nd ed.]
        p.   cm.
    Includes bibliographical references.
    ISBN 0-7923-9052-0
    1. Japan—Economic conditions—1945- 2. Japan—Economic
  policy—1945- 3. Japan—Foreign economic relations. I. Lauter,
  Geza P. (Geza Peter) II. Title.
  HC462.9.H45   1990
  337.52—dc20   89–20081
                                                       CIP

Printed in the United States of America

Contents

List of Tables and Figures

TABLES

Figures

Acknowledgments

Much of the information and insight presented in this book was obtained through personal interviews particularly with Japanese and, to a lesser extent, American government officials and business executives in Tokyo and Washington, D.C. While they are too numerous to mention individually, their willingness to take time out of their busy schedules is very much appreciated.

Mr. Donald Kopka and Ms. Scheherazade Rehman, both Ph.D. candidates at the School of Government and Business Administration of The George Washington University, provided invaluable support in preparing this second edition. They not only assisted in preparing the manuscript but Mr. Kopka also wrote the section on domestic consumer market trends while Ms. Rehman wrote the chapter on financial deregulation as well as the sections on research and development and the changing corporate strategies.

Foreword

In the first, 1987, edition of this book, Dr. Higashi and Dr. Lauter have discussed and analyzed the initial stages of the internationalization process

The authors with Michio Watanabe at a reception in Hakone, Japan, 1988.

of the Japanese economy as it had evolved between 1985 and 1986. In this, the second, edition, they explore the developments during 1985–1988 and show how the gradual transformation of the economy from export-led to domestic demand-led growth has taken place, what the results of the transformation process are, what remaining problems still have to be resolved, and what directions the Japanese economy might take in the future.

While the transformation process is by no means completed, Drs. Higashi and Lauter provide a broad, policy-analysis based overview that enables the reader to understand not only the economic but also the basic political and social issues involved in the internationalization process. In this sense, the authors stay away from the extreme positions that characterize so many of the publications on Japan today and attempt to provide a realistic view of the changes and the impact of these changes. I believe that this book is a fair and balanced representation of events.

> Michio Watanabe, Chairman
> LDP Policy Affairs Research Council 1988–1989
> Tokyo, May 1989
>
> Minister of International Trade and
> Industry, December 1985–July 1986
>
> Minister of Finance
> July 1980–November 1982

The Internationalization of the
Japanese Economy, Second Edition

1 THE PATH TO ECONOMIC POWER

Japan, known around the world as a small, resource-poor island country, has experienced a greater than tenfold increase in its gross national product (GNP) in real terms since 1950. Annual growth rates ranging from 10 percent during the 1960s to approximately 3-4 percent in the 1980s have not only resulted in continually increasing world GNP shares but will also enable Japan to match the Soviet Union as the second largest economy behind the United States by the beginning of the twenty-first century.

The statistics on United States-Japan bilateral trade reported in this book were obtained from both American and Japanese sources. Any discrepancy between the two sets of data is the result of the differing calculating methods used.

The U.S. Department of Commerce reports imports (Japanese exports) on a CIF (cost, insurance, and freight) basis, whereas Japan reports its custom-cleared exports on an FOB (free on board) basis, which excludes insurance and freight costs.

Because of exchange rate fluctuations, monetary amounts were changed into yen or dollars as indicated by the prevailing exchange rate or by the year in which the transactions took place.

TABLE 1-1.   World GNP shares of selected countries and regions:
1960–2000 (in percentages)

Country	World GNP share		
	1960	1980	2000
Japan	3	10	12
USA	33	22	20
Other OECD countries	26	31	26
Industrial countries	62	63	58
NICs*	3	4	7
LDCs	11	11	13
Developing countries	14	15	20
USSR	15	13	12
Eastern Europe	4	5	5
China	5	4	5
Communist Bloc	24	22	22
World, total	100	100	100

 * NICs = Newly industrializing countries (Republic of Korea, Hong Kong, Singapore, Brazil, Mexico, and Taiwan).
   Source: *Japan 1986: An International Comparison* (Tokyo: Keizai Koho Center, 1986), p. 8.

Table 1–1 shows the past and projected world GNP shares between 1960 and the year 2000.

This remarkable growth in Japan's economy was characterized by a rapid increase in export activity. In 1965 Japan's world export share was approximately 5 percent, and by 1985 its share exceeded 10 percent; during the same 20 year period, the United States' share decreased from 16 percent to approximately 11 percent. Japanese exporters established major world market shares while global economic growth decreased in real terms from 4.4 percent during 1970–1975, to 3.9 percent between 1975–1980, to approximately 3 percent by 1980. Japanese exports increased significantly as a percentage of imports by all Organization for Economic Cooperation and Development (OECD) countries between 1978 and 1983 particularly in advanced products as shown in table 1–2. It is noteworthy that these years were marked by generally low growth rates in most member countries.

As Japan's export market shares increased, current and trade account surpluses began to emerge during the second half of the 1960s, then became persistent and grew rapidly, particularly during the early 1980s. The Japanese current account surplus reached $24.2 billion in FY 1983, $37

TABLE 1-2. Japanese exports of advanced products as a percentage of
OECD imports: 1978 and 1983

Product	Year	
	1978	1983
Computers	5.2	18.0
Office machines	43.8	58.3
Telecommunications equipment	26.5	41.8
Stereos, televisions, VCRs, etc.	50.6	99.3

Source: *OECD Commodity and Trade Statistics* (Paris: Organization for Economic Cooperation and Development, issues 1975 through 1984).

billion in FY 1984, and $50 billion in FY 1985 which represented 3.7 percent
of GNP, and was, thus, larger than the Federal Republic of Germany's
postwar high of 2.7 percent achieved in 1974, and matched the U.S. record
of 3.7 percent set in 1947, shortly after World War II when the United States
dominated the world economy.[1]

Not surprisingly, such a performance generated a proliferation of literature attempting to explain this economic phenomenon. One extreme of this
literature is represented by such an adulatory work as *Japan as Number
One*, whereas the opposite extreme is represented by a book as hostile as
The Japanese Conspiracy.[2] Between these two extremes is a mixed bag
of publications dealing mostly with the sociocultural and managerial
dimensions of the Japanese success story. While these publications provide
some interesting insights, the authors' extreme or limited positions make
it difficult to obtain a reasonable and comprehensive understanding of the
Japanese experience.

There are, however, three recent books with differing but complementary
approaches that represent the best of the genre to date.[3] *The Competition:
Dealing With Japan* by Pepper, Janow, and Wheeler, of the Hudson
Institute, examines the macroeconomic issues surrounding Japan's growth,
while *Kaisha: The Japanese Corporation* by James C. Abegglen and George
Stalk, Jr., analyzes the microeconomic aspects of Japan's post-World War
II economic performance. *Japan in the World Economy* by Bela Balassa and
Marcus Noland is the first comprehensive analysis of the international
implications of the Japanese economic achievements. The authors argue that
unless the Japanese do away with a number of distorting domestic economic
policies, their external balances will continue to create problems for the rest
of the world in general and the United States in particular. They suggest
reforms in the tax system, land use policy, working hours, and other areas

to reduce the nation's external surpluses while improving the quality of life of its people. It is interesting to note that a number of their arguments and recommendations are similar to those developed and proposed by the Maekawa Commission in its 1986 and 1987 reports. But in contrast to the Commission, Balassa and Noland tend to ignore the political feasibility of some of their recommendations and, thus, while making a sound economic argument, reduce the practical relevance of their suggestions.

Nonetheless, together these three books provide an insightful analysis of Japan's evolution into an economic force, the implications of this evolution for other nations and of the possible measures through which it can fulfill its responsibilities as a global economic power.

Objectives of this Book

During 1985–1989 important developments took place in Japan. Partially in response to multilateral and bilateral pressures generated by the persistent current account surpluses, and partially as a result of self-initiated soul-searching aimed at a redefinition of the country's role in the twenty-first century, these years have generated much discussion about the nation's future, particularly in 1985 and 1986, and about economic policy changes, such as tax reform, in 1987 and 1988. New "visions" of the future— programs and reports as, for example, the original 1986 and 1987 follow-up Maekawa Commission reports, and a number of other studies—identified the basic issues in need of consideration and resolution. Although responsible politicians, government officials, business leaders, and aca-demicians, all of whom are so-called internationalists, agree that Japan's new status as an economic power calls for a revised global role and the assumption of a whole new set of responsibilities, many Japanese do not yet fully appreciate their country's impact on the world economy. They still see Japan as vulnerable and unique believing that their country should be treated as a special case among the world's nations. Others believe that Japan alone is asked to endure fundamental and often painful economic adjustments to please other nations suffering from symptoms of "advanced industrial nation's disease" such as the decline in international competitiveness due to low industrial productivity, high wages, prodigious spending habits, and a craving for leisure and comfort istead of working hard and saving for the future. Some express resentment over the fact that other nations never seem to consult Japan on anything except trade issues, and then only to lecture the Japanese about their "unfairness" or what they need to do to satisfy the demands of others. These views became especially pronounced during 1987–

1989 when, in spite of international and domestic claims of rapidly rising affluence, Japanese complaints about economic problems, such as rapidly increasing housing costs, heavy mortgage repayments, rising education costs, and social security contributions, were becoming more frequent and noticeable. This is particularly true among those who until recently saw themselves as members of a vast middle class with annual incomes up to approximately $70,000 in 1987–1988. In spite of the increasing national wealth and the appreciating yen; these Japanese do not understand why their standard of living is not reflecting the widespread characterizations of Japan as the world's wealthiest nation and are beginning to view themselves as members of an increasingly more stratified middle class with widening differences in the standard of living. Therefore, there is disagreement within Japan not only concerning the necessity to redefine the nation's international role but particularly with regard to who is going to pay the cost of the readjustment. Not surprisingly, those with vested interests and much to lose as, for example, the farmers, are the most vocal; but gradually even the previously "silent majority" of Japanese wage earners is also beginning to ask questions to which no satisfactory answers are forthcoming. The 1988 "Recruit" insider-trading stock scandal and the introduction of what most Japanese consider a regressive, 3-percent value-added (consumption) tax as part of the comprehensive 1988 tax-reform act, has added to the increasing dissatisfaction of large segments of society.

Most people, nonetheless, understand that something needs to be done. In a poll conducted by the New York Times, CBS news, and the Tokyo Broadcasting System in the spring of 1986, 62 percent of the Japanese agreed that their country is now a world economic power with international responsibilities; only 31 percent disagreed.[4] Informed people also understand that past attempts of pursuing only a balance between domestic demand and exports to reduce the huge current account surpluses are not realistic, because given the income elasticity of Japanese exports (1.7) and that of imports (0.7), such a policy would require domestic economic growth three of four times that of the world economy over extended periods of time to generate enough imports to balance the surpluses. Thus, in addition to the establishment of more stable and realistic exchange rates through the coordination of national economic policies by the major industrial nations, Japan needs to achieve a balanced combination of higher imports, increased foreign investment and aid, as well as growth of domestic demand to reduce the surpluses and to develop a new international role.

The objective of this book is to explore the nature of the domestic and international policy options the Japanese have chosen to internationalize their economy, to point out the problems associated with their implementation, and to review the results through the first half of 1989.[5] The word *internationalization (kokusaika)* lacks conceptual clarity, and by 1988 it had become a sort of buzzword. Nonetheless, its basic meaning is simple and straightforward: it refers to the switch from export-led to domestic demand-led economic growth, the gradual diminution of Japan's "uniqueness," and the sharing of the burdens of maintaining free trade and a growing world economy together with the United States and the European Community.

The 1985 Action Program, the 1986 original and the 1987 follow-up Maekawa Commission reports, and the various related "visions" of the future published in 1985 and 1986 are used as the framework for discussion. The program, reports, and visions were selected because they represent the different aspects of the internationalization process as it is taking place. The 1985 Action Program was import-oriented, and it was formulated primarily in response to strong foreign, particularly American, pressure. The 1986 Maekawa Commission Report was the result of both external pressures and a genuine, comprehensive domestic soul-serching process initiated by the internationalists under the leadership of then Prime Minister Yasuhiro Nakasone. The 1987 follow-up report provided a more detailed and expansive explanation of the overall recommendations of the Commission. The visions, such as the 1986 Ministry of International Trade and Industry (MITI) report on "Japan in the Global Community: Its Role and Contribution on the Eve of the Twenty-First Century," were produced to stimulate ideas in the then emerging society-wide debate.

In addition, the major events in Japan and the United States that have led to the 1985–1989 developments are also explored, as are the domestic controversies surrounding the internationalization process. The focus of this book is on Japan, but because the United States is its most important trading partner and the guarantor of its national security, the evolution of U.S.–Japan trade relations as they have led to a variety of American demands upon Japan to change its economic ways are also included in this discussion.

It is, however, not within the purview of this book to speculate about the "winners" and "losers" in the international economic arena of the future. International economic competition is not static nor is it a zero-sum game. While government policies are important influencing factors, and beyond a certain volume foreign direct investment raises justifiable questions, conspiratorial explanations of government business relations and xenophobic responses to foreign capital are not helpful in explaining what is happening in the world economy. A number of authors of a recent spade of books dealing either directly or indirectly with Japan have developed a set of propositions of questionable validity concerning the change processes in the global economy, foreign investment in the United States, and the

Japanese society[6]. However, nations do not "trade places," the "buying into America" is based on rational economic considerations and helps sustain the U.S. economy in the era of the twin-deficits and a political culture that discourages hard decisions. Most of all, as unacceptable as many of Japan's traditions may be to outsiders, the nation is not governed by an unidentifiable "System" that is devoid of a political power center and that manipulates the people. Its "unelected power centers," the various interest groups such as the farmers and others, are also well organized pressure groups in other nations as, for example, the European Community. While it is wrong and unfair to call these and other critical authors "Japan bashers," most of them have provided a simplistic picture of the global economic processes and of Japan. One does not have to buy the "uniqueness" argument every time the Japanese respond to outside criticism to acknowledge that in many respects Japan, for better or worse, is indeed quite different from the rest of the world. Referred to as "revisionists" in America, some of these authors even argue that Japan is not developing into a more open economy but . . ." is driven by economic conquest and must be treated with different rules."[7] No doubt, many of Japan's traditional political, economic and even social attributes and practices create problems for trade relations with the rest of the world in general and America in particular. In assuming its new role as a major global economic force, Japan will have to adjust or give up many of these attributes and practices without, however, giving up its national identity. But to argue that such changes must result in an American type economy regardless of what the Japanese believe works best for them, is as presumptuous as the proposition that the United States must become more like Japan if it wants to regain its economic strength. Moreover, the argument that the Japanese internationalization process is only fancy window-dressing leading to no change at all, ignores the mounting evidence indicating that fundamental changes are taking place, although they may be slow, controversial at home and not always what critics abroad want.

Scare scenarios prognosticating the downfall of America and the increasing, always harmful dominance of Japan also abound. In a book on Japan's "financial threat" to the United States, the author projected a scenario in which the newly elected American President repudiates the nation's debt to Japan in 2004. He does so because America is heavily indebted to Japan, the Japanese own a great deal of American industry and real estate, interest rates soar, a new oil shock is plaguing the world, the Japanese dominate all critical technology industries, and ". . . finally, in the tradition of Japan's many fanatical campaigns, the whole country will be thrown into a massive rearmament drive."[8] In the meanwhile, America's influence and standard of living are plunging. Although the author mentions that at present all of this is fictitious, he argues that a number of the assumed trends are already under way and, thus, the scenario is not beyond the realm of possibility. While such prognostications convey a sense of reality because undoubtedly some of the events assumed are, to a variable degree, happening, their uninterrupted convergence by the year 2004 cannot be taken seriously. What this author, and others, conveniently ignore is the high degree of interdependence that has evolved between the two nations. The Japanese and, for that matter, other nations have a vested interest in not only a healthy and growing global but also American economy. To put it bluntly, creditors and foreign investors are just about as much captives of borrowers and host countries as the latter may be of the former.

The increasing economic interdependence through capital movements, trade, foreign direct investment, traditional joint-ventures, new types of corporate strategic alliances in high-tech industries, and the formation of trade-blocks is going to cause all kinds of major and minor economic disagreements among the United States, Japan, and the post-1992 European Community. However, if nothing else, a realistic sense of self-interest requires that the Japanese and the Europeans help maintain a healthy and free-trade-oriented America. To exert economic pressure on the United States to an extent that these aims could be undermined would be self-defeating.

Prognostications of Japan's becoming more than an economic power and obtaining some kind of stranglehold over America as well as the claims of a rapid and unstoppable decline of America as a political and economic force make for captivating headlines; they sell books and provide titillating topics for TV talk-show hosts. It is, of course, true that the United States faces economic problems and that a readjustment of global economic relations involving Japan, the United States, and Western Europe, i.e., the European Community, is taking place, with the relative positions changing in favor of Japan. However, forces moving the world economy and individual nations are too complex and still not well understood enough to justify the simplistic claims and predictions so widespread today. Among other things, it is not nations but industries and firms that compete in global or individual markets; the magnitude and impact of often speculative capital movements are as important, if not more so, than trade flows as far as external balances are concerned. Fluctuating exchange rates make nations and businesses appear richer or poorer almost overnight; technological breakthroughs in a few key industries can unsettle competitive positions in short order; and the standards used to develop country-rankings are woefully inadequate and, more often than not, misleading. A few illustrations of the source of distortions are per capita income figures not adjusted for purchasing power, America's debtor position not corrected for the valuation of past American investments at market and not original cost, exchange rate movements, comparisons that do not take into account the law preventing U.S. banks from doing business across state lines and bank profitability, and which do not consider the unwillingness of numerous high-tech companies to patent their inventions because they want to keep them as "trade secrets." The historian Paul Kennedy's arguments that the global political and economic realignment is part of a long historical process whose final outcome is not yet clear are far more convincing than what the doomsday-scenario writers have postulated.[9]

It should also be noted that national wealth and a strong economy are necessary but not sufficient conditions of international political and economic leadership. Japan is already a formidable global economic force and will be even more so in the future. It is a nation already demanding more influence in global economic matters, and in many ways it is also more difficult to deal with, because with increased economic strength comes not only increased self-confidence but also occasional arrogance and high-handedness. But it is difficult to see Japan as replacing the United States as one of the two superpowers. America's military might, $5-trillion-plus economy, rich natural resources, and, in spite of counterclaims, still strong technological base, flexible political and social system, as well as huge reservoir of human resources cannot be so readily overcome. Moreover, the predictions of a Japanese drive for international political and economic leadership are based on the false premise that the Japanese want such leadership in the first place. Anyone acquainted with modern-day Japan knows that, apart from some possibly noisy extremists, the overwhelming majority of Japanese do not believe in a global mission for their nation, a condition that has to be met by any aspiring superpower.

What the Japanese aspire to is a larger role in the world economy as a "co-leader" of the United States and of the post-1992 European Community. Such ambitions are not only justified but necessary from the global point of view in general and the viewpoint of the United States in particular. Japan must take on more of the burden of re-establishing balanced global economic relations because only through the cooperation of the great powers can this task be accomplished. The problems at hand are too large and complex for the United States even to attempt to solve by itself as it often did in the post-World War II era when it dominated the world economy to such an extent that it caused discomfort and unease in many parts of the globe.

Undoubtedly, the Japanese aspiration to become co-leader is causing unease and discomfort in many parts of the world today. According to a 1986 survey of the *Nihon Keizai Shimbun* (The Japan Economic Journal), most people in the United States and Western Europe see Japan as an economic threat, although they think that the Japanese are a friendly people.[10] Given a list of 30 countries from which to choose international competitors posing an economic threat to their nations, respondents in the United States, the United Kingdom, France, and the Federal Republic of Germany chose Japan as the country that most concerns them. Japan was seen as the number 2 and 3 economic threat, respectively, in Canada and Italy. In other words, people throughout the world see Japan as practicing a single-minded and narrowly defined economic nationalism at the expense of the rest of the globe. Thus, a better appreciation abroad of Japan's domestic and international policy options in redefining its global role and the problems surrounding their implementation is far more important than predictions of who is going to be *Ichiban* (Number One) in the years to come. It is true that the Japanese are a very competitive people, and most of them believe in rankings of any kind. Undoubtedly, international economic competition is going to get tougher in the future, and in numerous industries the Japanese will be in the forefront of this competition. However, an increasingly large number of thoughtful Japanese are beginning to recognize that what the world needs is not economic domination by any nation but more effective multilateral cooperation or, in other words, a Japan that is known for its willingness to resolve economic problems together with others rather than for its single-minded and narrow economic nationalism.

Such a Japan is on the way. While the transformation process may be too sluggish and not transparent enough for many Americans and Europeans, the objectives, the pace and the nature of the internationalization process is for the Japanese to decide. Neither "Japan-bashing" nor unqualified support of what the Japanese are doing helps the process. What is needed abroad is constructive criticism tempered by the acknowledgement that Japan can become a responsible member of the world-economy while retaining its national identity however the Japanese define such identity. Anything less will only create problems for Japan and the rest of the world.

As indicated previously, the internationalization process is controversial. Quick and easy changes should not be expected. The process will extend over a number of years and will be marked by more debates, marginal changes, trial and error, and probably even some retreats. Many of the proposed policy options touch on fundamental values and call for wrenching adjustments within the Japanese society. Moreover, the rapid appreciation of the yen during 1987–1988 has unleashed economic forces that are contributing to the internationalization process, but at the same time are also creating a new set of domestic problems which need to be considered. To minimize these problems or to see the uneven progress as a clever plot either to delay the inevitable or perhaps not change anything at all, underestimates the difficulties associated with altering deeply ingrained habits and addressing new socioeconomic problems anywhere, let alone in a strongly tradition-bound society such as Japan.

The views expressed within some American and Western European political and business circles, that Japan's internationalization process represents fancy windowdressing since it will not quickly eliminate Japan's large current account and trade surpluses, are based on unrealistic expectations. The objective of the internationalization process is not to eliminate such imbalances *per se*, but to establish a more balanced multilateral trade environment in which both the benefits and the burdens of free trade are more equitably shared by all participants, including Japan. In such an environment, excessive long-term current account and trade imbalances will be less likely, and whenever they occur, they will be addressed through a more rational discourse than is presently the case. This, of course, assumes that in addition to Japan's internationalizing its economy the United States is going to address the problems of its "twin-deficits," the European Community resists the temptation of creating an inward-looking integrated market by 1993, and the sputtering Uruguay round of GATT (General Agreement on Tariffs and Trade) negotiations lead to, at least, a partial success.

The Evolution of the Japanese Economy

To discuss the domestic and international policy options chosen by the Japanese to internationalize the economy, it is first necessary to provide an overview of the evolution of Japan's post-World War II economy.

Japan entered its era of rapid economic growth at a time when the mass-production methods in a number of key industries, such as automobiles and consumer durables, began to mature, and worldwide demand for such products was strong. At the same time, the establishment of the GATT provided an environment in which nations could practice free trade. This was made possible by the enlightened economic leadership of the United States which, partially out of self-interest and partially out of the recognition that a 1930s-type protectionist environment could easily result in another economic disaster, convinced most nations of the noncommunist world that free trade benefits everyone.

Two countries that made the most of the new international economic environment are the Federal Republic of Germany and Japan. Free of any big politico-military ambitions and protected by U.S. military power in the East — West cold war, both nations devoted their considerable talents and energies to rebuilding their economies and continual development.[11] In a relatively short period of time, Germany and then Japan became formidable international competitors. For the former, this essentially meant the re-establishment of a pre-World World II position, but for Japan, it meant breaking new ground.

While for a long time it was fashionable to explain the rapid growth and continually improving international competitiveness of the postwar Japanese economy through the "Japan Inc." concept, recent analyses have revealed that more complex forces have been at work.[12] Undoubtedly, Japan did have a national strategy to develop its economy; this strategy consisted of goals, ideas on how to accomplish those goals, and specific policies and institutions needed to implement the ideas. However, as indicated in an insightful study of international competitiveness, "... key differences in strategies do not appear to be between those that are more coherent and those that are less so, but between those that are growth/pro-ductivity/opportunity oriented on the one hand and those that are distribu-tion/security/resources oriented on the other."[13] In other words, while close and systematic cooperation between business and government was important, the key elements in Japan's economic success were the strong growth and productivity orientation of both government and business. The validity of this argument can be demonstrated by simply considering the large number of nations whose close government — business relations did not produce the same results as occurred in Japan, because the growth-productivity orientation was absent. Abegglen and Stalk make the same point at the micro level.[14] According to them, it was primarily the growth orientation of the *kaisha* nurtured by strong domestic competition, that made the Japanese corporations such formidable international competitors, and not what others saw as "unfair" competitive practices.

This growth-productivity orientation was based on what Scott calls "the dynamic (revised) theory of comparative advantage" which the Japanese introduced, and which today is followed by a number of the newly indus-trializing countries (NICs), such as South Korea and Brazil.[15] According to the classical notion of comparative advantage, a country's resources are given, change very slowly over time, and once fully used, lead to increasing costs. Not subscribing to such a static view of the world economy, the Japanese decided to alter their "given" comparative advantage, labor. By creating other critical resources, such as technology, and by fully exploiting the benefits of the learning curve and the economies of scale of production, they quickly became internationally competitive in a number of selected industries. Simply stated, the Japanese did not accept the proposition that more than 100 million able and highly motivated people subscribing to a common set of values should be limited to the exploration of their "given" comparative advantage. The Japanese envisioned more for their country than simply specializing in labor-intensive products for the indefinite future. They did not accept the low standard of living and the chronic balance of payment deficits which the classical theory of comparative advantage ordains for those nations less fortunately endowed with resources.

Altering the "given" comparative advantage and enhancing the growth-productivity orientation called for an active government policy role. Growth areas needed to be identified, capital allocated, technology obtained, various means of increasing productivity had to be developed, and markets needed to be secured. This was done through a variety of measures that collectively became known as industrial policies. The following is an outline of these policies as they were applied in Japan from the early 1950s until the late 1960s.

Industrial Policies

Japan's postwar industrial policies have long been a topic of controversy. Those who subscribe to the conspiracy explanation of Japan's economic success consider such policies irrefutable proof of powerful government agencies, such as MITI, the Economic Planning Agency (EPA), and the Ministry of Finance (MOF), organizing and successfully managing a systematic economic assault on the rest of the unsuspecting world. In their view, most industrial policies violated international trading rules (GATT), thus providing Japan with unfair competitive advantages. Others, basing their analyses on the classical or "static" notion of comparatiive advantage, argued that the Japanese strategy did not involve anything new or very unusual.[16] As is the case with such controversies, the most reasonable explanation lies somewhere between the two extremes.

There can be no question that the Japanese introduced a more effective strategy for industrializing in general, and for achieving international competitiveness in particular. They had no choice, because rapid economic growth and increasing productivity and exports were needed to cope with the shortage of resources, the chronic balance of payment problems, and the low standard of living during the immediate postwar years. The homogeneous nature of the society and its tradition of discipline and goal orientation provided an environment in which industrial policies could be effectively developed and applied within a relatively short period of time.

A discussion of industrial policies immediately introduces a problem of definition. Equating such policies with "targeting," the practice of selecting winners and losers in the international marketplace, too narrowly defines these policies. The argument that all government economic policies somehow impact the economy and, therefore, are industrial policy, renders this concept analytically useless. The diversity of economic policies available and the multiple, broad impact of their combined applications make it difficult, if not impossible, to measure their effectiveness. So, while the Japanese undoubtedly developed and applied a new strategy, and while this strategy was successful, generalizations about its precise effectiveness, fairness, or unfairness are questionable at best, misleading at worst. The most that can be convincingly said is that within a relatively short period of time, Japan managed to create the critical resources necessary to becoming competitive in today's global economy.

Japan's example is inspiring. While most developing countries do not possess the societal characteristics needed to imitate Japan's success, many will at least try.[17] Few developing-country governments can afford to accept indefinitely the second-class economic citizenship that the traditional methods of industrialization confer. Thus, to avoid acrimonious trade conflicts, the international community needs to adjust current trade rules to accomodate the new industralization strategies which reflect the political and economic realities of the world as they exist, not as they ought to be according to some idealized notion of the past. While the concept of free trade should continue to play a central role, it should not be allowed to degenerate into a static article of faith to which nations pay lipservice but do not abide because it has little or no relevance to reality. Every nation knows that industrialization and trade are dynamic activities, and that domestic political necessities often override the principles of free trade as they are embodied in the current set of GATT rules.

If the Japanese experience is properly evaluated, a general understanding about the legitimacy of the various dynamic, industrial policy measures might be reached. The standard of "fairness" so often applied in the United States in this evaluation process has no practical significance because the international community cannot agree on the meaning of the term. Some argue that it reflects universally accepted values, while others point out that it is simply the expression of the idiosyncratic norms of a few countries. Thus, the emotional and essentially meaningless debates about fairness and unfairness should be replaced by a more useful discourse on how to provide for an effective industrialization process on the basis of the dynamic concept of free trade and competition and the economic realities of the last decade of the twentieth century. This, of course, is easier said than done. However, considering the alternatives, it is worth trying. Although these issues are not on the agenda of the current Uruguay round of GATT talks, perhaps the member nations will address them during the 1990s.

In the meanwhile, no generally accepted definition or interpretation of industrial policies as applied by Japan is available. Perhaps one of the most insightful explanations was given by Abegglen and Stalk who argued that

> ... the principal role of the government of Japan at the operating, business level of industrial change and growth has been to facilitate and accelerate the workings of the market, to speed the process of reduction of declining sectors, and to work clear the way for market forces to have full play in emerging growth sectors. At the broader level of national policy, the government of Japan has been a critical force in providing the social infrastructure, in providing supportive fiscal and monetary policy, and in providing general directions for the business community.[18]

Abegglen and Stalk see the industrial-policy and macroeconomic-policy combination provided by the Japanese government as a forceful guiding mechanism that paved the way for the economy to become internationally competitive. To this, one should add that until the mid-1960s, as in all developing countries, protection of infant industries was a centerpiece of this mechanism, and that the resulting protectionist attitudes were carried over by government and business circles into later years. Protectionism, however, was not only used to promote the development of emerging industries but was also meant to deal with the difficulties of an overvalued yen.[19] Japan was committed to a fixed exchange rate set under the Bretton Woods system in 1949, resulting in chronic balance of payment deficits until the mid-1960s. It responded to this problem with strong foreign exchange controls, including severe limitations on foreign investment both at home and abroad, import quotas, high tariffs, and a variety of tax and other incentives for exports. The balance of payments difficulties naturally promoted import substitution.

The industrial-policy and macroeconomic-policy combination used was neither routine nor a sophisticated conspiracy violating international trade rules; it was a well-conceived, uniquely Japanese way of accomplishing challenging objectives in the shortest possible time. It is worth noting that protectionism during the 1950s and 1960s did not necessarily violate international trade rules, because under the Bretton Woods system, nations with balance of payment problems were expected to reduce trade deficits and defend the exchange value of their currencies through protectionist measures.

The uniqueness of the Japanese strategy was not so much in its policy measures but in the combinations of those measures and in the societal framework within which the policies were applied. The homogeneous and well-educated population could be called upon to devote its considerable energies to the achievement of the growth-productivity objectives, to sacrifice consumption for savings, and consequently, to accept a lower standard of living than could have been realized. Such human qualities were harnessed by the elite bureaucracy and business leaders who were respected, trusted, and could provide the necessary leadership.

The theoretical foundations of Japan's industrial policies were developed by two different generations of economists.[20] The first generation was educated before or during World War II, and its influence was very noticeable between the early 1950s through approximately 1965, during which time MITI played a dominant role in developing and implementing industrial policies. This generation was dedicated to the transformation of a defeated, underdeveloped nation into a modern, developed state through the creation of an industrial base hidden behind protective barriers. These enconomists were influenced by the highly centralized planning systems emerging throughout the world in the late 1940s and early 1950s. They believed that the government must not only formulate development plans but also regulate the activities of the various sectors. Competition did not play an important role in their deliberations for the postwar economy.

During the 1950s and 1960s when Japan became a member of various international organizations, such as the GATT, this generation viewed the resulting external demands for economic liberalization not as an opportunity to participate in the emerging free trade system but as a cost that the nation, albeit grudgingly, had to pay to become a full member of the international community. During the mid-1960s when this first generation of economists was gradually replaced by the next generation, its influence did not suddenly disappear but was carried over into subsequent years.

The next generation of economists was educated mostly in the West, and came home with ideas that were largely unknown in Japan at the time. They subscribed to the general equilibrium theory of microeconomics, as well as the welfare, economic, and industrial organization concepts developed mainly in the United States. They argued that a competitive market mechanism was the only way to allocate resources efficiently, and that industrial policies were needed to upgrade industries when, for some reason, the market mechanism performed inadequately. Not surprisingly, the second generation clashed with the first, and in general, displayed a much less cooperative attitude toward government agencies and industrial policies. Second generation members were particularly critical of the formation of the Nippon Steel Corporation through the merger of two major steel companies, and supported the Fair Trade Commission (FTC), which had very little influence during the 1960s and 1970s.

Private sector economists of both generations were regularly consulted by the bureaucracy and its economists during the policy formulation process. They played an important role in the various councils established to advise government agencies. The most important of these, the Industrial Structure Council established by MITI, generated various medium-term and long-term policy reports called "visions" which the Japanese government published. While the recommendations of the council were not binding, they were reflected in the specific policies formulated by the administrative branch and approved by the Diet. After the mid-1960s, however, the two different generations of economists working in both the private and public sector began clashing over policy options. So except for the first two decades following the war, industrial policy formulation was not free of conflicts; in fact, it was marked by diverse arguments during the lengthy consensus formulation process which preceded final decisions.

From the outset, MITI led the development and implementation of industrial policies.[21] Its name and organizational structure reflected the indivisibility of production and international trade as national objectives, and its highly qualified staff orchestrated the various activities needed to achieve the aimes. Supported by other government institutions, such as the Economic Planning Agency (EPA), the Japan Development Bank (JDB), and the Export-Import Bank, MITI also maintained a cooperative relationship with the powerful Ministry of Finance (MOF) as well as other key ministries. However, behind the support and cooperation that eventually emerged once a consensus was reached were long and acrimonious disagreements and debates, and it was not always the views of MITI that characterized the emerging policy. More often than not, it was the powerful Ministry of Finance in charge of the purse strings that had the last word on important issues.

The industrial policies reflected consensus concerning the growth objectives which were based on an assumed set of domestic and international economic conditions.[22] Continuous improvements in productivity and international competitiveness in a "targeted" group of industries were the foremost considerations in deciding on the appropriate combination of policies. The specific instruments included infant industry protection and import substitution, as well as tax incentives to promote savings for investments. For example, no tax was levied on income from small savings accounts (*maruyu*), postal savings accounts, and central government bonds. Double taxation of corporate income was minimized, special depreciation measures were established for certain assets, tax-free reserve funds for a variety of purposes were allowed, and selected service export tax credits were given. In general, the tax measures were aimed at improving the financial situation of companies and at promoting exports.

Supportive tax policies were backed by direct government lending at favorable terms. The Fiscal Investment and Loan Program, administered by a special bureau of the Ministry of Finance, was the major program used. The key institution, the Japan Development Bank, provided long-term, low-interest loans primarily for capital investment in emerging industries, but research and development efforts generating innovations based on technologies originating elsewhere were also supported. The primary advantages of such loans over loans made by private banks were lower interest rates, longer life, and the absence of compensating balance requirements. In spite of claims to the contrary, Pepper and associates cite a U.S. International Trade Commission study, according to which only about 1.6–2.0 percent of the value of individual loans offered through such programs could be considered a subsidy.[23] They also found that as a percentage of all loans, lending by the Japan Development Bank was relatively insignificant.

Another important policy measure was the exemption of certain types of cartels from the Anti-Monopoly Law, which was introduced after World War II and based on the American antitrust laws. The Japanese have always been very pragmatic about their laws and have never elevated any of them to the position of sacred convenants. If the antimonopoly requirements were not conducive to economic growth and the continuous improvement of productivity, they were willing to make exceptions as needed. Thus, already during the mid-1950s, recession and rationalization cartels became legal subject to case-by-case approval by the Fair Trade Commission. Rules on interlocking directorates were changed, and the limits on bank ownership of corporate stock were raised. In addition, MITI sponsored a number of special industry laws, some of which exempted various types of joint economic behaviour from the antitrust laws. The total number of authorized cartels increased from 53 in 1953 to 1,079 in 1966, and then gradually declined to 886 in 1970, and 422 in 1986.[24]

Beginning in the mid-1960s when direct government control over many aspects of the economy was relaxed or eliminated. MITI and some of the other agencies continued to exert their influence through administrative guidance (*gyoseishido*). Japanese laws and directives are written in a general language so as to allow the bureaucracy to interpret their intent according to the special circumstances prevailing at the time of their application. Due to the respect and trust that the elite bureaucrats enjoyed, administrative guidance, although informal and not legally enforceable, was usually followed by those who received it.

The decline of industrial policies as major economic management tools continued without interruption throughout the 1960s and 1970s, and was completed by the early 1980s. Changes in both the international economic environment and in the domestic economy, the increasing plurality of Japanese society, and various external pressures all contributed to this process. Following MITI's loss of control over foreign exchange allocations during the 1960s, steps were taken to liberalize technology imports, foreign exchange controls, and import quotas. Tariffs were lowered, virtually all export promotion programs (except for a tax-break allowed for small and medium size firms) were eliminated, and because of the increasingly larger fiscal deficits, the Ministry of Finance granted fewer favourable tax treatments. The financing role of the Japan Development Bank was substantially reduced, and the number of cartel exemptions was also curtailed. Foreign investment controls were gradually eliminated, and a number of different market opening measures were introduced.

By the early 1980s, the goals of the Japanese economic policy became much broader than they had been in the past. Less emphasis was put on growth and more placed on environmental problems, social welfare, small business, and the macroeconomic problems associated with large budget deficits. The reduction in the size, cost, and influence of government through "administrative reform" also moved to the forefront. Business was doing well on its own; the private sector was successful, and it did not want government interference. Certain applications of industrial policy did continue, such as aid to structurally depressed industries, support to small-sized and medium-sized enterprises, development of visions, promotion of research and development (R&D), and administrative guidance; however, for the most part by the early 1980s the Japanese economy was not functioning much differently than that of the United States or Western Europe. This was noted by a number of American experts of Japan during a series of congressional hearings.[25] With some exaggeration a few experts even implied that the only major difference between the Japanese economy and others was its continuing strong growth and productivity orientation.

By most standards, the Japanese economy of the early 1980s was quite different from that of the 1960s and 1970s. Nevertheless, within certain American and European political and business circles Japan continued to be viewed in terms which, in some cases, would even have been an exaggeration years earlier. These circles ignored the liberalization efforts which took place and clung to an outdated, static picture of a dynamic economy that was undergoing constant changes. Impressed by the achievements of *kaishas* like Toyota or Sony, they perpetuated the myth that the Japanese economy was a fiercely efficient steamroller which, under the single-minded and often "unfair" leadership of MITI, was about to roll over the world and wipe out all of its competitors. Notwithstanding the accomplishments of the Japanese economy in general and the *kaisha* in particular, these views were erroneous in several respects.

When judged by growth and productivity standards over a 25-year to 30-year period, the Japanese economy performed consistently better than the American or European economies, yet MITI, EPA, and the other agencies did not posses any mystical powers to achieve that performance. For example, as table 1–3 shows, during the era of rapid worldwide growth (1956–1971), Japanese government forecasters regularly underestimated the growth of the domestic economy. At a time of relative international stability, such performance was hardly an indication of infallible leadership.

Although some non-Japanese observers argued that the underestimation was done on purpose by some ministries to obtain more funds for their favorite growth projects, whatever the case may have been, economic forecasting is a difficult task. American and European forecasters were and are plagued by the problems of over- or underestimation in trying to predict the course of their economies. The illustration should nevertheless correct the myth that the Japanese policy formulators had some sort of supernatural hold over the economy and, consequently, could manipulate it according to their will.

Table 1–4 shows that government forecasts for the 1970–1990 period were approximately of the same quality as those for the previous era, except that in a period of slower global growth, officials consistently overestimated the potential of the Japanese economy.

Government agencies made errors in more areas than forecasting. The automobile industry is a classic example of the problems MITI faced when picking its winners and losers. In the early days of the automobile industry, MITI strongly objected to that industry's plans to export, because the officials did not believe that there was a market for Japanese automobiles. Although by 1962 MITI was willing to support these exports, its officials insisted on certain structural changes, demanding that manufacturers merge, thus creating a dominant Japanese automobile *kaisha*. Only three small mergers took place, and simultaneously, against MITI's objections, several new producers entered the industry. When MITI finally left the industry alone around 1969, the individual manufacturers took off on the road to international success. Television, stereo equipment, camera equipment, and other types of manufacturers were not high on MITI's list of deserving industries, either. Nevertheless, through their own efforts, they also successfully penetrated world markets. Today these industries not only hold major market shares but they are also the technological leaders in their fields.

TABLE 1-3. Long-term economic forecasts and actual results: 1956–1971

Name:	Five-year plan for economic self-support	New long-range economic plan	Doubling national income plan	Medium-term economic plan	Economic and social development plan
Period:	1956–1960	1958–1962	1961–1970	1964–1968	1967–1971
Cabinet:	Hatoyama	Kishi	Ikeda	Sato	Sato
GNP growth forecast:	5.0%	6.5%	7.8%	8.1%	8.2%
Actual:	8.7%	9.9%	10.7%	10.6%	10.9%

Source: *Japan's Industrial Policies* (Washington, D.C.: The Japan Economic Institute, 1984), p. 13.

TABLE 1-4. Long-term economic forecasts and actual results: 1970–1990

Name:	New economic and social development plan	Basic economic and social plan	Economic plan for the second half of the 1970s	New economic and social seven-year plan	Outlook and guidelines for economic society in the 1980s
Period:	1970–1975	1973–1977	1976–1980	1979–1985	1983–1990
Cabinet:	Sato	Tanaka	Miki	Ohira	Nakasone
GNP growth forecast:	10.6%	9.4%	6%+	5.7%	4%
Actual:	5.9%	4.2%	5.7%	4.2%	—

Source: *Japan's Industrial Policies* (Washington, D.C.: The Japan Economic Institute, 1984), p. 13; and *Japan 1986: An International Comparison* (Tokyo: Keizai Koho Center, 1986), p. 12.

TABLE 1-5. International comparison of manufacturing productivity growth trends: 1950–1979 (in percentages)

Country	1950–1979	1950–1967	Time periods 1967–1973	1973–1979	1977–1978	1978–1979
United States	2.4	2.6	2.9	2.2	0.5	1.5
Japan	8.5	9.5	10.0	4.2	7.9	8.3
Canada	3.9	4.1	5.1	4.8	4.7	0.8
France	5.2	4.9	6.1	5.1	4.9	5.4
West Germany	5.7	6.1	5.3	5.0	3.4	5.2
Italy	6.0	6.4	7.2	3.3	3.0	2.2
United Kingdom	2.7	3.0	4.2	0.6	1.2	2.2

Source: *Report of the Japan-United States Economic Relations Group* (Washington, D.C., 1981), p. 41.

The Key Role of Productivity and Savings

While infant industry protection together with the macroeconomic-industrial policy combination played a major role in the rapid growth of the postwar Japanese economy, focusing only on these measures provides an incomplete picture. It was the growth-productivity orientation of the Japanese government and business that made the impressive results possible, particularly as it was reflected in the continual increase of manufacturing productivity and net household savings rates. International comparisons of these two key factors show why the Japanese economy developed so much faster than its competitors. Table 1–5 shows the growth trends in manufacturing productivity in the major industrialized countries over a period of nearly 30 years.

The data clearly show that except for the 1973–1979 period when the first oil shock and its aftermath caused manufacturing productivity to decline, for most of the 1950–1979 period Japan was well ahead of the other nations. However, when considering the Japanese performance, it must be noted that there were significant differences between the aggregate productivity levels and the productivity of individual industries or firms. Table 1–6 demonstrates the productivity differences according to plant size during the early 1980s. The productivity of companies with fewer than 300 employees, the small-sized to medium-sized firms, was just more than half that of companies with 1,000 or more employees.

TABLE 1–6. Productivity differences in the manufacturing sector according to plant size: 1981 (in percentages)

Number of employees	30–49	50–99	100–199	200–299	300–499	500–999	1000 or more
Productivity	46.1	48.6	58.8	67.7	78.2	88.0	100.0

Source: *Useful Labor Statistics* (Tokyo: Japan Productivity Center, 1984), p. 16.
Note: Firms with more than 1,000 employees represent 100 percent productivity.

So, it was the large *kaisha* that were in the forefront of continuous productivity improvements. These companies carried the improvements into the international marketplace through what Abegglen and Stalk call the "winners competitive cycle."[26] This is based on the proposition that for a company to succeed in a highly competitive environment, it must grow faster than others. A company can do this by increasing market share through the efficient manufacture and aggressive marketing of high quality products. The *kanban* (just-in-time) inventory system, aggressive price cutting through cost reduction based on the learning curve, or continuous new product introduction are some of the means to such an end. The funds generated through growing market shares are reinvested to finance the repetition of the cycle. Abegglen and Stalk also point out that the process is more effective in high-growth as opposed to low-growth economies. Thus, for many years the large Japanese *kaisha* had better opportunities to exploit this cycle than their American or European competitors.

The other major factor in the growth-productivity orientation that differentiated Japan from the rest of the industralized world was the high rate of personal savings. Once postwar inflation was brought under control in 1951 and real income began to rise, savings increased steadily throughout the years. While expected to level off once the economy stabilized in the 1960s, saving continued to grow, although at a slower pace. Table 1–7 provides an international comparison of net savings trends as a percentage of disposable household income over a 20-year period.

TABLE 1–7. A comparison of net household savings in selected countries: 1960–1981 (as a percentage of disposable income)

Countries	Years		
	1960–1966	*1967–1973*	*1974–1981*
Japan	17.2	18.1	21.4
United States	7.2	8.4	7.4
Federal Republic of Germany	16.0	16.1	12.2
France	12.2	12.8	13.1
United Kingdom	5.6	5.7	9.2
Italy	17.5	19.2	21.8

Source: *OECD Economic Outlook, Historical Statistics, 1960–81* (Paris: Organization for Economic Cooperation and Development, 1983), pp. 69–70.

The *maruyu* tax-exempt small savings) arrangements played a major role in the postwar savings system. Through the *maruyu*, small savers could exempt interest earned on deposits and make tax-free investments in government bonds and certain pension plans. While a number of different institutions offered savings opportunities, one of the most important of these was the postal system established in 1875 and managed by the Postal Savings Bureau of the Ministry of Posts and Telecommunications (MPT). By channelling the small deposits into government and industry, the postal savings system provided a substantial part of the capital needed to finance postwar growth. In the early 1980s, this accounted for more than 30 percent of individual savings deposits, worth approximately $500 billion.[27]

External Trade

As mentioned earlier, Japan needed rapid economic growth and constantly increasing exports to cope with the shortage of resources, the low standard of living, and the chronic balance of payment problems of the immediate postwar years. Promoted through infant industry protection and macro-economic-industrial policy combinations, external trade began to grow rapidly around 1960. Table 1–8 shows the evolution of Japan's global trade over a period of more than 30 years until 1983. Except for the stagnation due to the first oil price increase and its aftermath in the mid-1970s, Japan's external trade grew at a rapid pace until the early 1980s when it slowed again. As table 1–8 illustrates, the growth of exports gradually outstripped that of imports in the early 1960s, and by 1965 the trade balance showed a surplus which, except for the mid-1970s, lasted into the 1980s.

TABLE 1–8.   Japanese exports-imports and their share in world totals: 1950–1983

	Exports		Imports	
	Value ($ million)	Share of world total (%)	Value ($ million)	Share of world total (%)
1950	820	1.4	974	1.6
1955	2,011	2.3	2,471	2.7
1960	4,055	3.4	4,491	3.6
1965	8,452	5.0	8,169	4.5
1970	19,318	6.7	18,881	6.3
1975	55,753	6.9	57,863	7.0
1980	129,807	6.9	140,528	7.3
1981	152,030	8.2	143,290	7.5
1982	138,381	8.1	131,931	7.4
1983	146,927	8.8	126,393	7.3

Source: *Facts and Figures of Japan* (Tokyo: Foreign Press Center, 1985), p. 45.

In 1968 the current account balance also turned positive, and with the exception of the first and second oil shock years, it remained in surplus thereafter. Table 1–9 shows the evolution of the current account balances over a period of 20 years.

The chronic balance of payment problems of the postwar years initially required tight government controls over all external trade and foreign exchange activities. Consequently, until the early 1960s, all such transactions were monitored by the government. However, in June 1960 the General Principles of Liberalization Plans of Trade and Foreign Exchange were adopted, and Japan decided to increase the liberalization ratio of imports from 40 to 80 percent within three years. The plan was advanced in the fall of 1961, and a decision was made to increase the liberalization ratio to 90 percent by September 1962. In February 1963 Japan joined the GATT and,

TABLE 1–9.   Japanese current account balances: 1961–1982 (in $ millions)

Year	Balance
1961	−982
1962	−48
1963	−780
1964	−480
1965	932
1966	1,254
1967	−190
1968	1,048
1969	2,119
1970	1,970
1971	5,797
1972	6,624
1973	−136
1974	−4,693
1975	−682
1976	3,680
1977	10,918
1978	16,534
1979	−8,754
1980	−10,746
1981	4,770
1982	6,850

Source: Various editions of annual *International Financial Statistics* (Washington, D.C.: International Monetary Fund).

consequently, could no longer restrict imports on the basis of international payment difficulties. Additionally, in 1964 Japan ratified Article 8 of the International Monetary Fund (IMF). The gradual removal of control over foreign exchange transactions culminated in the amendment of the Foreign Exchange and Foreign Trade Control Law in December 1980. All restrictions were removed, although the Ministry of Finance retained some authority to reimpose capital controls if necessary.

Liberalization of trade, foreign exchange, and the oil price shocks were probably the major external factors that played an important role in changing Japan's export structure over the years. Unit the mid-1950s, exports consisted mainly of textiles, apparel, toys, china, and other light industrial products. However, as the industrial structure was gradually upgraded, exports increasingly shifted toward higher value-added items. In the 1960s, textiles and other light industrial products began to lose their international competitiveness, because domestic wage levels rose and a number of developing countries established light and labor-intensive industries, just as Japan had done in late nineteenth century. By the 1960s, steel, shipbuilding, petro-chemical, machine, and precision industries were becoming internationally competitive. In the 1970s, these industries continued to gain strength, although the shipbuilding industry had to operate at under-capacity because of a decline in worldwide demand. The automobile industry became competitive in the early 1970s, and established itself as one of the world leaders by the mid-1970s primarily through the fuel efficiency and high quality of its cars. Electronics, telecommunications, and other high technology industries broke into world markets during the late 1970s and early 1980s.

Japan's most important trading partner is the United States. The

TABLE 1-10. Japanese exports to and imports from the United States: 1960–1983 (in $ millions)

Year	Exports		Imports	
	To USA	% of total	From USA	% of total
1960	1,102	27.2	1,554	34.6
1970	5,940	30.7	5,560	29.4
1975	11,149	20.0	11,608	20.1
1980	31,367	24.2	24,408	17.4
1982	36,330	26.2	24,179	18.3
1983	42,829	29.1	24,647	19.5

Source: *Nippon: A Chartered Survey of Japan 1985–1986* (Tokyo: Kokusei-Sha, 1985). p. 89.

importance of America as a market for Japanese exports began in the early 1950s and has continued into the 1980s. Table 1–10 shows the evolution of Japanese trade with the United States between 1960 and 1983, including the share of this bilateral trade in total exports and imports. As the data show, the percentage of Japanese exports going to the United States has increased over time while the percentage of imports from America has decreased. Not surprisingly, the sharp growth in exports during the early 1980s, and the only slight increase in imports were harbingers of serious bilateral trade conflicts.

TABLE 1–11. Japan's merchandise trade balance with the United States: 1973–1983 (in $ millions)

	Exports	Imports	Balance
1973	9,449	9,270	179
1974	12,799	12,682	117
1975	11,149	11,608	−459
1976	15,690	11,809	3,881
1977	19,717	12,396	7,321
1978	24,915	14,790	10,125
1979	26,403	20,431	5,972
1980	31,367	24,408	6,959
1981	38,609	25,297	13,312
1982	36,330	24,179	12,151
1983	42,829	24,647	18,182

Source: *Japan 1986: An International Comparison* (Tokyo: Keizai Koho Center, 1986), p. 36.

Japan's merchandise trade balance with the United States was negative until 1965. The United States experienced an annual trade surplus of $200–300 million except in 1961, when the surplus grew to more than $700 million.[28] Table 1–11 shows the evolution of bilateral trade balances during the second half of the 1970s when the Japanese surpluses became increasingly larger.

During these 10 critical years, the composition of goods flowing from Japan to the United States was quite different from that which moved in the opposite direction. Japan's exports included only small amounts of agricultural products, crude materials, mineral fuels, or chemicals. The overwhelming majority of goods sent to the United States consisted of a wide range of manufactured items, including machinery, telecommunications equipment, transportation equipment, and other products, such as watches, toys, and sporting goods.

In contrast, American exports of manufactured goods and equipment in the same categories accounted for less than one-third of annual shipments to Japan. The majority of American exports were agricultural commodities, crude materials, and mineral fuels, including coal. While the United States also exported high-technology products to Japan, some observers likened the structure of trade between the two nations to trade between a developing and an industrialized nation. Such comparisons, although simplistic insofar as they ignore the resource endowments and structural differences between the two countries, were an indication of the emotional and often superficial nature of the debate that eventually engulfed U.S.-Japanese trade relations.

The Evolution of U.S.–Japan Trade Conflicts

Japan's international trade conflicts in general, and with the United States in particular, began during the late 1960s and early 1970s. Until then its increasingly competitive stance in the world markets and growing trade and current account surpluses were accepted. World trade was still increasing at a satisfactory pace; economic growth, although interrupted by periodic recessions, was still strong enough in the major industrial countries to mask the gradual loss of international competitiveness by certain American and European industries, and unemployment levels still fluctuated within politically tolerable limits. Bilateral disagreements over trade issues were usually short-lived and settled in a reasonably amicable manner.

Beginning with the 1969–1971 textile conflict with the United States, however, the frequency, nature, and duration of the trade disagreements began to change. There were multiple reasons, some of which were inherent in the political-economic development process of the competing nations while others were primarily attributable to domestic and international economic policy choices made by the governments. One of the most significant political-economic developments was the change in the role of the United States. Specifically, the relative decline in America's economic and political power in the 1960s and thereafter made it difficult for the United States to maintain its traditionally liberal and paternalistic trade policies toward Europe, Japan, and the developing countries. The beginning of this new era was marked by the first U.S. global trade deficit in 78 years, a deficit of just over $2 billion in 1971. This, combined with the emergence of a number of Japanese industries as major international competitors, created trade conflicts that were conducted in an increasingly acrimonious fashion over longer periods of time. The United States, as well as other countries, particularly the members of the European Community, began to argue that the Japanese who have benefited so much from free trade are not willing to shed their narrow national economic policies to help restore the global economic imbalances that were emerging.[29]

As far as the bilateral trade relations with the United States were concerned, in addition to the 1969–1971 textile conflicts, two other periods stand out during the 1970s and early 1980s.[30] The years 1976–1978 and 1981–1984 were marked by acrimonious and emotionally charged disagreements. These periods correspond with the years when Japan had large current and trade account surpluses, the United States and some Western European trading partners had large current and trade account deficits. With respect to the U.S.–Japan trade conflicts, the data show the following.[31] From 1967 through 1972, America's current account shifted from a surplus of over $2 billion to a deficit of approximately $6 billion. During the same time, the Japanese current account swung from a small deficit to a surplus of approximately $7 billion. From 1975 through 1978, the U.S. current account moved from a surplus of more than $18 billion to a deficit of approximately $14 billion; at the same time, Japan moved from a small deficit to a surplus greater than $16 billion. In terms of the bilateral trade balances, in the 1966–1972 period, America's bilateral trade deficit rose from an annual average of $0.5 billion to over $3.5 billion. Following a dip during 1973–1975, the U.S. deficit jumped to more than $8 billion in 1976–1978. In 1981 the deficit reached about $16 billion, and it continued to increase, reaching $20 billion in 1983. In the same year the United States experienced a current account deficit of $40.8 billion, whereas Japan's current account surplus jumped to $21 billion from $6.8 billion in the previous year.

The U.S.–Japan trade conflicts had several major dimensions.[32] The first category consisted of national trade policies involving market access, the fairness vs. unfairness debate, and the various nontariff barriers. Also included here was the question of the low level of Japanese manufactured imports. The conflicts usually emerged over either the sharp increase in Japanese exports of textiles, steel, color televisions, and automobiles, or the inability of American exporters to expand their sales of agricultural, telecommunications, and related high-technology equipment in Japan.

Macroeconomic issues and monetary policy comprised another dimension, particularly the implications of America's increasing budget deficits and Japan's efforts to control its budget in line with the administrative and fiscal reform policy. As Bergsten and Cline pointed out, the opposing trends of the national budgets had important implications for the bilateral trade balances and conflicts.

The structural differences of the two economies represented the last major dimension. The differences in household savings, Japan's traditionally close supplier relations (*keiretsu*), its complex distribution system, the American exporters lack of savvy and drive to penetrate the Japanese markets, the short-term orientation of U.S. corporate managers, the price, quality, and competitiveness of American products, and related matters were the issues raised most often. Naturally, throughout the course of the debates and the ensuing negotiations, issues frequently overlapped; the nature of the Japanese distribution and supplier systems, for example, were included in the discussions on market access in general, and on nontariff barriers in particular.

The most heatedly debated issues concerned trade policy. Specifically, market access and alleged unfair trade practices have dominated U.S.–Japan trade conflicts since the mid-1970s. As a number of American industries lost their international competitiveness, local unemployment became a problem; and as the U.S. bilateral trade deficits with Japan increased, more and more industries sought help in Washington. Members of Congress, understandably sensitive to pressures from their constituents, responded by lashing out at the Japanese, the most visible competitors making inroads into the U.S. markets. Concerns in other categories, such as monetary and macroeconomic policies, received less attention, because other than the experts, most people and the press on both sides of the Pacific did not fully understand the complex issues involved. So, other than discussions at the highest level, relatively little attention was paid to these other matters. Another relevant issue, the internationalization of the Japanese economy as envisioned during the second half of the 1980s, was not sufficiently discussed by the two governments either, although matters of domestic economic growth generated some heated debates in 1978. Moreover, little time was spent on the discussion of structural problems in the American economy or the trade implications of the increasing budgetary deficits. The Japanese tried to approach these matters jointly, but the United States found it expedient to focus on other points of disagreement.

This is not to say that international trade experts have not tried to assess realistically the causes of the huge U.S. trade account deficits. Some have argued that there were many causes with deep roots on both sides of the Pacific. They believed that these causes should be addressed through broad negotiations and coordinated multilateral actions, involving not only the United States and Japan but also the European Community and other nations.[33] On the American political scene, however, circumstances made it difficult, if not impossible, for even the most enlightened member of Congress to pursue such ideas. Pressures from single issue interest groups, a less orderly structure of Congress due to the demise of the once omnipotent committee chairman system, and the reduced influence of the White House after Watergate all combined with the uneven performance of the American economy to preclude a broader approach. Thus, members of Congress were conditioned to respond to specific pressures. The result was an increasingly assertive and protectionist Capitol Hill that paid more attention to trade policy issues than at any time since the mid-1930s, working against a free trade-oriented but hard-pressed Administration that tried to achieve a balance between the domestic pressures and America's international obligations.

Many members of Congress also believed that a clear and simple line could be drawn between fair and unfair trade practices. Ignoring differing value systems, the complex relationship between trade, macroeconomic, and structural policies as determinants of a nation's international competitiveness, they considered Japan's continuing bilateral trade surpluses as prima facie evidence of unfair Japanese trade practicese. A congressional axiom arose whereby the higher the bilateral trade imbalances became, the more unfair the Japanese actions had to be. Thus, by the late 1970s, the size of the annual bilateral trade imbalances dominated congressional debates on trade to the exclusion of most other relevant issues. This is not to argue that the growing bilateral imbalances were economically sustainable or politically acceptable, because clearly, something had to be done; however, focusing on the bilateral imbalance and using the amorphous notion of unfair trade practices as the single most important explanation for what was happening was an erroneous domestic political strategy at best, and a denial of reality at worst.[34]

From the beginning of the bilateral trade conflicts, the Japanese also adhered to some questionable views and practices. Perhaps the most basic of these was the inability, or in some cases the unwillingness, of the responsible leaders, such as the politicans and government officials, to publicly recognize the nation's transition from a weakling to an economic power during the second half of the 1970s. Consequently, at every level of society, the Japanese continued to exhibit the "small country" mentality which had been rooted in the nation's long history of isolation, lack of natural resources, and economic uncertainty. Inward-looking, uncertain about the economic future, and passive in international relations, the Japanese presented a two-sided Janus face to the world. The country's gradually emerging economic power and its aggressive international trade competitiveness contrasted the self-effacing and passive behavior exhibited by Japanese representatives in the international arena. The "little brother" attitude of military, political, and economic dependency toward the United States, the wait-and-see approach marked by defensiveness in international negotiations in general and in the trade conflict with America in particular, was a reflection of the unresolved clash between long-held self-perceptions and the sudden economic reality.

During the 1970s, only the Japan experts appreciated the nature of the clash between perception and reality taking place in Japan. Most others considered the contrasting behaviour patterns as convincing proof of duplicity. Some Japanese politicans and government officials may not have wanted to publicly admit the transition in order to continue benefitting from the "small and dependent" posture. It was, however, disingenuous to consider the inability of a people to quickly revise its self-perception under rapidly changing conditions as a single-minded, society-wide conspiracy, particularly since these changes did not equally benefit every sector of the economy.[35] The reverberations of the two oil-price shocks also dampened the enthusiasm of many Japanese to see their country as an emerging economic power. Finally, it is important to understand that during the 1970s and also the 1980s, the fruits of hard work and increasing national wealth manifested by the current account surpluses were not translated into a generally improved quality of life. While the standard of living as measured by the traditional — and often misleading — economic indicators, such as per capita income, was getting better every day,[36] quality of life measures, such as leisure time, housing conditions, and other similar socioeconomic considerations, did not reflect the enormous wealth the nation was accumulating. Thus, the average Japanese did not personally experience the country's transition into a world economic power.

Japan's limited international orientation also complicated the bilateral trade conflicts. Strange as it may seem in light of the country's international competitiveness and the remarkable individual successes of its major corporations, the Japanese were not adroit in understanding and dealing with the outside world. For historical reasons, such as the long, self-imposed isolation under the shoguns and the highly structured homogenous society, it took some time to develop and hone the skills needed to deal with the international community, some of whose members have on occasion taken advantage of the Japanese.

An inward looking island-people, the Japanese thus failed to grasp the deep sense of genuine frustration felt by American policy formulators, trade negotiators, and businessmen who suddenly confronted a rapidly changing world economy that was increasingly shaped by Japan's economic policies. The Americans were especially frustrated because as they saw it, Japan was becoming an economic power by taking full advantage of a post-World War II free-trade-oriented international economy whose chief architect, the United States, by the mid-1970s needed supportive cooperation but was not getting it from the Japanese who refused to change or give up their narrow nationalistic economic policies.

Manufacturing high quality products and aggressively marketing them throughout the world is one thing; however, negotiating political and economic matters in international fora in a foreign language is quite another matter. Until Yasuhiro Nakasone assumed the premiership in the early 1980s, Japan never had a prime minister of international stature who could speak to world leaders in English and deal with them as an equal. Previously, Japan had had a succession of prime ministers who had possessed strong domestic political bases but lacked broad international experience. Most members of the Diet had similarly limited backgrounds and qualifications. Only a few spoke foreign languages and had extensive international contacts. Among government career officials, with the exception of the staff of the Ministry of Foreign Affairs and to a lesser degree MITI, there were only a handful of influential officials who possessed the necessary skills and experience to effectively represent the nation's interests. In most other ministries a prolonged international involvement was seen as risking a promising career.

The Japanese generally believed that because they depended on the United States in a number of important ways, such as defense and markets, the Americans should be more understanding and supportive. They also resented the unequal relationship and resulting feeling of dependency because they believed that America had chosen Japan as its scapegoat in order to vent its frustrations about the declining international competitiveness of its industries. Most Japanese saw America as a big bully who wanted to pressure the small, defenseless Japan into unquestioningly following its commands. There was a tendency to regard the American trade laws and trade policy actions as specifically directed at Japan. The Japanese did not recognise that the trade laws in principle were directed at a certain type of economic behavior based on American values, and not against any individual country *per se* no matter how acrimonious its disagreements with the United States might have been. They listened to the Congressional rhetoric, and viewed the trade laws as instruments of intimidation. The agressive American approach and the way in which Japanese politicans and government officials often used the "American pressure" argument to obtain political and interministerial consensus, of course, did not help matters.[37] Suffice it to say that in the Japanese society, form has always been considered at least as important as substance, and thus, America's habit of exerting strong pressure may have received more attention than it needed.

The Japanese political decision-making process, based on a lengthy consensus-seeking approach, often involved intricate interministerial turf battles which led to long delayed responses to American trade negotiation demands.[38] While on occasion the Japanese side used the delays as a negotiation ploy, in most cases the delays could not be avoided. The American side, however, suspected that most of the time delays were planned and used as an excuse for inaction.

Thus, by the late 1970s, U.S.–Japan trade relations assumed the format of tiresome morality plays with predictable outcomes.[39] Undoubtedly, the domestic political realities in both America and Japan foreordained much of the routine process and results; nonetheless, it is regrettable that the leaders of both nations failed to acknowledge the futility and muster the political courage to address the trade imbalance question more realistically.[40]

Notes

1. The Japanese fiscal year (FY) begins of April 1 of each year and ends on the following March 31.

2. Ezra F. Vogel, *Japan as Number One* (Cambridge: Harvard University Press, 1979); Marvin Wolf, *The Japanese Conspiracy* (New York: Empire Books, 1983).

3. Thomas Pepper, Merit E. Janow, and Jimmy W. Wheeler, *The Competition: Dealing With Japan* (New York: Praeger Publishers, 1985); James C. Abegglen and George Stalk, Jr., *Kaisha: The Japanese Corporation* (New York: Basic Books, Inc., 1985); Bela Balassa and Marcus Noland, *Japan in the World Economy* Washington D.C.: Institute for International Economics, 1988).

4. *The New York Times* (May 3, 1986), p.1.

5. While both "restructuring" and "internationalization" are used to refer to the changes expected in Japan, hereafter the term internationalization will be used because it is more comprehensive and better conveys the intent of the changes.

6. Clyde V. Prestowitz, Jr., *Trading Places: How We Allowed Japan to Take the Lead* (New York: Basic Book, Inc., Publishers, 1988. Martin and Susan Tolchin, *Buying Into America* (New York: Time Books, 1988). Karel van Wolferen, *The Enigma of Japanese Power* (New York: Alfred A. Knopf, 1989).

7. "Rethinking Japan," *Business Week* (August 7, 1989), p. 44.

8. Daniel Burstein, *Yen! Japan's New Financial Empire and Its Threat to America* (New York: Simon and Schuster, 1988).

9. Paul Kennedy, *The Rise and Fall of Great Powers* (New York: Random House, 1987).

10. The *Japan Economic Journal* (May 3, 1986), p. 4.

11. For a more detailed exposition of this theme, see Richard Rosecrance, *The Rise of the Trading State* (New York: Basic Books, Inc., 1986).

12. The term "Japan Inc." was used sarcastically to characterize the close and systematic cooperation between the Japanese government and business community that prevailed for many years.

13. Bruce R. Scott, "National Strategies: Key to International Competition," *U.S. Competitiveness in the World Economy*, Bruce R. Scott and George C. Lodge, eds. (Boston: Harvard Business School Press, 1985), p. 72.

14. Abegglen and Stalk, Kaisha: *The Japanese Corporation*, op. cit., pp. 5–6.

15. Scott, *"National Strategies," op. cit.*, p. 93.

16. Scott, *Ibid*, p. 96.

17. A case in point is Brazil. In 1984 it passed a law that prohibited the import of small computers for eight years, and then it supplemented this action with an industry development plan. This United States responded with a Section 301 (unfair trade practices) action in the fall of 1985. The Brazilians, however, maintained that domestic law is sovereign and cannot be changed under foreign pressure. The disagreement was resolved in 1989.

18. Abegglen and Stalk, *Kaisha: The Japanese Corporation, op. cit.*, pp. 33–34.

19. Beginning in the mid-1960s, the yen was undervalued until 1971. During the following years, it was periodically undervalued to various degrees.

20. Ryutaro Komiya, "Industrial Policy's Generation Gap," *Economic Eye*, March 1986, pp. 22–24.

21. For a detailed discussion of MITI and its role, see Chalmers, Johnson, *MITI and the Japanese Miracle* (Stanford, CA: Stanford University Press, 1982).

22. For a detailed discussion of the various policy measures and their application over time, see chapter III in Pepper et al., *The Competition*, op. cit.

23. Ibid., p. 117. Other important public financing institutions were the Industrial Bank of Japan and the Long-Term Credit Bank of Japan.

24. Figures received during personal interviews with Fair Trade Commission officials in Tokyo, May 1986.

25. U.S. Congress, Joint Economic Committee, *Industrial Policy Movement in the United States: Is It the Answer?* (Washington, D.C.: U.S. Government Printing Office, 1984), pp. 44–47.

26. For a detailed discussion of how the kaisha continually increased productivity and how the "winner's competitive cycle" develops, see Abegglen and Stalk, *Kaisha: The Japanese Corporation, op. cit.*, chapter 4, 5, and 3, respectively.

27. *The Wall Street Journal* (December 13, 1985), p. 34.

28. Annual statistical summaries of Japan by the Keizai Koho Center.

29. For a detailed discussion of the narrow national economic policies that distorted international economic relations, see Balassa and Noland, *op. cit.*

30. For a detailed discussion of the specific issues involved in these conflicts and of their resolution, see I.M. Destler, Haruhiro Fukui, and Hideo Sata. *The Textile Wrangle: Conflicts in Japanese-American Relations 1969–1971* (Ithica, N.Y.: Cornell University Press, 1979), I.M. Destler and Hideo Sato, *Coping with U.S.–Japanese Economic Conflicts* (Lexington, MA: D.C. Heath, 1982).

31. The following data were obtained from the various annual issues of the International Financial Statistics of the International Monetary Fund and U.S. Department of Commerce publications.

32. For a detailed discussion of these issues, see C. Fred Bergsten and William R. Cline, *The United States-Japan Economic Problem* (Washington, D.C.: Institute for International Economics, 1985), pp. 3–13. This study was updated in a minor way in 1987.

33. See, for example, C. Fred Bergsten "What To Do About the U.S.–Japan Economic Conflict," *Foreign Affairs* (Summer 1982), pp. 1059–1075; and Gary R. Saxonhouse, "The Micro- and Macroeconomics of Foreign Sales to Japan," in *Trade Policy in the 1980s*, edited

by William R. Cline (Washington, D.C.: Institute for International Economics, 1983), pp. 259–304.

34. There were, of course, voices of reason as well. A good example is the General Accounting Office, which in its 1979 report on *United States-Japan Trade: Issues and Problems* (Washington, D.C.: General Accounting Office, 1979) presented a measured appraisal of U.S.-Japan trade relations to Congress.

35. See previous discussion regarding slower growth of the agriculture, textiles and shipbuilding industries.

36. See, for example, *1983 World Bank Atlas* (Washington, D.C.: The World Bank, 1983).

37. See, for example, Kazuo Ogura, *U.S.–Japan Economic Conflict* (Tokyo: Nihon Keizai Shimbun, 1982).

38. For a detailed discussion of the process, see Chikara Higashi, *Japanese Trade Policy Formulation* (New York: Praeger Publishers, 1983).

39. The repetitive pattern is discussed in appendix A.

40. Prior to the mid-1980s, the only major agreement that tried to address some of the fundamental causes of the bilateral trade imbalances was the Strauss-Ushiba communique of 1978. The agreement committed both the United States and Japan to take certain measures and to work together on others designed to achieve high levels of noninflationary growth, improve their respective balance of payments position, bring the MTN negotiations to a successful conclusion, and to increase assistance to developing countries.

2 THE ORIGINS OF INTERNATIONALIZATION

The years 1981–1984 were characterized by the interaction of a number of events in both in the United States and Japan which le to a head-on collision over trade matters between the two nations. Foremost among these events was the rapid increase of Japan's global trade surpluses while the global balances of the United States deteriorated year by year. Table 2–1 shows these trends.

TABLE 2-1. Japanese and United States global trade balances: 1981–1984 (in $ millions)

| Year | Country | |
	Japan	United States
1981	19,967	− 27,978
1982	18,079	− 36,444
1983	31,454	− 67,216
1984	44,257	− 114,107

Source: *Japan 1986: An International Comparison* (Tokyo: Keizai Koho Center, 1986), p. 33.

Concurrently, Japan's bilateral trade surpluses with the United States also grew at a rapid pace. Exports to America increased by about 55 percent between 1981 and 1984, whereas imports from the United States showed only a 4 percent increase over the same period, as shown in table 2-2.

Predictably, the aforementioned trade statistics caused concern around the world, particularly in Tokyo and Washington. The Japanese knew that the rapidly growing global and bilateral trade surpluses would intensify the already critical attitudes of the European Community (E.C.) and the United States. Japanese politicians and government officials braced themselves as best as they could against the new round of "unfair trade practices" charges. Since Japan's average tariff on industrial imports would be 2.9 percent versus 4.3 percent in the United States and 4.7 percent in the European Community when the Tokyo Round Tariff reductions would be completed in 1987, it was inevitable that the critics would point to nontariff barries as the means through which the Japanese kept their markets closed. Thus, during the early 1980s, the various traditional trade arrangements and practices of Japan came under increasing scrutiny and criticism particularly in the United States and Western Europe.

Major Controversies

Until the end of the 1970s, with some notable exceptions, most foreign companies found it difficult to enter the Japanese marketplace. A variety of formal measures carried over from the 1950s and 1960s as part of the strategy to develop the international competitiveness of selected industries as well as a number of other, mostly sociocultural nontariff barriers, created major entry problems. However, by the late 1970s, the formal protectionist measures were beginning to be dismantled in response to external pressures as well as domestic economic policy changes. But most of the sociocultural

TABLE 2-2.   Japanese exports to and imports from the United States: 1981–1984 (in $ millions)

Year	Exports	Imports	Balance
1981	38,609	25,297	13,312
1982	36,330	24,179	12,151
1983	42,829	24,647	18,182
1984	59,937	26,862	33,075

Source: *Japan 1986: An International Comparison* (Tokyo: Keizai Koho Center, 1985), p. 36.

nontariff barriers were not amenable to government-initiated changes and, thus, essentially remained intact for some time. Their gradual weakening had to wait for the dramatic rise of the yen (*endaka*) and the convergence of social, demographic, consumer behavior and technological developments which during 1986–1989 began to break down traditional structures and practices, particularly in the distribution area.

The policy changes initiated by the Japanese came about slowly. The consensus seeking a policy-formulation process which had to deal with the demands of a variety of vested interests and America's demands for quick action resulted in ponderous U.S.-Japan trade conflict negotiations. Throughout the discussions American and European government and business circles vehemently criticized Japan's negotiation strategy and apparent unwillingness to take the measures deemed necessary to "open up" the marketplace to foreign goods and services. Because this went on for years, the criticism was frequently based on information that did not take into account the changes already under way. The result was a combustible mix of myths, dated information, and realities that tended to confuse rather than clarify the issues at hand. While America and Europe criticized, the Japanese complained that the world's perception of Japanese economic policies and the marketplace lagged behind reality. At times this was part of an evasive strategy, but at other times it was true. The Japanese—in spite of their extensive use of high-priced Washington lobbyists—were inept at effective public relations and could not convincingly communicate their viewpoints. Their explanations were seen as typical excuses or were simply ignored. All the critics had to do was point to the rapidly increasing bilateral trade and global current account surpluses to validate their claims.

However, by 1986–1989 events have shown that a number of arguments that were voiced during the controversies of the early 1980s were indeed exaggerated, explained little of what was happening, and served mostly to inflame a difficult series of discussions.

The Closed Nature of the Japanese Market

While it became an article of faith that the sole cause of the growing Japanese surpluses were the result of the closed nature of the marketplace, scholarly studies and the annual Organization for Economic Cooperation and Development (OECD) country surveys presented analyses that arrived at different conclusions than the conventional wisdom so widespread during the early 1980s.[1] Bergsten and Cline, for example, found that over the 1980–1984 period, Japan's bilateral trade surplus with the United States as a percentage of total bilateral trade turnover increased by 18 percent.

However, during the same period of time, 17 of America's 25 most important trading partners did better than Japan; the median increase for their bilateral surpluses was 29 percent. Explaining the reasons for the Japanese surplus, Bergsten and Cline emphasize the differences in private sector saving rates, and the overvalued dollar during the years studied. They point out, the Japanese did not become more protectionist in his time, and consequently, market barriers could not have been the major cause of the growing trade imbalances between 1980 and 1984. They argue that by international standards, Japan's import/GNP ratio is not unusual, and that the relatively low share of manufactured goods in total imports reflects the country's comparative disadvantage in natural resources rather than a concerted effort to keep foreign products out. On the basis of structural considerations Bergsten and Cline conclude that Japan is likely to maintain a long-term global current account surplus of about 1–1.5 percent of GNP, and an annual bilateral trade surplus with America of approximately $20–25 billion, even if it immediately met all U.S. trade demands.

Bergsten and Cline's findings were controversial. Apart from legitimate methodological criticism by, for example, Balassa and Noland, they were accused of a bias in Japan's favor.[2] In a *Business Week* article on Japanese influence through the funding of American universities and research institutions, the authors pointed out that Bergsten's organization, the Institute for International Economics, of Washington, D.C., received about $280,000 of its annual budget of $3.6 million from Japanese sources. Moreover, the authors argued that the 1985 Bergsten and Cline study published by the institute said that "... an overvalued dollar, not protectionism, was responsible for Japan's trade surplus. ..."[3] In other words, any research finding that did not conform to the conventional wisdom, that the Japanese surpluses were generated entirely by the "closed marketplace," could only be the result of undue influence. It should be noted that Balassa and Noland, who were critical of the low levels of Japanese-manufactured imports and of the nation's domestic economic policies, agreed with Bergsten and Cline that the 1980–1984 rapid growth in Japan's bilateral surpluses could not have been caused by formal protectionism because during these years formal protectionism was declining. Thus, other more complex factors had to be at work. The increase in Japanese imports as the result of the sharply appreciating yen in 1986–1988 indicated that exchange rate changes — while no longer as effective as they used to be — continue to play an important influencing role. Thus, the argument that the 1980–1984 bilateral trade imbalances were strongly influenced by the overvalued dollar cannot be disputed. Of course, other forces had to be at work as well.

Other studies and the OECD country surveys cite the different export and import structure of Japan as compared to the rest of the world, the decrease in oil prices, reduction in the use of raw materials due to major changes in the structure of output, and the general decline in the raw material intensity of various industries, as reasons for the increasing global surpluses.[4] The U.S.–Japan bilateral trade imbalances were explained by the differing business cycles of the two nations and the overvalued dollar caused by the huge American fiscal deficits of the early 1980s.

During the 1960s and 1970s the Japanese marketplace was indeed difficult, albeit not impossible, to enter due to a combination of formal and informal restraints ranging from tariffs through nontariff barriers to sociocultural traditions. But by the early 1980s the formal restrictions were fast disappearing and could no longer serve as the sole explanation of the growing Japanese surpluses and American deficits. Undoubtedly, numerous informal (nontariff) barriers continued to hamper foreign companies, and the sociocultural traditions also tended to restrict imports. Bergsten and Cline and the OECD, for example, mentioned channels of distribution systems and the *keiretsu* arrangements as major problems. They emphasized, however, that the arguments supporting such views were mostly anecdotal, and that even if such arrangements reduced imports, their impact could not readily be measured. Other sources cited Japanese product standards, certification processes, and consumer behavior as important constraints.

The Distribution System

The 1984 OECD country survey emphasized that Japan's distribution may be a particularly difficult import obstacle. In subsequent years the OECD called for a reform of the system, because its practices and complex structure which has evolved over many years and differ substantially from what exists in other industrialized countries create market entry problems. The OECD analysts had a valid point. The Japanese primary, secondary, and even tertiary wholesalers, for example, are engaged in unusually complex relationships with retailers providing services not offered in other countries. Retailers are small and numerous by international standards; according to the Economic Planning Agency (EPA), there are 14 retail shops in the country for every 1,000 people.[5] This compares with 11 in France, 6 in the United Kingdom, 6 in the United States, and 5 in the Federal Republic of Germany. Thus, in essence, with half the population Japan has approximately the same number of retailers (1,260,000) as the United States, and according to MITI (the ministry that has jurisdiction over distribution matters), the average customer base of Japanese retailers is 69 compared to

136 in the United States, 166 in the Federal Republic of Germany, and 240 in the United Kingdom. The multiple stages in the distribution system undoubtedly hamper imports in that products may have to pass from an importer/manufacturer to a sales company, a regional sales office, a primary wholesaler, sub-wholesalers, a jobber, a purchasing agent, and, finally, the retailer. On the average, distribution channels may be three times longer than in other industrialized nations, which slows the flow of goods and substantially increases prices to consumers. Furthermore, imported goods are sold almost exclusively by large-scale stores located in large cities and not by the small neighborhood shopkeepers. Manufacturers in selected industries as, for example, consumer electronics, maintain a strong network of retailers who sell only the manufacturers' products. For instance, Matsushita maintains around 28,000 retail stores whose owners are part of the corporate system and sell the company's products at or close to the price recommended by Matsushita. Under such arrangements, the manufacturer usually owns the wholesaler, distributor, the retailer and even the inventory.

Wholesalers may return unsold goods (*henpin*), provide a variety of rebates, and send sales representatives to aid the retailer's operations. Shops expect to sell around 70 percent of the products obtained from wholesalers within 90 days. The other 30 percent are returned but the cost of this is included in the price of the items sold. Retailers receive interest-free credit through the 90-day promissory notes used. All of these practices, together with the high price of land and the resulting high rents, naturally increase the cost of distribution. These practices, not found elsewhere, are the result of a long evolutionary process and of Japanese consumer behavior which is characterized by frequent small purchases of goods, among other things. The practices also can be attributed to the desire of consumers to do business with shops that sponsor local social events, have a wide assortment of products used in everyday life, and are located in the neighborhood. Although the system is frustrating and difficult for both new domestic and foreign companies to enter, it contains an inner logic that is based on traditions. The traditional practices have become entrenched into the system due to customer preference and familiarity which supersede efficiency considerations.

However, it was the eventual recognition that this system did not fully allow for the "pass-through" of the 1985–1988 yen appreciation and in response to the increasing *gaiatsu* (external pressure) that the Japanese started to have second thoughts about the impact of the distribution system on both consumer welfare and imports. In 1985, the Fair Trade Commission (FTC), concerned about competitive restrictions, requisitioned a study of the distribution system. The study, published in 1986, concluded that the distribution arrangements and practices may indeed make it difficult for foreign companies to enter the market.[6] They recommended that the FTC consider measures that would eliminate or at least change some of the more burdensome features.

The continual *gaiatsu* and complaints voiced in Japan by members of the business community and mass media opinion-makers eventually prompted former prime minister Takeshita to announce at the June 1988 Toronto summit meetings of the industrialized nations that Japan was going to reform its distribution system. Shortly after his return to Tokyo, a new position of Director General for Commercial Affairs was created in MITI. The director general was put in charge of reviewing the distribution system and of developing recommendations for change. As usual, various committees were also created to study the problem at hand and to initiate the consensus-forming process that is necessary for any kind of reform. A subcommittee of the ad hoc Special Advisory Council on Enforcement of Administrative Reform convened in the summer of 1988 to formulate recommendations. MITI's Industrial Structure Council and the Small and Medium Enterprise Policy Making Council also opened joint discussions. Other agencies as, for example, the Economic Planning Agency (EPA), created its Distribution Problem Research Group which published an interim report in June 1988 that came out strongly in favor of reform.

Concurrently with these developments, the United States increased its pressure on Japan. At the U.S.–Japan Trade Committee meeting in Hawaii in September 1988, American negotiators emphasized that this was the first meeting intended to deal with the issue of a thorough and continuous reform of the Japanese distribution system. The U.S. side demanded concrete changes in three areas: the Large-Scale Retail Stores Control Law, the liquor sales licensing system, and the regulation of premiums and labeling. The Americans argued that the control law limits the number of large-scale stores which are the major sellers of imported goods. This, in turn, keeps up the high price of imports. Moreover, the 1938 liquor licensing system which is managed by local tax collection agencies requires applicants to file 20 different forms and, in most instances, obtain the consent of the existing retailers through the local chamber of commerce and industry. As a consequence, by the end of March 1988, only 371, or 8.7 percent, of the total 6,455 supermarket firms operated by the member firms of the Japan Chain Stores Association carried a license. According to the Association, this compares to 7.2 percent in 1973, some 15 years ago. The Americans also objected to the rules governing the use of premiums to spur sales and the labeling requirements which they considered unreasonable.

The U.S. position was supported by the 1988 OECD country report, the European Community, which also called for major changes in distribution, and by the head of public affairs committee of the *Keidanren* (Japan

Federation of Economic Organizations). In a speech at the Foreign Correspondents Club of Japan in the fall of 1988, the *Keidanren* representative pointed out that the retail industry is regulated by 12 laws and that the application process of opening large-scale retail stores involves 73 different approvals and permits from the government. Such criticism, together with the reform demands, prompted the editors of the *Weekly Toyo Keizai* to declare in their August 6, 1988, issue that the era of the *ryutsu kaikoku* (the opening of the Japanese distribution system) has begun.[7] George Fields, the chief executive of ASI Market Research (Japan), Inc., and one of the country's foremost marketing experts, observed that *kaikoku* was the term the Japanese used when Commodore Perry's fleet arrived in the last century. He added that the *Toyo Keizai* editors also made the point that the "... black ships have arrived again — in the form of relaxation of regulations."[8]

By late fall of 1988, the subcommittee of the ad hoc Special Advisory Council on Enforcement of Administrative Reform presented its recommendations to the prime minister. The Council's recommendations usually carry a great deal of weight; they were, for example, very instrumental in the privatization of Nippon Telegraph and Telephone (NTT) and the Japanese Railways. The Council, which also proposed deregulation in six other areas of the economy, recommended the issuing of an increased number of liquor licenses to retail stores and the relaxation of regular holiday business hours in addition to other measures. But it stopped short of recommending the elimination of the controversial Large-Scale Retail Stores Control Law and proposed only to enforce the law "properly" so as to correct "customs" that obstruct the opening of such stores. More specifically, it recommended the reduction of the time allowed for negotiations between the owners of the existing small-scale local ("mom and pop") stores and the large-scale retail outlets.

On December 13, 1988, the cabinet accepted the recommendations and announced its intention to implement the changes. In fact, before the end of the year, rules prohibiting comparative advertising were rescinded, prohibitions on loss-leaders of the "buy-one-get-one-free" type had been eliminated, and the limits on sales-context monetary prizes offered by manufacturers for retailers had been lifted. However, in a report on developments in the distribution system in the 1990's MITI's advisory group in June 1989 recommended only that the large retail stores law be applied more flexibly. It did not call for the repeal of the law.

The cautious recommendation to adjust but not to eliminate the Large-Scale Retail Stores Control Law confirmed that in spite of the strong external pressure and increasing domestic criticism, the Japanese are not willing to quickly dismantle the existing distribution system. The law, the centerpiece of the system, originated in the Department Stores Act of 1955 which was designed to limit the opening of large retail stores. At a later date it was replaced by the Adjustment of Retail Business Operations in Large-Scale Retail Stores law which was broader in scope and covered department stores and retail chain stores. However, because its regulations were so general as to allow the formation of new retail chain-stores, local retail associations pressured LDP politicians into passing the more restrictive current law in 1979.

This law divides retail stores into categories according to size. New stores with a proposed sales floor of more than 500 square meters must gain the approval of local residents and of small shopkeepers beforehand. If the new store is to be larger than 1,500 square meters, MITI's approval must also be obtained. Thus, small-scale local shopkeepers can veto the establishment of any store exceeding 500 square meters, the size of a modest convenience retail outlet in the United States or Western Europe. It is the resulting protracted negotiations with the small retailers that lengthen the approval procedure from the theoretical four months to possibly several years. It must, however, be pointed out that sometimes the resistance of the small local shopkeepers is organized by the owners of the already established large-scale stores in the area who are as much interested in keeping competitors out as are the small shopkeepers. But, whatever the case may be, the resulting limited competition increases prices and, thus, may constrain demand.

The Council's unwillingness to propose the elimination of the control law was controversial. A number of Japanese business leaders and the editorial writers of major newspapers (*Asahi Shimbun*) complained that the recommendations to deregulate the economy in general, and the distributions system in particular, did not go far enough. Japan's trading partners reacted angrily to the failure to eliminate what they consider to be the centerpiece of a major nontariff barrier. On the other hand, the Japanese labor unions claimed that the deregulation plan would inevitably deteriorate working conditions. In responding to the criticism, members of the Council pointed out that if they had made more drastic recommendations, the entire deregulation effort would have been dissipated by the various interest groups defending their own turf.

Although controversial, the cautious recommendations of the Council were based on a realistic assessment of the situation. Most Japanese retailers are small, but in spite of this they have strong political influence. They are numerous and well known in their communities. According to the EPA, approximately 20 percent of Japan's working population is engaged in distribution, with 1 out of 4 nonmanufacturing businesses being a wholesaler; in the United States this ratio is 1 out of 10; and in the Federal Republic of Germany, it is 1 out of 9. Based on such statistics, it is understandable that politicans are reluctant to support drastic changes in the distribution system which could provoke resentment at the polls. A 1989 survey by the *Nikkei Marketing Journal*, a major industry newspaper, for example, revealed that more than 800 local government bodies have drawn up measures to restrict the expansion of large-scale stores in their communities. Any interference from Tokyo with these measures could spell political trouble.

The dominance and, thus, the political influence of small shopkeepers, however, is going to decline over time due to a number of forces already at work. For the first time since such statistics have been kept, the 1985 Retail Census showed a 5 percent decline in the number of small stores from 1982 to 1985. Over the following three years the trend sharply accelerated and the number of retail stores dropped 55 percent between 1985 and 1988, as reported by the *Japan Economic Journal* in February 1989. While a similar trend is affecting small wholesalers whose number has fallen from over 420,000 in 1982 to under 400,000 in 1987, the number of convenience stores increased by 40.8 percent between 1985 and 1988. As reported by the *Japan Economic Journal*, applications for new retail shops exceeding 1,500 square meters were also up by 14 percent from July 1987 to June 1988.

The decline in the number of small-scale retailers and wholesalers is the combined result of several trends. Owners of small outlets are aging and dying off; and many of the younger family members do not want to follow in the footsteps of their parents. Others are trying to escape the inevitable by joining convenience store chains. For example, of the more than 3,000 7-Eleven franchisees, most are former small shopkeepers. Due to an increase in the number of working women and changing life-styles, consumers also are beginning to be more interested in time-convenience, i.e., 24-hour or mail-order services. *Endaka* (the sharp appreciation of the yen during 1986–1988) sprouted a number of new discount stores which offer previously unavailable low-priced imports from the Southeast Asian region that are appealing to price-conscious consumers, although lately a number of such products ran into difficulties due to poor warranty and service policies.

The acceptance of imports is also promoted by new types of import activities. For example, "parallel imports," where products are obtained directly from the country of origin or from a third country and not from the traditional "sole" manufacturers' agents, and "grey imports," where Japanese exports are re-imported to take advantage of their lower prices abroad, are becoming widespread. Original Equipment Manufacturer

(OEM) imports, which are Japanese-designed but foreign-produced products, and "reverse imports," that is, products manufactured by Japanese corporate subsidiaries abroad, are also mushrooming. A case in point is the very successful Honda Accord Coupe which is produced in America. According to MITI, such imports rose 76 percent in fiscal year (FY) 1988 over FY 1987, and are expected to continue to grow. As a result of these developments, the proportion of the independent retailers selling only the products of certain manufacturers (exclusive retailers) in the consumer electronics industry, for example, declined from well over 50 percent in the 1970s to around 40 percent by 1989. Not surprisingly, the result is a war between the major manufacturing companies and the discounters and other mass retailers which offer better prices and choice. MITI data also show that large retail outlets are buying and selling more imported products than ever before. In FY 1986 imports made up only 12 percent of total sales, by FY 1987 such sales increased to 16 percent. Nomura Research Institute's data show a more modest trend in that they found that the departments stores sales of imported products as a percentage of total sales has recently been increasing at 1 percent annually.

Technological developments such as the Point-of-Sale (POS) computer networks are also beginning to change traditional distribution practices which have long sustained the small intermediaries. For example, small retailers can now band together to order in bulk from large wholesalers and thereby reduce their dependence on the less efficient small wholesalers who have traditionally supplied them.

It is in this already changing context that the Council's cautious recommendations and MITI's reluctance to reform the system drastically should be considered. Undoubtedly, the evolutionary process combined with the gradual changes will take more time to show results than the quick adjustments that the United States, the Europeans, and a number of Japanese businessmen and opinion-makers have called for. On the other hand, such gradual change is more acceptable to the majority of Japanese who do not like solutions that cause social dislocations and economic hardship. Of course, this assumes that the various vested interests recognize the undercurrent and pay more attention to consumer welfare in the adjustment process.

By the spring of 1989, it became clear that the cautious change process caused disagreement with the United States and the European Community (EC). However, the Americans and Europeans cannot pressure the Japanese too much on this issue because the existing international trade laws consider a nation's distribution system a domestic concern, particularly as long as domestic manufacturers are subject to the same restraints as foreign companies, which by and large, is the case today and will be even more so as the gradual changes continue.

The Keiretsu Arrangements

The potential restraining effects of the *Keiretsu* system on imports has also received a great deal of attention outside Japan. The *Keiretsu* are groupings of manufacturing companies organized either around major (city) banks (*kin-yu*) or around large corporations (*Kigyo*).[9] The dominant form are the groupings organized around the six major (city) banks. Because of their potential to restrict competition, the FTC periodically investigates their activities.

Undoubtedly, the *Keiretsu* arrangements are based on a variety of interdependencies among the participating companies and their banks as, for example, financing, mutual shareholdings, buying and selling transactions, and personal ties. Although they are in some ways similar to the pre-World War II *zaibatsu*, they tend to function differently under the watchful eye of the FTC which is the enforcer of the relevant Law Relating to Prohibition of Private Monopoly and Maintenance of Fair Trade, or, as it is widely known, the Antimonopoly Law.

Over the years the governments and business circles of the United States and Western Europe have often charged that the *Keiretsu* companies reject business with firms outside the group in general and foreign companies in particular whenever the goods and services offered directly compete with those provided by the group members. Moreover, they claimed, this is true even if the services offered by the nongroup members are better in quality and price.

Historically, the major reason for the evolution of the pre-World War II *zaibatsu* and their successor, the *Keiretsu*, aside from financing, was the desire for the continuity of supplies and orders. Japanese businesses, just like Americans or Europeans, have always preferred certain suppliers over others for reasons of continuity as long as the price, quality, and other critical transaction considerations were within acceptable ranges. Thus, it is possible that restrictive intragroup practices occur even today. However, to argue that such practices are institutionalized through the *keiretsu* system regardless of the variations in transaction considerations ignores the highly competitive nature of the Japanese marketplace, and the aggressive growth and cost reduction orientation (i.e., price competitiveness) of the Japanese companies, as discussed in chapter 1. No Japanese company could consistently afford to violate basic economic considerations and still remain domestically and internationally competitive over the long-run, particularly after the sharp yen appreciation during 1986–1988.

The importance of the *keiretsu* system in the Japanese economy is also exaggerated abroad. According to a 1986 survey by the FTC, industrial corporations belonging to the six largest *keiretsu* (Mitsubishi, Mitsui, Sumitomo, Fuyo, Sanwa, and Dai-Ichi-Kangyo) accounted for only 4.6 percent of all employees, 15 percent of total assets, 16.5 percent of total sales, and 17.5 percent of total net profits of the Japanese industrial sector in 1984.[10] According to a 1989 report of the FTC, the 193 companies which are members of the six "keiretsu" own an average of a little over 22 percent of the total outstanding shares of the other member companies of the group. This compares with over 25 percent in 1981. Moreover, 68 percent of the 193 firms employ one or more executives of the other group companies, delegated primarily by the groups "lead bank." The FTC also found that the 163 manufacturing and trading companies of the six groups account for 15 percent of total sales and 15 percent of all assets made and held by Japanese firms. Thus, the importance of the groups seems to have somewhat declined since the 1984 report. The 1989 report, however, pointed out that if subsidiaries and other related companies are included, the "keiretsu" groups represent 25 percent of total sales and a little over 30 percent of total assets of Japanese companies. Corresponding data for 1984 shows that this figure has not changed over the years.

Even if loyalty influences business decisions, the magnitude of the *keiretsu* buying and selling transactions does not seem large enough to act as a major nontariff barrier as alleged. In 1984, the FTC reported, the six largest trading companies, each belonging to a different *keiretsu*, on the average obtained 11.5 percent of total purchases and made 4.6 percent of their total sales to other members of the group.[11] For the manufacturing companies of the same *keiretsu*, the proportions were 12.4 and 20.4 percent, respectively. Thus, even if the 11.5 and 12.4 percent of total purchases of trading and manufacturing companies, and the 4.6 and 20.4 percent of all of their sales were made entirely on the basis of group loyalty — an assumption that can neither be sustained nor challenged — the overwhelming majority of all purchases and of all sales by the trading and manufacturing *keiretsu* members were with nongroup companies.

According to the same FTC study, the intragroup transactions involved a number of broad product categories as shown in table 2–3. Except for

TABLE 2-3.   Proportion of major product categories in the intragroup transactions of the six major *Keiretsu*: 1984

Product categories	Purchases	Sales
Textiles and apparel	3.1%	1.2%
Food and agricultural products	0.5%	0.6%
Mining, metal materials, and chemicals	9.9%	6.7%
Machines and equipment	21.1%	2.8%

Source: Internal reference papers (Tokyo: Fair Trade Commission, and the Economic Planning Agency, 1986).

machines and equipment, the percentages of intragroup deals in the other categories are rather low.

At the present time it is not clear what the future holds for the *Keiretsu*. The structural changes in the economy, the sharp appreciation of the yen during 1986–1988, the liberalization of capital markets, and the new 1987 worldwide capital adequacy rules of the Bank of International Settlements (BIS) are just a few of the developments that may challenge their existence or merely alter some of their practices.

Equity financing by Japanese corporations is rapidly increasing as financial markets are internationalized and liberalized. The bullish stock market of 1986–1989 has prompted many corporations to issue convertible domestic bonds and to increase their capital through public offerings. The favorable business climate, the strong domestic demand, and the increase in research and development activities are the major reasons for corporations seeking massive infusions of new funds.

This trend is reinforced by the BIS requirement that banks engaged in international banking increase their capital adequacy ratios. The capital adequacy levels of Japanese banks were much lower than those of their American or European competitors, most of whom have already reached the required level. Faced with the necessity to increase their net worth rapidly, banks are thus forced, among other measures, to become more profit-conscious.

As the banks turn increasingly profit-conscious, i.e., stiffen their loan conditions and the corporate self-financing ability improves, the traditional influence of the large "city" banks over the *Keiretsu* members is likely to decline. Thus, just as in the case of the channel of distribution system, certain forces are already under way that are going to weaken the *raison d'être* for the traditional arrangements.

Product Standards and Consumer Behavior

In addition to singling out the distribution and *keiretsu* systems, critics of Japan have argued that Japanese product standards and consumer behavior also significantly limit imports. It is true that historically, the Japanese have always used a different system of establishing and enforcing product standards. In most industrialized nations, if a product fails or injures someone, the aggrieved users sue the manufacturer or distributor. In Japan, the public expects the government to establish and strictly enforce product standards and certification systems to protect the consumer, who very rarely sues the producer if anything goes wrong. Thus, Japan's comprehensive product standards and certification systems were developed to protect and satisfy the Japanese public, and not to keep foreign products out of the marketplace.

This is not to say that the complex standards and other requirements did not create problems for foreign companies trying to enter the Japanese marketplace. Their restrictive impact was reinforced by the Japanese legal system which is different from that of the rest of the world, particularly the United States. The absence of clearly written laws and recognizable underlying legal principles, together with the traditional administrative guidance, made it difficult for foreign companies to obtain the insight they needed to function within the Japanese regulatory system. This, and the lack of transparency in the governmental decision-making process which, compared to that of the United States, was subject to more cultural nuances reflected in the practice of administrative guidance, frustrated and irritated Americans and other nationalities dealing with Japanese government agencies in charge of product standards and certification.

Therefore, product standards and related requirements needed to be reviewed and changed to conform to international practices. It is, however, very difficult to obtain estimates of the impact of the standards and other requirements on Japan's trade balances with the rest of the world, and with the United States in particular. Nevertheless, Bergesten and Cline tried, and claim that about $5–8 billion in American exports may have been negatively affected by the Japanese practices.[12]

As a signatory of the products standards code of the 1979 MTN Agreement (Tokyo round), the Japanese obligated themselves to remedy the situation during the early 1980s. As part of a set of measures, they established the Office of the Trade Ombudsman (OTO) in 1982 to provide a central clearinghouse for complaints concerning the various standards, certification requirements, approval procedures, and other nontariff barriers. Eventually, changes were introduced and new measures were taken to increase the transparency of the standards formulation process. Thus, while remnants of the traditional arrangements still hindered foreign companies prior to the 1985 Action Program, product standards and certification systems were no longer as restrictive as in the past. The government, however, addressed the problem in a comprehensive and consistent fashion only in 1985 when, through its Action Program (to be discussed in the next chapter), it began simplifying and eliminating the remaining restrictive product standards and related requirements. This process was virtually finished by 1988.

Japanese consumer behavior was also strongly criticized for its discriminatory attitude toward foreign products during the early 1980s. Government officials and businessmen abroad argued that imports have very little chance to break into the Japanese marketplace because consumers have always preferred domestic products even if they were of a lesser quality and higher price. This point of view became an article of faith and, in a sense, a self-fulfilling prophecy in that it discouraged American, European, and other companies from even trying to enter the marketplace. Undoubtedly, Japanese consumers are difficult to please. They are demanding and are specially quality-conscious; they hold the providers of products are services to the highest standard of manufacturing and marketing. Consumers also exhibit strong loyalty to products that they have found to be satisfactory and do not readily switch to substitutes, domestic or foreign, unless the substitutes are superior, i.e., provide more consumer benefits. It is also very likely that the homogeneity of taste which had prevailed in the past as well as the strong sense of nationalism characteristic of the Japanese had influenced consumer behavior to an extent that may have led to the preference for domestic products over imported ones. It was, however, a gross exaggeration to argue that no matter what, the Japanese would not buy imported goods except as expensive gifts on special occasions. Already the findings of a 1983 consumer attitude survey indicated this much, as shown in table 2–4.

As the data show, while many Japanese consumers did prefer domestic products (26 percent), the majority (66 percent) did not differentiate among products on the basis of origin, but on the basis of total value provided. In this respect, the Japanese already, during the early 1980's were like Americans, Germans, French, or any other nationally. However, due to the complex, multi-layered distribution system, most foreign products were more expensive than domestic ones, and price was seen by Japanese consumers as a major disadvantage of imports. The results of a survey conducted by the Prime Minister's office, shown in table 2–5, confirmed this conclusion.

TABLE 2–4.   Japanese consumer attitudes toward foreign and domestic products: 1983

Consumers	Percentages
Do not differentiate between foreign and domestic products	66.3
Prefer domestic products	26.4
Prefer foreign products	2.3
Don't know	5.0

Source: *Analysis of and Proposals Concerning the Japanese Distribution System, Commercial Practices, and Other Corporate Behavior* (Tokyo: Manufactured Imports Promotion Committee, 1983), p. 12.

Thus, except for highly differentiated luxury imports purchased mostly as gifts which were expected to carry higher price tags than similar domestic products, it appeared that the high price rather than the foreign origin was what kept Japanese consumers from buying more imports. It is also noteworthy that for electrical appliances, which require careful postsales service, price was not the major consideration. Consumers were more concerned about the perceived inability to obtain service and parts on a continuous basis.

Although these and similar consumer-attitude survey results were available during the first half of the 1980s, they were not taken seriously abroad. Apart from legitimate methodological concerns that there may have been a gap between what consumers said and actually did, these results were dismissed as typical Japanese excuses to provide an explanation for the low level of imports. Anyone taking the findings seriously was considered to be either working for the Japanese or to have some other vested interest. These innuendos were similar to the ones directed at Bergsten and Cline when their findings showed that Japanese protectionism alone could not explain the increasing bilateral and current account surpluses during 1981–1984, and when they argued that some other forces had to be at work as well.

In spite of the widespread scepticism abroad, the findings of the consumer attitude surveys of the early 1980s were insightful. While some consumers preferred domestic products over imports, the majority did not differentiate between domestic and foreign products and it was the high price of imports and their often low level of service that discouraged purchases. But, not surprisingly, it took the sharp 1985–1988 appreciation of the yen to convince the sceptics that such findings reflected real consumer attitudes.

The September 1985 Plaza-Accord appreciated the world's major

TABLE 2–5.   Japanese views of the advantages and disadvantages of foreign products: 1984 (multiple response in percentages)

Advantages		Disadvantages	
Food products			
Taste good	50	Expensive	54
Make nice gifts	37	Unsure how to use because of	
Satisfying to eat or drink	36	insufficient instructions in	
Good quality	26	Japanese, etc.	22
Inexpensive	11	Taste bad	6
		Poor quality	3
Clothing			
Good colors, patterns, designs	57	Expensive	56
Satisfying to wear	42	Wrong shapes, sizes	16
Good quality	35	Poor quality	16
Inexpensive	26	Poor colors, patterns, designs	7
Macke nice gifts	15		
Electric appliances			
Work well	47	Inadequate after-sales service	53
Durable	36	Expensive	28
Satisfying to use	29	No instructions in Japanese	12
Good quality	22	Wrong shapes, sizes	11
Good colors, patterns, designs	19	Work poorly	9
Make nice gifts	11	Poor colors, patterns, designs	8
Inexpensive	9	Hard to use	5
		Poor quality	5
		Break easily	5

Source: *Imports in Daily Life* (Tokyo: The Prime Minister's Office, 1985).

currencies, particularly the yen, against the U.S. dollar. The strong yen, or *Endaka*, as the Japanese refer to this phenomenon, unleashed a set of forces whose effects are still reverberating in the Japanese economy and marketplace. The 41.5 percent appreciation of the yen against the U.S. dollar in 1986 was followed by a 16.5 percent increase 1987 and a 12.8 percent rise in 1988. This development, in conjunction with the domestic economic boom of 1986–1989, generated by the switch from export-led to domestic demand-led growth fueled by easy money and a more expansive fiscal policy, resulted in a dramatic increase of imports. Measured on a dollar-basis, imports went up by 18.2 percent in 1987 and by 25.4 percent in 1988, as reported by the Ministry of Finance in January 1989. Manufactured imports, only 31 percent of total imports in 1985, reached 44 percent in 1987 and 49 percent in 1988. This, however, by no means argues that Japan's overal import-performance is satisfactory; both its overall import/GNP ratio and manufactured goods to total imports ratio are still considerably lower than that of major Western European nations and the United States.

Nonetheless, these import data confirm that, given appropriate price incentives, Japanese consumers are willing to buy products regardless of their national origin as long as the quality and service meet their standards. It is particularly noteworthy that consumers have changed their price-quality perception of imports from the developing nations in general and the Newly Industrialized Countries (NICs) in particular. Products from South Korea, Taiwan, Singapore, and other nations, whose quality two or three years ago were suspect, are among the top-selling imports in the Japan of 1989. Of course, although the price-quality perception has changed, shoddy and poorly serviced products still have no chance in the marketplace.

The upsurge in imports occurred in spite of the fact that the yen's appreciation was not fully passed on to the consumers. According to the EPA, the yen's appreciation resulted in approximately $242 billion in exchange rate gains for Japan between 1985 and 1988. However, only about one-third of this gain ($74.2 billion) was passed on to the Japanese consumers. It is important to note that because a large percentage of Japanese imports consists of industrial and agricultural raw materials whose prices reflect changing global supply-demand conditions, it is difficult to interpret the data to determine the pass-through gains of consumers. Nonetheless, it is clear that consumers are not satisfied with the gains they obtained, according to a survey taken in February and March of 1988 and released by the Prime Minister's Office in the late summer of the same year. Only 40 percent of those polled saw foreign goods as less expensive than in the past, and approximately 40 percent claimed that import prices did not decline at all. About 8 percent believed that the benefits of the appreciated yen were passed along sufficiently. This was an important finding because 70 percent also pointed out that price was the most important consideration in the purchase of domestic or imported products, an insight that the 1983 surveys had already indicated.

The majority of respondents in the 1988 survey stated that they found the products of the Southeast Asian NICs much less expensive than those from Western Europe or the United States. This explains the dramatic upsurge in imports from South Korea, Taiwan, Hong Kong, and Singapore during the 1986–1989 period. It is believed in Japanese import circles that consumers are willing to buy the products of these countries if their prices are 40 percent lower than those of comparable domestic products. Apparently the NIC producers managed to overcome the price barrier since, according to MITI, imports from the "Four Tigers" increased by 60 percent in 1987 over 1986, and 24.2 percent in 1988 over 1987, totaling U.S. $48 billion in 1988. This compared with $46.9 billion in imports from the European Community in the same year. While these figures include the so-called "reverse imports," i.e., finished goods and parts or components manufactured by Japanese subsidiaries in these countries, the fact remains that these are imports from developing nations whose past import-share in Japan was very low by international standards (6.3 percent as opposed to 6.9 percent for the EC and 9.0 percent for the United States in 1987).

There are many import bargains in Japan today. According to the *Nikkei Trendy* magazine which regularly compares the prices of domestic and imported products, during the spring of 1988 a Japanese 20-inch color TV cost $617 while an import cost $375, a 65 percent difference. An imported BMX bike sold for $100 while the comparable domestic product sold for $233; foreign portable compact disc-players fetched $154 but the domestic equivalent had a price-tag of $232. It is no wonder that Japanese consumers have partially overcome their suspicions concerning the quality of low-priced imports and have begun to resist the high prices of domestic goods. While this resistance has not yet evolved into what could be called a "consumer revolution," it is significant that, according to the previously cited 1988 survey, the majority of the respondents who have expressed strong price-consciousness were under 30 years of age. It appears that the more traveled and probably better informed younger Japanese are no longer accepting the high domestic prices. Even more significant is the fact that more than 50 percent of the respondents polled expressed the view that it must be the complex domestic distribution system that enables domestic manufacturers to uphold their high prices and enables distributors to withhold a substantial part of the yen appreciation from the consumers. It should be noted that such consumer views were reinforced by the findings of a 1988 EPA study published about the same time as the survey results.

In light of these developments and as the previously discussed trends work themselves through the distribution system, the prices of imported goods should continue to decline. This may be particularly true for the high-priced luxury goods, because effective April 1, 1989, the 1988 tax reform act eliminated excise taxes, some as high as 30 percent, on what the previous tax code classified as luxury goods such as cars, refrigerators, TV sets, and liquor. The new consumption tax of 3 percent is applied uniformly to all goods, this should benefit not only consumers but also American and European firms marketing luxury goods in Japan.

The tax change together with the "wealth-effect," i.e., the increased propensity to spend as wealth increases, should, within the foreseeable future, bring Japanese import ratios in line with those of Western Europe and the United States. The findings of a 1988 Bank of Japan study concerning Japan's income import-elasticity supports this conclusion. This elasticity measures import increases in response to income growth, that is, the wealth-effect on the purchase of foreign goods. When this elasticity is at 1, imports grow at the same rate as income.

During the 1950s and the 1960s, a time of high economic growth when oil and capital equipment had to be purchased in large quantities from abroad, Japan's import elasticity against income was 1:1 and 1:2, respectively. The elasticity declined to 0.6–0.7 during the 1970s when growth slowed. However, in 1986 the elasticity began to increase and reached 0.96 in the April-June period of 1988, and surpassed 1 by early 1989. The recent growth of imports exceeded that of income due to the surge in domestic demand generated by the switch from export-led to domestic demand-led growth and was marked particularly by an increase in manufactured imports which are very income-sensitive.

It is interesting to note that some domestic critics have argued that part of the wealth-effect may be the result of the exorbitant land prices which convinced many Japanese that they cannot afford a home and, thus, should spend their income on manufactured imports and leisure services. While there is no clear evidence to support this argument, it may very well be true. However, whatever the case may be, the fact remains that imports are on an upswing. But it would be a mistake to expect this trend to calm the waters of the troubled U.S.–Japan economic relationship, because America's share in the import boom is disappointingly low, although, on a dollar-basis, in 1988 U.S. firms exported 33 percent more than they did in 1987. Most of this was accounted for by food, lumber, and computerized office equipment. Unfortunately, however, in the critical category of manufactured imports the U.S. share declined from 35.4 percent in 1985 to 26 percent in 1988 and a stunningly low 14.7 percent in 1988. This trend is even more disturbing when hourly manufacturing wages are considered. According to the Industrial Bank of Japan, such rates in Japan were nearly 25 percent higher than in the United States at the prevailing exchange rate during the first half of 1988, providing a price advantage to American sellers.

It is also noteworthy that the large U.S. share losses in Japanese-manufactured imports were to countries as, for example, the Federal Republic of Germany, whose currency depreciated less against the yen than the U.S. dollar, whose hourly manufacturing rates are also higher than those in America, and whose firms are exposed to the same import and distributions system as are all other exporters to Japan. Thus, it seems that

America's declining share of Japanese-manufactured imports is caused by forces other than the so often referred to "Japanese trade barriers." A case in point is the automobile market. According to a survey by the *Japan Economic Journal* published in November 1988, the top 10 imported automobiles the Japanese want to buy were: 5 German, 2 Swedish, 1 British, 1 French. The only U.S.-manufactured car listed in eighth place was the Honda Accord Coupe, a Japanese "reverse import."

In its 1989 "Economic White Paper" the Economic Planning Agency stressed that Japan must move faster to ease various regulations and to restructure its economy in the interest of increasing imports. The report, which serves as a guideline for future economic policies, also restated the nation's commitment to promote economic growth through the increase of domestic demand rather than the growth of exports.

In the fall of 1989 MITI announced a plan to boost imports based on a tax-relief scheme and low interest rate loans available to retailers and wholesalers buying imported goods. Effective April 1, 1990, the plan allows importers to deduct a small percentage of the cost of foreign goods from their annual tax bill and encourages particularly small retailers and wholesalers to finance their imports through low-interest rate loans provided by the Small Business Finance Corporation.

A discussion of the trade controversies, particularly as they apply to U.S.--Japan bilateral trade relations, would be incomplete without a discussion of two additional considerations. The first is the international competitiveness of the U.S. economy. While it is an exaggeration to refer to this process as de-industrialization, it is undeniable that the American economy is not doing as well internationally as it should to maintain a leading role in the world.

The second consideration involves the use of trade balances as the sole measure of the overall economic relations between nations. Although, as discussed later, there are some limitations to the use of more comprehensive measures, particularly in U.S.–Japan trade, there is increasing evidence that trade balance measures alone are an inadequate basis for international economic policy formulation.

America's International Competitiveness

The measurement of a nation's international competitiveness is a complex and somewhat uncertain undertaking, because competition takes place at the industry level and is conducted by individual firms. Moreover, the traditional standards such as the trade imbalances, import penetration ratios, or declining export shares in the global marketplace are at best unreliable. Nonetheless, if such standards show negative trends over extended periods of time, it is reasonable to suspect that the nation in question has problems "producing goods and services under free market conditions which meet the test of the international marketplace while simultaneously maintaining and expanding the real income of its citizens."[13] By most of the standards used to measure the overall international competitive performance of a nation, the American economy appears to have reached this stage in recent years while the Japanese and the West Europeans have improve their performance.

It would, however, be an exaggeration to argue — as a number of observers have done in the United States and abroad — that America is in the process of being deindustrialized or losing its eminent position in the world economy. What is happening is an economic realignment of the most advanced nations which undoubtedly reduces the dominant position of America but does not eliminate it. Moreover, while there are no easy solutions, through a concerted effort of the business community, the educational establishment, Congress, and the Administration, the vast economic, technological, and human resources of the nation could be mobilized in a manner that would allow the United States to regain much of the strength that eroded during the last two decades. As mentioned in the first chapter, this is not a matter of being "Number One" again but a matter of participating in the global marketplace to the optimum capacity of the American economy which continues to be considerable.

The major reason for the declining international competitiveness of the United States is, among others, the slow industrial productivity growth of the last two decades. Table 2–6 shows a summary of comparative industrial productivity trends published in the 1986 report of the Bureau of Labor Statistics of the U.S. Department of Labor.

While in terms of aggregate productivity (Gross Domestic Product per hour worked) the United States is still the world's most productive economy, other industrialized nations such as France and the Federal Republic of Germany are beginning to close the gap. Although America's industrial productivity growth rate has somewhat improved during the second half of the 1980s, the growth rate is still less than half that of Japan and about 40 percent below that of Canada, the Federal Republic of Germany, France, Italy, and the United Kingdom. Moreover, according to studies by the Congressional Office of Technology and others, even the improvement shown beginning in 1985 may have been the result of the Department of Commerce's measurement errors rather than of real improvement.

Tentative explanations for the slow growth in industrial productivity in

TABLE 2-6. Comparison of industrial productivity increases in selected industrialized countries: 1985 and 1973–1985 (in percentages)

Country	1985	1973–1985 (Average annual increase)
Belgium	n.a.	5.7
Federal Republic of Germany	5.7	3.8
France	3.8	4.5
Japan	5.0	5.6
United Kingdom	2.8	2.8
United States	2.8	2.2

Source: *International Comparisons of Manufacturing Productivity and Labor Costs* (Washington, D.C.: Bureau of Labor Statistics. U.S. Department of Labor, 1986), pp. 2 and 6.

the United States abound; conclusive evidence concerning the restraining effect of a specific set of factors, however, is not available. The following is an overview of the nature of those factors which productivity researchers regularly identify as contributing to the slowdown.[14]

One of the most frequently mentioned major reasons for the declining international competitiveness of the United States is its poor savings-investment balance during recent years. From the mid-1970s to 1982, the balance averaged out to about zero, but beginning in 1983, the situation changed, and the savings shortfall began to take on serious proportions. It reached 2.4 percent of GNP in 1984, and this unfavorable trend continued into 1985–1986. The savings shortfalls were exacerbated by rapidly increasing federal deficits and the resulting government demand for funds, which necessitated capital inflows from abroad, particularly from Japan where the savings-investment balance was reversed.

Thus, from the late 1970s to the early 1980s, America's low saving rate, together with the growing demand of the federal government for funds, contributed to the growth of the current account deficit. It also generated high real interest rates which made it too costly to invest to maintain international competitiveness. In today's world markets effective competition requires not only low real manufacturing costs but also the production and marketing of modern, high quality products; many American industries have not invested sufficiently to meet this requirement. For example, between 1981 and 1984, total business expenditures for new plant and equipment increased from $315 billion to only $354 billion, or about 3 percent annually.

The situation had not changed by the late 1980s. America's national, or total, savings rate (savings by households, corporations, and governments at all levels) was under 2 percent — less than one-eighth of the Japanese, one-fifth of the West German, and less than one-third of the British national savings rate during this period. This continued to keep the cost of capital high (about twice as high as in Japan), necessitated increased borrowing from abroad, and restrained investments in plant and equipment. American businesses invested at less than half of the average investment rate of their major competitors in the highly industrialized nations.

During the 1980s research and development (R&D) expenditures also declined; as a percentage of GNP they sunk lower than in Japan and Western Europe. As a result, from 1980 to 1986 America went from having a $26.7 billion trade surplus in high-technology products to a $2.6 billion deficit. According to R&D experts, a major reason for this was the diversion of research and development funds from the civilian sector to the military sector in recent years. Military R&D, in turn, lost its relevance to the civilian markets because it calls primarily for high performance at any cost, while civilian R&D is more interested in low cost, reliability, ease of maintenance, and long production runs. These differences make it difficult to transfer military technological advances to more mundane civilian use.

A faltering public secondary educational system which produces large numbers of high-school graduates who are functional illiterates is another often cited reason.[15] Although the United States has an official literacy rate of 99 percent and 25 percent of all American workers are college graduates (as reported by the Department of Labor in 1988) compared with only 20 percent just 10 years ago, there are millions of workers who cannot read, write, or think well enough to meet the demands of the industrial workplace. Corporations are finding that their new workers are not up to the demands of even their nontechnical entry-level jobs. Thus, they have to spend a great deal of time and financial resources to test and to re-train workers. According to a Hudson Institute report ("Workforce 2000"), the situation will be even more difficult in the future, because by the year 2000 those groups whose educational skills have historically lagged will make up more than 80 percent of the people entering the workforce.

Certain government policies have also negatively affected industrial productivity growth rates beginning during the mid-1970s. Although the magnitude of the negative impact of the Environmental Protection Agency (EPA) and of the Occupational Safety and Health Administration (OSHA) regulations on industrial productivity growth is controversial, most studies on the topic found that a restraining effect was present, particularly until 1981 when the incoming Reagan Administration tried to reduce the impact of these regulations.

In a less direct but equally demaging fashion, management practices have also contributed to the declining international competitiveness of the United States. While the executives of some major corporations are trying to be growth/productivity/opportunity oriented, the majority of them show a preoccupation with short-term objectives, with financial coups rather than with long-term competitiveness.

A major reason for this is the recent shift in control over corporations from individual to institutional investors, such as pensions funds, insurance companies, trust funds, and banks. Whereas individual investors are chiefly interested in long-term gains, institutional investors demand quick results. If certain stocks do not perform, they are unceremoniously dropped. Thus, corporate executives are at the mercy of such impatient investors and have to produce the quick, steady gains demanded. Under the resulting speculative, short-term-oriented economic conditions, only large corporations can generate enough profits to simultaneously achieve short-term expectations and fulfill the long-term commitments that international competition requires. Most U.S. corporations cannot simultaneously pursue such diverse objectives, and thus must opt for the domestic short-term goals, particularly since managerial rewards are usually attached to such goals and not to long-term international achievements.

Even today, the American financial community not only favors short-term over long-term results but also considers the reshuffling of existing assets over the creation of new ones a more important management responsibility. Mergers and acquisitions (M&As) and leverages-buyouts (LBOs) are praised for the supposed financial benefits they bring to stockholders, and the economic sense they embody. True, under pre-1987 tax laws, by marking up asset values and then re-depreciating them, the tax bills of the acquirers could be reduced. Furthermore, debt interest payments remained tax deductible and, thus, not surprisingly, takeover activities of every type mushroomed. In 1988, the total value of such activities reached $311.4 billion, and Wall Street firms received an all-time high of $1.28 billion for their roles in the deals. These amounts involved a total of 3,637 mergers and acquisitions, an increase of 41.6 percent over the 1987 totals of 3,637 deals valued at $219.5 billion. As a result of all this activity, by the end of 1988, American corporations had taken on a staggering $1.8 trillion in debt since 1982 and had retired more than $400 billion in equity. Although due to a fairly strong economy the heavy new corporate debt did not create any major problems during the first few years of the M&A and LBO mania, the softening of the junk-bond market and the increasing number of companies facing debt-repayment problems beginning in the summer of 1989 considerably reduced the enthusiasm for such transactions. In its September 11, 1989 issue "Business Week" devoted the lead-article to the potential problems caused by this financial practice of Wall Street. This debt explosion has not created any short-term problems because of moderate growth, low-inflation, and reasonably stable interest rates which characterized the economy during 1986–1988 and into 1989.

Certain academic and financial advisers maintain that there is nothing wrong with financing business with such huge debt. To support their arguments they point to Japanese and West German companies which have long carried a much higher debt than their American counterparts. What such arguments ignore, however, is that in both of these countries the governments provide a much more supportive environment for taking on debt, and that the Japanese and West German companies have much closer links with their lenders. A bank that has a long association with a company and is both a lender and an equity holder is much more interested in the financial well-being of the company in the long run. Moreover, if a company's debt burden is too high, Japanese and German banks can replace some of the debt with equity. Undoubtedly, the current use of LBOs is, for all practical purposes, creating a closer "ad hoc" relationship among American lenders, equity holders, and the firms involved. The question is, however, how will the lenders react when the benign economic conditions turn into a slowdown or a recessing that places the highly leveraged companies under financial squeeze.

In the meanwhile, the American public is still waiting for the arrival of the "leaner-meaner" and, thus, internationally more competitive corporations which the M&A and LBO activity is supposed to have generated. Wall-Street dealmakers have long claimed that their actions help improve the manufacturing capabilities, cost structures, research and development skills, quality and scope of product assortment, and marketing ability of America's corporations. While all the evidence is not yet in and giving Wall Street the benefit of the doubt, it is still hard to see how managements, which have to spend most of their time on financial transactions involving billions of dollars of new debt, can undertake the long-term steps necessary for the formation of internationally competitive companies. A study of the National Science Foundation on the effects of M&A and LBO activities on research spending published in 1989 lends considerable weight to such doubts. According to the study, firms involved in M&As and LBOs slowed their R&D spending in 1986 and 1987 when most other companies were increasing such outlays. Based on the evaluation of 200 major corporations, which together account for 90 percent of total industrial R&D spending, the Foundation concluded that after a decade of annual increases averaging almost 6 percent by the group of firms, growth in R&D spending all but disappeared in 1986–1987. The increase in such expenditures by the firms was offset by the combined cuts of 5.3 percent by the 24 firms in the group which were involved in recent M&A, LBO, or other corporate restructuring efforts. The cutbacks were most significant among the eight firms that engaged in LBO or share-buy-back strategies to avoid becoming takeover targets. They decreased their R&D spending by nearly 13 percent. Moreover, almost all the companies that had reduced R&D spending also reported a 4.1 percent decline in the employment of R&D scientists and engineers between 1986–1987, while industry as a whole employed 1.8 percent more of such technical specialists during the same time period. Such findings, together with the 1986–1988 insider information scandals on Wall Street and the involvement of major investment banking houses in high-risk financing methods, put a new light on the M&A-LBO mania of recent years.

To respond to the competitive problems in the short-term, U.S. managers have also experimented with managment techniques that promised a "quick fix," including Japanese ones. There is, of course, nothing wrong with experimenting with new ideas. On the contrary, managers must keep an open mind and remain receptive to new developments. However, the short life-cycle of many of the techniques tried indicates that they were fads rather than serious innovations that could solve the problems of low productivity, poor product quality, and low employee motivation, problems that plague many U.S. corporations.

Moreover, America's international competitiveness is also curtailed by its trade policies which are designed to dispense equity to anyone who seeks remedies for narrowly defined "injuries." Thus, the broader issues surrounding international trade, such as the improvement of the international competitiveness of the economy or the interests of consumers, are not usually considered. As a result, in most cases U.S. trade policy formulators represent the narrowly defined concerns of certain interest groups quite well but cannot adequately protect the economic interests of the nation as a whole.

The passage of the Omnibus Trade and Competitiveness Act of 1988 was hailed by its supporters as a major step in restructuring the trade laws so as to restore America's international competitiveness. The Act, however, has not changed the tendency of trade laws to allow narrow interests to challenge larger interests; on the contrary, it has actually reinforced it. The new law tightens the process of trade regulation in a number of ways so that future presidents who are inclined to adopt a laissezfaire attitude toward alleged "unfair" foreign trade practices will find it hard to do so. The law, at the same time, allows for a wide interpretation of, for example, whether the cost of protecting a domestic industry from full import competition outweighs the benefits. This procedural protectionism is an invitation to narrowly defined sectoral interests to exert political pressure to gain protection at the expense of the larger interests of society.

The Act includes provisions that amend Section 301 of the 1974 Trade Act that authorized presidential action to eliminate foreign trade practices that violate trade agreements or that are unjustified, unreasonable, or discriminatory. It also transferred the retaliatory authority from the president to the U.S. trade representative. Moreover, the changes include a tightening of deadlines for action, mandatory retaliation against the violation of trade agreements, and other "unjustifiable" practices. Particularly troublesome is the addition of the Super 301 section that targets the "systematic practices" of "priority" trade partners which "prevent market access." This section implies that the United States intends to declare unilaterally what are "fair" or "unfair" business practices so that it can "punish" offending trade partners as it sees fit. Never before has America come up with a potentially more dangerous piece of trade legislation.

Although the 1988 Act turned out to be less protectionist than its earlier versions, it represents a potentially troublesome development. True, its impact depends on how future presidents want to use it; nonetheless, its thrust is protectionist and unilateral. The few provisions as, for example, the reduction of strategic export controls and the expansion of existing export promotion programs, which are designed to further international competitiveness, are anemic and do not address the basic issues. Most of all, they do not outweigh the protectionist potential of the law.

Finally, the limited international orientation of most U.S. companies must also be mentioned. While there are exceptions to this, and whereas a great deal of the information concerning the problem is unsubstantiated hearsay, there is an undeniable kernel of truth in the allegations. A case in point is a 1986 incident reported in *The Wall Street Journal* which illustrates the difference between American and Japanese companies' attitudes toward global market opportunities.

In 1984 the U.S. Census Bureau reached an agreement with the Central Statistical Office of the People's Republic of China concerning the exchange of data. In late 1985, the Chinese provided the Census Bureau with a great deal of socioeconomic and demographic statistics useful for evaluating Chinese consumer good markets. The bureau's staff analyzed the information, and the Department of Commerce included the results in its "Country Market Profile: The People's Republic of China," and offered it to American firms for $300 per copy. Between December 1985 and the fall of 1986, less than 10 copies were sold.

In early 1986 the Japan External Trade Organization (JETRO) obtained a copy and, because the report was not copyrighted, had it translated and published in book form. JETRO distributed the book at no charge to over 700 Japanese member organizations interested in trade with China, including trading companies, manufacturers, department stores, financial and research institutions, and universities. Following this distribution, JETRO printed another 500 copies that quickly sold at $20 per copy.

In the spring of 1989 a Small Business Administration (SBA) seminar on export prospects to the Republic of Korea and Taiwan had a dismally low turnout. A joint trade-mission organized by the SBA and the Department of Commerce to the European Community and later in the spring to Japan had only a dozen companies sign up, a number well below the minimum number of 20–25 to make such missions worthwhile. It is interesting to note that, except for Taiwan, the countries mentioned above were on the list of nations "unfairly limiting U.S. exports" that the U.S. government announced at the end of April 1989.

Measures such as the 1988 trade act and the depreciation of the dollar against major currencies between 1985–1988 are not addressing the fundamental issues and cannot, therefore, be expected to improve America's international competitiveness. Despite some improvements, the nation's merchandise and current accounts have not responded well to the dollar depreciation. When the dollar was undervalued in the late 1970s and overvalued in the early 1980s, prices, and thus the trade balance, responded the way economists predicted they would. However, during the long slide of the dollar since 1985 the expected price changes have, in most cases, not materialized.

The intense attention paid to the exchange value of the dollar is justified up to a certain point beyond which other factors must also be considered as, for example, the ability of Japanese competitors to keep their prices down in spite of the yen appreciation through dramatic improvements in efficiency, or the unwillingness of American consumers to give up high-quality imports even if they cost more than their domestic counterparts. Of course, a "cheap dollar" would at some level dramatically reduce the trade imbalances. However, the social and economic cost of such a dollar in terms of America's standard of living is not an acceptable outcome nor is it necessary. By addressing the problems in an imaginative and constructive manner, America's international competitiveness could be restored to a level where it could continue to play a major role in the global economy. The alleged lack of technological progress is not the major issue; basic research is strong and new inventions abound. The problem is with the commercialization of inventions, i.e., the manufacture of high quality products at a low cost, or industrial productivity and quality control. It is imperative that this area be improved. Time is of the essence, however, and halfway solutions not addressing the real problems won't do. The willingness of the Bush

Administration's economic policy formulators to take a fresh look at the problem of international competitiveness in 1989 and to devise ways to encourage American businesses to focus more on productivity growth and less on quick profits and financial manipulations, is encouraging. While there are no quick and easy solutions to the problems, a change in the outlook and attitudes of corporate management would be a good starting point on the road to improvement.

It is interesting to note that at a time when the trade-policy team of the Bush Administration was trying to formulate a "tougher" and more "aggressive" stance toward trade partners in general and Japan in particular in the spring of 1989, the General Accounting Office (GAO) published a report berating U.S. government efforts in promoting exports to Japan. The GAO report stated that in FY 1988, the U.S. Foreign and Commercial Service (FCS) had a budget of little over $200,000 to promote trade efforts in Japan. In comparison, during the same time the Japanese spent over $13 million on trade promotion in America, 67 times the U.S. amount. The report also noted that FCS staff normally do not return long-distance telephone calls to American businesses in the United States. Of course, government promotion is not the answer to America's trade problems, but the GAO findings underline the U.S. government's haphazard, inconsistent, and uncoordinated approach to improving the trade balance.

The Inadequacy of the Trade Balance Measure

A number of students of U.S.–Japan trade relations and some U.S. government officials have recently indicated that the trade balance measure by itself can result in myopic trade views.[16] According to this argument, U.S–Japan relations are more complex than the traditional bilateral trade balance measure implies. For example, the shifting of U.S. manufacturing operations to Japan resulted in about $4–5 billion in annual Japanese exports to the United States which are actually produced by American companies. Furthermore, approximately $15 billion in exports are specifically ordered by American original equipment manufacturers (OEMs), and in 1985 alone, American subsidiaries in Japan manufactured and marketed about $50 billion worth of goods there. By 1988–1989 the land, buildings, and other assets that American companies have assembled in a variety of subsidiaries and joint ventures in Japan multiplied in value as a result of the yen appreciation. Thus, once such transactions and developments are taken into account, bilateral economic relations take on a different meaning than when trade balance measures alone are considered.

Thus, in a world economy that is characterized by global networks of multinational corporations as well as by huge nontrade-related financial flows, reliance on the trade balance measure alone does not accurately reflect the scope of U.S.–Japan economic relations. A new set of more comprehensive measures is therefore long overdue. It is, however, difficult to gain widespread acceptance for this, because U.S.–Japan trade relations are not conducted in a rational economic but in an emotional political context. Members of Congress, for example, are angry about the huge bilateral trade imbalances mostly because of the unemployment implications in their electoral districts. These concerns are not groundless; a U.S. Department of Commerce study found that between 1979 and 1985, more than 1.5 million manufacturing jobs had been lost.[17] The authors estimated that while in 1977 exports accounted for a 7.1 percent of employment, imports accounted for a 6 percent loss of jobs. By 1984, export-related employment stood at 6.5 percent whereas imports resulted in a 7.8 percent job loss. In the same year, the net loss of jobs (the difference between jobs created by exports and jobs lost through imports) was 1.1 million, or 1.3 percent of total employment. By estimating that a $1 billion loss of exports reduces employment by approximately 21,000 jobs, the Department of Commerce provided members of Congress with a useful argument against Japan. Whereas such evidence is tenuous at best, the argument is politically effective because it can be backed up by the huge bilateral trade imbalances, whatever their causes may have been. This reported trade-employment relationship was welcomed by the Democratic members of Congress who had been looking for an effective political issue to use against the Republicans. They found this combination irresistible because it linked their traditional concern for working men and women with a problem of the 1980s which gained more prominence daily. The Democrats believed that they could finally expose the weaknesses of Reaganomics, at least as they saw them.

The Democratic views were additionally supported by newly formed interpretations of the employment implications of free trade.[18] According to some American scholars, in the second half of the 1980s, trade is not based on comparative advantages but on wage-cutting. Therefore, only through strict limits on imports could the negative effects of lower wages on the American economy in general and on the standard of living in particular be limited. The logical outcome of this and of similar type arguments was, of course, the trade act of 1988.

Notes

1. See, for example, the Saxonhouse study cited in chapter 1: the Federal Reserve Board of New York, "Japan's Intangible Barriers to Trade in Manufactures," *Quarterly Review* (Winter

1985–86), pp. 11–18, and C. Fred Bergsten and William R. Cline, *op. cit.* Also, *Japan* (Paris: Organization for Economic Cooperation and Development, 1985), particularly pp. 39–54.

2. Balassa and Noland, *op. cit.*, p. 69.

3. *Business Week* (July 11, 1988), p. 72.

4. Japan shows high export and low import income elasticity relative to the rest of the world. High income elasticity for exports has resulted from Japan's concentration in commodities and areas that have high demand growth rates. The low income elasticity of imports is caused by Japan's industrial structure which is geared toward high value added products designed to save resources and reduce imports of raw materials, particularly fuel.

5. All EPA data reported were obtained through personal interviews and from internal working papers in Tokyo, in March and May 1986.

6. *The Japan Economic Journal* (July 5, 1986), p. 7.

7. *Tokyo Business Today* (October 1988), p. 21.

8. *Ibid.*

9. Robert I. Ballou and Iwo Tomita, *The Financial Behavior of Japanese Corporations* (Tokyo: Kodansha International, 1988), pp. 58–59.

10. FTC and EPA Internal working papers obtained during personal interviews at these agencies in Tokyo, in March and May 1986.

11. *Ibid.*

12. Bergsten and Cline, *The United-States-Japan Economic Problem, op. cit.*, p. 124. For a discussion of these issues, see also *Progress Report: 1984* (Tokyo: U.S.–Japan Trade Study Group, 1984).

13. From the definition of international competitiveness by the President's Commission on Industrial Competitiveness, 1986.

14. Martin N. Baily and Alik K. Chakrabarti, *Innovation and the Productivity Crisis* (Washington, D.C.: The Brookings Institution, 1988).

15. For a detailed discussion see the "Special Report" of *Business Week* (September 19, 1988), pp. 100–135.

16. See, for example, John M. Cline, "Inter-MNC Arrangements: Shaping the Options for U.S. Trade Policy," *The Washington Quarterly* (Fall 1985), pp. 57–71; Jane Sneddon Little, "Intra-Firm Trade and U.S. Protectionism: Thoughts Based on a Small Survey," *New England Economic Review* (January-February 1986); and Kenichi Ohmae, "Rising Yen But No Falling Trade Gap," *The Wall Street Journal* (July 1, 1986), p. 26. In April 1986, Allen Wallis, Undersecretary of State for Economic Affairs, reportedly said of this subject: ". . . If we base our trade policy toward Japan — and indeed, our attitude toward that country and its people — on one number, we will have a bad policy and provoke results that are not in our interest." From *Asahi Evening News* (April 25, 1986), p. 9.

17. Office of Business Analysis, *Trade Ripples Across U.S. Industries*, a working paper (Washington, D.C.: U.S. Department of Commerce, 1986).

18. John M. Culbertson, "Free Trade is Impoverishing the West," "Control Imports Through Bilateral Pacts," and "Importing a Lower Standard of Living," in *The New York Times* (July 28, August 11, 1985, and August 17, 1986), pp. F3, F3, and F3, respectively.

3 THE ACTION PROGRAM AND ONGOING U.S.-JAPAN TRADE CONFLICTS

Since the reasons for the rapidly growing Japanese current and trade account surpluses, particularly with the United States during the late 1970s and early 1980s, were complex, it would have been very important to address the imbalances through cooperative multilateral efforts. However, with the advent of the Reagan administration in 1981, the United States unilaterally focused its trade policy on the "opening" of the Japanese marketplace to the exclusion of most other relevant factors. Through this narrowly conceived approach, the Administration wanted to rapidly reduce the high bilateral trade imbalances.

The major reason for this strategy was the desire to obtain maximum domestic visibility for the Reagan trade policy. It was simpler to point to a set of unilateral Japanese measures developed in response to U.S. demands to improve market access than to obtain political benefits from complex agreements on mutually acceptable macroeconomic policies which would have been more effective but which only experts could have understood. Moreover, through tough sounding demands the Administration hoped to contain the periodic protectionist outbursts on Capitol Hill. The American side also believed that specific demands made it more difficult for the Japanese to equivocate, and that unilaterally exerted pressures made it easier for the United States to evade the necessary but politically painful domestic measures such as curtailment of budgetary deficits through spending cuts or tax increases.

The 1981–1984 Japanese Market Opening 'Packages'

Not surprisingly, the Japanese saw things differently. From their point of view, the market opening measures did not address the fundamentals of the trade imbalances and, consequently, could not lead to a lasting resolution of the trade conflicts. Furthermore, most of the measures were seen as unilateral concessions, and the Japanese government was also being required to prefer one industry over another. This caused political problems as, for example, when Japanese farmers charged that the government was selling them out during the bilateral agricultural negotiations of the late 1970s and early 1980s, to secure the American markets for manufactured exports. Neither did the Japanese approve of the American tendency to use specific cases to symbolize the generally closed nature of the Japanese marketplace. Lastly, the Japanese objected to the excessive politicization of some issues because this unnecessarily exacerbated the overall conflict.

As usual, the United States prevailed, and in response to American demands, the Japanese government developed a series of market opening measures or "packages." They typically included the elimination and/or reduction of tariffs on selected products, the simplification of import procedures, increased transparency in economic decision-making, and other similar measures. The Japanese tried to quickly generate as much goodwill as possible, and thus, usually announced the packages in advance. Often, they anticipated and developed packages to blunt congressional anger or to provide the Prime Minister with a suitable *Miyage* (gift) when visiting Washington.

Since most of the measures were hastily developed in a piecemeal fashion under intense American pressure, the packages did not add up to a systematic approach. As a matter of fact, they usually represented what was politically possible at a time when the state of the bilateral trade relations called for some visible action; which is not to say that they were entirely opportunistic or ineffective. The gradual import procedure changes, the increased transparency in economic decision-making, and other related steps helped American companies to enter the highly competitive Japanese market with less frustration. Such benefits, while not immediately reducing the trade imbalances, were bound to be helpful over the long run.

Moreover, on the Japanese side, the review of procedures, requirements, institutions, and the consideration of the nation's global image prior to reaching a consensus on the packages raised the awareness of politicans, government officials, businessmen, and the general public. They began to realize that decisions concerning the new international role of Japan could not be postponed any longer. While the government's response to American demands was always controversial, the resulting debates paved the way for the 1985 Action Program, the 1986 and subsequent Maekawa Commission Reports, and the other "visions" which gave strong impetus to the internationalization of the economy as envisioned during the second half of the 1980s.

The number of market-opening packages introduced depends upon the interpretation of the measures the Japanese have taken over the years.[1] For example, already prior to 1981, several sets of measures were designed to improve market access. The 1985 report of the Japanese Advisory Committee for External Economic Issues, known as the Okita Committee, identified six different sets of measures introduced between December 1981 and 1984.[2] Although the committee divided the packages into three categories such as external economic measures, market opening measures and the promotion of immediate external economic measures ostensibly to differentiate between those that improved market access and those which increased imports in the short-run vs. the long-run, from a practical point of view this differentiation is unimportant. All the packages were developed to meet the American, as well as the increasingly vocal European Community, demands for the opening of the Japanese market. The specific measures, among others, included the two-year advanced implementation of tariff reductions agreed upon in the Tokyo round (December 1981), the elimination and reduction of tariff rates on 215 items (May 1982), improvement of certification systems (January 1983), import promotion campaigns (October 1983), the submission of bills to the Diet to reform the tobacco monopoly (April 1984), and the increase of industrial imports under the Generalized System of Preference (GSP) from developing countries (December 1984).

International receiption of the packages was generally critical. However, while prior to 1981 the criticism had come mostly from the United States and usually consisted of an angry and threatening "too little, too late," this time both the sources and the views were more diversified. The Asian Pacific nations such as the Republic of Korea complained that the measures favored America and Western Europe, and the Oceanic countries felt neglected because they were not even considered. The Americans and Western Europeans jointly complained that despite a number of successive packages, the trade imbalances have not improved, and that economic decision-making continued to lack transparency, leaving too much scope for administrative guidance. Complaints were heard about the lack of followthrough of high-level policy decisions by the operational staff, particularly by customs officials processing imports.

Unilateral American criticism turned out to be much harsher, but this was to be expected. Between 1981 and 1984 America's bilateral trade deficit with Japan jumped from a little cover $13 billion to over $33 billion, an increase of approximately 250 percent. Furthermore, Japan's manufactured imports as a percentage of total imports grew only about 3 percent from 21 to 24 percent, and its manufactured imports from the United Stated increased only marginally from $10.1 billion $11.8 billion, or about 16 percent over the same time period.[3] In the opinion of Washington political circles, the trade statistics proved the closed nature of Japan's market and the ineffectiveness of the 1981–1984 liberalization measures.

The trade imbalances were announced against a backdrop of bilateral negotiations. The topics included, among other things, the level of Japanese car exports, defense contributions, and the increase of beef and citrus imports. The negotiations were made more difficult than usual by the mixed reception of a high-level Liberal Democratic Party (LDP) delegation (the Easki mission) in Washington in 1982, the Hitachi-IBM industrial espionage case in the same year, and the 1983 Congressional debates on industrial policies.

As usual, the Administration was restrained in its response and even praised a couple of the packages (for example, the May 1982 and January 1983 measures) as proper steps in the right direction. While it criticized others, it was not as aggressive as many members of Congress, who were in an angry mood and dismissed the packages; these Congressmen wanted immediate and forceful action to reduce the trade deficit. For example, Senator John Danforth introduced the trade-reciprocity bill in 1982 to "force open Japanese markets." Local content legislation continued to be on the congressional agenda as was the unfair nature of Japanese industrial policies.

More moderate voices, however, were also heard. The Council of Economic Advisors, for example, in its 1983 annual report stated that Japan was not the sole cause of America's overall trade problem even though some import barriers burdened bilateral relationships. The fall 1984 USTR report on five (except the December 1984) packages introduced between 1981 and 1984 identified a series of problems as seen by the Administration but also pointed out that the measures opened up new opportunities for U.S. exporters and investors. It was noteworthy that the report relied on an increase in such opportunities as its evaluation standard and not on the impact of the measures on the trade balances. It was also encouraging that during the Congressional hearings on Japan's industrial policies in 1983 and afterwards, an extensive debate took place on the structure, international competitiveness, monetary, exchange rate, and macroeconomic policies of the United States. As a consequence, the fundamental causes of America's growing global and the bilateral trade deficits were beginning to be recognized in Washington, and, at least temporarily Japan was no longer viewed as the sole cause of the nation's international economic problems.

The Spring 1985 U.S.-Japan Trade Developments

American-Japanese trade relations were off to a good start in 1985. The "Ron-Yasu" meeting in Los Angeles on Janauary 2 was dominated by the now familiar issue of U.S. access to Japanese markets, and the two leaders came away from the meeting with an agreement concerning a new negotiation format. The "Market-Oriented, Sector-Specific" (MOSS) approach was initially to address specific barriers in specific markets, such as telecommunications, medical equipment and pharmaceuticals, electronics, and forest products. Other industrial sectors were to be added to this list at a later date. The items to be reviewed included production, imports, distribution, demand, laws, restrictive rules, business practices, traditions, and consumer preferences.

The MOSS format was proposed by the American side which was dissatisfied with the effects of the market-opening packages to date. The United States argued that the packages were too general, and were very slowly implemented, if at all. American negotiators believed that focusing on specific markets and issues would provide quicker, and most of all, politically more visible results in the form of increased U.S. market shares, and eventually, improved trade balances.

The Japanese were not enthusiastic about the MOSS negotiations because these, too, were narrowly focused and did not include a review of the underlying causes of the bilateral trade imbalances. While the Japanese did not expect too much, they went along with the negotiations because they knew that as a result of the huge bilateral trade imbalances, U.S.-Japan trade relations would be under tremendous pressure during 1985.

Anger was rising in the United States. According to an early 1985 media poll, almost 9 out 10 Americans regarded the trade problem with Japan as either "very serious" or "somewhat serious."[4] Furthermore, by a margin of 3 to 2, they believed that the President did only a "fair" to "poor" job in gaining access to the Japanese markets. Not surprisingly, many members of Congress exploited the resulting rhetorical opportunities for their own political ends. They called upon the Administration and Japan to introduce more measures through which the trade imbalances could be reduced. While such behaviour was understandable the protectionist demands created problems for the Administration which tried to maintain its credibility in the world as a champion of free trade.

It was the 1984 trade data showing a $33 billion ($37 billion by U.S. standards) American deficit that set off the spring 1985 trade conflict cycle which culminated in the Japanese market opening Action Program in July of the same year. After the release of these figures, members of Congress talked angrily about the "dismantling" of American industries. One senator referred to free-trade as "unilateral disarmament," while others started a flurry of activities which eventually led to the introduction of more than 300 protectionist bills.

Of course, not all of the bills were directed against Japan, but a number of them were introduced with the clear intent of "sending a message to Japan" that America's patience with the trade imbalances and all of the past market opening measures had "worn thin."[5] Amidst a series of hearings on America's trade position in general, and U.S.–Japan trade in particular, the idea of an import-surcharge bill surfaced. Eventually the bill was introduced by a troika of leading Democrats, Senator Bentsen, Representatives Rostenkowski and Gephart, not with the expectation that it would pass, but with the intention to shock the White House and the Japanese into "action." Thus, "Japan bashing" got its start.

The bill was the most protectionist legislation introduced in Congress since the Smoot-Hawley Act of 1930, a measure which had disastrous results not only for the United States but for the entire world. In light of this, the import surcharge bill was widely denounced not only in the United States but also by most of the international community.[6] The White House, the mass media, and trade experts agreed that the bill was a bad idea and that it could only damage the United States and the rest of the world. At the same time, all interested parties acknowledged that it reflected the prevailing anti-Japanese sentiment in Congress as well as in many other parts of the nation.

Two additional events fueled the already aggressive mood of Congress during early 1985. First, on March 28, MITI announced that Japan would maintain and raise car export quota ceilings from 1.85 million to 2.3 million vehicles for the April 1985–March 1986 period. The Japanese were concerned that if quotas were lifted, shipments would quickly increase to approximately 2.7 million units because American consumers would purchase more of the Japanese cars in such high demand. In a sense, this was a no-win situation. Whatever the Japanese government decided, one group or another, such as the American car manufacturers, union, members of Congress, or the Japanese automobile exporters, would have been upset. Expectedly, in the end, all sides were equally dissatisfied with the decision, including the White House, whose alleged signals concerning the matter had been "misread" by the Japanese.

The MOSS negotiations were not going well either, particularly in the area of telecommunications, where the United States had high hopes for increased sales following the privatization of Nippon Telegraph and Telephone (NTT) in the spring of 1985. The Americans wanted fewer regulations, less stringent technical standards, and the right to sell equipment without any restrictions. As usual, they believed that the Japanese were dragging their feet during the negotiations to continue the protection of the domestic marketplace. Among Japanese government officials, there was widespread resentment of the American demands; they privately complained that the United States behaved as if it were still an occupying power. To resolve the stalemate, and to forestall the import-surcharge bill, President Reagan sent a special emmisary to Prime Minister Nakasone to ask for some action which would convince Congress that progress was being made toward the reduction of the trade deficits. Thus, pressure on the Japanese steadily increased.

A tense situation resulted which was complicated by the inability of most Japanese, including responsible government officials, politcans, and the mass media, to understand the nuances of the American political system. They did not sufficiently appreciate the constitutional principle of the separation of power which shaped U.S. trade policy through the interaction between the Executive Branch and Congress. Most Japanese accepted the views put forth by their mass media, particularly the newspapers, that the protectionist sentiments expressed in Congress, chiefly for domestic political reasons, represented America's trade policy towards Japan. They did not realize that U.S. trade policy is formulated through the iterative relationship of Congress and the White House, not by Congress alone. They failed to see that the final outcome is always a much more moderate policy than the Congressional statements and debates usually imply.

The Japanese Debate on Demand Stimulation

In a bid to contain the mushrooming bilateral trade conflict, Prime Minister Nakasone appointed State Minister Komoto in March 1985 to formulate a set of specific trade measures based on the recommendations of the Committee on External Economic Relations (the Okita Committee), concerning the trade problem. The Prime Minister was anxious to make an advance announcement on April 9 of what was later to become the Action Program because he wanted to fend off criticism of Japan at the April 11–12 OECD meeting in Paris, and hoped to defuse the anti-Japanese sentiments on Capitol Hall.

Such advance announcement of trade measures was done regulary by the Japanese, who after a slow process of consensus building, were always in a hurry to assure the rest of the world, especially the United States, that they are anxious to satisfy the various demands put upon them. By doing so, however, they raise expectations to such high levels that the formal measures eventually announced always fall short of expectations abroad. Consequently, international response is always negative, and the unrealized expectations reinforce an image of Japan as the insincere trading partner who cannot be trusted. This was part of the reason behind the "Japanbashing" frenzy which engulfed Washington in the spring and summer of 1985.

Prime Minister Nakasone held his intended press conference on April 9 in which he outlined the proposed market opening measures. The White House received the announcement in a friendly, but guarded manner; Capitol Hill and American business circles reacted cooly and skeptically. Key members of Congress stated that the measures could not deflect oncoming retaliatory legislation. Others, not aware of the gradual shift of power from the bureaucrats to the politicians, argued that while the Prime Minister probably meant what he said, the Japanese bureaucracy would not accept the proposals. Western European reactions, by the large, echoed U.S. sentiments, and at the April OECD meeting in Paris, Japan was severely criticised; Foreign Minister Abe declared afterwards that the conference was one of the most difficult he had ever attended.

To help resolve the increasing trade conflicts, the Okita committee recomended a reconsideration of Japan's traditional savings and consumption patterns, and the stimulation of domestic demand to increase imports. This recommendation initiated a spirited political fight among top LDP politicians, with a hidden agenda from Nakasone's opponents, in the spring of 1985.[7] This argument was not over the desirability of demand stimulation; almost everyone agreed that it was necessary. Rather, the clash seemed to be about how to do it. Prime Minister Nakasone opposed demand stimulation through increased public spending because of his firm commitment to fiscal austerity. He wanted a new, comprehensive set of market access measures and a revitalized private sector to stimulate demand. The Prime Minister was supported by Minister of Finance Takeshita and Minister of Foreign Affairs Abe.

The opposition was led by LDP Vice President Nikaido and the Chairman of the LDP Executive Council, Miyazawa, who wanted fiscal stimuli. They argued that fiscal policy was unnecessarily austere, and that because there was a large surplus of domestic savings over investment, public borrowing would not crowd out private investment and reignite inflation, among other things. Thus, an expansionary fiscal policy would encourage investments without any negative consequences, and would also raise import demand. Although to the outside world the debate appeared to be over economic policy, in reality Nikaido and Miyazawa tried to use the disagreement to engineer an early removal of Nakasone. They both wanted to be Prime Minister, and believed that the debate over demand stimulation provided them with the right issue to realize their aspiration.

In the midst of the increasingly vocal debate, U.S. Secretary of State Shultz gave a speech at Princeton on April 11. Addressing the problems of the world economy, Shultz reviewed the current economic policies of America and of the other industrialized nations, including Japan. He pointed out that for the sake of global prosperity, each nation had to make individual as well as multilateral efforts to moderate trade imbalances. Not mincing words about the U.S. fiscal deficits and their impact on the dollar exchange rate, and thus on trade, the Secretary also discussed Japan's high savings rate and the necessity of domestic demand stimulation without, however, suggesting the fiscal means to do so.

Nevertheless, true to form, the Japanese mass media ignored those aspects of the speech which did not fit their preconceived notions, and declared that America demanded immediate domestic demand stimulation through fiscal means. Such manipulation of Shultz's speech and the appearance of foreign pressure were welcomed by Nikaido and Miyazawa, who capitalized on the distortions to further their hidden agenda. Although the misinterpretation of Shultz's speech was eventually rectified through a personal meeting between Shultz and Minister of Foreign Affairs Abe, bilteral relations were burdened by the unwarranted exaggerations of the Japanese media.

Other interested parties also joined the debate.[8] The president of the influential Keidanren explained in a press conference on April 17 that he was against domestic demand stimulation. Instead, he argued, Japan should develop an "export adjustment" (restraint) policy to pacify foreign critics. The Chairman of the LDP Policy Affairs Research Council and the Chairman of the LDP Tax System Research Commission concurred. Others, such as the head of the Keizai Doyukai and president of Nissan, and the vice president of Keidanren and president of Toyota, disagreed; they wanted additional market access measures and the expansion of domestic demand through the revitalization of the private sector. While the latter views had merit, the previous arguments in favor of export adjustment reflected a curiously short-sighted view of the interests of the Japanese economy. A substantial curtailment of the exports of Japan's internationally most successful industries would have meant giving up hard-earned competitive advantages just to assuage nations whose industries did not keep pace with the world-market developments.

Throughout the debate Prime Minister Nakasone remained firm on his position. He rejected demand stimulation through fiscal means, and instructed the various ministries and government agencies to prepare a broad set of economic measures which focused on market access and increased imports, which he eventually presented to the world as the Action Program of July 1985.

In retrospect, it is noteworthy that during the entire debate underlying the development of the 1985 Action Program, none of the participants ever justified increasing domestic demand to raise the living standards of the Japanese people. The focus of the debate was always on how foreign demands, particularly those coming from the United States, could best be satisfied regardless of how this affected the Japanese themselves. Such a reactive, as opposed to proactive, stance has long been characteristic of Japanese international economic policy formulation to the detriment of the nation's long-term interests.

Reasons for the Action Program

In his April 9, 1985, nationally televised speech Prime Minister Nakasone was surrounded by line-charts and bar-charts, and used a schoolmaster's pointer to urge his countrymen to increase their purchase of foreign products. Moreover, he also explained the economic rationale for his request, but did not dwell on the more subtle motives. The Prime Minister wanted to achieve several objectives with his bold and unusual move. First, he wanted to demonstrate to the United States, particularly to members of Congress, that his government understood the dangerous state of U.S.– Japanese trade relations. At the same time, he also wanted to show sensitivity to the general international economic situation, marked by huge Japanese current and trade account surpluses, and convince a skeptical world that Japan would do its share to reduce the imbalances.

Prime Minister Nakasone also wanted to reestablish his policy priorities domestically, particularly among the LDP politicians who attacked him during the debate on demand stimulation. Thus, what to many critics appeared to be a unique but superficial public relations move by Japanese political standards, was in fact a carefully planned political strategy designed to impress domestic and international friends and foes alike. In taking his case to the people through television, Nakasone not only demonstrated his unique political style but also tried to obtain much needed public support for the measures which eventually became known as the Action Program of July 1985.

At the same time, by making an early announcement, Nakasone raised expectations abroad to a level that, in its final form, the Action Program could not fulfill. Moreover, according to some cynical Japanese and foreign observers, through his television plea for more imports, he unintentionally strengthened the perception abroad that the Japanese discriminated against foreign products. Finally, others have pointed out that by choosing such a dramatic method to address the trade balance problem, particularly in relation to the United States, Nakasone may have also created the impression that his government was succumbing to American pressures. However, while the strategy was controversial, there was no disagreement that the Prime Minister's unique personal leadership style influenced the development of the Action Program and of the other measures which were aimed at the internationalization of the Japanese economy. Furthermore, his style was well received abroad, particularly in the United States.

Prime Ministerial Leadership Styles

When Yasuhiro Nakasone became Prime Minister in 1982, most Japanese were skeptical, and some even expressed a dislike for the new head of government. Among his critics, Nakasone had an image of a calculating wheeler-dealer who always followed the political winds. A number of domestic political pundits called him a "weathervane" and gave him little more than six months in office.

However, Nakasone proved his detractors wrong, and by the summer of 1986, when he dissolved the Lower House and called elections for both the Lower and Upper Houses on the same day, he had been Prime Minister for three and one-half years, with consistently high public poll approval ratings (over 50 percent), outlasting the tenure of his three predecessors. After the overwhelming electoral victory of the LDP on July 6, 1986, the party leadership decided that he would continue in office at least one year beyond October 1986, when his term as LDP President should have ended and, according to party rules, he should have been replaced as Prime Minister.

He achieved this against great odds, particularly after the May 1986

Tokyo summit went awry. Many of his domestic critics, particularly a couple of influential leaders of the LDP who wanted to take over as Prime Minister, considered the summit a failure for Japan in general and for Nakasone in particular. The summit achieved as much as could be realistically expected, but his critics judged it only for one outcome: the inability of Nakasone to convince the other participants that the steep appreciation of the yen had gone far enough. Only Chancellor Kohl of the Federal Republic of Germany paid any attention to the Prime Minister's concern; the others said that a strong yen was long overdue to correct the trade imbalances. Even President Reagan could not support Nakasone, because the growing U.S. trade imbalances and the upcoming fall 1986 congressional elections made this politicially impossible. Nonetheless, critics seized the opportunity and declared that the much publicized "Ron-Yasu" relationship had no substance to it. By mid-May, the Prime Minister's opponents declared that he was in no position to call double elections, and even if he did, he could not possibly lead his party to a margin of victory that would enable him to stay in power beyond October 1986.

However, the critics again underestimated Nakasone's political savvy. He engineered the overwhelming LDP electoral victory, and as a result, he was seen as a forceful leader both at home and abroad; in this, he surpassed former Prime Minister Tanaka, who for many years was the acknowledged strongman of Japanese politics. While many of Nakasone's critics continued to view him as a crafty politician, most Japanese have learned to like his political manner which combined traditional Japanese philosophy and respect for old values with an appreciation of the Western world. The result was a unique leadership style which was characterized by flair and a degree of publicity consciousness never seen before in a nation where reticence remains a virtue.

Nakasone aspired to the prime ministership for a long time, and in the interim developed his policy priorities so that when the day arrived, he was ready to move forward with his plans. His domestic program was based on the desire to "settle all outstanding accounts in postwar politics." By this he meant a restructuring of the broad socioeconomic and educational framework within which the nation's political parties have operated since the 1950s. The framework was the legacy of the LDP which monopolized power for 30 years, and whose policies began to flounder when Nakasone began his rise in the early 1980s. At that time, while the government reached the outer limits of its financial capabilities, expenditures were still mounting, and the ratio of budget deficits to GNP not only reached new heights but also significantly surpassed those of America and of the Western European nations, except Italy. Abroad, Japanese prime ministers were the "odd-man-out" in international conferences; at home, most politicans, government officials, and the general public were still prisoners of the *shimaguni konjo* (insular, small-country mentality) which was becoming increasingly incongruous with the nation's mounting economic power.

Nakasone began implementing his domestic program while he was still director general of the Administrative Management Agency in 1980. To reduce the size of government and to revitalize the private sector, he recommended the formation of a special reform council to Prime Minister Suzuki. The recommendation was accepted, and by 1981, administrative and financial reforms without tax increases were under way.

Nakasone displayed a strong sense of history and of patriotism. To bolster the nation's self-respect, in 1985 he made an official visit to the Yasukuni Shrine, which is the spiritual home of Japan's war dead; he was the first post-World War II prime minister to make this visit.[9] Undaunted by the resulting domestic and foreign criticism, he continued to express his strong personal conviction that the Japanese must re-enter the world as a confident people if they are to accept new international responsibilities. He believed that in addition to knowledge and modern technology, this can be accomplished only through a renewed respect for old values and traditions which have shaped the nation throughout its long history.

Nakasone also had a global perspective of Japan's role. From his first day in office, he had made internationalism a major theme of his government. This global orientation and his vision of Japan's future as an economic power, in combination with his leadership style, has earned him the respect of world leaders which past Japanese prime ministers lacked. When Nakasone met with the heads of other Western nations, he displayed an aggressive sense of self-confidence which was missing in his predecessors, who never managed to act as equals among their peers.

While Nakasone was well liked and respected as a Prime Minister outside Japan, and many of his countrymen appreciated his style, his personality and nontraditional leadership occasionally created problems in the LDP and the government. Articulate and telegenic, he showed authoritarian tendencies which most of the top LDP politicians and the bureaucrats resented. Critics overwhelmed by the range of Nakasone's ideas and his leadership style referred to him as a "presidential prime minister" who made decisions by himself in a "top-down" as opposed to the traditional "bottom-up" manner. While Nakasone respected traditional Japanese practices, he believed that because the world is complex and changes rapidly, the top-down decision-making process is more effective. Undoubtedly, this individualistic, Western style leadership and his relative negligence to engage in the extensive *nemawashi* so important in Japan, as well as his lukewarm support of those who have helped him in the past were not in accordance with traditional Japanese political behavior.[10] This, and his heavy reliance on "brain trusts," or private advisory committees, in the policy formulation process were seen by many politicians and bureaucrats as an attempt to undermine their influence. Most senior politicians believed that he was not relying enough on their advice, did not seek their agreement in time, and used the brain trusts to endorse his views, thereby gaining public acceptance for, as well as overcoming intraparty resistance, to his policy plans. This criticism has some merit because in contrast to past prime ministers, Nakasone did not view himself as an organizer-coordinator of routine matters but rather as an orignator-executer of ideas which he also wanted to realize in his own fashion. Examples of this included his views on the controversial tax and educational reforms and the internationalization of the Japanese economy as set forth in the 1986–1987 Maekawa Commission Reports prepared by one of his brain trusts.

Some critics faulted Nakasone for realizing his political program at the expense of the weaker social groups such as the aged, who had been hit the hardest by his insistence on fiscal austerity. Although he had inherited the various economic and social problems, such as the increases in medical costs and the inadequate support system for the elderly, the critics charged that his fiscal policies magnified the problems and led to a loss of "warmth" in the relationship between government and the people, which is an important aspect of Japanese political life. Other cirtics considered Nakasone's tendency to seclude himself at times instead of informally socializing with other politicians as more proof of his "aloofness" and lack of warmth. It is noteworthy, however, that the same public which Nakasone's critics believed was alienated from him had consistently rewarded him with high public poll ratings and gave the LDP their sweeping electoral victory in July 1986.

The views put forth by a small group of young Dietmen in their May 1986 newsletter typified the criticism of Nakasone within the LDP. These parliamentarians, none of whom belonged to the Prime Minister's faction, accused Nakasone of not developing appropriate economic policies which led to the dramatic appreciation of the yen against the dollar. They called the MOSS negotiations and the 1985 Action Program stopgap measures which could not resolve the basic underlying problems, and disapproved of the Prime Minister's management of U.S.–Japanese relations. In their view, close personal ties with the President resulted in Japan's uncritical acceptance of American demands. Furthermore, they claimed, Nakasone's "showmanship" changed the LDP tradition of carrying out policies without posturing, and they called on him to exhibit some warmth and address the problems associated with daily life. The group also objected to the extensive use of brain trusts because the substitution of private advisory groups for political parties and elected representatives endangered the established political process.

In November 1987 Nakasone stepped down from the presidency of the LDP which carries with it the premiership. Although after leading the LDP to a landslide victory in the double elections of 1986, he failed to carry out the long-planned tax reform. But it was not because of this or of a power struggle that he did so. He stepped down because he was required by the LDP rules on the presidency.

Foreign expectations of a Japanese Prime Minister's performance vary with his perceived political style. Thus when Nakasone picked Noboru Takeshita, a former Minister of Finance, as his successor in the fall of 1987, the news was received with concern abroad. Political observers were speculating about Takeshita's quiet behind-the-scenes deal-making style and noted that while he may be able to get "things done," he was too pragmatic, lacked the sophistication of his predecessor, and had no political philosophy. They saw him as a "bureaucrats' bureaucrat" who would be incapable of inspiring his countrymen to recognize the new international realities which require changes in the society in general and the economy in particular. Or, to put it differently, they feared that the internationalization process set on the way by Nakasone would slow down considerably or perhaps even come to a halt. Takeshita's advocacy of the *furasato* concept or the boosting of the quality of life outside major population centers, i.e., the promotion of decentralization as the basic theme of his government, seemed too inward-looking to insure the continuation of Nakasone's internationalization process. The widespread view that Takeshita is a *nihonteki* (a typical Japanese), his "bottom up" leadership style previously exhibited as Minister of Finance, and his close relationship with the bureaucracy, particularly Ministry of Finance, as well as the various interest groups, was seen abroad as an indication that Nakasone's cosmopolitan and cooperative attitude as well as assertiveness towards the bureaucracy would be replaced. The replacement would be a safe but sluggish inward-oriented bureaucracy-led government that would be far less responsive to the outside world than the Nakasone administration was. These concerns were reinforced when it became apparent in late 1987 and early 1988 that while the Japanese respected Nakasone, many actually prefered a prime minister who is modest and indirect like Takeshita.

The Changing Policy Formulation Process

While a Japanese prime minister's style is important in that it sets the overall tone of his government, the views expressed abroad about the transfer of the prime ministership from Nakasone to Takeshita were exaggerated. No Japanese prime minister can through his political style decisively influence the policy formulation process, although adjustments are possible as, for example, Nakasone's reliance on his private "braintrusts" rather than the bureaucracy or Takeshita's generally better relations with the bureaucrats. While appealing, Japanese political life is too complex for simple, personality and leadership style-based interpretations nor is it dominated by an unidentifiable "System" without a political core. An understanding of Japanese political life requires a differentiation between personality- and leadership style on the one hand and the policy-formulation process on the other hand. The former can have a minor effect on the process but has no influence on the substance of the policies themselves.

The same arguments were made again when as a consequence of the 1988–1989 Recruit-scandal Takeshita was replaced by Sosuke Uno and then as a result of personal indiscretions, Uno by Toshiki Kaifu during the summer of 1989. American and European political observers again speculated about the possible policy changes the new prime minister would initiate. They continued to make the mistake of associating personality and leadership style differences which could have a minor impact on the policy formulation process, with changes in the policies themselves.

More important than prime ministerial leadership styles are the basic changes that have taken place in the nation's policy formulation process during the last decade in response to gradually evolving trends. While the change process has not yet ended and will continue in the future, the fundamental trends have already been established as discussed in the following section.

The Declining Influence of the Bureaucracy

Historically, Japan's highly efficient bureaucracy dominated the policy formulation process. Well educated by the nation's top universities and selected through a demanding examination system, these bureaucrats represented the best talent that the country had to offer. Bound together by a common educational background, but divided by loyalty to their ministries, they nevertheless developed unified policies which served the country well through a long consensus-seeking process. Respected and well informed, they advised and influenced politicians in the Diet and the cabinet. At the same time, politicians could satisfy their constituencies' wishes by simply following the policies developed by the bureaucrats because the economy was rapidly growing and government finances were in good shape.

When the time came to look for a postretirement career, many a select group of bureaucrats ran for a seat in the Diet. While those who eventually were elected represented a relatively small percentage of all bureaucrats, they made up a large part of the Diet membership. So, it is not an exaggeration to say that for many years the bureaucrats governed Japan.

This governmental process was so characteristically Japanese and lasted for such a long time that the outside world, and even many Japanese, failed to notice the evolution of historical changes during the 1970s. Gradually and against its will, the bureaucracy was forced to share its nearly exclusive control over policy formulation with the politicians. This is not to say that bureaucrats no longer exert influence; they continue to play a major role in the resolution of routine matters, and throughout the entire nonroutine policy formulation process, politicians, still listen carefully to their views. However, bureaucrats no longer enjoy a unique status, and to exert their influence, they must now form alliances with group of well-placed politicians.

A case in point is the once omnipotent Ministry of Finance's (MOF) gradual loss of power to politicians and, to some extent, to other ministries which spend the public funds allocated by MOF. Not surprisingly, the battle between MOF and the politicians as well as the other government ministries is over the budget and fiscal policy in general. The traditionally conservative MOF bureaucracy believes in strict fiscal discipline and abhors the more free-spending ways of politicans, but it no longer has the decisive power to always stop them. Recognizing this, the other ministries have aligned themselves with the powerful LDP politicans and now also challenge the MOF bureaucracy.

The bureaucrats themselves agree that they no longer have exclusive control over the policy formulation process. According to the results of a survey published in the March 12, 1986, edition of the *Mainichi Shimbum*, 60.3 percent of the officials polled in 18 different ministries agreed that postwar prosperity was the result of their leadership. However, only 20 percent claimed that the Japanese economy is still led by bureaucrats in the second half of the 1980s.

Bureaucrats gradually lost their exclusive control over policy formulation for a number of reasons. First, over the years a U.S. style political democracy based on elected representatives as opposed to appointed government officials has evolved. Furthermore, by the early 1980s the government was no longer in a position to expand its budgets freely, and politicians would have lost their constituencies' support if they had simply continued to follow the bureaucracy's advice which was no longer supported by generous funding. Moreover, a number of Diet members who have specialized in areas such as education or tax matters for 10 to 20 years have obtained a much better grasp of issues than the officials who are frequently rotated through the various sections of the ministries. Consequently, over the years the politicians' and bureaucrats' "visions" began to diverge, and politicians as a group have become much more knowledgeable. Thus, in contrast to past years when more than 90 percent of the legislation was written by bureaucrats and after closed-door (LDP) committee meetings rubber-stamped by the Diet, in recent years as much as 25 to 50 percent of the submitted legislation was written by the Diet members themselves. Bureaucrats nonetheless provided valuable expertise throughout the process.

This trend has been accelerated by the increasing number of bureaucrats entering political life at a younger age than their predecessors. Currently, more bureaucrats are leaving in their thirties and forties to run for office than in the past, when officials stood for election in their late forties or fifties after having obtained a considerable amount of seniority in their ministries or agencies. The present day bureaucrats move into politics earlier for a couple of reasons. First, as a general rule, LDP Diet members must have won at least five or more elections, meaning that they must have spent at least 10–15 years in the Diet before they can be considered for cabinet appointments. Thus, bureaucrats entering the political arena after the age of 50 cannot obtain the necessary two or three cabinet appointments to become influential senior politicians. Furthermore, retiring bureaucrats have recently seen their options reduced as the nature of traditional *amakudari* management positions in large corporations usually offered to them has changed.[11] With the gradual deregulation of the economy, corporations are now more independent and, thus, consider it less useful to employ retiring officials. These officials can, of course, still find jobs as advisors, but the road to the top of large corporations is no longer as open as in previous years. It is noteworthy that many of the new advisory positions are with foreign companies, some of which as, for example, IBM and Texas Instruments, already employed former bureaucrats in the 1960s. However, the practice became widespread only after foreign banks and securities companies moved into Japan during the second half of the 1980s and began worrying about the advantages *amakudari* could give to their Japanese competitors.

To obtain the services of a former bureaucrat, foreign companies have to proceed differently than their Japanese counterparts because they are not tied in with the *amakudari* system that the various ministries maintain with industries and firms. Foreign companies have to ask the retiring government of officials and offer them formal contracts. Costs may be high; they can reach $500,000 for a highly placed former bureaucrat such as a division-chief or vice-minister. While foreign companies are concerned that the close ties of the retired bureaucrats could result in corporate secrets leaking out, many nonetheless employ them because they consider both the costs and the risks worth the benefits. Companies such as IBM, Solomon Brothers, Merrill-Lynch, Dupont, and Motorola, to mention just a few, have obtained the advisory services of a number of well-known former officials. As a matter of fact, foreign companies have recently become quite popular among the bureaucrats about to retire because they offer not only better financial terms but also greater challenges and opportunities.

Another development that may contribute to the continual loss of power of the bureacracy is a 1988 GATT panel finding that concluded that the time-honored tradition of "administrative guidance" has the same effect as statutory regulations and, thus, contravenes the GATT provisions. Formulated in response to a European Community (EC) complaint, the finding stated that Japan's price monitoring system on semiconductor exports, put into effect through administrative guidance under American pressure, ran counter to GATT's ban on quantitative restrictions. Thus Japan's bureaucracy was put on notice that one of its favorite policy instruments violated international trading rules. This, together with the increasing reluctance of many Japanese companies to respond to administrative guidance, may mean the eventual demise of this instrument and, thus, the continued erosion of the bureaucracy's once almost unchallenged power.

The swift replacement of two prime ministers during the summer of 1989 prompted American and European observers to argue that because of the LDP's serious political problems the transfer of policy-formulation power from the bureaucrats to the politicians has ended. Moreover, the observers emphasized, now that the bureaucrats are in charge again, the slow and controversial internationalization process will also come to a halt. The bureaucracy will again exercise its power and influence to deflect external pressures for change.

Such views, however, fail to realize that the transfer of policy formulating power from the bureaucrats to the politicians is a fundamental process that may be temporarily slowed down but not halted by political uncertainty. While the LDP is trying to come to terms with the political problems generated by the Recruit-scandal and its aftermath, the bureaucrats may exercise a stronger influence over the policy implementation process as well as the routine policy formulation process. However, the policy issues facing Japan today and in the future are not routine matters but criticial choices which only politicians, however handicapped in the short-run, can decide. The resolution of trade-conflicts with the United States and the European Community, the aging of the population and related matters involve major policy choices and not routine considerations. Thus, the shift of policy-formulating power from the bureaucrats to the politicians continues regardless of temporary slowdowns and/or interruptions.

Changes Within the Liberal Democratic Party

The gradual shift of policy formulation from the bureaucrats to the politicians has been accompanied by changes within the LDP itself.[12] Whereas in the past, policy formulation within the party was the domain of the different factions who hammered out an agreement concerning the bureaucracy's policy proposals behind closed doors, in time the Policy Affairs Research Council and its divisions (*bukai*), transcending factions in accordance with policy issues, became the focal point of the process. The number of Council meetings steadily increased over the years, peaked in the mid 1960s, and then gradually declined until the early 1980s, when their frequency again increased to slightly over 1,200 per year, where the number is now stabilizing.[13]

The divisions or *bukai* combine specialized knowledge with political authority within the framework of smaller and therefore more manageable organizational units than the full Policy Affairs Research Council. They are organized along policy, that is, ministry or agency lines and cover the spectrum of government. There are, for example, agricultural and forestry, postal, highway, telecommunications, finance, construction, and aviation divisions, among others. Membership is open to all Dietmen who are interested; each may be a registered member of up to three divisions. However, nonmembers may freely attend divisional meetings of their choice and participate in the discussions.

The heads of divisions are experts in their fields, who have served at least three to five terms in the Diet. They have long-standing associations with the various interest groups formed around the divisions and may have seen years of administrative service as cabinet members, parliamentary vice ministers, or Diet committee chairmen. The divisional heads manage the relationship between the divisions, administrative organs such as the ministries, and outside interest groups.

The evolution of the divisions as influential, deliberative bodies is illustrated by the number of organizations lobbying the tax division for favors between 1966 and 1986, particularly after 1983 when the pressures for tax reform were beginning to mount. As Figure 3–1 shows, in 1968 there were 48 organizations, and just two years later in 1970, this figure nearly doubled, reaching 95. In the 1970–1976 period, there was a steady increase although

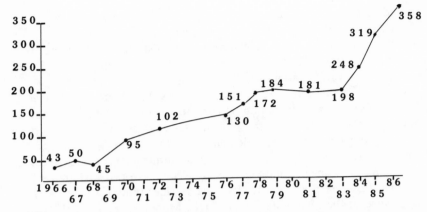

Figure 3-1.   Number of Organizations Lobbying for Tax Reform with the Tax System Research Commission of the LDP Policy Affairs Research Council: 1966–1986. *Source*: Seizaburo Sato and Tetsuhisa Matsuzaki, *Jiminto Seiken*, (LDP Regime), originally published by Chuckoron-Sha, Inc. (Tokyo: 1986), p. 113. Courtesy of authors and Chuckoron-Sha, Inc.

less rapid, of 35 more organizations, bringing the total number to 130 in 1976. The next three years saw another dramatic increase when 54 more organizations became active. While these numerical increases were great at the time, the largest increase occurred between 1983 and 1986, from 198 to 358 groups. This represents an increase of 80.8 percent between 1983 and 1986, and 732.6 percent between 1966 and 1986, the year in which tax reform was considered.

A critical role in the policy formulation process is played by the *zoku giin*, or political cliques/tribes. These informal groups have evolved along the lines of the specialized divisions but sometimes transcend both factional and divisional lines. There is no limit to the number of *zokus* Dietmen may join. Thus, the *zoku* unite LDP Diet members of varying backgrounds and seniority under the banner of certain special interests. Leadership is in the hands of influential senior politicians ("bosses") who wield a great deal of politial power.Membership continually changes according to the issues at hand and over time, and may include active cabinet members as well as first-term representatives who get equal opportunity to present their views at the *zoku* meetings.[14]

The *zokus'* ability to prevent the acceptance of a policy contrary to their perceived interest is based on traditional political practice. Throughout the policy formulation process, politicans whose interests are not directly affected usually do not comment on the views expressed by those whose interests are directly involved. As a consequence, the ultimately agreed upon policies alway strongly reflect the views of the most affected *zoku* members even though they may be in a minority and some othe members of the LDP may have reservations about the overall wisdom of these policies.

A case in point is the agricultural *zoku*. Although it is no longer as dominant as in the past, it continues to be one of the most important political interest groups in the Diet. In spite of its disagreements with industrial interest groups as, for example, the *Keidanren* which challenges the protectionist agricultural policies, the agricultural *zoku* continues to collect large sums of money, obtain blocks of electoral votes, and in general, influence Japanese political life. Its considerable strength is rooted in the importance of the farm vote for the LDP. Moreover, most of the LDP's senior politicians have rural backgrounds; for example, ten prime ministers who held office since 1960 began their political careers in rural prefectures.

Opposition to the Action Program

Due to the *zokus'* powerful membership, access to information, and strong ties to interest groups (including the relevant bureaucracy), no policy can be formulated and no legislation can be passed into law in Japan today without the support of the relevant *zoku*. Therefore, it is no longer the bureaucracy, but the special interest *zoku* which can make it difficult or even impossible for a Prime Minister to be an effective leader. Whereas the officials of the various ministries can deliberately sabotage the Prime Minister's orders through delaying tactics or other means, they cannot openly challenge him. Only the *zoku* can do that, and this is what happened during the preparation of the Action Program.

While the outside world watched with fascination what it believed to be a struggle between Prime Minister Nakasone and the bureaucracy over the specifics of the program, in reality the Prime Minister had to do battle with the various *zoku* which protected the special interests they represented. Armed with the necessary information from the bureaucrats and support from the special interests groups, they were, thus, in a position to prevent the necessary consensus on any issue they opposed.

One area of particular contention centered on the tariff schedules for agricultural and marine products. While the government proposed a flat tariff rate decrease on these products, the agricultural-forestry *zoku* rejected the idea and agreed to other features of the program only after difficult negotiations. When the Prime Minister tried to reduce plywood tariffs, he had to postpone the move because the *zoku* again resisted. He had to provide an extra budget allocation of more than $1 billion to help the industry modernize before the *zoku* members were willing to agree to the tariff reductions, which, even then, would take effect only three years from the date of the discussions.

To expedite the formulation of the Action Program, Nakasone, in an unusual demonstration of his resolve while negotiating with the *zoku*, also pressured the bureaucracy. He invited the vice ministers and bureau chiefs of the various ministries to his office to convince them of his intentions to increase imports. This was unusual because traditionally Japanese prime ministers talk to cabinet ministers first, who tell bureaucrats what they should do. Not surprisingly, a number of officials disagreed with the Prime Minister's approach and plans. An official of the domestically oriented Ministry of Posts and Telecommunications, for example, was quoted as saying that "... Prime Minister Nakasone does not have the power to enforce his personal choice, so it's risky to put your life in the hands of such a man. You never can tell when you will be betrayed."[15]

To increase the effectiveness of the planned measures, to obtain international publicity, and to pressure the bureaucracy, Prime Minister Nakasone also urged foreign participation in the rescheduling of tariffs, simplification of product standards, and import certification procedures because "the world is watching for this as the key to realizing a free market in Japan through the Action Program."[16] Thus, at a meeting of the Director Generals of 22 ministries and agencies, seven guests from the United States, European Community and Asian Pacific region countries were given an opportunity to provide input for the program. The United States promptly submitted a request for market opening measures in 13 areas including the right for U.S. lawyers to practice in Japan, and the expansion of imports of American automobiles, shoes, and wine, among other things; the other foreign representatives also submitted requests, equally detailed, on behalf of their special trade concerns.

Scope of the Action Program

The Japanese Government-Ruling Parties Joint Headquarters for the Promotion of External Economic Measures, headed by Prime Minister Nakasone, officially announced on July 30, 1985, the Action Program for Improved Market Access, to be implemented over a three-year period. The Program included three basic principles broadly outlining Japan's intentions for increased participation in world economic affairs and aimed specifically at creating wider access in six areas of the Japanese marketplace. The plan further sought to promote international participation in this market-opening process through a new round of multilateral trade negotiations. Herein, Japan declared itself a full-fledged member of the international economic community, willing to accept its status and responsibility as a major economic power.

The underlying premise of the Action Program was stated as a willingness on the part of the Japanese to achieve a market openess "greatly exceeding that of the international level." With this in mind, the plan set out the following principles:

1. From the basic standpoint of "freedom-in-principle, restrictions only as exception," government intervention would be reduced to a minimum so as to leave the choice and responsibility to consumers.
2. A positive attitude, as befitting Japan's position, would be taken in promoting the new round of GATT negotiations.
3. Special considerations in plan provisions would be given so that the Action Program could help promote the economic growth of developing nations.

These basic principles signaled a shift in the Japanese world position from a small country to an economic power, and indicated a restructuring of not only the traditional relationships between Japan and the outside world but also of domestic economic practices and relations between the Japanese government and its citizens.

Selected Program Areas

The opening of the Japanese market outlined in the Action Program included measures in six areas, which were tariff schedules, import quotas, standards and certification of imports, government procurement, financial and capital markets, and services and import promotion measures. Tariff rates on 1,853 items, including products from the Generalized System of Preferences, were to be eliminated beginning in 1986; tariffs on other products were to be reduced by 20 percent starting the same time, and other products, such as wine, would remain on the same schedules until Arpil 1, 1987. With respect to import quotas, action on the remaining quantitative restrictions, would be taken in consultations and negotiations at GATT talks and other meetings of interested parties.

The Japanese government hoped that revisions of the certification system, traditionally under its strict control, would help alleviate foreign criticism of the system as a nontariff barrier and facilitate market access for imports. The new program envisioned that the number of import items subject to self-certification be expanded to include 14 new products such as carbonated beverages and some electrical appliances. Another measure proposed that data on imported products obtained in laboratories abroad be accepted by Japanese authorities "to the extent possible."

With respect to import procedures, the Japanese also addressed the issue of "transparency" in the policy-formulating process. The program stated that foreign representatives would be allowed to participate in advisory councils, subcommittees, and other policy-formulating bodies to express their views. The Japanese wanted to reflect the opinions of foreign interests in the drafting or revision of standards.

This section also announced an effort to simplify the administrative procedures associated with imports. Measures, such as the publication of schedules for import approvals, were designed to reduce the time involved in these procedures. Other measures reduced the import notification requirements at points of entry and increased authority of customs officials to handle point-of-entry problems.

The program also included a section providing for additional "transparency" in government procurement. The measures promised better access to information concerning the tendering of bids. Among other provisions proposed in this section, bid times would be extended from 30 to 40 days to increase foreign competitiveness on government contracts, and delivery times would be extended "as far as possible." Lastly, while the GATT Agreement on Government Procurement (Tokyo Round, 1979) is applicable to 45 government organizations, Japan proposed to apply the agreement to another 16 government-related organizations likely to request foreign contract bidding.

Efforts to liberalize Japan's financial and capital markets had been underway before the Action Program was drafted, but the Action Program formalized Japan's commitment to market opening measures in this area. The major provisions of this section included a relaxation and ultimate removal of interest rate ceilings on large denomination deposits by the spring of 1987. They also promoted liberalization of interest rate ceilings on small denomination deposits provided that necessary provisions were established to protect depositors. Another feature of this section authorized nine eligible foreign banks to participate in trust banking business. One last provision, which related to the opening of financial markets, liberalized the issuance of floating rate Euroyen notes.

The final area affected by the Action Program was services and import promotion. Many of the Japanese service industries had been sharply criticized by foreigners for maintaining nontariff barriers, particularly in distribution, legal, and insurance services. This section proposed to allow foreigners to participate in these service areas to a limited extent. For example, new legislation was drafted to amend the Lawyers Law to enable foreign lawyers to practice in Japan. With regard to insurance, National Health Insurance, previously provided only to Japanese citizens, would be made available to all foreign residents of Japan. The government further proposed to formulate an international framework for trade in services as another facet of the planned new round of multilateral trade negotiations.

Import promotion fell into several categories. First, in order to encourage private industries' efforts to increase imports, the interest rate of the Export-Import Bank of Japan for import credit on manufactured goods and government procurement would be lowered, and direct investment by foreign firms would be encouraged. Next, the government proposed to enhance the public's "awareness of the importance of imports" through officially sponsored promotions, particularly large-scale import fairs organized by the Japan External Trade Organization (JETRO). In conjunction with this, it also proposed to encourage its citizens to travel abroad to generate demand for imports. Finally, the program also addressed two key foreign concerns: the elimination of counterfeiting and improved distribution.

Counterfeiting of popular trademarks and brand name items of consumer goods had become a serious problem all over the world, but especially in Japan where consumers are particularly brand-conscious, and the manufacturing skills necessary to produce high quality copies are available. Here the Japanese government proposed to actively enforce laws by establishing anticounterfeiting agencies and prosecuting counterfeiters. With regard to the distribution system, the government proposed to conduct a fact-finding study on the distribution paths of imported goods and provide the results to consumers. Also, the function of the Office of Trade and Investment Ombudsman was to be strengthened to settle foreign complaints concerning market access.

While the program sets out specific timetables and implementation plans for its measures, it contains certain caveats. For instance, the Economic Planning Agency proposed eliminating or reducing tariffs on 1,853 products starting in March 1986; however, some products such as wine remained on their original schedules for an additional year as a political concession to the agricultural interests. Moreover, the very sensitive product issues were relegated to the area of "future consultations with interested parties." Tariff rates on industrial products would be reduced by 20 percent in principle, unless injuries to Japan's "domestic industries are caused to the extent by import surges or other circumstances due to this measure" in which case "suspension of the measure on related products may be introduced."[17] In other sections, such as the measures related to import quotas, the program did not ignore the politicially sensitive issues, but neither did it take concrete steps toward their resolution. With respect to import quotas on beef, citrus fruit, and other agricultural products, for example, the Japanese promised to observe existing arrangement "in good faith." The program proposed that upon the expiration of the present arrangements, Japan would start new "consultations . . . and shall take appropriate actions with sincerity."[18]

Import Campaigns

To raise public awareness of the trade problem and to urge consumers to buy more foreign products, the government in cooperation with the private sector also staged an import campaign in October and November 1985. Some 100 leading figures from the art, sports, and entertainment world were enlisted to help. Import fairs were organized at more than 1,000 sites across the country; Prime Minister Nakasone himself made a much publicized appearance at the Tokyo Fair.

The Japanese government knew that the program could not succeed without the full support of the large private-sector companies. Consequently, already on April 22, 1985, MITI called in the executives of the 60 leading export-oriented corporations and trading companies, asking them to develop their own "action programs." By the end of May, MITI announced that the 60 companies planned to import goods worth more than $96 billion during FY 1985, an increase of $5 billion or 5.5 percent over FY 1984.

On August 23, MITI asked another 74 companies to join the import promotion effort, and by early 1986 projected that the total of 134 corporations intended to import goods worth $104.6 billion in FY 1985, an increase of 7.5 percent from the previous year. Some of the increase was expected from the *sogo-shosha* (trading companies), electronics and machinery manufacturers, department stores, supermarket chains, and energy companies. Most of it, however, was to be generated by the car manufacturing industry that pledged to procure from foreign sources whenever possible. Imports by all companies affiliated with the Toyota group, for example, were expected to reach $917 million in FY 1985, an increase of 9 percent over FY 1984. The parts and components to be imported included tires, windshields, machine tools, and aluminum wheels. Other car manufacturers, such as Nissan and Mazda, expressed similar intentions.

Among the *sogo-shosha*, Marubeni Corp., Sumitomo Corp., C.Itoh & Co., and Nissho Iwai Corp. were the most active. They instituted import incentive systems and other measures to motivate employees to obtain more products from abroad. According to a MITI survey, the combined imports of the top 13 *sogo-shosha* in FY 1985 were expected to increase by $5.9 billion, or 6.7 percent over FY 1984.

Reactions Abroad

Reactions to the Action Program abroad ranged from a wait-and-see attitude to dejected deja vu to outright hostility. As usual, the early announcement of these measures on April 9 raised expectations to a level that could not be met by a program that was shaped through the traditional consensus-formulation process. Furthermore, like all the previous market-access packages, the Action Program was a unilateral response to strong foreign pressures for specific measures within a short period of time. Thus, the program could not address the fundamental issues of the current and trade account surpluses that Japan was amassing. Such a move would have necessitated a broad, coordinated multilateral effort which neither the American nor West European nor most developing country governments were prepared to undertake. A joint effort would have forced these governments to alter many domestic economic policies, which would have been politically unacceptable.

Criticism was immediately widespread. In the developing world, for example, the South Korean press criticized Japan for not directly responding to Korean expectations, while Singapore newspapers argued that the entire program was developed to pacify the United States. Others, such as the Thai and Malaysian press, were less negative and looked forward to some improvement in their trade with Japan. Among the industrialized countries, official circles and the media in Britain expressed scepticism about the entire effort, while the French had doubts about Nakasone's ability to implement the program over the objections of all the vested interests. The Federal Republic of Germany and Australia, on the other hand, were somewhat more positive, and speculated that a fully implemented Action Program might be beneficial.

American Criticism and the Japanese Response

From the Japanese point of view, America's reaction was the most important. Unfortunately, the official announcement of the program came on the same day as the U.S. Department of Commerce published its monthly trade statistics showing that in June the United States had incurred its second highest monthly trade deficit of all time ($13.4 billion), 34 percent or $4.6 billion of which was with Japan. Thus, when Tokyo made its announcement, the anti-Japanese mood in Washington, particularly on Capitol Hill, was intensifying.

The White House reaction was cool, and although it referred to some parts of the program as "promising," it suggested that the three-year implementation schedule should be enacted "in a more timely fashion." This contrasted the warm praise that the Administration gave the initial announcement in April, and was part of a strategy to dampen the protectionist forces in Congress while keeping pressure on the Japanese. Some U.S. government officials greeted the program with guarded praise; staff members of the U.S. Embassy in Tokyo, for example, said that it would probably help the sales of some foreign products in Japan, such as cosmetics, processed foods, and appliances. Others in Washington noted that the program made no provisions for the removal of agricultural quotas, and that it did not seem to clearly address the admission of foreign lawyers, nor did it include steps to dismantle the structural import restraints such as the distribution system.

Reactions in Congress were uniformly hostile. Leading proponents of the protectionist movement, which by the summer of 1985 overwhelmed both the House and Senate with over 300 bills, expressed scepticism about not only the effectiveness of the Action Program but also the sincerity of the Japanese government.[19] The resulting "Japan-bashing" involved a great deal of "bureaucracy-bashing" because even members of Congress did not realize the shift of policy-formulating power from the bureaucracy to the LDP *zoku* and, thus, vented their anger at the government officials.

One of the key sponsors of the import surcharge bill, Senator Lloyd Bentsen (D-Texas) was reported to have said that while he has not had a chance to look at the program, he was skeptical from past experience because the Japanese bureaucracy "is a master of the hidden trade barriers." Senator John Danforth (R-Missouri), chairman of the Senate International Trade Subcommittee, stated that the Japanese announcement of the program was just another set of fine-sounding words which probably would not lead to any concrete results. Senator John Heinz (R-Pennsylvania) went even further, he called U.S.–Japanese negotiations a con-game in which the United States was the willing dupe. The Japanese, Sen. Heinz added, would not open up their marketplace because they knew that the United States would not take any strong actions against them[20]

On the other side of the Pacific, the Japanese mass media conveyed the U.S. reactions in their usual style. The reporters did not differentiate between the White House and Congressional views, nor did they explain the motivation behind the Administration's strategy to respond in a guarded manner. Above all, they emphasized the statement made by the various members of Congress, and provided details of some of the 300 protectionist bills pending at that time. Most reporters paid little attention to the American domestic political situation which was the major reason that members of Congress, who were already thinking ahead to the next elections, tried to outdo each other's protectionist rhetoric.

Not surprisingly, such exaggerated reports stoked the fires of resentment in Tokyo. The Japanese could not understand what it was the Americans wanted when, given their domestic political circumstances, they had done as much as possible. They were frustrated by the expectation that they should rapidly change long-standing arrangements and practices, and consequently, they fell back on the only explanation that seemed reasonable. The Japanese believed that America was inefficient and unwilling to take the painful but necessary steps to put its economic house in order, and found it easier to blame Japan for its problems.

Such views, although containing some truth, were as oversimplified as the often repeated American charge that the root of all bilateral trade problems was the closed nature of the Japanese marketplace. While Japan no longer maintained the protectionist barriers of an era past, traditional arrangements and practices, such as product standards, continued to hamper market access.

The Action Program was designed to eliminate these constraints and thereby improve market access. It was unfortunate that the emotional responses on both sides of the Pacific clouded the introduction of the program. A less emotional examination would have shown that the program was neither a quick and easy way to fix the trade imbalances nor a cynical public relations exercise. It would have revealed the simple truth that the program was a unilateral move in the right direction with possible future benefits for Japan and the rest of the world.

The 1985–1986 MOSS Negotiation Results

The Japanese government published its official report on the first-year implementation results of the Action Program on August 1, 1986. However, already earlier in the year, in January, the American and Japanese governments released a joint communique on the achievements of the Market-Oriented Sector-Specific (MOSS) negotiations, which overlapped with the program in that they also dealt with questions of market access, albeit only in selected industries.[21]

The MOSS talks began in the spring of 1985, and addressed the Japanese telecommunications, medical equipment, pharmaceutical, electronics, and forestry markets. Both governments agreed to pinpoint and reduce regulatory, tariff, and other existing import barriers in these markets. While officially termed successful in the end, the negotiations had their ups and downs; in some of the highly technical discussions, ill-informed American negotiators were lectured by Japanese bureaucrats on their lack of understanding, which led to frustrations on both sides. Moreover, in late 1985 a disagreement concerning forestry products nearly led to a breakdown; Foreign Minister Abe had to personally intervene to save the situation at the last minute.

In their joint communique, Secretary of State Shutz and Foreign Minister Abe praised the talks. In his individual statement to the press, Abe cited unilateral tariff cuts, a sharp rise in the yen, and substantial changes in the regulation of the telecommunications, medical equipment, pharmaceutical, and electronics markets as positive developments. Secretary Shultz supported Abe's remarks but emphasized that little progress was made toward resolution of the disagreement over forestry products.

While the agreement was noteworthy, the major reason for the optimism and satisfaction expressed in the joint statement was the desire to dampen protectionist sentiments on Capitol Hill, where another cycle of Japan-bashing was expected to begin in the spring of 1986. Nonetheless, representatives of the telecommunications, medical equipment, pharmaceutical, and electronic industries believed that the MOSS agreements would make it easier for their firms to enter the Japanese marketplace.

The First Year of the Action Program

Following the conclusion of the MOSS talks, the Japanese government, later in the year, announced in its first year Action Program report that Japan had made good on most of its promises to reduce tariffs and to eliminate remaining nontariff barriers.[22] The exception was the slow progress in the expansion of agricultural import quotas and the government procurement of foreign products.

While the government's report of the first-year Action Program implementation results was upbeat, the trade data for FY 1985, ending on March 31, 1986, were much less encouraging. According to the customs statistics published by the Ministry of Finance, while total exports increased by 3.3 percent, imports were down by 5.1 percent.

The import decline was mainly caused by the stagnating demand for food, crude oil, coal, and liquefied gas, items which represented more than 40 percent of Japan's annual imports. Also, the total figures reported in U.S. dollars were affected by the unexpectedly rapid decline in the price of some of these items.

In the midst of these discouraging data, there was, however, one ray of hope. Manufactured imports showed a more than expected increase and reached a 31 percent share in total imports, including fuels, an all-time high since World War II and substantially higher than the preceeding year's 20 percent. This positive trend was reinforced by JETRO's August 1986 report which announced that during the first six months of 1986, manufactured imports grew by 23.7 percent to $24.7 billion, representing a 38 percent share in total imports.[23] According to JETRO, the first six-month data indicated that by the end of FY 1986 manufactured imports could surpass the FY 1985 high of 31 percent.

The first-year private sector action program results were also modest. According to MITI data, by the end of FY 1985 the 134 participating corporations reported only a slight 3 percent increase in the value of imports over the previous fiscal year.[24]

To meet their commitments in the future, some of the 134 corporations planned to increase their manufactured goods imports during FY 1986. The 26 member Hitachi group, for example, set an overall goal of $980 million, an increase of 13 percent over FY 1985. Of this amount, Hitachi planned to spend $400 million in the United States, an increase of 12 percent over the previous year.

The results were disappointing, but it was unrealistic to have expected that the Action Program could greatly increase overall imports within a single year, particularly with conditions of stagnating demand in the major import markets. Most knowledgeable observes knew this, and also understood that long-established buying patterns and habits could not be changed overnight, regardless of concentrated import promotion efforts. As one Japanese government official explained, "The aim (of import promotion) is not to make them (the Japanese) buy—the amount is negligible—but to stop them from opposing the idea of increasing imports.[25] The chairman of Marubeni Corporation stated that "... import expansion calls are similar to Buddhist chants, constants recitation eventually enables them to seep into one's mind.[26]

One of the reasons that the import—often high-price—promotion campaigns were not very effective was that in addition to the strong loyalty and high quality expectations of Japanese consumers in general, industrial buyers had their own loyalties and very selective standards. Most original equipment manufacturers (OEMs) considered imported parts and components a major problem. They found that many imported items, regardless of the source, did not meet quality standards. As a consequence, in many companies even though the purchasing department heads wanted to increase imports, technical staff on the shop floor often resisted. With the sharp appreciation of the yen, such intraorganizational conflicts became more frequent in the second half of 1986 because purchasing managers could point to the considerable cost savings derived from imports, while the technical specialists continued to worry about quality. Generally, such debates were won by the quality-control technicians whose arguments carried more weight than those of the purchasing specialists. Many Japanese companies had established a worldwide reputation as high quality producers; not surprisingly, they were not willing to risk such a reputation just because the government wanted to increase imports. Official exhortations worked in the past, but they did not have the same effect in the second half of the 1980s.

Industrial imports were also limited by manufacturing considerations, particularly the widely used *kanban* (just-in-time) inventory system. Successful application of the *kanban* depends largely on the firm's suppliers. In this system, suppliers must provide the buyers with small lots of high quality parts delivered frequently and coordinated precisely with the buying firms' manufacturing schedules. There is very little or no safety stock; thus, the quality, quantity, and timing of the deliveries are extremely critical. Dependable and readily available suppliers are a necessary.

Other traditions and long-established practices also hampered imports. Most of these were rooted in the commercial practices of the past, and thus, could not be as readily changed through government directives as, for example, product standards or import procedures. Government surveys showed that despite the yen appreciation, the price of many foreign products had not decreased during the first half of 1986, because traditional importers of such products wanted to obtain higher profits or maintain brand image or both. While the government wanted the benefits of the yen appreciation passed on to the consumers, there was no easy way to convince importers to reduce prices since it could not dictate price-policy to private sector companies.

The effectiveness of the Action Program during the first year was also reduced because it was not possible to raise the export-orientation of foreign, particularly American, companies. The Japanese import promoting delegations of the large, private sector corporations, for instance, came back with mixed feelings from America.[27] The representatives of Toyota and Hitachi reported that they found U.S. companies whose products they liked, but the managements of these firms were indifferent to exporting. Others were reluctant to adapt their products to the Japanese marketplace. Moreover, even companies which were export-oriented could not take advantage of the new opportunities on such short notice. Managers needed time to develop business plans and to undertake the necessary financial as well as human investments required for entering the very competitive Japanese marketplace.

The Japanese government was concerned about the modest results and, in August 1986, urged the top managers of Japan's major department stores and supermarkets to increase the import of consumer goods manufactured abroad under licensing arrangements. The MITI minister personally told mangers to purchase more clothes and household merchandise produced mostly in Asian countries. Moreover, the minister asked that managers develop plans to return the windfall profits obtained through the yen appreciation to the consumers. The requests were made in August because department stores and supermarkets import about two-thirds of their foreign products during the fall and winter seasons. The heads of the retail firms promised to do their best, but such admonitions no longer carried the same weight as in the past.

By the second half of 1986 the much-publicized and -criticized Action Program was almost forgotten. Although the Japanese government issued regular reports on the results during 1986 and 1987, its final report published in 1988 was barely noticed. This is understandable because by the middle of 1986 the program was overshadowed by the Maekawa Commission report concerning the restructuring of the economy and the shift from export-led to domestic demand-led growth. Moreover, the dramatic appreciation of the yen during 1986–1988 unleashed forces that began reshaping the Japanese marketplace in a fashion that no government-sponsored import promotion program could even approximate.

The Action Program was the result of specific American demands backed by moralistic rhetoric and the threat of punitive congressional action together with the Japanese desire to somehow contain American anger through a set of measures that addressed at least some of the U.S. concerns. Not surprisingly, because the program did not address the fundamentals and focused on what was politically possible in a short period of time, it had little or no effect on the bilateral trade balance and on Japan's global current account surpluses.

The Action Program, however, did result in some lasting long-term benefits which were not recognized on either side of the Pacific. During program formulation and implementation, the Japanese government, politicians, and the public at large were repeatedly forced to scrutinize the image of their nation within the global context. The debates surrounding the consensus formulation process helped the Japanese understand that their nation is no longer seen around the world as a small weakling country, but as an economic power whose actions, or inactions, affect the entire world economy. It was in this sense that even the hastily and narrowly conceived Action Program stimulated the long-overdue debate about the broader aspects of the internationalization of the Japanese economy which took a momentum of its own beginning in 1986 when the Maekawa Commission report outlined the nation's new growth objectives and the appreciating yen began the restructuring of the economy in earnest.

Ongoing U.S.–Japan Trade Conflicts[28]

Japan's FY 1985 trade statistics were received abroad with the usual critical comments. Most of the response emphasized that the decline in imports was more proof of the closed nature of the Japanese marketplace.

Shortly after the Japanese data were published, the U.S. trade figures for July 1986 were announced. The merchandise trade deficit had soared to $18 billion, a new monthly record. Administration officials and members of Congress expected that trade would be a major issue in the Congressional elections later that year, therefore, they focused on these trade statistics.

As expected, the U.S. government continued to pressure Japan on what it considered to be several unresolved issues. These included the admission of foreign lawyers under the Action Program and increased access to the Japanese tobacco and car parts markets under the new round of MOSS negotiations which began in mid-1986.

The Admission of Foreign Lawyers

In May 1986, in accordance with the Action Program commitment, the Diet passed legislation admitting foreign lawyers (*gai-ben*) to practice in Japan beginning April 1, 1987. The United States had been pressuring Japan on this issue for some time; Americans viewed the admission of lawyers as a part of the campaign to open Japan's service markets. Moreover, they told the Japanese that admitting foreign lawyers was in Japan's interest because specialized legal services were needed to undertake the complex international transactions in the newly liberalized financial markets.

Not surprisingly, the Japanese lawyers disagreed, and *Nichibenren*, the Japanese Federation of Bar Associations, strongly rejected the American arguments and formed a countermeasures committee to deal with the matter. Members of the organization were concerned about the influence foreign lawyers could have on the legal profession's traditionally harmonious interaction with Japan's consensus-based society.[29] Moreover, they claimed, the standards of the legal profession are among the highest in Japan; thus, the admission of foreign lawyers could affect these standards.

The legal profession in Japan is very selective. To become a lawyer, candidates must first complete an undergraduate university education, and then apply to the nation's only law school, the Legal Training and Research Institute. Of the several thousand applicants, only a maximum of 500 are admitted annually if they pass the rigid admissions exam. In 1984, for example, of the 35,000 applicants, 500 passed and were admitted, a success rate of 1.4 percent. The curriculum is based on a two-year apprenticeship in trial practices, drafting legal documents, and other related matters. At the end of two years, candidates must sit for a routine final examination which all of them pass. The graduates may then become assistant judges, public prosecutors, or *bengoshi*. Although approximately 25,000 candidates take the *bengoshi* exam annually, including those who failed before and graduates of other fields, the number of new *bengoshi* annually is about the same: for example, 448 in 1986 and 445 in 1987.

The *bengoshi* are specialists in civil law and criminal defense, and may, therefore, represent clients in court. Others, such as patent or tax attorneys, differ from the *bengoshi* in that they represent clients only in their special fields. Most of the *bengoshi* practice in Tokyo where they are members of small firms, usually comprised of two to five lawyers.

Of course, in addition to the legitimate concern about how foreign lawyers would fit into such a differently structured legal system, the *Nichibenren* was also trying to protect the vested interests of its members. Most Japanese lawyers were afraid that their small firms would be overrun by New York-based or Washington-based law firms with hundreds of lawyers and support staff.[30]

The legislation ultimately approved by the Diet became effective on April 1, 1987. It is based on the principle of reciprocity insofar as it admits only those foreign lawyers whose native countries admit lawyers from other nations, including Japan. Approval to practice requires five years of experience, is limited to the lawyer's home country law, and prohibits the formation of partnerships, the employment of Japanese lawyers, and participation in arbitration proceedings. Moreover, while the Ministry of Justice maintains general oversight, *Nichibenren* was authorized to exercise disciplinary control over foreign lawyers.

The American Chamber of Commerce in Japan and the European Business Council in Tokyo were among the first to object to the specifics of the legislation. They argued that the law was not an internationally appropriate solution as promised by the Action Program. They were joined by a group of American lawyers who petitioned the United States Trade Representative (USTR) to begin an investigation under Section 301 (Unfair Trade Practices) of the 1974 Trade Act. Corporate executives complained that the system requires them to pay two firms for legal services: their American legal representatives who, however, could not handle issues involving Japanese law, and, therefore, a Japanese law firm which they need to retain.

American lawyers objected to most features of the legislation, but were particularly upset by the reciprocity requirement. Their concern stémmed from the fact that in the United States, legal licenses are issued by the states, and because in 1986, only New York, Michigan, Hawaii, and the District of Columbia had a policy of reciprocity, lawyers from all but these four areas were barred from Japan. To placate American critics, the Japanese government promised to continue consultations on the ordinances implementing the bill, but it also made clear that "the basic framework is not going to change."

The legislation is undoubtedly restrictive, but it was the best that could be achieved under the circumstances. The *Nichibenren* had an agreement with the government dating from the early 1980s in which it agreed to solve the admission problem on its own. Moreover, the bar association is politically influential association with strong ties to the legal *zoku* in the LDP policy-formulating apparatus. The association effectively used its influence during the consensus formulation process that preceded the submission of the bill to the Diet. Thus, the government had no choice but to go along even though the legislation did not meet all the expectations at home and abroad.

The events surrounding this legislation have shown that as far as the vested interests of professional groups are concerned, the Japanese government is subject to the same kind of pressures as, for example, the American or West German state and federal governments. The political influence and restrictive practices of the American and German Medical Associations exercised under the guise of maintaining professional standards are legendary. Naturally, for the sake of the world economy, restrictive professional practices, whether in Japan or abroad, should not be accepted indefinitely. Changes, however, must be introduced gradually and multilaterally; otherwise the vested professional interest groups throughout the world will continue to fight even the most modest proposals for change.

At the same time, the strong reaction of U.S. lawyers to the Japanese legislation reflected a curious point of view. Reciprocity limitations are not unusual in the world's professional service markets. In the United States, lawyers licensed in one state wishing to practice in some other state must often pass the bar examination of that other state before being allowed to practice there, regardless of their previous experience. Most importantly, the exclusion of American lawyers from Japan, except those from New York, Michigan, Hawaii, and the District of Columbia, could easily be remedied through the acceptance of the reciprocity principle by those states that presently reject it.

Thus, the lawyers' petition requesting an "unfair trade practices" investigation by the USTR was more of a reflection of a narrowly defined self-interest than a genuine concern over general access to Japanese service markets. American lawyers were motivated by the same self-serving considerations as the *Nichibenren* which was trying to keep them out of Japan.

Fortunately, despite the unreasonable position taken by the American lawyers, reason prevailed in Washington. On June 10, 1986, the USTR declined to initiate a Section 301 action. He did so because of the continued exchange of views and because the Japanese legislation became effective only one year later, in 1987, at which time the implementation process could be reviewed to see if any additional action was necessary. Thus, this curious episode in U.S.–Japan trade relations came to a well-deserved ending.

By 1989 only 49 foreign lawyers have registered in Japan, 34 of them from the United States. The majority of them reside in Tokyo and deal with foreign financial companies which handle Japanese firms' M&A activities and real estate purchases abroad. The others provide legal counsel in trade disputes, particularly with the United States. As a consequence of the passage of the Omnibus Competitiveness and Trade Act of 1988 most American lawyers expect an increase in such cases in the future.

After two years of experience in Japan, foreign lawyers complain most about the prohibition on employing Japanese lawyers while the "bengoshi" hire young American lawyers in Tokyo to provide services concerning American law. Moreover, they argue, Japanese lawyers may now open offices in New York and eight American states as well as in the District of Columbia on a reciprocity basis and, thus, hire American lawyers to expand their international activities. To this the "Nichibenren" responds that 42 states continue to reject reciprocity to keep Japanese lawyers out of the United States. Thus, by the end of 1989 it became apparent that the legal issue may very well again develop into a major disagreement between the two countries in the near future.

Tobacco and Car Parts Imports

In the fall of 1986, the United States also expressed concern about the tobacco and car parts markets to which, the Americans argued, access was still restricted. This claim was made within the framework of the new 1986 MOSS talks, as well as in reference to the overall market access commitments made by the Japanese government in the Action Program.

The American demand for more access to the tobacco market presented a difficult problem for Japan. When the former Japan Tobacco and Salt Public Corporation monopoly was replaced by the Japan Tobacco, Inc., to increase competition, conditions in the marketplace remained restrictive because the new company retained a monopoly over domestic leaf buying, tobacco processing, and cigarette manufacturing. This was demanded by the tobacco *zoku* which claimed to protect the livelihood of the approximately 90,000 domestic tobacco leaf growers against low-cost foreign competition. Prime Minister Nakasone had no choice but to agree to the demand, because otherwise he could not have obtained a consensus for even the partial dismantling of the monopoly.

While politically unavoidable, the arrangements made little economic sense. The Japan Tobacco, Inc., paid about three times the world market price for tobacco leaves to growers, and as a result of this price support, by 1985 more than a year's supply of surplus leaf tobacco had accumulated in the warehouses. Even under the best of circumstances, such a surplus could be eliminated only in three to five years, or around 1988, at the earliest. Circumstances, however, were not the best, because the demand for cigarettes appeared to be stagnating or perhaps decreasing.

Although over 310 billion cigarettes were sold in FY 1985, this represented a 0.6 percent decrease from the previous fiscal year. While the evidence was not entirely clear, it was possible that the Japanese were beginning to pay more attention to the health hazards associated with smoking. In a January 1987 report the Japan Tobacco Inc. announced that the estimated number of smokers declined by about 3.6 million from the 1978 peak of around 35 million to a little over 31 million in 1986. Moreover, the report emphasized, the estimated smoking population decreased by slightly over 1 million during 1985–1986 alone. Such developments, if they turned into long-term trends, could have had a very adverse effect on the domestic leaf growers because the share of foreign tobacco (cigarettes and pipe smoking tobacco) rose to 2.4 percent in FY 1985 and 3.3 percent by June 1986, from 1.8 percent in FY 1984.[31] Increased sales of imported cigarettes were attributed to the narrowing price gap due to an increase in domestic prices, as well as the diversification of consumer tastes.

Thus, by the fall of 1986, the Japanese government was in a difficult situation. The partial dismantling of the tobacco monopoly satisfied neither the American government nor the other foreign governments. At the same time, the influential *zoku* was not about to give up its protectionist stance to satisfy foreign, particularly American demands for a more open market. The *zoku* members believed that the Japanese government should not be concerned about the foreign demands because the former public monopoly became a private firm and the market share of imported cigarettes was on the rise. Others, including members of the Diet, were angry at the United States because just as American medical and government authorities were trying to reduce smoking, U.S. negotiators pressured Japan to buy more tobacco. Moreover, they argued, in response to an October 1986 report by the U.S. Academy of Sciences concerning the negative effects of "passive smoking" or the involuntary inhalation of smoke by nonsmokers, the American authorities were more ready than ever to limit smoking at home. This reminded some of the Japanese of imperial Britain which forced the Chinese to consume opium during the nineteenth century to achieve its commercial aims.

However, from the outset, the United States argued that were it not for the restrictive practices, American producers could obtain a substantial share of the estimated $14.8 billion Japanese market. To lend weight to the criticism, the Office of the USTR independently initiated a Section 301 investigation in September 1985. The American position was further hardened when the Japanese introduced an excise tax of 11 cents per package in May 1986, thereby effectively nullifying the anticipated price benefits of the declining dollar. It is noteworthy, however, that in the fall of 1986 when the yen had already apreciated more than 40 percent against the dollar, American cigarettes continued to sell at Y280 or $1.81 in 1986, per pack, a price which U.S. manufacturers had maintained for a long time. In other words, they were not willing to take advantage of the stronger yen and reduce the price of their cigarettes to be more competitive with the domestic brands which sold for Y200–220 or $1.30–1.50 per pack. The Americans took the position that they did not increase the Y 280 price when the dollar was strong or when the Japanese government imposed a higher excise tax in May 1986; thus, they should not be expected to reduce their prices now. This was a curious response from a marketing viewpoint insofar as increased market shares are usually achieved through price reductions when other competitive factors remain unchanged.

The U.S. government's demands were straightforward. It asked the Japanese either to eliminate the high import and excise taxes or, if they wanted to retain them, to allow foreign manufacturers to produce cigarettes in Japan. To underline the seriousness of its demands, the United States set September 15, 1986, as the deadline by which the Japanese should respond or suffer retaliatory action. September 15, however, coincided with the opening day of preparatory talks for the new GATT round, and the United

States did not want to add to the already tense atmosphere in Punta del Este, Uruguay, and consequently postponed announcing the measures it planned to take against Japan for three weeks.

However, shortly before the new deadline expired, the Japanese, after intense negotiations between the government and the tobacco *zoku*, accepted the American demands and "suspended" the 20 percent tariff on foreign tobacco effective April 1, 1987. Japan also agreed to introduce a formula for the automatic approval of retail prices, to shorten the minimum application period for price changes from 60 to 30 days beginning on January 1, 1987, and improve cigarette distribution based on "fair and mutually advantageous" commercial terms. Thus, the threat that America would restrict a wide range of Japanese manufactured imports unless the tobacco conflict was resolved was effective, and as a consequence the average price of U.S. cigarettes declined from $1.81 to about $1.64.

The accord was important politically to the Reagan Administration, particularly in the Southern states, where Republican candidates for the 1986 congressional elections were already under strong fire for the President's veto of the textile-quota legislation earlier that year. As soon as the agreement was reached, the President instructed the USTR to suspend the Section 301 proceedings against Japan, but emphasized that the office should monitor implementation of the Japanese measures.

While the political aspects of the disagreement were settled, the economic effects were open to question in that the agreement still left American cigarettes more expensive than the domestic brands which sold for $1.30–$1.50 per pack. Thus, the American cigarette manufacturers still had to demonstrate that they could take advantage of a long-term market share opportunity instead of just cashing in on windfall profits.

By mid-1987 it was clear that the American and other foreign companies intended to take full advantage of the opportunities provided by the elimination of the 20 percent tariff, the easing of distribution, and the continually appreciating yen. In a very short time they matched the price of the domestic brands, and a full-scale *tabaco senso* (war) errupted between the domestic and foreign sellers. The Japan Tobacco Inc. (JTI), the former public monopoly, competed as a private corporation with 66 brands. Opposing it were the foreign companies, spearhaded by American brands that represented 95 percent of the rapidly growing import market share which amounted to 2.4 percent in FY 1985, 8.8 percent in FY 1987, and rose to 12.1 percent in FY 1988. This increase was attributed to reduced prices, the introduction of new brands designed for Japanese tastes, and effective marketing. All of this happened while the number of smokers stagnated and the U.S. anti-smoking campaign made headlines in Tokyo.

In mid-1987 an unfortunate incident almost put a stop to the rapid growth of cigarette imports. The American company R.J. Reynolds inadvertently shipped 160 million cigarettes with high herbicide levels to Japan. Japan does not have legal standards to regulate the use of herbicide, but the cigarettes sent to Japan had an average of 1.4 parts per million (ppm) compared to the U.S. legal limit of 0.5 ppm. However, R.J. Renynolds handled the situation adroitly; it held all affected cigarettes in warehouses and immediately replaced them by air. A news conference was called, and the head of the company apologized for the mistake. In a relatively short time the incident was forgotten, and imported cigarettes continued to make inroads; by the end of 1988 their market share was over 12 percent.

Thus another chapter in U.S.–Japan trade relations came to a mutually acceptable end. And the solution to the problem was found through the release of market forces prompted by more open competition and the appreciating yen rather than direct government action. Of course, in light of the U.S. Surgeon General's 1988 smoking report and the continuous and increasingly stronger anti-smoking campaigns in the United States, the Japanese may ask some hard questions in the near future which foreign cigarette manufacturers must be prepared to answer in a satisfactory manner.

In early 1986 the United States also raised the issue of Japanese car and truck parts imports. The U.S. side insisted that Japan must provide American parts manufacturers with equal business opportunities to sell original equipment and repair or replacement components to Japanese car and truck manufacturers. They supported the demand by pointing out that U.S. producers had only a relatively small share of the parts market whereas the Japanese car and truck manufacturers had more than $24 billion in annual sales in America. They advised the Japanese that this amounted to almost half the entire trade deficit with Japan in 1985, and that in the same year, America had exported only $130 million in parts to Japan, whereas its imports of such parts had amounted to more than $2 billion.

Thus, intraindustry trade in car and truck parts between the two nations was tilted in Japan's favor. Both the American and the Japanese governments wanted to diffuse this issue before it erupted into a full-scale conflict. Consequently, in May 1986 they announced the addition of "Transportation Machinery" as the fifth sector to be included in the MOSS talks. The Americans wanted the Japanese to remove the barriers that prevented U.S. manufacturers from selling, while the Japanese pointed out that it was not formal barriers but manufacturing differences and divergent buying practices that caused the problem.

According to the Japanese, one of the major manufacturing differences was the extensive use of *kanban* by Japanese car and truck makers. In addition to all the well-known requirements of the system, *kanban* users normally do only random checks on parts obtained from Japanese suppliers who have low defect rates, whereas American suppliers themselves admitted that they had quality problems with 5 to 10 percent of their output in 1986. This quality problem was compounded by the traditional practice of Japanese manufacturers to work with their suppliers when designing parts specifications. Since U.S. suppliers did not participate in the developments of the specifications, they could not always meet the manufacturers' exact requirements.

Buying practices also differed in the two countries. While U.S. car and truck manufacturers selected parts suppliers annually, the Japanese maintained long-term relations with the parts producers. Most American manufacturers also used a larger number of suppliers than their Japanese rivals. According to industry reports, during the first half of the 1980s General Motors still used more than 3,500 suppliers whereas Toyota made do with less than 250. Moreover, Japanese manufactuers often invested in the parts producers, and provided them with a variety of services to maintain a reliable and high quality supply line. Thus, most Japanese manufacturers were reluctant to replace such a well-established system with arrangements that they considered untested and potentially troublesome.

During the initial August 1986 meeting of the two sides the Americans acknowledged that the different Japanese manufacturing and buying practices and not formal barriers created the problems for U.S. sellers. Nonetheless, they wanted a government-to-government agreement to remedy the situation while the Japanese argued that the firms themselves should address and resolve the issues at the technical level through a coordination of the manufacturing and buying processes.

The outcome of the negotiations were modest. Both sides agreed that Japanese car and truck builders had to review their purchasing practices while American parts producers had to meet Japanese quality, price, and delivery expectations. The most concrete result of the agreement was the establishment of a system to monitor the purchase of U.S.-made parts, accessories, and materials by Japanese car and truck manufacturers and their U.S. subsidiaries over a period of five years beginning in April 1987. Moreover, the Japan Automobile Manufacturers Association (JAMA) was appointed to keep track of the number of purchasing agreements which Japanese car and truck manufacturers or their American subsidiaries establish with U.S. parts suppliers through 1991. Finally, the Japanese government also agreed to cooperate with the automobile industry in staging seminars and trade shows and promised to resolve any new problems with Washington as soon as they surfaced.

The first results following the agreement were promising. In 1987 U.S.

exports of parts to Japan increased by 16 percent over 1986. According to JAMA, $1.7 billion worth of American-made parts were purchased by the Japanese car and truck manufacturers and their U.S. subsidiaries between October 1987 and March 1988. This represented a 32.2 percent increase over the same period a year earlier. For all of FY 1987, sales were up 25.9 percent to a total of $3.14 billion, a substantial improvement over the puny $130 million worth of parts sold in 1985. Of course, the 3.14 billion figure for all of FY 1987 included the purchase by Japanese car and truck manufacturing companies located in America from both domestic and Japanese-owned parts producers which followed the large manufacturing companies to the United States. Nonetheless, the trend was encouraging for both sides.

The increasing purchases were caused primarily by the American suppliers' better appreciation of what the Japanese car and truck manufacturing companies expected. American suppliers invested in new production technologies and displayed a willingness to accommodate the special wishes of the Japanese buyers. They displayed staying power in correcting mistakes and provided better quality parts together with service and on-time delivery. Most of all, because of the sharp appreciation of the yen against the dollar, they offered low prices and aggressively sought new sales opportunities. A number of them established permanent liaison offices in Japan as well as assembly operations either wholly owned or through joint-ventures with well-established local partners.

U.S. parts suppliers also began selling to major Japanese car and truck manufacturing companies in the United States. While disagreement over quality, service, and delivery were still occuring, the overall relationships between the two sides turned cooperative rather than confrontational. American suppliers, however, started facing a new threat. Beginning in 1985 approximately 250 Japanese car parts manufacturers moved to the United States through the establishment of subsidiaries, joint ventures, or buyouts of existing domestic producers; and by the end of 1990 their number was expected to reach 300. According to industry experts, what started out as a small-scale attempt at diversification became a survival strategy for Japanese parts manufacturers due to the sharp appreciation of the yen against the dollar during 1986–1988.

Included among the U.S.-based Japanese companies are producers of car electronics, tires, plastic and rubber components, and basic materials like steel. Also present are producers of aluminum wheels, air conditioners, and engine parts. These companies include some of Japan's largest corporations such as NKK Corp., Bridgestone, and Nippondenso Co., while others are on the way. In February 1989 an American steel giant, for example, announced that it will join Japan's Kobe Steel Ltd. in a venture to produce high-quality steel for automakers manufacturing cars and trucks in the United States. The two companies agreed on a 50–50 percent ownership of an existing USX plant in Ohio. Industry experts noted that the quest of American and foreign car and truck manufacturers for high-quality, rust-resistant, electro-galvanized steel brought the two sides together. Japanese steel companies like Kobe have the specialized know-how to produce galvanized metal which will be produced by the new joint-venture.

Increasingly Ford Motor Co., General Motors, and even Chrysler Corp. are also becoming dependent on the Japanese suppliers. In 1987, for example, Nippondenso sold $350 million of components to the three U.S. automobile manufacturers, up from $60 million in 1983. These develop-ments do not bode well for the approximately 40,000 American parts suppliers, most of which are small and undercapitalized. In the long run it is likely that only the most competitive and flexible of them will survive; marginal producers are going to be eliminated. This outcome is underscored by the car industry expectation that by 1990 the Japanese will be building as many cars in North America as Ford Motor Co., and thus the demand for high-quality parts, service, on-time delivery, and competitive prices will be even more pronounced than it already is. Honda Motor Co., for example, announced in 1988 that it wants 75 percent U.S.-content by 1991 for the cars it builds in Ohio, up from the current 63 percent. At the same time Honda officials intend to regularly subject U.S.-made car parts to *zenbara* (tearing apart — analyzing) and *higahikaku* (comparison) with Japanese parts.

Thus, it appears that by 1988 another previously hotly contested U.S.–Japan trade conflict was resolved primarily through market forces such as competition in quality, service, and delivery. While the government-to-government MOSS negotiations set the stage and emphasized the key issues involved, it was left to the firms of the involved industries to find a way out of the morass of charges and countercharges. In fact, the resolution of the disagreements over the admission of foreign lawyers to Japan, the market access of cigarettes, and the sale of U.S. car parts to Japanese car and truck manufacturers have shown that trade disagreements can be handled in a reasonable and effective manner. The United States was right in pressuring the Japanese to do away with some of the institutional restrictions affecting lawyers, cigarettes, and, to a much more limited extent, car parts. The Japanese were correct in pointing out that the removal of institutional restrictions alone would not help to resolve the conflicts and that the involved American companies had to become more competitive and use the benefits obtained through the yen appreciation against the dollar to reduce prices and not to obtain extra profits.

The resolution of these three trade conflicts in a mutually acceptable and beneficial manner by the end of 1988 proved that U.S.-Japan trade disagreements do not have to degenerate into lengthy and conflict-laden morality plays. In particular, they showed that a sense of realism and goodwill on both sides can lead to much more effective resolutions than demagoguery and threats.

Notes

1. For a detailed chronological discussion of all the various economic measures introduced through 1983, see the successive yearbooks on U.S.-Japan economic relations published by the Japan Economic Institute of America, now known as the Japan Economic Institute.

2. "Report of the Advisory Committee for External Economic Issues" (Tokyo, April 9, 1985). The establishment of the Office of Trade Ombudsman in 1982 was also part of the first package.

3. *Japan 1986, An International Comparison* (Tokyo: Keizai Koho Center, 1985), p. 36; and "The Japanese Government, External Measures: The U.S. Government's Assessment of Their Implementation and Impact" (Washington, D.C.: Office of the United States Trade Representative, 1984), p. 2.

4. *Business Week* (April 8, 1984), p. 53.

5. Much of this was political "grand-standing."

6. Staff Working Paper, "The Effects of Targeted Import Surcharges" (Washington, D.C.: Congressional Budget Office, 1986); and "Costs and Benefits of Protection" (Paris: Organization for Economic Cooperation and Development, 1985).

7. This debate had its roots in the past because Japan's experience with Keynesian demand stimulation methods during the late 1970s was controversial. In response to U.S. pressure, the government adopted the "locomotive" thesis of economic growth, and set a real growth target of 7 percent in 1978. Prime Minister Fukuda encouraged "provisional and exceptional fiscal policies for positive expansion" in order to implement a proposal to help end the world recession caused by increased oil prices. The result was a dramatic increase in Japan's annual fiscal deficits, from 7 trillion yen to 14 trillion yen in one year. By FY 1985, Japan's ratio of outstanding long-term debt to GNP was 48.8 percent, and the debt service absorbed about 20 percent of the annual budget. (In FY 1984, the U.S. public debt/GNP was 33.8 percent. See Takuji Matsuzawa, "Keidanren's Viewpoint on Government Spending and Future Administrative & Fiscal Reform, *Keidanren Review* (October 1985), p. 3.

8. The *Keidanren* (Japan Federation of Economic Organizations) is a private, nonprofit organization representing all branches of economic activity in Japan. It influence national policy formulation. The *Keizai Doyukai* is an economic organization for national policy studies. It is also a private, nonprofit organization, and is financed entirely through subscriptions; it, too, is quite influential.

9. In 1986, out of consideration for the sensitivities of neighboring Asian countries, he refrained from visiting the shrine again. A number of his cabinet members, however, made the pilgrimage.

10. *Nemawashi* is an informal, private, and usually face-to-race exchange of views in advance of reaching a decision. It involves persuasion to obtain understanding, agreement, and support.

11. *Amakudari*, or descent from heaven, is the traditional one-way retirement of government

officials to industry. In the past, former high-level officials frequently became top managers in the industries which they regulated while in the bureaucracy. Until the mid-1970s, this was one of the key factors in the close government-business relationship.

12. Seizaburo Sato and Tetsuhisa Matsuzaki, "Policy Leadership by the Liberral Democrats," *Economic Eye* (December 1984), pp. 25–32.

13. *Ibid.*, p. 26.

14. It is interesting to note that never before have so many *zoku* bosses been appointed simultaneously to ministerial posts as they were in December 1985 when Prime Minister Nakasone reshuffled his cabinet. Among them were then Finance Minister Takeshita, Transport Minister Mitsuzuka, and Agriculture, Forestry and Fisheries Minister Hata, each boss of the respective *zoku*.

15. "Bureaucrats Rebellion Against Nakasone," *The Oriental Economist* (July 1985), p. 12.

16. Remarks made at a policy review meeting, Tokyo, June 18, 1985.

17. *The Action Program for Improved Market Access*, chapter I, sec. 2.2

18. *The Action Program for Improved Market Access*, chapter II, sec. 2.

19. *The Washington Post* (July 31, 1985), p. F-1.

20. *Ibid.*

21. "U.S.–Japan Joint Report on Sectoral Discussions," by Secretary of State George Shultz and Foreign Minister Shintaro Abe (Washington, D.C.: U.S. Department of State, January 10, 1986).

22. A report on the progress of the Action Program, released in September 1986 by the joint U.S.–Japan Trade Study Group (TSG), reviewed specific trade issues on a product-by-product and service-by-service basis, comparing observations and conclusions of its 1984 report with the Action Program progress. This study group, consisting of Japanese and American businessmen, found that although a great deal of work still had to be done, a lot of progress has been made in opening the Japanese marketplace to foreign goods and services. See "TSG Progress Report 1986" (Tokyo, September 1986).

23. *The Wall street Journal* (August 29, 1986), p. 20.

24. The value of imports amounted to $100.4 billion, $4.3 billion less than the expected $104.7 billion.

25. *The New York Times* (January 18, 1986), p. 36.

26. *The Japan Economic Journal* (March 29, 1986), p. 5.

27. *The Wall Street Journal* (October 23, 1985), p. 36.

28. The continuing controversy over agricultural imports is discussed in the next chapter.

29. The majority of Japanese were afraid that the admission of foreign lawyers would reduce the traditional emphasis on social harmony.

30. In 1986, Japan had just over 12,000 lawyers; in the United States, there were more than 600,000, with the largest American law firms employing between 400–800 attorneys. From *The Washington Post* (September 15, 1986), p. A10.

31. *The Japan Economic Journal* (September 6, 1986), p. 28.

4 THE MAEKAWA COMMISSION REPORTS AND THE POTENTIAL CONSTRAINTS ON INTERNATIONALIZATION

The original Maekawa Commission Report was released amid a lot of domestic and international publicity on April 7, 1986, and, expectedly, it received a great deal of attention around the world. Most people abroad believed that this was the first time that the topic of internationalization of the economy was raised in Japan. Consequently, they characterized the report as a historic event. Undoubtedly, the report was important because it was prepared by Prime Minister Nakasone's private "brain trust," therefore reflecting his views. Moreover, the report was released at a time when Japan's current and trade account surpluses had reached new heights.

Following the publication of the first report, Prime Minister Nakasone asked Maekawa to continue to study the problems, propose solutions and to develop more concrete details for a follow-up report. The follow-up report was published in April 1987, almost exactly one year after the original document.

However, the Maekawa Commission was not the first to investigate the idea of internationalization. Other groups, most notably MITI's Industrial Structure Council, have broached the subject before 1986. Therefore, the idea was not new, although the previous studies and reports treated it in a more general and speculative fashion. Furthermore, in most cases, internationalization played a secondary role to problems such as energy dependence and industrial restructuring. Nonetheless, the earlier publications raised the same questions and considered measures which were similar to those the Maekawa Commission eventually included in its recommendations.

Selected MITI Visions and Other Views

One of the first MITI visions which raised the question of internationalization was published in March of 1980.[1] The document, which was prepared by the Industrial Structure Council, emphasized that during the 1970s Japan had become a major economic power whose actions impact the rest of the world. Based on this recognition, the Council suggested three national goals for the 1980s and beyond: (1) increased international contributions; (2) the reduction of resource dependency; and (3) development of private-sector vitality and improvement of the quality of life ("relaxed ease").

The section on internationalization was brief and general; nonetheless, its inclusion indicated that the Council recognized the changing role of the Japanese economy in the world. It called for the maintenance of the free trade system through improved market access and an increased international division of labor. Furthermore, it emphasized that Japan must increase manufactured imports and modify institutions and practices which restrict imports and, thus, internationalize.

A similar document was prepared by the Economic Planning Agency (EPA) in 1983.[2] This study concluded that Japan was undergoing major changes marked by internationalization, the arrival of a maturing economy, and an aging society. The report emphasized that Japan no longer tried to "catch up" with the industrialized world because it was now part of it. Thus, to move into the 21st century, the nation needed a "grand design" charting a new long-term course. However, because there were no appropriate development models to adopt, the Japanese had to create their own. This model needed to be Japanese, but at the same time, it also had to take into account the effect of Japanese actions on the world economy. In particular, the model needed measures to help revitalize international economic growth, improve market access, and aid in the resolution of global food and environmental problems.

In August 1983, the Economic Planning Agency published another set of future views which the Nakasone government adopted as policy guidelines for the period FY 1983 through FY 1990.[3] This document identified the

1983–1990 period as a turning point for Japan and listed four policy priorities. First, there was the completion of administrative and fiscal reforms, focusing on the reduction of the size of government and the fiscal deficits; second, the revision of the existing industrial structures to provide for more economic growth; third, the integration of the private sector in the economy; and finally, the promotion of international cooperation and Japan's assumption of leadership in this area. To achieve all this, the EPA paper called for stable international relations, an economy and society full of vitality, and a secure and affluent life for the people.

The Industrial Structure Council of MITI published another vision "in search of Japan's contribution and cooperation in bringing about innovative growth of the international economic system" in early 1986.[4] The objective was to determine the desirable form of industrial structures in the new age, moving toward the year 2000. The new structures were sought with regard to three concerns: (1) the contribution of the structures to the international economy and community; (2) changes in domestic economic factors; and (3) new lifestyles.

The Council recognized the undesirability of the growing current and trade account surpluses for both the world economy and Japan. At the same time, it emphasized that although Japan could begin to reshape its macroeconomic policies to moderate the surpluses, by itself Japan could not significantly reduce the imbalances; only a comprehensive, multilateral effort could accomplish this. Nonetheless, the report urged the Japanese government to develop economic policies to support the growth of the world economy and to help preserve the free trade system. It also urged the country to adapt its savings and technological development patterns to the needs of the world economy and to establish global rapport with other nations. The Council further recommended that the Japanese government help stabilize exchange rates at a reasonable level, foster economic growth through the increase of domestic demand, continue with the implementation of the Action Program, and show initiative and leadership in cooperating with other nations. Thus, in contrast to the others, this MITI vision went beyond generalities and identified the shift from export-led to domestic demand-led growth as a key element of the internationalization process, and outlined the various means through which this should be done.

Another MITI report was published in April 1986 by a mixed group of Japanese and non-Japanese academicians and business executives.[5] Rather idealistically, they argued that nations must work together to build a new global economic system in which emphasis on the common good replaced self-interest.

However, in a more realistic fashion, the group also pointed out that

Japan is a major economic power, and thus, its policies must respond to the new global situation. Specifically, the nation must begin to take on a leadership position; it can no longer sit idly by while other countries try to resolve international economic problems. To this end, Japan should continue to foster domestic economic growth in a way that will help the international community, and it should share its economic achievements with others. Finally, Japan should encourage free trade particularly in its region, and thereby improve the economic well-being of Asia and the other developing countries.

The group recommended several specific ways to achieve these goals. These included the promotion of free trade through increased market access, the coordination of international economic policies with other nations to stabilize exchange rates and to minimize imbalances, and the encouragement of foreign direct investment. In addition, Japan should also provide for the economic growth of the less-developed nations through the international exchange of human, specific, and technological values and knowledge. While not specifically identifying the need to shift from export-led economic growth to domestic demand-led growth, the group's recommendations were similar to those made by other groups.

The private sector's views on Japan's future was published in March 1986.[6] Although not a detailed long-range vision of the future, this policy statement was important because it represented the opinions of the *Keidanren* (the Japan Federation of Economic Organizations), an influential private sector business group. The *Keidanren* recognized that the Japanese government had made progress toward internationalization, but believed that even greater efforts were necessary, because as a major economic power, Japan must help protect the free trade system which is vital to its long-range interest. More specifically, the federation urged the government to implement the 1985 Action Program, to play a major role in the preparation and management of the new GATT round, to help liberalize trade in services, to promote foreign direct investment and to provide for a more constructive exchange on international economic matters throughout the world.

Thus, when the Maekawa Commission began its work in the fall of 1985, it had a number of previous contributions concerning the internationalization of the economy from which to draw. This is not to minimize the Commission's insights and efforts; it achieved as much as possible in a relatively short period of time and under intense pressure from abroad. Nonetheless, the past efforts of the other groups should be credited with laying the groundwork for the Commission's recommendations.

The Original Maekawa Commission Report and Its Reception

Prime Minister Nakasone appointed the 17–member brain trust composed of academic, business, and government leaders and chaired by former Bank of Japan governor Haruo Maekawa, in early November 1985. The Prime Minister created this group at a time when he had two things uppermost in his mind: the increasing trade conflict between Japan and the United States, and the annual economic summit conference of the industrialized nations scheduled for Tokyo in May of 1986.

At its first meeting, Nakasone defined the group's mission as the search for policy options through which the government could pursue the "harmonization of Japan's economic relations with other countries." The assignment was difficult because by the fall of 1985, Japan already faced a stronger yen, slower growth, weakening export markets, and generally increasing foreign criticism. Because the Prime Minister wanted to use the Commission's recommendations to shift Japan's export-led economy to a domestic demand-led one in the interests of the world community, the government once again found itself in a reactive rather than proactive stance. Thus, in a sense, the Maekawa Commission began its work where the Okita committee, whose recommendations also formed a basis for the Action Program, left off a year earlier.

The final Maekawa Commission report was released on April 7, 1986, just in time for the Prime Minister's visit with President Reagan in Washington, and approximately four weeks before the Tokyo summit. Expectedly, it cited the need for long-term changes to reduce exports and expand domestic demand in order to "transform the Japanese economic structure into one oriented toward international coordination."[7] Rather than establishing any blueprints for these structural changes, the report set forth six general recommendations:[8]

1. The government should strive for economic growth.
2. The government should promote basic transformations in the nation's trade and industrial structure.
3. The government must work for the realization and stabilization of the exchange rate at an appropriate level.
4. The government must further promote the liberalization and internationalization of the nation's financial markets.
5. Japan must actively contribute to the well-being of the world community through international cooperation.
6. The government should review the preferential tax treatment of savings.

Under these six broad recommendations, the report suggested guidelines on meeting the overall internationalization goals. It indicated that measures derived from these recommendations and the guidelines should be implemented on the basis of market principles as well as from global and long-term perspectives to strengthen the free trade system.

The report called upon the government to open Japan's market wider to imported goods, including farm products and manufactured goods. In this respect, it called for the thorough derregulation of cumbersome government rules from the premise of "freedom in principle, restrictions only as exceptions," language taken directly from the Action Program. Furthermore, the Commission suggested that coal mining and other declining industries be phased out, and that their products be replaced by imports.

As for suggestions to expand domestic demand, the Commission cited housing construction and urban redevelopment through private sector "vitality," stimulation of private consumption through tax reductions, and local government promotion of investments aimed at improving the infrastructure. Another consideration focused on revising labor laws to reduce average working hours and to increase the minimum number of paid holidays.

One last noteworthy area of reform investigated by the Commission was Japan's international role with respect to less developed countries. The report proposed expansion of official development assistance (ODA) to these countries and an increase in the importation of their goods. The Commission also urged the government to encourage the international division of labor through positive industrial adjustment and an increase in foreign direct investment, without sacrificing small-sized and medium-sized enterprises.

Two weeks after the release of the report, the government, in an effort to follow through on the Maekawa Commission recommendations, unveiled its own guidelines containing a list of measures designed to produce an economy driven by domestic demand and to promote imports. These guidelines were formally approved May 1, 1986, at a meeting of a special task force established under the chief cabinet secretary to implement an overall program based on the Maekawa report. In addition to elaborating on the contents of the report, the guidelines called upon the government to influence the business community to be more flexible about raising wages and increasing summer vacations to allow consumers to increase leisure spending, and to ensure that the benefits of economic growth were passed along to all citizens.

The guidelines also recommend that in order to change the national economy as dramatically as proposed by the Maekawa Commission, the bureaucracy should manage the allocation of resources, particularly fiscal resources. However, the guidelines stressed the necessity to maintain the nation's basic economic position by limiting any new issues of deficit-financing government bonds.

The Domestic Response

Shortly after the publication of the Maekawa report, the Japanese government also announced a set of economic measures designed to ease the . deflationary effects of the sharp rise in the yen's exchange value and to expand domestic demand in the short run.[9] Thus, domestic reaction to the Maekawa Commission's recommendations was influenced by the views on the short-term economic stimuli.

Not surprisingly, public reaction was mixed. Most mass media commentators agreed with the long-term aims of the proposed changes but questioned the generality and abstract nature of the recommendations. They claimed that the absence of specific measures to implement the proposals could partly be attributed to the composition of the committee in which 8 out of the 17 members were former high level government officials. The exbureaucrats supposedly favored realism over idealism and managed to prevail in the writing of the final report. Some critics referred to the report as *sakubun*, a clever piece of work without any practical significance because it lacked clear operational definition. Others pointed out that the government can no longer dictate to private industry; consequently, the recommendations may be difficult to implement regardless of their degree of specificity, Moreover, they argued, the various *zoku*, whose interests are affected by the recommendations, would not support proposed changes such as substantially increasing agriculture imports or phasing out some of the declining industries.

Economists were concerned that the short-term economic stimuli announced in conjunction with the report were not strong enough to propel the economy forward, and that this would make the implementation of the long-term recommendations impossible. Most of them speculated that the officially predicted 1986 growth rate of 4 percent could not be achieved, particularly in light of the continued appreciation of the yen. Such views were supported by private research institutions which forecast the average growth for FY 1986 at about 3 percent or less, a notch below government expectations.

Opinions in political circles were also splintered. The Prime Minister's supporters agreed with the necessity to restructure the economy over the long run, although most of them were concerned about the specific ways to do so. In contrast, Nakasone's political rivals seized the opportunity to reignite the debate over domestic demand stimulation which preceded the Action Program. They wanted to take Nakasone's place, and thus, they tried to raise their political visibility by highlighting policy differences with the Prime Minister. Again they called for sweeping measures to expand domestic demand, including the reissue of government bonds, the issue of construction bonds to finance public works projects, and broad tax incentives for new housing. However, before another major debate on demand stimulation could fully develop, Nakasone caused a political uproar in Japan.

Armed with the proper *Miyage* (present), that is, the Maekawa report and the package of economic stimuli, Prime Minister Nakasone met with President Reagan in Washington on April 12–14, 1986. Although the meeting was intended as a preparatory session for the Tokyo summit in May, it was devoted mostly to a discussion of the bilateral trade problems. In order to moderate strong American criticism of his economic policies, Nakasone tried to convince the Administration and Congress that Japan would shift from export-led to domestic demand-led growth in the future, substantially increase imports, and thereby, reduce the current account and trade imbalances as recommended by the Maekawa Commission. He emphasized that the government would set up a special headquarters to work out the schedule for the implementation of the recommendations. Furthermore, he agreed to the creation of a joint Japanese-American advisory board which would monitor the entire process. Following his meetings with the President, Nakasone also met with members of Congress and declared that Japan accepted "the challenge" of implementing recommendations to fight protectionism and to improve relations with the United States.

Top level Administration officials expressed satisfaction that the Prime Minister was serious about implementing the "historic changes," and speculated that the new measures could signal a turning point in bilateral trade relations. They also suggested that Nakasone's remarks to the President and Congress implied that he accepted virtually all of the Maekawa Commission's recommendations. None of the officials, however, claimed that the Prime Minister had made a formal commitment.

Nonetheless, Nakasone's statements in Washington were interpreted by his political opponents in Tokyo as a "casually made national pledge of a mere set of proposals formulated by a privately appointed advisory committee." The critics charged that Nakasone made a *koyaku*, an internationally binding commitment, to the United States without first obtaining the necessary consensus through *nemawashi* within the LDP and the bureaucracy. From the critics' point of view, the Prime Minister violated the most basic tenet of Japanese political life, and exposed the nation and the party to potential harm. The critics claimed that changing industrial structures to increase imports is the same as sacrificing certain economic sectors which are not internationally competitive, such as agriculture. Others argued that the joint Japanese–American monitoring of the implementation process is unfair because Japan alone is to be monitored even though a number of reasons for the bilateral trade imbalances are rooted in America's domestic economic policies. Even a number of the Prime Minister's supporters believed that he acted hastily, and that by generally endorsing the Maekawa recommendations in Washington, he provided the Americans with an opportunity to exert unilateral pressure on Japan.

As soon as he returned to Tokyo, Nakasone met with his critics in a government–LDP liaison meeting comprised of 11 cabinet members and 11 key officials of the party. He explained that the did not make a *koyaku* or formal commitment to the United States, and that the mass media had made a mountain out of a molehill. Still, he was strongly criticized for "going his own way" and not consulting adequately with the LDP leadership before commenting on matters of national importance. The chairman of the Policy Affairs Research Council even refused to accept the Maekawa report as a basis for policy deliberations because the advisory panel that prepared the report "lacked authority," and therefore, in legal terms, the document represented little more than the private views of it members. While Nakasone's explanations were eventually accepted, the LDP party leadership's dissatisfaction with his method of placing private advisory groups ahead of the party policy formulation apparatus continued. Thus, by late spring of 1986, the Prime Minister was walking a narrow path between the demands of the United States and the demands of his LDP critics.

Not surprisingly, Nakasone's explanations to the LDP leadership were not well received in the United States. The mass media and a number of politicians on Capitol Hill viewed his statements as soft-pedaling the commitments to implement the Maekawa recommendations, and thus, to reduce Japan's current and trade account surpluses. Some in the media made critical references to the Prime Minister as a politician who "keeps reading from two different scripts" and who cannot be relied upon.[10] More importantly, in a speech to a group of businessmen in Washington, USTR Yeutter stated that when Nakasone returned to Tokyo, his government started to back away from the Maekawa recommendations. Yeutter emphasized that this was a dangerous game that could lead to very harmful consequences for Japan. Already under pressure at home, the Japanese government's response to such high level criticism from abroad was immediate and tough; a spokesman labeled the remarks "irresponsible," and stated that the USTR and other American government officials did not appreciate the Japanese efforts. While the matter was eventually settled, the USTR's remarks provided Nakasone's critics and opponents with a weighty political argument. They could point to the remarks as proof of their predictions that the Americans would use the Prime Minister's Washington statements to immediately increase pressure on Japan.

Nakasone's political opponents used the Washington incident to attack the Prime Minister continuously. Moreover, in early June the Chairman of the LDP Executive Council and the Chairman of the LDP's Policy Affairs Research Council unveiled a set of economic proposals which were critical of the government's fiscal austerity policies. They argued that as a result of the yen's sharp appreciation, Japan was in a critical situation, and that only a comprehensive set of pump priming measures could save the economy from stagnation. Such proposals were in line with the policy adopted at an earlier LDP leadership meeting concerning the provision of a more than $20 billion supplementary budget during the second half of 1986. Although Nakasone endorsed the supplementary budget in order to win support for his double-section plans in July, he referred to the proposals as "personal opinions" prevalent in the party.

Expectedly, the LDP's overwhelming electoral victory in July 1986 reduced the volume of criticism and substantially enhanced Nakasone's position. While the Maekawa Commission's report was not an election issue, and Nakasone was criticized during the campaign for the rapid appreciation of the yen, the voters seemed to endorse his plans for the future. Following the election, the Prime Minister declared his intention to move ahead and shift Japan's economy to domestic demand-led growth. He told the mass media that the government would "faithfully" follow the recommendations of the Maekawa Commission.

To emphasize his commitment, Nakasone again stressed the necessity of structural adjustments at a meeting of the Economic Council in September 1986. The Council established a special committee headed by Haruo Maekawa, to promote economic restructuring and to increase imports. As a first step, the Committee set a specific numerical target for the reduction of Japan's current account surplus which amounted to an all-time high of 3.7 percent of GNP in 1985, and was expected to be more than 4 percent in 1986. The Committee announced that this proportion should be reduced to about 1.5 to 2 percent over the next five to seven years, and it considered the target as a reasonably well-defined goal for the internationalization process. While the Council is a highly respected body that usually prepares the five-year social and economic outlook for the government its recommendations are not binding. Moreover, in the past some of its recommendations were made irrelevant by the rapid change of economic circumstances. Nonetheless, it is significant that it has tried to set a specific goal for the internationalization process, and that it also formed two additional subcommittees to study the problems of stimulating domestic demand and of the potential rise in unemployment.

Thus, despite strong opposition within the party and criticism from other circles, Prime Minister Nakasone not only engineered an electoral victory but eventually also managed to have the basic propositions of the Maekawa Commission accepted by the LDP leadership as the centerpiece of future economic policies. While the details still had to be worked out through the customary consensus-seeking procedure, the overall direction of the Japanese economy was set. The extension of his LDP presidency and, thus, Prime Ministership for another year beyond October 1986, and the inclusion of his strongest LDP opponents in the newly formed government, provided Nakasone with the political flexibility he needed to begin the consensus-seeking process in earnest.[11]

Reactions Abroad

The international response to the Maekawa report was muted. European media and government circles, for example, expressed scepticism and took a wait-and-see attitude. They argued that the Japanese had issued too many reports and market access packages in the past, none of which had substantially altered the massive current and trade account surpluses. A number of commentators criticized the absence of specific details and concluded that the report was just another window-dressing exercise to promote Nakasone's April visit to Washington and his stewardship of the May Tokyo summit.

In the United States, the White House expressed optimism and hailed the report as a turning point in Japanese history. Administration officials calculated that in praising the recommendations, they could enhance the probability of their implementation. Furthermore, they also wanted to strengthen Nakasone's domestic position because he was known to be in favor of harmonious international economic relations. Thus, when USTR Yeutter's critical remarks caused indignation in Tokyo, top Administration officials quickly distanced the White House and said that Yeutter spoke only for himself.

The Administration's view of the Maekawa report reflected a shift in policy from emphasizing procedural market access to encouraging domestic growth as a means of reducing the bilateral trade imbalances. American policy formulaters were clearly concerned about the delayed impact of the dollar devaluation, the persistent budget deficits, and the continuing decline of American's international competitiveness. They were searching for more comprehensive and effective measures than the market access packages of the past. Thus, the Maekawa Commission's recommendations were in accord with the United States' new approach to international economic problems in general and to bilateral trade conflicts with Japan in particular.

Congressional views were less enthusiastic. While even the most vehement critics of Japan conceded that the recommendations were important and that if implemented, they could go along way toward easing U.S.–Japan trade relations, many members of Congress expressed scepticism about the readiness of the Japanese to follow through. Some senators cited past experiences with market access plans, and as usual, did not recognize the power of the *zoku* and placed the blame on Kasumigaseki, Tokyo's government district by arguing that the Japanese bureaucracy would not accept most of the recommendations. Others stated that only time would reveal how serious the Japanese are about internationalizing the economy, and cautioned that if the recommendations were not implemented at an early date, protectionist pressures in the United States would reach new heights in the fall 1986 midterm elections, and possibly beyond, since the Democrats could gain control of Congress, as they did.

The U.S. media response was mixed. Some newspapers compared the recommendations with changes that took place in Japan during the Meiji Restoration in the nineteenth century. A few argued that the plan called for a switch from the mercantilist policies of the past to policies which may redress the global imbalances Japan created over the past 30 years. Others, however, criticized the report for a lack of specifics and noted that the recommendations were more philosophical than pragmatic in nature. Moreover, they also claimed, the Prime Minister did not have the support of the bureaucracy for the proposed changes. All of this, the U.S. critics claimed, would make it very difficult, if not impossible, for the Prime Minister to call double elections and remain in office beyond October 1986, let alone obtain censensus for the recommendations. As it turned out, such views, as usual, underestimated Nakasone's political skills.

Not surprisingly, the harsh views were moderated after the July 1986 electoral victory. Critical members of Congress and the media conceded that the Prime Minister apparently had sufficient support among the voters and in the party to realize his plans. Some even considered the election results a direct vote of confidence in the Maekawa Commission's recommendations.

The Follow-up Maekawa Comission Report

Shortly after the publication of the original (1986) Maekawa Commission report and in light of domestic and foreign criticism that the report was too vague, Prime Minister Nakasone asked for a second follow-up report containing more concrete details. To preclude charges that the Commission was only one of his private braintrusts and, thus, had no authority, he asked Maekawa to form a subcommittee, to be known as the Special Committee on Economic Restructuring, under the auspieces of the Economic Council, a highly respected government advisory body. The follow-up report was published in April 1987 and added the following major points to the original report:

1. Financial support and tax breaks for home buyers
2. Changes in land use, including agricultural land
3. Measures to invigorate provincial economies and to decentralize urban areas
4. Promotion of adequate wages, of price stability, and of the yen appreciation pass-through to consumers
5. Reduction of annual working hours to 1,800 and the provision of 20-day vacations by the year 2000
6. Reform of the distributions system for the petroleum, construction, telecommunications, and agricultural industries
7. Increased overseas development assistance and a larger Japanese role in the resolution of the debt crisis
8. Increased participation in international scientific undertakings and reform of the educational system through participation from abroad.

The follow-up report was well received in both Japan and abroad. Newspaper editorials and commentators as well as others praised the specificity of the recommendations and observed that they addressed most of the previous concerns in a realistic fashion. Washington particularly appreciated the deadlines that the Commission set for some, albeit not all, actions outlined in the report.

It is noteworthy that because Prime Minister Nakasone restructured the Commission from one of his private braintrusts to a governmental advisory body, the political fallout that followed the original report did not recur. Thus, the recommendations were adopted by the LDP and the government bureaucracy, and while the public's reaction was more ambivalent, most Japanese accepted the follow-up recommendations in the spirit of "kokusaika" or internationalization.

The Domestic Discussion of Internationalization

The beginning of a new year in Japan is traditionally a time for introspection by individuals, families, and society as a whole. At such times, people think about the past year's events and speculate about the future. The media usually play a major role in this self-examination; newspapers with circulations of several million copies and the major television stations present articles, commentaries, and special programs on where Japan stands and what the next few years may bring.

At the beginning of 1986, the major theme of the national self-reflection was the necessity to live in harmony with the rest of the world. The question of coexistence with other nations is, of course, not new in Japan. It had been discussed many times, in a number of settings, with varying intensity and results since the Meiji restoration. However, never before had the discussion been as intense and focused as at this time. The media, government officials, politicians, intellectuals, business leaders, and others referred to the internationalization of society in general and the economy in particular as one of the great new tasks. It is not an exaggeration to say that by the early months of 1986, there was a consensus on the desirability of internationalization, and anyone opposed to the process was regarded by most people as acting against the national interest. However, this consensus was at a philosophical level and did not include an appreciation of the practical measures which would have to be taken, or more importantly, on how such measures could affect the daily lives of people. Apart from the speculative newspapers and magazine articles, no other interpretations of the potential effects of the internationalization process were available.

The tone of the 1987 and 1988 new years' introspections was essentially the same as in 1986. The mass media and other opinion-makers continued to discuss the meaning of internationalizing the society and the economy and expounded on Japan's new responsibilities.

However, at the beginning of 1989 a new theme was added to the national soul-searching process. Newspaper editorials displayed titles such as "Where Do We Stand?" "On Japan's Image," "New Image Needed," and "Ugly Japanese". Editorials posed questions as, for example," ... why cannot Japan gain respect, trust, and popularity, at a time when its motto is peace and culture?" (*Asahi Shimbun*, January 1, 1989). In answering the question, the writer lamented that ". . . as long as the Japanese people fail to clean up politics, oppress free speech through intimidation, unleash aggressive trading companies abroad, buy up foreign land, and permit rude behavior in public and the abnormal shopping behavior of rude package tourists in foreign countries," respect, trust, and popularity cannot be forthcoming from abroad.

Others referred to the Recruit insider stock-trading scandal that engulfed the nation's interest in 1988 and complained that people seemed to have become so money-hungry that the traditional values that made the country economically strong were being ignored or entirely given up. Again, others pointed out that it was imperative that Japan no longer be seen as an "inscrutable society" or a "peculiar country" if it wanted to be on good terms with free and democratic societies whose media, politicians, businessmen, and other opinion-makers were beginning to refer to the Japanese as "arrogant."

While some of what was said in these editorials represents exaggerations and too-severe criticism, the main thrust of the arguments addressed the key concerns of many Japanese at the end of the 1980s with respect to the nation's role in the global economy. There is in Japan an increasing recognition that "a tall tree catches much wind," or that as a major economic power the nation can no longer expect others to display a benign neglect toward habits and practices that offend friend and foe alike.

Some of the 1989 New Year's editorials pointed to all the changes that had taken place in 1988 and, thus, drew a more positive picture of the nation's status. The journalists emphasized the changes in rice policies, construction, the employment of foreign workers, and the Ministry of Finance's efforts to establish some stock-trading rules. They mentioned that agricultural products lost some of their "sacred" image as the public began to embrace the need for some import competition. It was in this spirit that Japan dropped the quotas on beef and oranges as a result of hard negotiation with the United States in 1988. Moreover, the writers underlined, all of this has happened to promote *kokusaika* or internationalization which had become a kind of buzzword but nonetheless had affected a number of domestic interests which were considered sacrosanct even a short while ago.

Of course, the internationalization of an entire society and its economy is an immensely complicated undertaking, and it is, thus, well-nigh impossible to identify the measures and changes that are needed to reach what is, in essence, a vaguely defined and continually moving target. Not surprisingly, this caused confusion among the public, and even today many Japanese fear that the changes could be destructive. They are concerned that the emphasis on increasing domestic demand, or spending, could turn into self-indulgence and undermine the Japanese tradition of self-sacrifice and hard work which made the economic achievements possible. Others, influenced by the intense foreign pressures for increased market access, believe that internationalization means simple procedural adjustments as exemplified by the numerous market access packages of the past, including the 1985 Action Program.

Some critics noted that internationalization is too partial to the United States and does not involve sufficient consideration of other nations.[12] The adoption of a lot of "Americana" during the postwar years, the argument goes, has created the illusion that internationalization is the same as accepting American influence and recognizing English as the *lingua franca*. These critical observers sought a broader interpretation of internationalization because although other nations do not complain as noisily as the United States, the economic gap between them and Japan is rapidly increasing. Hence, Japan must pay attention to their expectations as much as it does to those of the United States and, to a lesser degree, Asia.

The Japanese preoccupation with the United States and Asia was confirmed by the result of the Public Polls on Japan's Foreign Relations, released by the Office of the Prime Minister already in June 1985. The findings showed that North American and Asia are the highest scoring among the geographic areas in which the Japanese showed the most interest. Over the period May 1980 to June 1985, interest in North America and Asia ranged from between 30 to 40 percent, reaching a virtual equality of 35 percent in June 1985. The remainder of the world accounted for only 30 percent of interest. Subsequent polls reported similar findings.

Sociocultural Considerations

All nations have images of themselves and of how others perceive them. Usually, such images are a mix of reality and myths, and are perpetuated by the educational system, the mass media, writers, social scientists, and politicians, among others, for a variety of reasons. In the case of Japan, there are a variety of *nihonjinron* or Japan theories which supposedly explain the nature of society and its implications for fields of human endeavor from economic behavior through politics to the arts. While such views are usually oversimplifications of very complex issues, they are still seen by most people in Japan and abroad as helpful explanations of how society functions and how it interacts with the outside world. Thus, although many propositions of current *nihonjinron* may be questionable, they are widely accepted and seem to contain enough truth to shed some light on the potential sociocultural restraints on internationalization.[13]

Although the Maekawa Reports deal only with the economic aspects of internationalization, their basic recommendation, the shift from an export-led growth to a domestic demand-led growth, cannot be accomplished without some modification of the sociocultural aspects of *nihonjinron*. Naturally, this cannot mean the eradication of the Japanese self-image, however disagreeable this image may have become to some nations which have difficulties accepting Japan's growing self-assertiveness. The modifications, however, must be made to the degree that the Japanese can accept them without damaging their sense of identity, and which at the same time, is enough to halt the world's growing perception that Japan wants to be treated as an equal but continues to insist on considering itself unique.

Such abstract interpretations of what internationalization ought to mean cannot be readily translated into pragmatic policy proposals. Consequently, it is not surprising that the Japanese are still searching for the practical measures through which internationalization can become a reality without the loss of a strong self-identity based on a centuries-old heritage. The debate continues, and in light of clashing generational values, external pressures, the appreciation of the yen, and increasing wealth, the search for possible answers is not getting any easier with the passage of time. Whereas abroad this may be construed as hesitation, reluctance, or even diversionary tactics to maintain the status quo, uncertainty and uneven progress are an unavoidable consequence of the immense scope of the internationalization task.

The author of one of the recent books on Japan argues that the two Maekawa reports were useless exercises which mislead the United States and the rest of the world.[14] He claims that neither the reports nor the appreciating yen had achieved any of the structural changes envisioned. Such views ignore the changes in the country's overall current and trade account balances, the changing import structures, the increase in overseas foreign direct investment, and overseas development assistance, the deregulation of the financial markets, to mention only a few of the structural changes referred to in the Maekawa reports.

Self-Perception — 'The Ugly Japanese'?

Most contributors to the conventional "Japan theories" have long noted that Japan is a group-oriented society that values reciprocity and social harmony above all else. Whereas the Western societies, particularly the United States, focus on individual rights and legalistic procedures, the

Japanese rely on a complex network of unspoken mutual obligations and pragmatic ad hoc adjustments. Moreover, while the Japanese were receptive to Western influence, particularly after the Meiji restoration, they themselves always decide what to accept and how to modify it. For example, the Japanese rejected two of the most conspicuous elements of Western culture, the Christian religion and the Roman alphabet. Instead, they adapted Buddhism to their values without forfeiting Shinto and assimilated Chinese characters into written Japanese. It is this pragmatic and flexible manner of absorbing foreign influences that helped the Japanese to maintain their self-perception as a unique nation. At first such an attitude was viewed with curiosity by the rest of the world, but it was gradually resented when combined with economic success. The attitude of uniqueness became particularly distressing to the industrialized nations because they believed that the Japanese were using this notion to justify a variety of trade practices that conflicted with the customary standards of international economic behavior.

Not surprisingly, many Japanese are, therefore, uneasy about internationalization. They see it as an externally imposed demand that may damage their identity. This is particularly worrisome because many Japanese believe that it was their uniqueness that made the economic success possible in the first place. In their view, foreign demands for change may endanger the economy's international competitiveness created through hard work. Such opinions are unintentionally reinforced by the Japanese government's reactive rather than proactive foreign policy in general and international economic policy in particular. The government initially promoted internationalization more as a necessary survival response to external forces than as a transition from an industrializing nation to a mature economy with corresponding improvements in the quality of life. Only in 1988 did it begin seriously to publicize how the quality of life of the Japanese people could be improved through the internationalization process.

Because of the uncertainties throughout the national self-examination process and subsequent discussions, many thoughtful Japanese raised questions about the willingness of the nation to internationalize.[15] A major catalyst for such doubts was an article by the late Theodore White.[16] The American author argued that 40 years after it lost the Pacific War, Japan is defeating the United States in trade, and that the "real winner of the war" will be decided in 10 years. He argued that the United States must never again be merciful and generous toward Japan because such policies allowed the Japanese to protect their markets while launching an assault on the U.S. economy, thereby dismantling American industries.

Although most Japanese understood that White's views did not represent the majority opinion in the United States, his harsh words raised concerns about how various long-standing domestic practicees may be perceived abroad. Newspaper editorials, for example, referred to the multiple fingerprinting of the Korean minority living in Japan and of other non-Japanese residents on working visas as a "relic of postwar Japan" that stands in the way of internationalization.[17] Others pointed to the rejection of Vietnamese refuges and the Labor Ministry's frequent denial of visas to foreigners as well as the limited number of foreign students in Japan's universities as a reflection of an insular attitude that may be difficult to overcome.[18] There were references to the low number of international conferences held in Japan relative to other nations and to the Japanese "cultural free ride" mentality which, from the outside, shows the nation as a combination of a "third-rate culture" with a "first-rate economy."[19] Some described the plight of new arrivals in Tokyo who find it very difficult to overcome the discrimination of Japanese landlords against foreigners.[20] Others criticized the practice of some corporations that still reject Japanese graduates of foreign universities because they do not want employees shaped by a *gaikoku daigaku* (foreign university), but young men and women with characteristics that can be honed only in Japanese universities.[21].

An EPA survey found that the attitudes in which such practices and behavior are rooted are still widespread and strong.[22] The survey asked 3,000 male and female respondents between the ages of 15–74 their views about the influx of people, products, and information from abroad. The overall finding indicated that whereas the Japanese are receptive to foreign products and information, they are uncomfortable with the idea of more people moving to Japan from abroad and, thus, decreasing the homogeneity of their society. Many Japanese still share a closed mentality toward foreigners living in their country either for work or study, the EPA noted in its report.

More specifically, the survey found that 73.3 percent welcome foreign technology, 79.2 percent foreign news, 78.6 percent foreign tourists, and more than 50 percent are in favor of increasing food imports and bringing more students from abroad. However, only 28.3 percent had no objection to more foreign workers, and a mere 26.7 percent supported the idea of international marriages. Moreover, increased foreign direct investment in Japan and an increase in the number of Japanese children educated abroad was acceptable to only 40 percent. A large percentage of respondents, 73.8 percent, rejected overseas assignments for themselves and their families, and 50.1 percent had negative views on renting living space to students from abroad.

Another survey published by the Prime Minister's Office in 1987 found that 42.5 percent of the respondents gave priority to national interests over global responsibilities, while only 38.2 percent believed that the nation needs to focus on its international role during the final decade of the century. While most other peoples would probably respond in a similar way if they had to choose between their national interests and some ill-defined and rather vague international commitment, in view of Japan's long isolation from the rest of the world such findings are cause for some concern. They indicate that the majority of Japanese still have to be convinced that *kokusaika* or internationalization means more than "going overseas," as they now do in large numbers for short visits.

A number of eminent Japanese express deep concern about these *shimaguni konjo* (insular attitudes). Some are particularly worried that these attitudes might turn into prolonged arrogance toward other nations, especially America. A high level government official and member of the Maekawa Commission pointed out that "... a growing number of politicians, businessmen, mass media people and other opinion leaders here are becoming undeservedly smug and prone to cavalier utterances."[23] Such people argue that only the Japanese can manufacture first-class products, and if the Europeans and Americans worked harder, they would not fall behind in economic competition. Moreover, they accept the idea that "Made in U.S.A." is a label of lesser quality as an article of faith, regardless of the nature of the products in question. They believe that Americans do not pay enough attention to detail, since, for example, their cars sound tinny and appliances waste energy.

Conversely, concerned Japanese point out, the executives of large Japanese corporations which are very successful in the American markets are firm believers in the principles of free competition, and believe that there is nothing wrong with sending large quantities of products to the United States as long as American consumers want them. They are particularly proud of the fact that they never received any government support, and argue that their success is due to superior productivity, constant technological improvements, and the provision of high quality products. American industries which cannot meet such competition should not complain because they have created their own problems. While there is truth in these arguments, if repeated too often and too loudly, they create the impression of arrogance and lack of concern for the economic well-being of other people, and thus, generate an image of "the ugly Japanese."

The strength of the *shimaguni konjo* mentality based on the "uniquely homogeneous" nature of Japanese society is well illustrated by the events surrounding Prime Minister Nakasone's remarks about American minorities and educational levels in September 1986. In a speech to young LDP political workers in the Shizukoka foothills of Mount Fuji, Nakasone explained that the minorities, particularly blacks and Hispanics, have negatively affected the American intellectual and educational levels.

While his remarks created an uproar in the United States, some of Japan's national newspapers did not even mention the speech until after the U.S. reaction. Others put it into inside-page columns which usually chronicle various minor political developments. Only Nakasone's political opponents in the Japan Socialist Party and other critics immediately recognized the potential international implications of the remarks. Most other Japanese believed that he was talking common sense, saying that ethnic diversity creates confusion and discord, and that societies function best when they are homogenous. Those who faulted him did so mostly for voicing his opinion, not for having it. The uproar in America was eventually moderated through an explanation and a formal apology by the Prime Minister addressed not only to the United States but also to the Japanese people for embarrassing them. Moreover, a number of U.S. newspaper articles informed the American public about the background and context of Nakasone's remarks, and thereby helped settle the matter.[24] This was important because most Americans did not know that the Japanese lived in isolation from the rest of the world for 250 years, and that even today, less than 2 percent of the population represent minorities.

The issue of Japanese racism was reopened in 1988 when it became known that toymakers manufactured and distributed large numbers of "Little Black Sambo" dolls with grotesquely pronounced racial characteristics. Moreover, about the same time a high official of the LDP remarked that blacks do not mind going bankrupt in the United States because they would not have to pay anything back. Not surprisingly, the Japanese Embassy in Washington received many phone calls from angry American blacks after these incidents. A short while later, the offensive toys were recalled from stores and the manufacturers stopped producing them. The high LDP official apologized and expressed his regret. However, abroad, particularly in America, such recurring remarks and incidents were seen as evidence of a lingering racism among older Japanese who were drilled throughout their school years in the notion that Japan is a unique country with superior people, a notion that seems to be resurfacing in direct proportion to the nation's economic success.

Such incidents are regrettable, but accusing the Japanese of conscious racism is an oversimplification. It can be argued that the experience of living in a homogenous society and growing up through a regimented educational system combined with economic power generates arrogance and a sense of superiority, but the offensive incidents are more rooted in ignorance than conscious racism. The overwhelming majority of Japanese simply do not understand the black experience in America just as they do not appreciate the implications of the limitations imposed on the 700,000 Koreans, many of them second or third generation residents, currently living in Japan. Conversely, the critics abroad fail to take into account that in the nineteenth century the Japanese were declared an inferior race by Western "scientists" and that many Japanese even today ascribe racial motives to the "Japan bashing" in the United States.

Related to the social undercurrents is the issue of Japan's newly emerging nationalism. In conjunction with the nation's emerging economic power, occasional arrogance, and sense of superiority, Japan is experiencing a re-awakening of what many observers call soft nationalism." This is not a nationalism of xenophobic or militaristic nature, although some extremist individuals and groups have expressed views in the spirit of the former. But such groups, although nosity, are few and far between.

The new soft nationalism starts from a sense of pride in the nation's economic achievements. Mixed with increased materialism, rooted in a higher standard of living, combined with the traditional sense of uniqueness and the fact that World War II ended before 60 percent of the current population was born, the new nationalism is not threatening the rest of the world. Rather, it is a new sense of assertiveness in international economic matters. Japan wants a larger role in those international organizations to which it provides substantial amounts of money. Moreover, its newly emerging political leaders, particularly those who will take the reins of power in eight to ten years, are not burdened by World War II guilt feelings. Thus, buttressed by a powerful economy and rooted in a rich cultural heritage, they will not be playing the "little brother" role to the United States any longer. In this sense, the new soft nationalism is in reality an expression of a regained self-confidence. Of course, such self-confidence can easily exceed the tolerable levels of arrogance and sense of superiority which nowadays is displayed on occasion. It is the responsibility of the new leaderships, particularly of those who spent years studying and working abroad, to understand the dangers lurking behind such attitudes and to speak up if they appear to be more than just sporadic outbreaks by people with extreme views.

A number of eminent Japanese consider the passage of the nation from the *Showa* to the *Heisei* period, resulting from the death of Emperor Hirohito in January 1989, as an excellent opportunity to learn from the lessons of the *Showa* period and to develop a comprehensive philosophy of national conduct for the future. They argue that it is difficult for a nation to play a major global role on the basis of a single strength and, thus, Japan may be reduced to nothing in the eyes of the world if and when its economic power declines. Therefore, to avoid such a fate, Japan must develop strong abilities in such areas as politics, diplomacy, and leadership.

The Communication Gap

Throughout their history, the Japanese have never been good at communicating with the rest of the world. This is partially due to the insular mentality, that is, the strong sense of uniqueness just discussed, lack of exposure to the international community, and their inability to master Western languages well because of the substantial grammatical differences between Japanese and Western languages. Other reasons include the reticence to strike up casual conversations with foreigners who are not well known to them or accepted as friends.

Moreover, Japanese political and business life are characterized by phraseology that is often skillfully used to obfuscate meaning whenever the speaker does not want to take a position or make a commitment without offending the listener. Politicians who speak of "making efforts with the greatest expedition possible" and businessmen who respond to an inquiry by saying "let me think about it" are politely saying that they intend to do little if anything at all. Such and similar ambiguity is sometimes difficult to understand even for some Japanese, let alone non-Japanese interested in quick and concrete responses, particularly if they are American. Most of this is the result of the Japanese language's dependence on emotions and feelings; specificity and concreteness are not as much part of the language as, for example, in English or German. The Japanese sometimes convey intentions and ideas through glances, stares, meaningful silences, or even grunts. Because of the nation's homogeneity, most people understand such communications although some older Japanese argue that the younger generation is not picking up these skills as well as they should.

What is true for society at large is also true at the official level. The Japanese government's reactive rather than proactive stance has been mentioned several times, in different contexts, as a restraint on Japan's foreign relations. The extensive use of lobbyists abroad, particularly in Washington, is another case in point. Given the nature of the American political system, foreign governments or businesses must have knowledge-able representatives in Washington other than their diplomats because the city is not only the seat of political power but also a rich source of information provided by the federal agencies and private think-tanks. Regardless, the Japanese probably employ far more lobbyists than necessary to obtain the benefits of direct unofficial representation. Whereas the impression outside of and in Washington is that heavy representation is effective in influencing U.S. policy toward Japan, the reality is more somber. The Japan lobby is a large but rather diversified conglomerate of economic and political interests which do not act in unison and, thus, are usually not that influential.

In July 1988, *Business Week* published a cover story arguing that Japanese lobbying in Washington is not only overwhelming and very effective but is also bordering on unethical behavior.[25] The authors showed that of the approximately $310 million spent by various Japanese organizations in the United States in 1988, more than 45 percent or $140 million went for corporate philanthropy and $50 million or 16 percent were spent on Washington lobbyists. For this money, they argued, the Japanese not only want to promote specific political objectives but also want to "shape the American agenda and reinforce the notion that America's economic problems are mainly homegrown."

The authors proposed that large numbers of American lawyers, public relations advisers, academics, journalists, and political consultants are used by the Japanese to influence U.S. political and public opinion in return for generous fees and donations. The efforts to obtain the services of such Americans by far exceed those of the Middle-Eastern oil producers who during the 1970s also tried to unduly influence American public opinion.

The purpose of lobbying is to get across a message to protect interests. As such, lobbying is a well-established practice in Washington, and in this sense the Japanese are only following a time-honored American tradition. As mentioned in an earlier chapter, by 1988 major American corporations were also busy employing former high-level Japanese bureaucrats in Tokyo with payments reaching several hundred-thousand dollars. As a matter of fact, in 1988, Solomon Brothers succeeded in getting a former MITI Vice-Minister to advise its Japanese operations as well as its headquarters in New York.

One of the major reasons for the mutual lobbying activities is the increasing interdependence of the two economies. To put it bluntly, the Japanese have substantial interests in the form of direct investments, major markets, and financial instruments in America while American companies cannot afford to stay out of Japan's burgeoning product and services marketplace if they want to remain global competitors in, for example, telecommunications or financial services. Thus, both sides are entitled to monitor and, within limits, to try to influence developments that may affect their interests. This is not to say that lobbying cannot be misused or that there are no legitimate ethical concerns that must be considered. However, to the extent that Americans are uncomfortable with the Japanese lobbying presence, particularly as it involves former high-level U.S. government officials, they should see to it that a significant amount of time elaspses between an official's resignation from a government position and his acceptance of a Japanese lobbying position. The new lobbying ethic law signed in November 1989 and affecting former members and staff of Congress as well as government officials may help. However, the one-year ban on lobbying following resignation from a Congressional or government position is too short to reduce the number of eager volunteers wanting to work for Japanese and other foreign interests.

By the beginning of 1989 Japanese lobbying in Washington was undergoing some changes. Over the years the Japanese have realized that they may have wasted a great deal of money on individuals who did not perform well. Moreover, there are now more young Japanese available who have been educated in the United States, speak English well, and are acquainted with the ways of Washington. They can represent Japanese interests as well and at a much lower cost. Of course, those with real and direct influence in the Administration and Congress, the "heavyweights," will remain the same few select individuals to whom access is going to remain very expensive.

The Japanese often think of themselves as a nation misunderstood by the rest of the world. While such contentions are sometimes self-serving, in many instances, they are true. One of the major reasons for this is the often poor foreign press coverage of Japan. This is partially due to the inability of most foreign correspondents to speak Japanese and their editors' demands for sensational headlines rather than solid, informative news. Moreover, in the case of the U.S. press, newspapers regularly report more about European than Japanese political, economic, and social affairs because most Americans have European heritages. However, this does not mean that there is a shortage of news about Japan. But it does mean that the articles published have not yet aroused genuine and lasting interest abroad.

There are, however, other reasons for the often superficial coverage. The more than 500 foreign journalists permanently assigned to Japan have difficulties obtaining insightful information because of the traditional Japanese press club system. Although the Foreign Press Center was established as a commercial venture in 1976 to help foreign reporters by providing various services, the press club system continues to tightly control the flow of reliable information from the source to the media. The *kisha kurabu* clubs are omnipresent; they cover the cabinet, the Diet, and every one of the 37 government ministries and agencies. Special clubs cover the Tokyo Stock Exchange and even religious affairs in Kyoto. Only the staff of the newspaper companies of the Japanese Newspaper Publishers and Editors Association can be full members. Foreign correspondents and even Japanese journalists who are not members cannot take advantage of the benefits the clubs provide through the government ministries, agencies, or other institutions that sponsor them. The benefits include, among others, furnished offices, administrative help, free domestic and international telephone calls, and guaranteed access to a continuous flow of information. Foreign journalists may be admitted as special members upon application. At press conferences, however, they must ask questions in Japanese; thus, for practical purposes, most foreign reporters do not join the clubs. Consequently, they find it difficult, if not impossible, to obtain information directly from primary sources.

The traditional reticence of most Japanese to communicate openly with foreigners also makes reporting about the country difficult. This is particularly true if the journalists are more aggressive and probing than the standard Japanese reporter. Therefore, direct insights into Japanese political, economic, and social life may be distorted or simply unavailable through primary sources, forcing reporters to rely on secondary sources provided by others which may be quite accurate, but still lack the journalistic intimacy so important to good reporting.

At a time when Japan is undergoing a series of economic adjustments, the policy formulation process is shifting from the bureaucracy to the politicians and the nation is assuming the role of a global economic power, the rarity of insightful, nonsensational reporting casts a shadow on the internationalization process. Friend and foe alike find it difficult, if not impossible, to keep up with the scope and complexity of events happening in Japan. The result is what many Japanese lament as the uninformed perceptions abroad that lag behind the events in Japan at best or distort the reality at worst. The latter particularly pertains to stories about how the well-oiled ruthlessly efficient Japanese economic machine buys up America or plans to take over the world within the foreseeable future. Such views create interest abroad because they sensationalize issues that contain an element of reality, but whose understanding takes more effort than just the unquestioning acceptance of superficialities and impressions based on fear and/or concern, however real they may be.

Education

Because of their highly competitive and demanding educational system, the Japanese are among the most literate people in the world. In international academic competitions, Japanese students are consistently among the top performers, particularly in mathematics and the sciences. Compared to the United States, Japanese students must learn as much math by the ninth grade as American students need to graduate from high school. Moreover, while only 75 percent of high school students graduate in the United States, more than 90 percent graduate from high school in Japan. At the higher educational level, with a university population one-fifth that of America, Japan produces about 75,000 graduate engineers annually as compared to 72,000 in the United States. However, in spite of such impressive results, the Japanese basic and higher education systems are under increasing scrutiny today. There is a debate about the future of the systems, and the outcome of these discussions may have implications for the internationalization process.

Educational reform ranked high on Prime Minister Nakasone's list of policy objectives. In 1984–85 he stimulated a public debate on education, and as a consequence, the Special Education Council has put forward various plans to revamp the educational system.[26] However, the Prime Minister was not pleased with the recommendations because they did not address what he considered to be the basic problems inherent in the post-World War II system developed during the occupation. Nakasone argues that the current 6–3 system (six years in primary school followed by three years in junior high school) is a "borrowed system that has no roots in Japanese society." He believes that the current educational system produces a generation which is devoid of discipline, respect for its elders, and love of the nation. The Prime Minister and the private advisory group he appointed to study the matter were convinced that a strong dose of moral education and more emphasis on responsibility to society are the answers. This, of course, is a reference to the nation's traditional values of loyalty, discipline, and hard work which the former Prime Minister wanted to see reinforced.

Debate over educational reform has a long history in Japan. Immediately after the establishment of an educational structure modeled after the West in 1872, there was an intense discussion of how such an alien model should be adapted to Japanese conditions. After World War II the system was again changed under the orders of the Allied Occupation Authorities, and thus, a discussion evolved over how the American model should be modified to fit the Japanese context characterized by a rapidly growing school-age population. When economic growth accelerated, another discussion began over how the educational system could be made more responsive to the needs of the economy.

The major issues of the current debate, however, are different from those of the past. The rapid growth of the educational system is slowing: the population of five-year-olds peaked in 1989 and then began to decline. For example, the Ministry of Education already noted in August 1988 that the number of primary school students fell below 10 million in 1987 for the first time in 15 years. Moreover, industry no longer demands continuous reform because there is a balance between the needs of the economy and the quality of individuals available for employment.

Today's education debate centers on the attitudes of the new generation of students. More Japanese students exhibit an "anti-school" attitude than ever before. Disillusionment, dislike of school, and violence have become so widespread that they have aroused concern throughout the nation. According to a poll conducted by the Prime Minister's Office in the summer of 1988, 63 percent of the Japanese adults believe that the parents' ability to discipline their children had dropped in recent years. The majority believed that parents are not able to inculcate tenacity and the strength to endure difficulties in their children. Others (25 percent) lamented the children's independence and expressed concern about the decline in the parents' ability to teach good life habits. That there is a problem was confirmed by the National Policy Agency which reported that scholastic pressures rank as the most important reason for driving young Japanese men and women to suicide. For instance, in 1986, 136 and, in 1987, 207 Japanese youth killed themselves because of such pressures.

Most education experts consider the high level of *gakureki shakai* (educational credentialism), which generated one of the world's toughest entrance examination systems, the major culprit for such resentful attitudes. Unless exceptionally bright, most youngsters must attend the *juku* (special cram school) to pass through the "examination hell," and be able to attend a prestigious high school or university. Moreover, the Headquarters for Youth and Children of the Management Coordination Agency reported in 1986 that young Japanese between the ages of six and the early twenties are not anxious to take on the responsibilities of adulthood, and want to maintain their present status as long as possible. The Agency found that almost all the young men and women are satisfied with their present way of life; in the case of senior high school and university students, over 80 percent were content, and in the case of young workers, over 70 percent. The majority of them are optimistic about the future and believe they can fulfill their personal expectations about life in general and their careers in particular within about 10 years. However, only 5 to 10 percent of the total expect to serve society or to have a career through which they can contribute to the improvement of society. The report concludes that today's youth is very different from the young people of the past in that they exhibit a strong desire to embark on an individualistic way of life rather than to follow a "grand dream based on a noble spirit."[27] The young men and women value their chosen lifestyles and want to lead a life that pleases them. Unlike their parents' generation which experienced the devastation of World War II and was subjected to deprivations, they prefer to spend their money on the goods and services they desire today and pay less attention to the need to save for the future. Not surprisingly, the older generation, with some discomfort, refers to the young as *shinjinrui* (the new human breed).

Thus, according to most Japanese, a far-reaching education reform is in order. The interim report released by the Advisory Curriculum Council of the Ministry of Education in October 1986 called for nurturing of the young generation's consciousness and sense of duty as Japanese in the world community, as well as the teaching of the cultural traditions of the nation.

Another report published by the Ad Hoc Commission on Education in the summer of 1987 stated that reform is necessary ". . . to eradicate the deeply ingrained uniformity, rigidity and national exclusiveness that afflict Japanese society." Moreover, the authors of the report argued, any reform should be guided by the "principle of individuality and individual dignity." Following the Ad Hoc Commission's report, a special Education Advisory Council was created to review the educational curricula from the kindergarten to the senior high school level. Once the review was completed, the Council recommended a new curriculum for each level for which, subsequently, new courses of study were developed. As before, the emphasis was on individuality.

In early 1989 the Ministry of Education announced its reform plans, the first since 1977. The proposed new curricula eliminates a number of restrictions and provides students with more flexibility in selecting courses. It also introduces computers in middle-school and high-school mathematics classes. Overall, the changes are designed to prepare the children for their new role as global citizens and to reinforce Japanese identity. In this sense, the thrust of the reforms is toward patriotism and traditional values as envisioned by former Prime Minister Nakasone when he initiated the reform process in the mid-1980s. Kenichi Fukui, the Nobel Prize-winning chemist who chaired the curriculum commission, announced that the new curricula provide an opportunity to "bring up children with the necessary qualities to carry the nation into the 21st century." In particular, he emphasized, the new measures are intended to develop children who "can think for themselves and who can study by themselves." The reform measures are going to be implemented in 1990.

While most Japanese applauded the reforms, some were concerned about the nationalistic dimensions such as the requirement to raise the *Hinomaru* (national flag) and to sing the *Kimigayo* (national anthem) at all commencement and graduation exercises. (Under the pre-reform regulations this was merely "advisable," i.e., left to the individual school authorities.) Moreover, critics charge, the increased emphasis on "moral education," the abolishment of social science courses in high school, and the proposed changes in the textbooks which, beginning in 1990, will include discussions of historical figures previously shunned (for instance, Admiral Togo, the hero of the Russo-Japanese War of 1904–1905), are potentially troublesome in that they may create problems with Japan's Asian neighbors. *Nikkyoso*, the Japan Teachers' Union, for example, immediately denounced the revisions as an effort to revive nationalistic ideologies. On February 12, 1989, the *Asahi Shimbum* newspaper editorialized that while the reformers propose the education of the intellect on an individual basis, they want to continue the education of the heart and spirit in a collective manner, just like during the pre-World War II years when moral education based on Confuscian values and nationalism were the order of the day.

Of course, the reform of an educational system is always controversial. Thus, the disagreements were unavoidable and perhaps even desirable in that they raise questions that eventually need to be answered by the educational establishment. Nonetheless, the overall thrust of the reforms is in line with what most Japanese believe is the proper role and method of education on the threshold of the twenty-first century.

The Japanese higher educational system is also undergoing a review and restructuring. Currently, competition for admission to the leading universities is intense; passing the university entrance examination is the major educational concern of most high school seniors.

Competition is intensified by the stratified nature of the higher educational system which was the result of the rapid increase in such institutions during the postwar years. At the end of World War II, there were 48 universities and colleges; by 1985, that number had increased to 446. Most of the new institutions are private, and many of them are not well endowed; thus, they must rely on tuition as the major source of income. Although all universities are officially equal and employers no longer offer pay differentials according to a university's ranking, most Japanese continue to evaluate institutions in terms of unofficial rankings. Moreover, the present structure and practices of even the most prestigious Japanese higher education institutions are not entirely in accord with international customs. Although these institutions provide a quality education, through their traditions, they continue to promote the image of Japan as a close-knit, homogenous, and thus unique society which is difficult for foreigners to penetrate.

Demand for higher education is growing in Japan. According to a report published by the Education Ministry in 1988, during the 1987–1988 academic year the number of university students nationwide increased by 60,000 from 1,800,000 to 1,860,000. Moreover, in 1988 more than 690,000 young men and women entered universities and junior colleges, and the ratio of applicants among high school students to universities and junior colleges reached 48 percent compared to 44.5 percent just a decade ago. As a consequence, the ratio of admittees to total applicants was the lowest in history in spite of a considerable increase in the capacity of universities and junior colleges. To deal with this problem, the Ministry of Education developed a plan with emphasis on the creation of new and the expansion of existing universities to meet the growing population of 18-year-olds which is expected to peak in 1992.

In the meanwhile, because of the highly stratified nature of the higher education system, the prestige institutions as, for example, Tokyo University or *Todai* continue to dominate. For example, a 1987 survey of the *Toyo Kezai* or publication showed that one out of every six executives of the country's leading corporations and one out of two career bureaucrats is a graduate of Tokyo University. Moreover, one out of five members of the national parliament in 1987 were also alumni. As a matter of fact, about 50 percent of the nation's top political, industrial, and bureaucratic positions were filled by the graduates of Tokyo and of four other leading universities.

At the same time, in an effort to internationalize their staff, a number of large corporations are opening their doors to graduates who have studied abroad. This, however, does not mean that they are welcoming them with open arms. Companies that are hiring Japanese graduates or foreign universities tend to be very choosy and watch their new hirees closely to see if they are fitting into the organizations. Nonetheless, it appears that the previous condition in which students who studied overseas were excluded from Japanese companies is beginning to change. More and more firms need staff members who not only speak fluent English but who can also understand other cultures and effectively interact with people from all over the world. Major corporations such as Sony are employing overseas educated Japanese in increasingly large numbers because they want to have more diversity in their homogenous workforce. As they are increasing foreign direct investments, they are having painful experiences abroad due to the lack of internationally adaptable staff. Recently even a number of small-sized to medium-sized companies have expressed an interest in employing the graduates of foreign universities because they are not finding enough graduates of domestic institutions and because they are becoming internationally more active as well.

The search by Japanese corporations for capable graduates abroad is somewhat hampered by the fact that many corporations do not have overseas contacts. This has created a new type of intermediary service such as the Center for International Cultural Studies and Education, a Tokyo-based firm providing guidance to Japanese students who want to study abroad. The company also publishes a bulletin called *Career News* which carries job announcements of domestic companies that want to hire the graduates of foreign institutions.

At the same time, the internationalization of Japan's higher educational system is proceeding at a slow pace. For instance, as of May 1, 1985, there were only 15,009 foreign students in Japan, most of them from Taiwan (29.4 percent), the Republic of Korea (20.9 percent), and the People's Republic of China (18.2 percent).[28] This number grew to 22,154 by May 1, 1987, and to 25,643 by May 1, 1988, respectively, an increase of 15.7 percent over a period of one year. Most of them still come from the same nations as in 1985, although the proportion of North Americans (4.1 percent) and Europeans (2.3 percent) has increased. But the total still pales in comparison to the number of foreign students in the United States (more than 350,000) and the major West European countries.

One of the reasons for this relatively low number is the time and effort involved in learning the language necessary to benefit from instruction. Another, and perhaps even more compelling, reason is the cost of education which increased sharply as a result of the appreciation of the yen during 1986–1988. Of those who were in Japan in 1988, for example, approximately 80 percent, or 20,549, were studying at their own expense at universities, graduate schools, junior colleges, or vocational schools across the nation. This represented an increase of 2,848 over 1987. Many of these students face extreme hardships, although major corporations, local governments, a special committee of the LDP, and the government have all considered the problem and have either come up with some short-term ways to help or have developed propositions to deal with the problem in the long run.

In 1988 the Education Ministry financed 16 percent, or 4,118, foreign students, an increase of about 600 over 1987, while close to 1,000 students were supported by their own governments. Most of the Japanese funding came from the Overseas Development Assistance (ODA) budget which increased by 26 percent in FY 1988 over FY 1987. While the Japanese government intends to increase its support through ODA in the years to come, ultimately the burden of supporting foreign students will fall on the private sector which has not done this sort of thing before. At the request of the Ministry of Education and MITI, major corporations have begun to offer dormitory space and scholarships, although the initial efforts are not too promising. By the end of 1988, only about 60 organizations agreed to sponsor 1,800, or about 1 percent, of all foreign students in Japan.

However, all of these arrangements can be effective only if the Japanese institutions also allow foreign faculty to become active participants in the universities. At present, the hierarchical structures of Japan colleges and universities make it difficult for foreign faculty, even if they speak Japanese, to become integrated into the decision-making system. Many institutions use the traditional *senpai-kohai* (senior-junior) system which is based on the employment of their own graduates as faculty, and thus leads to a certain amount of inbreeding and isolation. Students who want to become faculty members are guided by individual professors for whom they develop an intense personal loyalty for the rest of their career. In the resulting close-knit institutional environment in which conformity is highly valued, it is still difficult for foreign faculty members who are outside the *senpai-kohai* system to become tenured, and thus to participate fully in the academic and administrative decision-making process.

To promote the process of change, Prime Minister Nakasone in 1986 announced a policy of increasing the number of faculty members and students from abroad, and rescinded a law that barred foreigners from obtaining tenure at national universities. According to his plan, by the year 2000, a total of 100,000 foreign students, many from neighboring Asian countries, would study in public and private colleges, universities, and research institutions. The objective for this influx of foreign students is to have a large number of young people learn *nihongo* (Japanese language, history, and culture). Another motive is the desire to have more Japanese faculty and students interact with people from abroad in a domestic setting.

By 1988 the special committee of the LDP studying the issue of bringing more foreign students to Japan concluded that it may be too difficult to realize such ambitious plans. Rather than aiming for a total of 100,000 by the year 2000, the committee proposed to increase the number of officially sponsored foreign students from the current 4,000 to 20,000. In other words, the LDP now believes that providing better quality support is more important than just increasing the quantity of foreign students studying in Japan.

The problem is complicated by the rapidly increasing arrival of foreign workers from developing Asian nations in recent years. Employee shortages, the unwillingness of the Japanese to do certain types of menial work, and the sharp appreciation of the yen have motivated thousands to try their luck, even if it means becoming illegal aliens. According to the Ministry of Labor, by the fall of 1989 the number of foreign workers with work permits reached 60,000, but the number of illegal aliens may have grown to well over 150,000. Of these, anywhere from 100,000 to 110,000 are estimated to be working illegally, including many students who came to Japan under false pretenses or who are forced to work illegally in low-paying menial or entertainment jobs to survive.

The public is, of course, very much concerned about the increase in illegal aliens in general and the increase in illegal workers in particular. Moreover, while the Ministry of Justice and the Ministry of Labor are engaged in a turf-battle over jurisdiction governing the treatment of foreign workers, others

154   THE INTERNATIONALIZATION OF THE JAPANESE ECONOMY

such as the Ministry of Construction want such workers to fill low-paying menial positions. At the same time, the Ministry of Foreign Affairs is concerned about the impact the public's reaction and the bureaucratic infighting may have on the nations of the Asian region where Japan has image problems.

Under these circumstances the plan to bring 100,000 foreign students to Japan by the year 2000 is not feasible. Nonetheless, the internationalization of the higher education system can be promoted through other more realistic means. A particularly noteworthy effort is the attempt of the United States-Japan Committee for Promoting Trade Expansion (CPTE) to have American universities open branch campuses throughout Japan. By the end of 1988 four institutions maintained campuses in Japan of which Temple University of Philadelphia came to Japan first in 1982. Another four are tentatively scheduled to open during the early 1990s. Such institutions offer a number of benefits such as new educational opportunities for Japanese students who fail to gain entrance to domestic universities, a potential boost to local economies, and possibly improved U.S.–Japan relations. For the American institutions the move to Japan helps increase revenues at a time of stable or declining enrollments back home and opens up new possibilities to promote international relations.

In all of these arrangements the academic standards are under the control of the American institution while the administrative and, most of all, financial end is handled by the Japanese side, often a private language or college preparatory school. How the entry of American universities into Japan is viewed by the educational establishment is not entirely clear. But companies are, in some cases, specifically recruiting their graduates because of language skills and the demonstrated ability to work in non-Japanese settings. The public in general has also come to learn more about these institutions and is now less reluctant to accept them, although the Ministry of Education has not yet officially recognized any of them.

Before a number of other American universities can be expected to follow the pioneers, certain problems have to be resolved. There is the question of quality control, of high costs due to the sharply appreciated yen, and of the difficulty in obtaining scholarships for students. Moreover, the local communities must develop more concrete and realistic plans to locate non-Japanese institutions of higher learning in their midst; enthusiasm is not enough. Nonetheless, the program is imaginative, and even if only a small number of universities succeed in establishing themselves, their presence can contribute to the internationalization of the Japanese higher educational system which, in turn, is critical to the internationalization of the society in general and the economy in particular.

Economic Policy Contraints

In addition to the sociocultural traditions and practices that interfere with internationalization, there are also several potential economic policy constraints. These policies are designated to protect economic sectors which are not internationally competitive, such as agriculture and several declining industries. Other policies as, for example, the administrative and fiscal reforms, are necessary to reduce the size of government and to moderate the fiscal burden accumulated over many years.

Agriculture

When considering Japan's role in the world economy, the outside world usually sees only the immensely successful large *kaisha*. Toyota, Hitachi, and Sony, among others, dominate the world's perception of an economy which, however, also has some "soft" spots. Behind the phalanx of the industrial giants, there is for example, a small-scale, low-productivity but politically influential agricultural sector which is protected by interacting socioeconomic and political forces.

Agriculture is an economic activity with special characteristics. GATT recognizes this and provides a unique status for agriculture which is greatly affected by a variety of socioeconomic and even climatic conditions. Based on this, Japan's farm policy is governed by the Basic Agriculture Law, enacted 25 years ago to help agriculture improve its international competitiveness. This is still the objective, although the policies formulated under the law have undoubtedly placed more emphasis on the protection of farmers, and generally neglected the improvement of competitiveness as well as the Japanese consumers.

A cornerstone of these policies were the 22 residual quantitative import restrictions that Japan maintained on processed agricultural commodities and food products well into the second half of the 1980s. Not surprisingly, these import quotas were a continuous source of friction with the United States which wanted wider market-access for agricultural exports. As bilateral negotiations proved fruitless, the United States filed a complaint with the GATT concerning import quotas on 12 categories in 1986. In December 1987 the GATT dispute panel ruled that in ten categories the import quotas violated international trading rules. This finding was adopted by the GATT Council in February 1988.

Due to the strong opposition among the politically influential farm bloc, the Japanese government at first refused to accept the ruling but eventually relented and decided to comply. While the liberalization of the ten food item imports were expected to reduce the U.S.–Japan bilateral trade deficit only by approximately $200 million out of $50 billion, the move was necessary to maintain smooth relations with the Americans, particularly since Prime Minister Takeshita was just about to meet with President Reagan in early 1988 and needed a *Miyage* (gift) to take to Washington.

The food categories involved such items as skim milk, processed cheese, beef and pork products, fruit puree and paste, fruit pulp and canned pinapples, noncitrus juice and tomato juice, tomato ketchup and sauce, starch, glucose, and other minor processed foods. The immediate and total liberalization of imports of these items would have certainly dealt a mortal blow to domestic producers. The political sensitivity of the issue was appreciated in Washington; consequently, the two sides got together and worked out an agreement by mid-1988 of gradually eliminating quotas on eight of the ten categories in a mutually acceptable manner.

Japan agreed to remove quotas on seven categories, including processessed cheese, fruit purees and pastes, canned pineapple and fruit pulp, tomato juice and noncitrus fruit juices, ketchup and tomato sauce, sugar and sugar syrups, and some other sugar-related food products in four stages, beginning October 1, 1988, and ending April 1, 1990. Two additional categories, including various milk and cream products and starches, the Japanese could not completely liberalize, and thus the two sides agreed that Tokyo will remove import restrictions on items of interest to the United States. Moreover, to compensate the United States for continued restrictions on nonfat dried milk, evaporated milk, some other dairy products, and starches, Japan agreed to cut tariffs on 15 types of farm commodities and processed foods as, for example, breakfast cereals, popcorn, soup, mayonnaise, and chewing gum, as of April 1, 1989.

With respect to the two categories, (peanuts, and dried beans and peas) in which the GATT ruled that Japan could maintain import quotas if it increased import volumes, the two sides agreed to raise the import ceiling for peanuts by 36.4 percent over three years and eliminate lentils and chickpeas from the quotas governing dried peas and beans.

During the summer of 1988 the United States and Japan worked out another major agreement concerning import restrictions on beef and citrus products which had grown into a festering trade problem over the years. As in the case of the 12 residual import quotas the United States had challenged, bilateral negotiations dealing with these two product groups proceeded slowly and, consequently, the United States filed another GATT complaint. The summer 1988 agreement, however, was reached before the GATT issued its ruling, and America agreed to retract its complaint.

Under the agreement Japan agreed to lift beef import quotas as of April 1, 1991. After that it is going to set a temporary tariff of 70 percent in FY 1991, 60 percent in FY 1992, and 50 percent in FY 1993. Subsequent tariff levels are going to be discussed within the framework of the Uruguay Round of GATT negotiations. However, if imports during 1991–1993 exceed the level of 120 percent of the previous year's imports, Japan has the right to take "safeguard" measures and impose an additional *ad valorem* tariff after consultation with the beef-exporting countries. But, after April 1, 1994, Japan may apply only those safeguard measures that are legal under GATT rules. The agreement also called for a three-year phase-out of import management operations by the Livestock Industry Promotion Corporation which had a virtual (80 percent) monopoly on beef imports and distribution.[29]

Import quotas on fresh oranges are set to be lifted as of April 1, 1991, although the tariffs remain at the levels of 40 percent in-season and 20 percent off-season. Moreover, during FYs 1988–1990, the imports of fresh oranges were going to be expanded by 22,000 metric tons annually to reach 192,000 tons by 1990.

The Japanese, furthermore, agreed to lift orange juice import quotas beginning April 1, 1992, and to maintain tariffs at the current levels of 25–35 percent, depending on the sugar content. The requirement that imported orange juice be mixed with *mikan* juice produced domestically was to be eliminated as of April 1, 1990, while during FYs 1988–1991 orange juice concentrate import volumes are going to rise.

In return for the maintenance of current tariffs on fresh oranges and orange juice, Japan agreed to reduce tariffs on a select group of food imports including grapefruits, lemons, nuts, pet foods, sausages, pork, and beans.

To deal with the domestic problems resulting from the agreement, the government and the LDP worked out a Y156 billion ($1.3 billion, at $1 = Y125) assistance program by August 1988. Of this amount cattle farmers received about Y50 billion ($400 million) in subsidies and loans during FY 1988 and FY 1989. While some of these funds come from beef tariffs, most of it is provided for in the budget; additional funds will be provided out of tariff proceeds beginning in FY 1990. Another substantial amount was earmarked for interest subsidies on the bank loans of cattle raisers and feeders. The *mikan* growers receive about Y106 billion or $848 million as part of an acreage-reduction plan. Additional funds are going to be provided to deal with some of the other problems the *mikan* growers will face as a result of the agreement.

With these two agreements Japan has substantially reduced its quotas on agricultural commodities and food products beginning in the early 1990s.

Aside from various dairy products and another few items, currently only flour and certain food preparations made from wheat, rice, and barley, edible seaweeds, and, of course, rice remain on the restricted list. Of these, rice and wheat are "state-traded" items whose import, therefore, may be limited according to GATT rules.

Nonetheless, rice imports became another bone of contention between the United States and Japan, and in 1986 the U.S. rice industry filed a petition with the Office of the USTR to seek retaliation against Japan's import restrictions on the grounds that it constitutes "unfair trade" under Section 301 of the 1974 U.S. Trade Act. The industry was represented by the Rice Millers' Association (RMA), consisting of 27 members and including farmer-owned cooperatives and independently owned rice milling companies located in Arkansas, California, and other Southern states. Others, such as 23 associate rice exporter members, have also joined the action.

The Association argued that the protectionist measures force Japanese consumers to pay $25 billion more annually for rice, and that this equals approximately half of the U.S. trade deficit with Japan in 1985. Thus, they claimed, the elimination of the restrictions would increase the purchasing power of the Japanese consumers and moderate the bilateral trade imbalance, both major goals of the Nakasone government's internationaliztion policy.[30]

The Reagan Administration, however, recognized the political sensitivity in Japan of the American rice growers' demand. In late October 1986, the Office of the USTR rejected the petition to retaliate against the Japanese if bilateral negotiations failed to increase U.S. rice imports. USTR Yeutter explained that he would ask the Japanese government to bring its rice policy to the table at the new round of multilateral trade talks (GATT) scheduled to begin in early 1987. According to Yeutter, an agreement reached in the preliminary trade talks at Punta del Este in September 1986 included two key provisions which could be applied to the Japanese rice policy. The first provision declares the liberalization of agricutural trade a major goal of the multilateral discussions, and the second would require GATT member countries to roll back policy measures which restrict or distort trade.

However, America's rice growers were not satisfied with the decision of the USTR and the position of the Administration, and they raised the issue again in the fall of 1988. In the midst of the Presidential campaign, the Rice Millers Association (RMA) and the Rice Council for Market Development (RCMD) representing 11,000 millers and 25,000 growers respectively filed another petition with the White House under Section 301 of the new 1988 trade act. The petition called for an initial import quota of 5 percent to be raised to 10 percent in four years. Japan's annual rice consumption is approximately 12 million tons; thus, the rice millers and growers demanded initial imports of 600,000 tons, rising to 1.2 million tons. The U.S. rice industry argued that the 1987 GATT ruling on agricultural import quotas undercut the Japanese position that its rice policies are GATT-compatible, particularly the proposition that rice is not covered by the ruling because it is state-traded. Moreover, the petitioners stated, Japan cannot claim an exemption for its rice import controls on the grounds that national security considerations call for rice self-sufficiency.

It is noteworthy that major American farm organizations did not rally behind the rice industry's petition. Groups representing producers of other crops as well as the American Agricultural Movement and the American Farm Bureau Federation were concerned about a Japanese blacklash against products such as soybeans, beef, and grains. Meanwhile, the U.S. Department of Agriculture reported that American rice exports were expected to grow by about 7 percent during the 1988–1989 marketing year in stark contrast to the 14 percent decline in 1987–1988, a year in which the rice industry faced major problems. Also, shortly after the petition was filed, the Lower House of the Diet unanimously adopted a resolution against the further opening of the nation's rice market to foreign imports. The resolution, passed in a plenary session of the 512-member Diet was not binding, but it expressed the strong sentiment of Japanese legislators that the approximately 20,000-ton annual rice import quota should not be raised, at least not yet. Part of these limited imports are set aside for Okinawa where local brewers prefer the long-grained Southeast Asian rice to produce *awamori*, a strong local drink, while the rest comes from the Republic of Korea on an occasional basis.

Rice, which has been cultivated in Japan for over 2,000 years, is a sensitive issue. Its social significance is far out of proportion to its economic importance. The literal translation of the Japanese terms for lunch and dinner, for example, are "midday rice" and "evening rice." It is not an exaggeration to say that to the majority of Japanese, rice is associated with national identity and security. Rumor has it, for instance that when the late Emperor Hirohito awoke from his sickbed in the early fall of 1988, his first concern was the rice harvest prospects.

Thus, the petition of the American rice industry received a great deal of publicity throughout the country. The results of a poll conducted by the Prime Minister's Office published in 1988 showed that more than 70 percent of all Japanese want rice self-sufficiency, and 95.4 percent believe that rice is the most desirable staple. This last finding was particularly interesting because per capita rice consumption was actually declining during recent years. Apparently many people are now rediscovering rice as a key part of their diet.

Of course, while rice occupies an important role in the national life,

Japan's rice policies also have a lot to do with vested interests. The small and inefficient, offen part-time, farmers produce more than the nation can consume but are politically very influential. Thus, they receive an annual subsidy of more than $4 billion in price-support payments. The government buys the bulk of the rice crop and then resells it at a loss based on a rationing system to licensed rice dealers. The remainder, consisting mostly of the better quality, is sold freely through stores.

Under the circumstances the Reagan Administration courageously again rejected the rice industry's petition in October 1988, just a few weeks before the Presidential election in November. USTR Yeutter explained that he trusted the Japanese assurances that while they cannot do anything in the short run, they are willing to put the issue of rice imports on the table as part of the overall Uruguay Round of the GATT negotiations process. He added, however, that if it turns out that the Japanese do not live up to their assurances, the United States would reconsider the decision.

Democrats and Republicans in Congress blasted the decision as a "cave-in" to the Japanese, and Presidential candidate George Bush prepared for the worst, although he endorsed the rice industry's petition. The Japanese, naturally, welcomed the decision but expressed concern about the possibility of reconsidering the decision following the December 1988 mid-term review of the GATT talks scheduled for Montreal, Canada. They were somewhat relieved a few days later when USTR Yeutter explained that the United States does not expect Japan to offer an end to the import restrictions in Montreal, but would merely have to agree to the elimination of agricultural subsidies sometimes in the 1990s which is America's major objective in the GATT talks. A narrow quarrel with Japan over rice would have distracted from this larger purpose, particularly since rice is not ever likely to be a major American export to Japan. If and when the import restrictions are removed, Thai and Chinese producers are likely to undersell all other producers and capture the major part of the import market. Moreover, while the elimination of rice import restrictions has symbolic value to the U.S. side, through the acceptance of the 1987 GATT ruling on the ten residual agricultural import quotas and the 1988 beef and citrus fruit agreement, Japan has done about as much as was politically feasible within a relatively short period of time. The United States needed to concentrate on its agricultural trade with the European Community which protected its farmers as strongly as, if not more than the Japanese do.

Nonetheless, the Japanese began gradually to streamline the antiquated rice production and distribution system in force since 1942 when the rigid controls were introduced to deal with the wartime shortages of food. Already in the summer of 1987 the government approved a 5.9 percent reduction in the producer rice price in accordance with the recommendation of the Rice Price Council, an advisory body to the Ministry of Agriculture, Forestry and Fisheries (MAFF). This first price cut since 1956 was followed by a 4.6 percent price reduction in 1988 which should have been twice as high except for the vehement opposition by the rice-*zoku* in the Diet. Such opposition may grow stronger in the future, because in line with the pricing formula developed by the Council, producer prices for rice are expected to decline at least 30 percent within the next five years. The formula, based on the production costs of the highly efficient farmers rather than on the cost of small-scale inefficient farmers, is a step in the right direction but is politically controversial. The complex nature of the controversy is illustrated by the fact that in the fall of 1988 even the *Keizai Doyukai* (The Japanese Association of Corporate Executives) and the *Keidanren* (The Federation of Economic Organizations) entered the melee by calling for dramatic cuts in the cost of production and increasing the percentage of free rice marketing within five years. Not surprisingly, the MAFF and the rice producers called the plan "unrealistic"; they preferred to cut rice output by 30 percent by the year 2000.

Other small changes were also introduced during 1988. In the summer, for example, the MAFF approved the sale of 100 metric tons of rice among 27 major wholesalers throughout the country, a major departure from traditional marketing practices. This was followed by another MAFF announcement concerning the sale of rice by retailers on the street and the installation of more than one rice vending machine in individual food retail shops. Moreover, the MAFF also allowed more retailers to sell rice in their shops as long as they did not deliver it. From abroad such measures seem inconsequential if not ridiculous. However, such small steps must be evaluated in light of the role and importance of agriculture in general and of rice in particular in the nation's life.

Agriculture and Politics

Japan has a high population density, small farms, and fertile but expensive land. The average two-acre or three-acre farms cannot compete with the large-scale farms and agrobusiness operations which are more dominant in other parts of the world. Moreover, the nation with its narrow territory, large population, and vulnerable sea-routes depends on foreign supply sources for approximately 50 percent of its food measured in calories and around 33 percent measured in value, proportions which are higher than in other industrialized nations. The 1973 unilateral American export-ban on soy-beans is frequently cited as an example of what can happen if the nation relied too heavily on supplies from abroad.

Japanese agriculture would undoubtedly be more efficient and thus more internationally competitive if it were recoganized into larger units so that modern production methods and equipment could be applied. However, this would mean the end of the rural socioeconomic structures which have existed for centuries and which form the basis of the rural communities throughout the country. This is not a realistic option for a government dominated by the LDP which has its major political support in such areas.

According to MAFF data published in 1988, Japan currently has 4.3 million farming households and 8 million farmers working on two or three hectares of land, many of them on a part-time basis. For agriculture to be internationally competitive, the farming population would have to be reduced by about two-thirds to approximately 1 million households farming an average of five or six hectares. Although the agricultural population is already declining because young people are leaving the land, such a decline would be politically and socially unacceptable.

Farmers are a major political force. The Zen-Chu or Central Union of Agricultural Cooperatives, comprises about 4,300 cooperatives representing 4.4 million farms and approximately 12 percent of all households. The organization controls all aspects of Japanese agriculture including the distribution of credit, fertilizers, and animal feed-stuffs. Its political influence is very strong; 360 of the current Diet members or 80 percent of the total belong to the LDP's Farming Promotion Council. In recent years, the LDP's farm support has been declining, but the MAFF backed by the still-influential farm-*zoku* in the Diet represents the interest of the Zen-Chu membership quite well. Any sudden or major change in the nation's agricultural policies could spell trouble for Japanese politicians at the polls, a prospect they obviously do not cherish.

It is, however, important to keep in mind that the restrictive agricultural import policies and the high subsidies provided to farmers also provide socially desirable benefits. It plays a major role in Japan's income equality between farmers and urban workers. Life on the farms has never been easy, but it is much better today than it used to be. After centuries of hardship, farmers are enjoying a measure of comfort. People have running water, electricity, color TV sets, telephones, and cars. Thus, not surprisingly, the Japanese are not ready and willing to completely and quickly dismantle the system that proved to be beneficial to an important, albeit small, segment of the population.

Japan's agricultural policy which protects the small farmers, yet results in high domestic food prices, has, by and large, been accepted by the

Japanese, most of whom have family roots in the rural areas. Most people still believe that national security in terms of stable food supplies justifies current policies, particularly since it became known that during the last few years the nation's self-sufficiency in grain has fallen to about 33 percent, the lowest ratio for any industrialized nation. This has created a psychological fear of shortages in an emergency. Naturally, the Zen-Chu and its allies fan such fears to secure the support they need to maintain the price support system even at its high cost to the consumer. Table 4–1 shows to what extent consumers subsidize agricutlural producers through the higher domestic prices.

Nonetheless, a survey by the Prime Minister's Office published in early 1988 indicated that 71.2 percent of the respondents wanted the nation to be self-sufficient in food production; of these, 39.3 percent were willing to support this goal even if it meant higher food costs. It is noteworthy that only about 20 percent declared that they favored low-cost imports to domestically produced food, while approximately 70 percent predicted that Japanese eating habits are going to remain rice-based. Such views were reinforced by the "Shodanren" (National Liaison Committee of Consumers' Organization) which is comprised of 18 consumer groups and publicly cautioned against "indiscriminate import expansion which could endanger the national economy." The country's biggest consumer union, *Seikyo*, or the Consumers Cooperative Union, did not criticize high food prices although it campaigned strongly for the reduction of electricity and gas fees in response to the yen appreciation.

However, recently some consumer groups took a less supportive attitude

TABLE 4-1. Comparison of domestic Japanese agricultural prices to import prices: 1985–1986*

| Products | Import source | | | |
	France	Britain	W. Germany	USA
Rice	—	—	—	8.3
Wheat	3.7	3.7	4.1	7.8
Sugar	1.8	1.5	2.3	2.9
Beef	1.2	1.3	1.7	2.6
Milk, Cream	1.4	1.5	1.5	1.9
Pork	—	1.2	1.4	2.4

* Figures shown represent the number of times that the domestic price exceeds the import price.

Source: *The Japan Economic Journal*, October 18, 1986, p. 3.

toward farmers. The Japan Housewives' Association, for example, argued that food prices must be lowered even if it means withdrawing support from the farmers. Others, such as the *Keidanren* (Federation of Economic Organizations) have long argued that the protectionist farm system must be dismantled and replaced with a competitive market system regardless of social and political concerns. Leading industrialists maintain that Japan's future depends on the industrial sector; thus, the protection of the agricultural sector is too heavy a price to pay because it creates resentment against industrial products abroad. In contrast, the farm lobby argues that it is both unreasonable and selfish to use farm products as a pawn in the attempt to earn conflict-free industrial trade relations with other nations.

The sensitivity of the farm issue notwithstanding, Japan's internationally minded politicians and government officials understand that the nation's farm policy has to be revised in the long run. This is why they agreed to put agriculture, including the restrictive rice import policies, on the agenda of the Uruguary Round of GATT negotiations that began in 1987. But, at the same time, they also emphasized that while they are willing to discuss rice with other issues such as the U.S. waivers on imports of some farm products and the European Community's (EC) import surcharges, they are not willing to give up rice as an essential staple of food self-sufficiency.

As soon as the talks began it became clear that there were major disagreements involving all sides. The United States, which promoted the new talks, wanted to eliminate all import barriers and subsidies by the year 2000, if not sooner. The EC expressed an unwillingness to discuss long-term measures and wanted to focus on the gradual reduction of subsidies in the short run using as standards the Producer Subsidy Equivalents (PSE) and the Consumer Subsidy Equivalents (CSE) measures developed by the OECD. The Japanese rejected these measures as misleading because, despite the fact that their farm subsidies are already on the decline, the high domestic food prices are driven up even higher in dollar terms due to the appreciation of the yen. The Cairns Group of 13 food-exporting nations which include, among others, Canada, Australia, and Argentina, were supportive of the U.S. proposal but wanted to put off its discussion until 1990

The Montreal mid-term review meeting in December 1988 failed to reach an agreement on the agenda for additional talks. To salvage the negotiations, the United States changed its position in early 1989. In his first news conference as the Secretary of Agriculture of the Bush Administration, former USTR Yeutter declared in February 1989 that while he still believed that all agricultural subsidies should be eliminated, he realized that it could be done only with the cooperation of other nations such as Japan and the EC. Furthermore, during the farm talks in Geneva on February 13–15, 1989, the United States expressed its readiness to explore short-term measures and to consider the propositions made by other nations. Although substantial differences remained, in April 1989 all parties agreed to negotiate "substantial progressive reductions" in agricultural subsides over the long run, aiming at a "fair and market-oriented system." Participants also agreed not to introduce new protective measures and to try to cut subsidies by an unspecified amount by 1990.

Thus, Japan may be able to realize, at least partially, its negotiation objectives which include the revision of the GATT code to allow nations with low food self-sufficiency to maintain some import restrictions, the assurance of the continuity of food supplies in case of temporary worldwide shortages, the gradual phasing out of export subsidies, and the maintenance of agricultural subsidies that do not adversely distort trade. Given the domestic social, economic, and political considerations, these objectives reflect a realistic assessment of how far Japan can go in removing subsidies and restrictions on agricultural imports. While the United States may disagree with these goals, the EC is more than likely to support them because they are similar to its own objectives.

Declining Industries

In addition to agriculture, the Japanese economy has other weak areas. These consist of industries which have experienced structural problems, mainly due to the major increase in the cost of energy and raw materials obtained from abroad, and lower demand for their products in Japan and throughout the world. Most are producers of basic materials as, for example, petrochemicals, fertilizer, paper, and aluminum, but others such as shipbuilding and steel are also included. In accord with changes in the world economy, they must be restructured to survive in the long run.

Government assistance to depressed industries is not new in Japan. It began with the recession cartels which, during the 1970s, allowed companies in an industry plagued by a temporary decrease in demand to reduce output systematically rather than to engage in destructive price competition. However, in time, MITI found that such short-term measures were no longer adequate because a number of industries became subject to long-term excess capacity problems.

As a result, MITI proposed the Temporary Measures Law for the Stabilization of Specific Depressed Industries which the Diet passed in May 1978, and which was in force until 1983. The law was designed to improve the competitiveness of depressed industries through systematic cutbacks of excess capacity. Industries identified as structurally depressed received antitrust exemption to do this according to a plan developed by MITI which was based on supply and demand projections, and included proposed cutbacks concerning surplus plant and equipment. By 1983, six industries producing 14 different products were authorized under the law to make the necessary adjustments.[13] In May 1983, the Diet renewed the law because the 1979 oil price crisis and economic recession of 1980–82 interfered with the restructuring schedule. Renamed the Temporary Measures Law for the Structural Adjustment of Specific Industries, it put more emphasis on revitalization than the previous version. Quite controversial throughout the years, the law was allowed to expire on June 30, 1988, thus removing another concern that industrialized nations in general and the United States in particular had about Japan's industrial policies.

According to the expired law, an industry was designated as structurally depressed if the majority of its firms lost money and at least two-thirds of them agreed to a restructuring. Once this requirement was satisfied, MITI, together with its Industrial Structure Council, developed a detailed plan the firms had to follow. Furthermore, if necessary, MITI could ask industry members to form a cartel to reduce capacity. The industries included produced mostly basic materials, although, at various times, others, such as sugar refining, were also designated. The 1983 legislation covered 26 different products, including 11 holdovers from the original law, but by the time the measure expired in 1988, the list was down to 13 products.

Firms in the designated industries could receive loan guarantees to ease the problems of scrapping plant and equipment, and could also obtain low-cost funds through the Japan Development Bank to introduce new technologies and products and to increase production and marketing efficiency. Modernization and the reduction of capacity were also promoted through tax laws, but no direct operating subsidies were provided. Following the expiration of the law, industries facing declining demand for their products are now on their own, although an April 1987 law provides some assistance to firms who lost their international competitiveness due to the sharp appreciation of the yen. The aid is designed to promote the switch from exports to producing for and selling in the domestic marketplace.

One of the industries facing severe problems is coal mining, which has lost its competitive edge against foreign coal producers because of large price differentials due to the combined effects of the global coal glut, lower oil prices, and the rapid appreciation of the yen. In September 1985, MITI established the Coal Mining Council, which, after lengthy deliberations, came to the conclusion that a scaling down of the industry is unavoidable. This finding is in accord with the recommendations made by the Maekawa Commission, which proposed that industries with declining international competitiveness be permitted to scale down to promote the international division of labor. The Commission specifically called for a "sizeable reduction in the domestic output of coal" and argued that coal imports be increased.

In 1960, Japan produced approximately 50 million metric tons of coal annually. By 1970 the volume declined to 32 million tons, and by FY 1985 the country imported 94 million tons, or 85 percent of its need from Australia, Canada, South Africa, the United States, the Soviet Union, and the People's Republic of China, by then all lower cost producers than the domestic mines. It was with the continually sharp appreciation of the yen and this high degree of import penetration ratio in mind that MITI officials developed an industry restructuring plan by 1986. It called for a reduction of production in steaming coal from 16.4 million metric tons in FY 1985 to less than 10 million tons by 1991, and that of coking coal for the steel industry from the 1986 level of 2.9 million metric tons to zero by the same year. Moreover, the plan indicated that eight of the country's 11 mines would gradually have to be closed down.

The major reason for the decline in the competitiveness of domestic coal producers is that coal lies in deep, widely staggered veins, and labor costs are very high. Depending on the mine involved and the quality as well as the type of coal in question, Japanese coal was priced around $170 or more per metric ton in 1988. In contrast, imported coal averaged $60–$66 per ton, or less than half the price of the domestic variety. Naturally, the nation's steel and electric power industries, the major users of coal, are not willing to pay the extremely high price for domestic coal. Thus, local collieries, a number of which run monthly deficits between $1 or $2 million, have no choice but to close down operations which were the economic mainstay of many small communities for decades.

To ease the transition to the final close-down, the Japanese government began to purchase unsold local coal in 1987. By buying such coal and selling it back at a later date, the government, for all practical purposes, provided coal producers with an interest-free loan. While this is a helpful interim measure, the government intends to stop such assistance by April 1992.

The government also provides financial assistance to the small communities built around troubled mines, but such funds are going to be sharply reduced after the next census in 1990. Many of the previously thriving communities are gradually turning into ghost-towns due to a rapid decline in population, particularly due to the departure of young men and women. Thousands of families experienced serious financial problems because the head of the household lost his job, and no other employment opportunities exist in the dying regions.

The painful social consequences of the restructuring plan were well illustrated by the closing down of a colliery of the Mitsubishi Coal Mining Company in November 1986. The colliery, the oldest in the country, was losing an estimated $2.6 million each month, with its cummulative deficit reaching $225 million by 1986. While the economic reasons for the shutdown were compelling, it resulted in the dismissal of 900 workers in a region where jobs were always scarce.

The restructuring of the industry, however, is not necessarily resulting in higher coal imports from the United States. American coal, while less expensive than Japanese coal, is not always price-competitive with Australian, Canadian, Soviet, or Chinese coal. Although due to a large number of miners' strikes in Australia and the rapid recovery of the Japanese steel industry in 1988, U.S. coal exports increased sharply, the long-term outlook for American coal is still modest. Steel producers, for example, view U.S. coal as a "swing source," that is, a source they can quickly turn to or away from depending on the supply conditions in the more price-competitive nations such as Australia or Canada and in response to the demand for steel. U.S. coal, however, may obtain a more stable market-share if the slight price-upturn of 1988 continues into the 1990s due to the closing of domestic mines, the strong global economic expansion, and the expected shutdown of a number of European mines in 1989–1990. Pressure by the U.S. government on Japan to reduce the huge bilateral trade imbalance through the increased purchase of American coal may, of course, also help.

Steel manufacturing was another industry in deep trouble during the 1985–1988 period due to the sharp appreciation of the yen and the loss of market-share to the producers from the Republic of Korea, Brazil, and Taiwan who had lower labor costs and more modern facilities. To survive, Japanese steel producers decided to cut the work force drastically, to integrate or close down production facilities, to reduce fixed costs, and to insure profits even if sales volume decreased. Such strategy was based on increased product diversification and the manufacture of high value-added products involving new technologies.

The reduction of the labor force was a painful process. For example, Nippon Steel reduced the number of employees from 64,000 to 57,000 between March 1987 and March 1989; Kawasaki Steel moved from 24,000 employees to 18,500 during the same time period, while Kobe Steel cut the size of the workforce from 26,000 to 20,000 over the same two-year period, to mention only a few of the major steel manufacturing corporations. Because the labor unions reject layoffs, the workforce reduction was done mostly through retirement and diversification into new lines of business. Nippon Steel, for instance, established more than 50 new subsidiaries beginning in 1986 and is transferring approximately 13,000 steel workers to these new businesses such as urban redevelopment, telecommunications, electronics, new basic materials, and biotechnology. The scope of diversification is such that management expects to boost the sales of the new businesses to equal the Y2 trillion ($16 billion) steel sales by 1995. To ease the transfer process, Nippon Steel picks up any wage differentials, and the welfare benefits are continued at the new place of employment without change or interruptions.

A major part of the industry restructuring process consisted of the closing down of plants throughout the country. Nippon Steel reduced its 12 plants to eight by the end of 1988 so as to bring down fixed costs to approximately 30 percent of the 1986 level. While some of the communities were negatively affected by the shutdowns, the results were not as painful as in the coal-mining communities because the transfor of the steel workers to new businesses was well conceived and executed. Moreover, the company has plans for the land freed by the mill or furnace closings as about 25 percent of the 70 million square meters freed has good redevelopment potential.

The steel industry survived the restructuring process, so far, not only quite well but, by 1988, also quite profitably. The turnaround was caused by a growing world-demand for steel, increased production efficiencies, the introduction of new technologies, and the effectiveness of the diversification strategy. According to industry experts, the steelmakers' major concern by the end of 1988 was no longer how to boost demand and how to restore competitiveness, but how to invest or spend the recently generated cash. Many producers reached the point where previously developed but not-yet-implemented restructuring programs were placed on temporary hold. At the same time industry executives agreed that much of the current capacity still has to be reduced in the long run and that the number of workers employed still must be brought down. The Nomura Research Institute, for example, predicted in 1988 that the competitive position of Japanese and South Korean steel producers may be equalized once the Japanese corporations complete their restructuring, particularly the paring down of the headquarters workforce. It is interesting to note that to restore their global competitive positions many of the steel manufacturing companies have also established joint ventures with American companies in the United States. The growing presence of Japanese car manufacturers in America provides excellent opportunities for such ventures in which the two sides combine their differing but complementary manufacturing skills.

Japan's shipbuilding industry is also undergoing structural changes due to declining demand for new shipping capacity. Worldwide shipbuilding orders reached more than 34 million gross tons in 1975 but rapidly declined to 12 million in 1987. Japan's market share was reduced from 17 million gross tons or approximately 50 percent to 6.7 million tons or less than 50 percent during the same time period. To address the problem, the Transportation Ministry's advisory group, the Shipping and Shipbuilding Rationalization Council, recommended a drastic reduction of production capacity in the summer of 1986 which was completed by early 1988. The number of shipbuilding companies with 5,000 gross tons of capacity or more was reduced from the original 44 to 26, organized into eight rather than 21 groups. The resulting 24 percent reduction in output was achieved through a cartel arrangement which the Fair Trade Commission (FTC) authorized under Section 24 of the nation's Antimonopoly Law for both FY 1987 and FY 1988.

However, by the middle of 1988 it became apparent that additional capacity reductions would be necessary if the industry were to survive into the next century. After a review of the various options, the Shipping and Shipbuilding Rationalization Council recommended several possible measures. These included additional concentration through increased cooperation among shipbuilding firms, international cooperation with the leading shipbuilding nations such as the Republic of Korea and the Members of the European Community, introduction of new technologies to manufacture more high value-added ships, and the development of new diversification opportunities. Transportation Ministry officials pointed out that the industry still has a workforce that is equivalent to 3 million gross tons of production while there is only a little over 2 million of work to be done. Thus, in September 1988 Mitsubishi Heavy Industries Ltd. announced that it would lay off 1,900 of the 6,000 employees in its shipbuilding division beginning in April 1989. However, Mitsubishi executives emphasized that those not scheduled for retirement would not be fired but transferred to other divisions or affiliated companies.

To support the industry's survival efforts the FTC in the spring of 1989 authorized the continuation of the FY 1987 and FY 1988 cartel arrangement for FY 1989, ending in March 1990. the arrangement involved 24 shipbuilding companies which are allowed to limit the total combined volume of merchant vessel construction to 2.4 million gross tons. About the same time as the FTC decision became known, the Shipbuilders Association of Japan, which oversees the cartel, announced that approximately half of the newly authorized output has been allocated to the seven largest shipbuilding companies and to the other half of the 17 other members of the cartel. But by September 1989 the FTC decided that the industry was recovering so rapidly that the cartel was no longer justified and instructed the 24 companies to disband it by November 1 of the same year, five months ahead of the original March 31, 1990 termination date.

While the overall Japanese industrial restructuring policy appears to enable some of the declining industries to partially restore competitiveness, the social cost of these policies is quite high. Employment statistics published in 1988 have shown that while the nation's overall unemployment rate fell to 2.4 percent in July 1988, unemployment in the regions affected by the closing down of mines and plants as, for example, in Kyushu and Hokkaido, remains higher than 3 percent. Moreover, over 50 percent of the workers laid off tend to be middle-aged and lacking in the skills and disposition necessary to take jobs in new industries such as biotechnology which are looking for younger and more flexible employees. A forecast issued by the Labor Ministry in January 1988 predicted that the mismatching of job opportunities and the middle-aged is going to get worse until about 1995. The report also pointed out that if the economy continues to grow at a 4 percent annual rate through 1995, unemployment is likely to remain at approximately 2.5 to 2.9 percent, but even such solid economic growth cannot resolve the problem of the mismatch between available positions and the qualifications of job seekers.

The government's policy of supporting structurally depressed and declining industries, particularly until the June 1988 expiration of the Temporary Measures law for the Structural Adjustment of Specific Industries, was controversial both at home and abroad. The FTC, charged with the enforcement of the anti-trust laws, has often tried to prevent MITI from realizing its restructuring plans. It argued that MITI's efforts were in vain because, due to market forces, the capacity reductions would have occurred anyway, and that the government-orchestrated cutbacks allowed inefficient producers to survive. Other domestic critics questioned the long-range relevance of the program that called for only capacity reductions in industries that lost their international competitiveness and, therefore, should be phased out. Doubts were also expressed about the ability of the government to help industries plagued by declining demand or high labor costs, magnified by the appreciation of the yen.

Criticism from abroad, particularly the United States, was even more vocal. High level American government officials often described the Japanese government's involvement in the restructuring processes as "critical," "thorough," and "definitive," implying that such involvement violated international trade laws. The Americans supported by the European Community, argued that the restructuring policies were inherently import-restrictive and, thus, added to the trade imbalances. The various joint activities such as officially sanctioned cartels and the "administrative guidance" issued by the different ministries, enable the high-cost domestic producers to keep low-cost imports out of the country. To this the Japanese responded by saying that the restructuring law did not contain any import-restriction clause and the low import penetrations levels in the affected industries were not by themselves proof of restrictions. MITI and the other ministries also denied that their administrative guidance" resulted in protectionism.

The validity of some of the domestic and foreign criticism notwithstanding, Japan's record in dealing with structurally depressed and declining industries, on the whole, is impressive. While a number of the industries are still struggling years after they began the restructuring process, the country has been spared most of the traumatic socioeconomic dislocations that depressed industries created in other industrialized nations as, for example, the United Kingdom. The Japanese realize that structural changes are necessary, but they try to minimize the human suffering normally associated with capacity reductions. In their view, while certain industries such as coal mining have to be phased out regardless of the consequences, their attempts to restructure others are socially and politically justified.

Administrative and Fiscal Reform

The problem of large government and rapidly increasing expenditures together with deficit financing is shared by all industrialized nations. Since Japan is no exception, former Prime Minister Nakasone made reduction in the size of government and the reestablishment of sound fiscal conditions, or administrative and fiscal reform, a centerpiece of his domestic policy program while in office.

Administrative and fiscal reform has a long, although not entirely successful, history in Japan. In the early 1960s, Prime Minister Ikeda created the first Special Administrative Research Council headed by a well-known businessman, but resistance from the bureaucracy and special interest groups prevented any reforms. Prime Minister Suzuki, at the recommendation of Nakasone, who served in his cabinet, formed the Second Special Administrative Research Council to explore ways to introduce reforms in 1981. When Nakasone took over as Prime Minister, he formed the Administrative Reform Promotion Council in July 1983 to monitor the implementation of the reform measures recommended in the Research Council's five previous reports.

Nakasone's concern about *Zaisei Saiken* (Fiscal Reform) were rooted in the mid-1970s when as a consequence of the recession triggered by the oil crisis in 1973, the government started its deficit financing binge. Although the Public Finance Law prohibits budget deficits, the government got by this through a loophole in the law which allows deficits generated by appropriations for investments such as public works, as long as the Diet approves. Bonds issued for this purpose were known as "construction bonds," and they accounted for about 50 percent of the deficit while the other half was comprised of deficit bonds which are sold to cover current expenditures. Beginning in the 1970s, both types of bonds were issued in increasing quantities to stimulate growth. Moreover, during subsequent years, social security outlays also increased rapidly because the government wanted to raise the standards of a system which was no longer adequate for an industrialized nation.

Deficits increased dramatically when in 1978, at the urging of the United States, Prime Minister Fukuda resorted to large-scale deficit spending on public works to expand domestic demand in accordance with the "locomotive thesis" which proposed that the Federal Republic of Germany and Japan stimulate their economies to pull the world out of the recession. This action together with increased fiscal spending in subsequent years unhinged the nation's fiscal structure. Large amounts of "deficit-financing" bonds were issued, and by FY 1986, total accumulated debt amounted to more than $900 billion, the annual deficit to $70 billion; interest alone represented 20.9 percent of the budget, and total government debt as a percentage of GNP reached new heights. By international comparison, Japan was ahead of the United States and all other major industrialized countries except Italy. Table 4–2 illustrates this point.

In light of these developments, throughout the years Prime Minister Nakasone stood firm on his commitment to fiscal reform. He pledged to eliminate reliance on deficit financing bonds by FY 1990; however, by late 1986, this had become a very difficult task. According to MOF officials, the original target was to cut bond issues by more than $7 billion each year beginning in 1984, but the actual reductions were around $3.7 billion in FY 1984, $4 billion in FY 1985, and $3.2 billion in FY 1986. In order to moderate the high deficits, the Prime Minister also attacked three of the major financial drains, the so-called three Ks: *Kokutetsu* (Japan National Railroads), *kome* (rice), and *kenpo* (the medical insurance system). Privatization of the railroads (discussed in the next chapter) became a reality in April 1987, and this was a major success because for some time, the railroads generated an annual deficit of nearly $10 billion. The high cost of the medical insurance system had also been, reduced through an increase in payments by the patients for medical services. However, while he was Prime Minister, Nakasone failed to overcome resistance from the *zoku* to reduce the subsidy payments on rice.

TABLE 4-2. Total government debt to GNP ratio in selected countries: 1985

Country	Total government debt to GNP ratio
USA[a]	48.8
Japan[b,c]	52.1
U.K.	49.1[c]
Italy[f]	76.3
France	18.5[f]
F.R. of Germany	21.4

[a] U.S. dollar figures are calculated according to the annual average exchange rates of the IMF, International Financial Statistics.
[b] Fiscal year.
[c] U.S.$1.00 = Y238.54.
[d] End of 1985.
[e] End of March 1985.
[f] 1984
Source: *Japan 1986: An International Comparison* (Tokyo: Keizai Koho Center, 1986), p. 83.

An unexpected tax revenue shortfall of more than $6.5 billion for FY 1986 made the situation even worse. It was the first time in four years that tax revenues had decreased by more than $6.5 billion of that was estimated in the budget for the year. As a consequence, the amount of deficit financing bonds issued for FY 1986 exceeded that for the previous year for the first time in three years. The unexpectedly low tax revenues were the result of a drop in corporate tax receipts due to the declining earnings generated by the sharply appreciated yen.

Prime Minister Nakasone's cautious and austere fiscal policies did not go unchallenged. While he was supported by the Ministry of Finance, the Keidanren, and others, his policies were criticized within the LDP and by a number of private sector economists who forecast a much lower growth rate for FY 1986 and up to 1990 than the 4 percent predicted by the government. One of the private sector economists argued that fiscal austerity was a mistake because healthy public finances could be achieved by the restoration of equilibrium in the economy through an increase in government expenditures, or pump priming.[32] Through simulation he showed that in addition to accommodative monetary policy, reduced personal, and lower corporate income taxes, the government should spend about $13 billion annually on public works between 1986 and 1990 to achieve a growth rate of about 4.4 percent which would restore fiscal health. While he did not make any specific proposals concerning the funding of the tax cuts and the spending increases, he concluded that the fiscal austerity policy is incompatible with the measures which are required to reflate domestic demand, reduce the external imbalances by 1990, and set the economy on its way toward internationalization in accordance with the recommendations of the Maekawa Commission.

The Nakasone government, however, did not change its austere fiscal policies. In December 1986 it announced the FY 1987 budget which envisioned the spending of $335.09 billion, up only 0.02 percent from FY 1986, the smallest increase since FY 1955. Of the total, $201.8 billion was allocated for general expenditures, with the remainder going to debt-servicing and local government funding.

The off-budget fund for loan programs and infrastructure projects, also known as the "second budget," however, was increased by 14.1 percent to $156.58 billion. The source of these funds include deposits in the postal savings bank, pension payments, and proceeds from bond issues. At the same time, public works spending by the central government was decreased by 2.3 percent from FY 1986; this decline, however, was more than offset by the new construction projects planned by local governments. As a consequence, overall public works spending should rise by 5 percent to almost $90 billion. Government officials expected that such spending would provide some stimulation to the economy in the upcoming years.

Government borrowing was expected to amount to $65 billion in FY 1987, down $2.8 billion from the previous fiscal year but still higher than the cuts required to meet the goal of a balanced budget by FY 1990.

While the FY 1987 budget was in keeping with the government's fiscal austerity policy, private economists in Tokyo expressed continued concern about the future of the economy. Most believed that the continual emphasis on fiscal austerity would make the achievement of the expected average 4 percent growth rate during the 1986–1990 period virtually impossible.

In contrast to the 0.02 percent increase in the FY 1987 budget, which was the lowest rise in 32 years, the FY 1988 budget was expansionary in that it called for an increase in spending of 4.8 percent, the largest in six years. The increase was engineered by Nakasone's successor, Prime Minister Takeshita, who responded to the pressures from the United States and other nations to stimulate domestic demand, to bolster imports, and to reduce the large current account surplus. Significantly, the deficit was estimated to be down by 16 percent from FY 1987, but the government still financed this shortfall with the so-called deficit-financing bonds. Nonetheless, by the beginning of the FY 1988 the accumulated long-term government debt stood at 51.9 percent of GNP, down from the 52.1 percent in calendar year 1985, as shown in table 4–2 but still well above the ratio of the United States which showed a decline from 48.8 percent to 41.1 percent during the same time period. The general expenditures of the FY 1988 budget included a 20 percent increase in public works spending, the steepest rise since 1979. This was made possible in large party by the government's continuing sale of shares in the privatized Nippon Telegraph and Telephone Company (NTT), generating more than $10 billion. Of this, more than 90 percent was earmarked to the public works projects. Additional revenue was generated by surging corporate profits thanks to the growing economy which began to shake off the effects of the yen appreciation. It is noteworthy that due to the unexpected windfall in revenues, the FY 1988 budget negotiations proceeded, without major tensions and battles, in an unusually relaxed mood compared to preceding years when the policy of *zaisei saiken* was discussed in a much more tense setting.

Based on the continuing strong economic growth in 1988 and a sharp rise in revenues, the government called for a 6.6 percent increase in the FY 1989 budget, the largest rise since 1981. However, the budget was seen by private economists and businessmen as only mildly expansionary or even neutral, because it provided for only a modest increase in public works expenditures. This was due to the fact that the economy did not absorb well the large increase in public works spending during FY 1988, and this led to some concern about inflation in general and the effects of such spending in particular. To compensate for the shortfall, the separately financed Fiscal Investment and Loan Program (FILP) capital (or "second") budget, however, was increased by 9.3 percent, most of which went to public works projects. The strong surge in expected revenues also led to a sharp increase of 22.6 percent in the allocation for revenue-sharing with local governments over FY 1988. The tax revenue increase combined with other revenues as, for example, the sale of NTT shares also enabled the government to reduce government bond issues by approximately 20 percent which cut the dependence on borrowing to 11.8 percent of total spending, considerably below FY 1988's ratio of 15.6 percent. As usual, the "supplementary budget" adopted by the cabinet in January 1989 slightly increased the total spending on the general account. Such supplemental budgets have become customary in recent years to stimulate the economy.

A study published by the MOF in early 1989 showed that if general expenditures (national outlays excluding costs of government bond redemptions and the allocations for revenue-sharing with local governments) increase by less than 1 percent on a year-by-year basis over the next two years, realization of the government's *zaisei saiken* plan, without the issuance of deficit-financing bonds by FY 1990, is a possibility. The study was based on the assumption that tax revenues would expand at an annual rate of 5.5 percent and that the current limits on operating outlays could be maintained. Furthermore, a suspension of the transfer of funds from the general to the special account to redeem government bonds was also assumed. It must be noted, however, that while the FY 1988 increase in general expenditures was kept to 1.2 percent over the previous fiscal year, the FY 1989 increase in such expenditures was budgeted at 3.3 percent, considerably higher than the MOF study considered acceptable. Thus, forecasts for the completion of the fiscal reform program by FY 1990 may be too optimistic, at least by the MOF's standards.

Due to the sharp rise in revenues during 1987–1988, the government in 1989 began to trim the amount of debt issues. For example, while in all of FY 1988 it put out 36 issues, between April and October of FY 1989 it placed only 14, a clear indication of a declining trend. Financial analysts were concerned that the reduced bond issues combined with large-scale redemptions of high yield bonds coming due could reduce the liquidity of the bond market. This could put pressure on the profit margins of major Japanese an non-Japanese banks and securities houses because all of these institutions were relying more and more on commissions and income from the increasingly more competitive bond market. In line with such developments, by early 1989 many large Japanese securities houses reported large losses or very limited earnings in bond-trading because as a result of deregulation, both the banks and non-Japanese securities companies have become important competitors. In contrast to such pessimistic views, the MOF took a much more optimistic stance and pointed out that even though deficit-financing bonds are going to be gradually phased out, there would still be a lot of other types of bonds to be traded because the government would continue issuing them in the future as well.

Thus, in spite of the controversy surrounding it, the government's fiscal reform policy was headed toward a successful completion by the early 1990s. The fears expressed in 1986–1987 that a continuation of the policy would make it difficult for the Japanese economy to grow at a 3.5 to 4.5 percent real growth rate, which was considered to be necessary to reduce the current account surplus to a more acceptable level by the early 1990s, seem to have been misplaced.

Notes

1. Industrial Structure Council, *The Vision of MITI Policies in the 1980s* (Tokyo: Ministry of International Trade and Industry, March 1980).

178   THE INTERNATIONALIZATION OF THE JAPANESE ECONOMY

2. Long Term Outlook Committee, Economic Council, Economic Planning Agency, *Japan in the Year 2000* (Tokyo: The Japan Times Ltd., 1983).

3. *Outlook and Guidelines for the Economy and Society in the 1980s* (Tokyo: Economic Planning Agency, August 1983).

4. Industrial Structure Council, Coordination Committee, Planning Subcommittee, *An Outlook for Japan's Industrial Society Towards the 21st Century* (Interim Report Focusing on International Perspective), (Tokyo: Ministry of International Trade and Industry, February 1986).

5. *Japan In the Global Community: Its Role and Contributions on the Eve of the Twenty-First Century*, Report of Roundtable Discussion on "Japan in the Global Community" (Tokyo: Ministry of International Trade and Industry, April 1986).

6. *How Can Japan Contribute to a Healthy World Economy* (Tokyo: Keizai Koho Center, March 1986).

7. *The Report of the Advisory Group on Economic Structural Adjustment for International Harmony* (April 7, 1986), p. 2.

8. *Ibid.*, p. 4.

9. Among others, the $23 billion measures included public works, the promotion of housing construction by individuals, the lowering of electricity and gas rates to pass on the exchange rate gains of the appreciated yen to consumers, and more relief to small-sized and medium-sized enterprises hurt by the stronger yen.

10. See for example, *Business Week* (May 5, 1986), p. 44.

11. For example, Kiichi Miyazawa, one of the Prime Minister's major opponents in the debate over domestic demand stimulation, became Minister of Finance, a position which made it more difficult for him to argue against fiscal austerity because the ministry is one of the major proponents of such policy.

12. *Asahi Evening News* (September 16, 1986), p. 7.

13. Two sociologists have recently challenged most of the current *nihonjinron*. See Ross Mouer and Yoshio Sugimoto, *Images of Japanese Society* (London: KPI Limited, 1986).

14. Karel van Wolferen, "The Enigma of Japanese Power," *op. cit.* pp. 412–413.

15. See, for example, Susumu Ohara, "An Island Unto Itself: The Roots of Japan's International Isolation," *Speaking of Japan* (May 1986), pp. 18–21; also "Thoughts on August 15," *Asahi Shimbun* (August 16, 1986), p. 9.

16. Theodore White, "The Danger of Japan," *The New York Times Magazine* (July 28, 1985), pp. 18–22 + .

17. *The Japan Times* (August 28, 1986), p. 14; *Asahi Shimbun* (August 2, 1986), p. 11.

18. *The Japan Economic Journal* (January 18, 1986), p. 6.

19. *Asahi Evening News* (September 13, 1986), p. 7; and Asahi *Shimbun* (May 20, 1986), p. 11, respectively.

20. *The Japan Economic Journal* (December 13, 1986), p. 6.

21. *Asahi Evening News* (May 22, 1986), p. 3.

22. *The Japan Economic Journal* (October 11, 1986), p. 11, and (November 1, 1986), p. 3.

23. Takashi Hosomi, "The Ugly Japanese," *Tokyo Business Today* (March 1986), p. 8; see also, Masahiko Ishizuka, "New Self-Assertion. But Whither," *The Japan Economic Journal* (October 11, 1986), p. 6; Yoshio Okawara, "Constructive Approaches Are What We Need," *Tokyo Business Today* (November 1986), p. 10; and "The Dangers of Neonationalism," *Tokyo Business Today* (November 1986), pp. 22-26.

24. See, for example, Nathaniel B. Thayer, "Nakasone Is Not a Racist," *The Washington Post* (September 30, 1986), p. A15; and "Japan Under Nakasone: Image of National Pride?" *The New York Times* (September 26, 1986), A13, as well as Carl T. Rowan, "The Real Issue Nakasone Raised," *The Washington Post* (October 7, 1986), p. A17.

25. "Japan's Clout in the U.S.," *Business Week* (July 11, 1988).

26. For a list of these recommendations, see *The Japan Times* (April 24, 1986), p. 1.

27. *Asahi Evening News* (December 20, 1986), p. 7.

28. Ministry of Education (Tokyo, March 1986 and February 1989).

29. The potential benefits of eliminating the beef import system by 1991 were underlined by an FTC investigation of beef trading companies and the Japan Meet Importers Association in the spring of 1989. FTC investigators raided 29 trading companies and found evidence that the firms secretly fixed bidding shares, thereby jacking up retail prices to consumers, practices that violated Japan's Antimonopoly Law. Industry sources charged that in 1987 alone the traders of imported beef pocketed about $15.5 million in unlawful profits by conspiring to raise prices for meat by as much as 10 percent over what it should have been.

30. The Association also claimed that the liberalization of the Japanese rice market would double U.S. exports from the present 18 percent world-export share to 36 percent.

31. The industries included, among others, nonferrous metals, shipbuilding, steel textiles, and chemicals.

32. Susumu Kato, "Three Scenarios for Economic Policy," *Economic Eye* (September 1986), pp. 19–22.

5 SELECTED TRENDS IN THE DOMESTIC ECONOMY

While the Japanese government made the decision to internationalize the domestic economy through the gradual implementation of the Maekawa Commission's recommendations as well as other policy options, a number of economic trends were already underway. Some of these were unleashed on a short notice by the sharp appreciation of the yen during 1985–1986. Others were introduced earlier by the government, and others still were subtly initiated by fundamental socioeconomic forces which were shaped by the Japanese political, social, and cultural environment, but which by and large are common to highly developed nations.

The extent and rate at which the economic trends promote the internationalization process is difficult to determine. They are, however, instrumental to the process and are an integral part of what some astute observers of global economic developments have referred to as the emergence of the "triad power," or the convergence of the economies and markets of the United States, Western Europe, and Japan.[1]

Economic Trends

At the beginning of 1986, Japan faced a much stronger yen and slowing exports; nevertheless, the government estimated an annual economic growth rate of 4 percent in real terms. This optimistic rate was predicated on a substantial increase in domestic demand; official forecasters were certain that prices would remain stable and real income would increase as commodity and other import prices declined as a result of the higher value of the yen. The optimism seemed justified by the surprising fourth quarter results of 1985 when the economy grew at a healthy, inflation-adjusted rate of 1.7 percent, or at an annual pace of 7.2 percent; the 1.7 percent rate was accelerated from the July-September quarter, when the economy had expanded a more modest 0.7 percent. Domestic demand accounted for 1.5 percentage points of the 1.7 percent growth during the July-September 1985 period, with external demand accounting for remaining 0.2 percent share.

The last quarter figures for 1985 were a surprise to most economists, who had been expecting sluggish growth as a result of a slowdown in exports and the sudden appreciation of the yen following the Group-of-Five (G-5) agreement in September 1985. Even government economists conceded that the statistics did not accurately portray the state of the economy. A case in point was the large increase in inventories which in the last quarter of 1985 rose by 31 percent from the previous quarter, when they dropped 21 percent. Although most of the blame for this was placed on the yen's appreciation, which severely hurt export-oriented industries, the increase happened before the full effects of the yen's sharp rise were felt.

As the yen moved from Y170 to Y160, deflationary effects of the appreciation became more visible, and the calls for stimulation of the domestic economy were becoming louder both at home and abroad. Since the government was committed to fiscal austerity, increased public spending could not be used to stimulate domestic demand. Thus, the attention turned to monetary policy. Eventually, the Bank of Japan decided to reduce the official discount rate on October 31, 1986, for the fourth time that year; the first three reductions had taken place in January, March, and August, and between these cuts, the discount rate fell to 3.0 percent per annum.

The central bank's action was notable because it gave the impression that monetary policy, which had remained steady for so long, was beginning to show signs of flexibility. The discount rate drops were orchestrated through close multilateral consultations with the United States, the Federal Republic of Germany, as well as other nations, as agreed the previous year in New York. This move was also a signal to the rest of the world that Japan was serious about stimulating domestic demand.

While the reductions in the discount rate eased the burden on small businesses, many small exporters were badly affected by the yen appreciation; in 1986 alone, more than 430 businesses were forced to close their doors. Corporate profits also plummeted causing companies to slash their labor forces wherever possible, and thus unemployment rose slightly to 2.9 percent in the first quarter of 1986, when the economy showed its worst performance in 11 years. Moreover, according to a Bank of Japan survey, manufacturing profits for 1986 were expected to drop 22 percent from 1985 levels. The private sector forecasters revised the optimistic 4 percent economic growth rate downward to 1.8 percent, less than half of what it had been the previous year.

While most of Japan's large corporations were cushioned by large profits from 1984 and the first half of 1985, and were thus able to weather the rough economic climate, it became clear by mid-1986 that flexible monetary policy alone would not be sufficient to reverse the ominous trends. Thus, in an attempt to revitalize the economy, on September 19, 1986, the government announced a $23 billion set of Comprehensive Economic Measures aimed primarily at public works projects.

The reflationary package had been championed by MITI, which insisted that a sizeable increase in public spending was necessary to boost domestic demand and thereby, to reduce trade conflicts with Japan's major trading partners. This action has long been resisted by the Ministry of Finance, which spent the past five years trying to bring public spending under control. MOF officials wanted fiscal measures which were consistent with the goals of the fiscal austerity policy, such as the reallocation of funds to finance construction, regulatory changes to encourage private investment, measures to pass on the benefits of the yen's appreciation to consumers, and increased aid to small businesses hurt by the strong yen. Even so, MOF officials did not believe that expanding domestic demand could significantly reduce the trade surplus.[2]

When the Comprehensive Economic Measures were announced in September 1986, it was not clear how the government planned to raise the $23 billion to revitalize the economy; by October 31, the government announced a supplementary budget, cutting back the original FY 1986 budget by $1.6 billion and also adding a $3.75 billion construction bond issue to help finance public works. The expected shortfall in revenue due to lower individual and corporate earnings, customs, and other revenues was covered by reserves from FY 1985 and savings from other expenditures. The total amount to be spent, including additional capital expenditures by the private sector, added up to the largest package of this type in Japanese financial history. Nevertheless, many questioned whether this was too little, too late.

Thus, due to the appreciating yen by the second half of 1986, the mood in the country was distinctly pessimistic and the economy began to slow down. Business circles, government, and private sector economists were concerned that regardless of the government's reflationary efforts, the economy could go into a tailspin. However, in the end, the efforts of Japanese manufacturing companies to increase efficiency and thereby to counter the rising yen, increasing consumption generated by government fiscal policy, and the gradually increasing private investments in plant and equipment resulted in a rapid upswing during FY 1987. This upturn had also been aided by technological innovations, particularly in information technology, by the deregulation of various sectors and by the decline in the price of imported oil and other raw materials which enabled the *kaisha* to obtain the dramatic improvements in efficiency.

The results of FY 1987 were impressive. They economy grew a real 5.2 percent, and while exports were sluggish, domestic demand increased in response to a rise in government spending and tax reductions. The ratio of the current account surplus to nominal GNP declined from 4.5 percent in FY 1986 to 3.3 percent, and the unemployment rate fell from 3.1 percent in May 1987 to below 3 percent while prices remained stable.

FY 1988 marked the third year of economic expansion. Real growth continued at a rapid pace fueled by housing, public spending, capital investments, and consumer spending. The latter grew at 5.1 percent, thus sustaining the spending cycle which began a FY 1987 based on the purchase of primarily clothes, durable goods, and services. Prices continued to remain stable, but the decline in the current account surplus slowed down. Merchandise exports began to increase again, and the gains in imports were beginning to level off. While pockets of unemployment, particularly in the coal mining, steel, and ship-building industries, continued, the unemployment rate was down. All in all, by the beginning of FY 1989 relative to the other industrialized nations the Japanese economy was in excellent shape and was about to enter the last decade of the twentieth century with confidence and cautious optimism.

Endaka or the High Yen

The gradually increasing exports in late 1988 and early 1989 reflected the ability of Japan's major manufacturing corporations to maintain their international competitiveness even under the most adverse conditions. While at first most of them responded to the soaring yen of 1986–1987 by turning to *zaitech* i.e., sophisticated stock-and bond-based financial management, to combat the fall in profits, by mid-1987 they were already busily engaged in *risutora* or restructuring.

Just like during the first oil-crisis in 1973, Japan's *kaisha* have responded to the challenge of the appreciating yen with vigor, imagination, and determination. They tried to maintain and, as it turned out, even improve their international competitiveness through concerted efforts to reduce manufacturing costs through a variety of methods. These included work-process changes, labor force reductions through reassignments, the introduction of new manufacturing technologies, pay squeezes, penny-pinching programs, and the increased sourcing of parts and components from abroad, particularly from the Southeast Asian region. Moreover, the *kaisha* also shifted to the manufacture of higher value-added products. Of course, the decline in the price of oil and other imported raw materials due to the soaring yen provided the foundation for the considerable cost savings.

   However, not just the large *kaisha* responded to the challenge. Even many small and medium-sized companies which supply parts to the large corporations under the *shitauke* (subcontracting) system managed to rationalize operations, reduce costs, and, thus, stay competitive. They formed cooperative relationships through which they obtained contracts from the *kaisha* on a joint basis to become somewhat more independent of the large corporations. Of course, a considerable number of small and medium-sized businesses could not handle the challenge and went bankrupt. Others, even including some large corporations, are still struggling to reestablish themselves or have given up on the international marketplace and focus instead on domestic opportunities.

   Nonetheless, overall most major *kaisha* came out of the two-year hiatus "meaner and leaner." By the end of FY 1987, 232 of them showed a 51.4 percent gain in profits and a 5.8 percent increase in sales. While in 1986 a Y140–160 exchange rate to the dollar spelled trouble for many of these corporations, by late 1988 they were ready to remain internationally competitive even at Y105 to the dollar.

   While Japanese industry has undoubtedly responded well to the *risutora* challenge, it is important to point out that the adversity they faced was not as daunting as it is generally believed. According to the International Monetary Fund's (IMF) trade-weighted data on the yen appreciation, in reality Japanese manufacturing companies had more time to adjust than just the 1986–1988 period. During the three years between the fall of 1985 and 1988, the real trade-weighted value of the yen increased by 36 percent, a figure considerably lower than usually mentioned. Taking the entire period between 1980 and 1988, the yen appreciated by 34 percent, or almost the same amount. Thus, during the eight years (1980–1988) while the yen's value periodically fell and rose, the trade-adjusted and inflation-adjusted value of the currency on the average appreciated only 3.7 percent annually.

   Moreover, by reflating the economy through several special "packages" and generous public works spending while keeping inflation and the cost of money low, the Japanese government provided a conducive domestic environment for the *risutora* process. The deregulation of the financial sector added to the opportunities of the *kaisha* by enabling them to replace expensive bank loans with a variety of new financial instruments that helped to reduce the burdens.

Changing Social Stratification

Traditionally, the Japanese have subscribed to the belief that they were overwhelmingly (90 percent) middle class. However, this is changing as wealth and lifestyle differences are leading to a socioeconomic stratification that departs from the homogeneous, self-described, middle-class society.

"The White Paper on National Life," issued in November 1988 by the Economic Planning Agency (EPA), publicized the growing economic disparities under the term *kakusa* (differential or gap). *Kakusa* was given great attention in Japan, for the term suggested an unexpected departure from the country's presumed equality. The evidence for such a departure comes largely from the changed consumption habits among the rich, rather than from extensive shifts in the spending patterns across all income groups. The 1988 Ministry of Labor's "Trends in Household Expenditure," for example, revealed that only the top quintile in income experienced a growth in expenditure in 1987. This group's spending increased by 4.6 percent, which exceeded its real income growth of 3.6 percent. However, the remaining 80 percent did not achieve gains in either income or expenditures, since their real incomes grew by only 0.6 percent, while their expenditures actually declined by 0.6 percent. These results suggest a growing economic gap between the wealthy and the majority of Japanese.

Real estate is a major source of these new class divisions due to the tremendous rise in land prices and unsatisfactory housing conditions. The EPA's "1988 White Paper on Economic Life" indicated that between 1985 and 1987, the 20 percent of households owning the most valuable pieces of land experienced a 180 percent increase in the average value of their property to Y98,640,000 ($759,000); this was nine times larger than the value of property held by people in the middle 40 percent of land owners. During the same period, the gap in land values between the top 20 percent and the middle groups in Tokyo increased from a five-fold difference in 1985 to a more than eight-fold difference in 1987. These rises have created multimillionaires out of many people, who have used their newfound wealth to engage in conspicuous consumption of expensive luxury and imported products. People who have not benefited from the rise in land prices sense a breakdown in the former egalitarianism, leading to a resentment of the extravagant lifestyles of the landed-wealthy.

Housing conditions are another cause of class differences. The price of housing has become onerous for the middle class. In Tokyo's suburbs, the price of an average-sized house has jumped from $70,000 in the mid-1970s to more than $1 million in many instances in 1988, and the construction of an average-sized Japanese house would cost $530,700 for land acquisition and $124,600 for erection of the building. At such prices, homeownership is out of reach for most newly formed families other than the wealthiest, although more than 60 percent of the Japanese have obtained their own homes in the past. Recently tighter government restrictions intended to curb speculative deals have helped to slow the escalation in land prices, which rose nationally by only 8.3 percent in 1988 compared to a 21.7 percent increase in 1987.

In addition to real estate and housing, recent changes in income and wages have also contributed to rising class differences. At the end of 1988, Rengo, Japan's largest labor organization, released a survey indicating little change in workers' disposable income between 1985 and 1988. The survey indicated that average disposable income was Y267,000 ($2,136) per month in 1988, an increase of only 3.9 percent or Y10,000 ($80) from 1985. Even as labor's income remained static, employers pressed for continued wage restraint during the *shunto*, or spring labor offensive, when unions negotiate for wage increases. *Nikkeiren* (Japanese Federation of Employers' Associations) regularly advocated lower wage settlements in order to avoid price increases that could reduce domestic consumption and hurt the international competitiveness of industries. At the same time, employers sought productivity improvements, cost reductions, and increased work time from employees to maintain and improve competitiveness. There existed an expectation that labor would sacrifice and reduce its demands for the welfare of the nation and the company. During the mid-1980s, wage increases in the range of 3.5 to 4.5 percent were consistent with such employer objectives. For the 1989 *shunto*, however, *Rengo* sought wage increases of 6 to 8 percent, but eventually settled for a 5.2 percent pay hike.

Results of various national surveys have also detected rising dissatisfaction among the general population. An EPA study in 1988 found that 27.5 percent of respondents were dissatisfied with their lives, an increase from 15.1 percent in 1984. In the same study, the proportion of people who were satisfied declined from 64.2 percent in 1984 to 43.2 percent in 1988. The respondents suggested that their lives could be improved through lower prices, tax reform, and reduction in work hours. Another study released by the Prime Minister's Office in January 1989 found that seven of ten Japanese do not believe that they live an affluent life. Heavy tax burdens and social security premiums, long working hours, unsatisfactory housing, and high prices were sources of dissatisfaction for this group of respondents. The Recruit scandal of 1988–1989 was another cause of public disenchantment. The scandal fed the middle-class's sense of gradual exclusion from wealth. While still in the nascent stage, the appearance of inequality and class differences and the consequent fraying of the social consensus has led to attitudinal changes. The ultimate effects of these changes are not yet clear, but the deterioration in social cohesion is potentially one of the most unsettling results of the economy's internationalization.

Consumer Market Trends

During the post-World War II years Japan's rapid economic growth was focused on the rebuilding of the economy and the development of the international competitiveness of selected industries. Domestic consumption needs were, by and large, ignored, and most Japanese thought of themselves as producers rather than consumers. This attitude shaped the propensity to save which was motivated by a readiness to sacrifice current consumption for future industrial development. Thus, the Japanese reputation as very demanding consumers is rooted in their traditional desire to purchase the best possible quality products and services within the constraints of a tight household budget characterized by high levels of savings.

By 1987, Japan achieved the highest GNP per capita in the world, $23,022, compared to $18,163 for Americans at the appreciated exchange rate. Yet in terms of what that income buys—in purchasing-power parity terms (PPP)—the Japanese are not nearly so affluent. Balassa and Noland estimated their per capita PPP income to be only $7,302 in 1987 compared with $9,009 for Americans.[3] Figure 5–1 provides a comparison of GDP per capita at prevailing exchange rates and at computed PPP levels in 1987 for a number of countries; the lower PPP of Japan is quite revealing.

The underlying price differentials are evident in a number of areas. Housing costs are the most noteworthy. The purchase of a three-room 700-square-foot apartment in Tokyo required monthly mortgage payments of $2,200, or 57 percent of a typical family's gross income in 1988. Construction of a new two-story house was out of reach for most people, with annual payments of $51,538, or 24 percent more than the average after-tax income of a Tokyo salaried worker. Renting was no better, with an average monthly rent of $1,430 compared to $1,150 in New York.

Table 5–1 from the EPA's 1988 "White Paper on the Economy" shows the price differences between Tokyo and New York with respect to a number of selected products. The data indicate that basic food products are considerably more expensive in Tokyo, but consumer durable goods are also

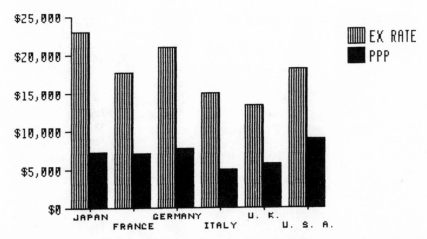

Figure 5-1.   Per Capita GNP of Selected Countries (at 1987 exchange rates and purchasing power parity (PPP) rates). *Source*: Data from Bela Balassa and Marcus Noland, *Japan in the World Economy* (Washington, D.C.: Institute for International Economics, 1988), p. 4.

more expensive, as are utilities, entertainment, and services. Prices are also comparatively higher for imports than in other industrialized countries. In early 1989, MITI found that import prices for the same products were 30 to 60 percent higher in Japan than in foreign countries. Travel abroad has raised doubts about the domestic prices as Japanese tourists have been astonished to find Japanese electronic goods selling at lower prices in, for example, New York, than at home. A joint U.S. Department of Commerce and MITI study of comparative prices in the two nations published in November 1989 provided additional confirmation of the price differentials. Comparing 122 brand name products, the study found that the Japanese prices were higher for 84 and the American prices for 38 products. An interesting finding of the study was that of the 27 electronic products considered 18 were less expensive in Japanese discount houses. In addition, studies by both the EPA and the Bank of Japan revealed that barriers within the distribution system have inhibited price declines on imported products that would have contributed to further expansion of imports. There has also been a growing awareness that Japan has an inadequate infrastructure with improvements needed in roads, sewerage, bridges, schools, and other facilities. The recognition of these "quality-of-life" problems contributes to the currently popular Japanese self-assessment that they are "a rich country of poor people."

Other evidence, however, contradicts this dismal view. For instance, typical Japanese housing space is small in comparison with America's, but

TABLE 5-1. Price differences between Tokyo and New York: 1987 (price in Japanese yen)

Item	Unit	Tokyo	New York
Pork	grams, 100	146	96
Onion	Per Kg.	144	104
Banana	Per Kg.	229	106
Bread	Per Kg.	371	293
Whiskey	One Bottle	3,569	1,168
Subcompact car	Car, 1900–2000 cc	1,941,000	1,181,856
Color TV set	Set, 20 inch	125,600	62,615
Color film	Roll	535	364
Cassette tape	One pack	357	177
Beef	Grams, 100	354	141
Gasoline	One liter	125	38
Kerosine	Eighteen liters	872	542
Electricity	Per month, 200 KWH	4,863	3,711
Water	Per month, 30 cubic meters	3,735	1,485
Bus fare	Minimum bus fare	160	128
Movie theater	Per Admission	1,492	830
Haircut	Per haircut	2,755	1,816

Source: *White Paper on the Economy, 1988* (Tokyo: Economic Planning Agency, 1988), p. 87.

it is about equivalent in size to the average European home. Japan is relatively crime free, and there are no appalling inner city neighborhoods as in the United States. Unemployment is relatively low, people are well-educated, and life expectancy is longer than in the rest of the developed world. The Japanese also sense that, in spite of their self-assessment, they are now a prosperous people and that the country's economic progress has served their living standard quite well. The advent of the Heisei era is also expected to demonstrate an upgrading of lifestyle with a diversified demand for quality goods among consumers. The increased use of microelectronics among corporations is expected enable the production of higher value-added goods to satisfy these consumer interests. Of course, the ultimate answer to the question of the adequacy of domestic living standards can be given only in another five to ten years when the shift from export-led to domestic demand-led growth is completed and its effects are fully experienced by the Japanese people.

Consumer Spending

A number of changes occurring in Japan are leading to increased consumption. Economists and marketing experts have detailed various developments that suggest new behaviors and attitudes which are contributing to a more consumer-oriented society. This is illustrated by the graph in figure 5–2 which depicts the interactive effects of domestic demand and exports on GNP growth. While domestic demand and exports had an additive impact on GNP growth prior to 1986, in 1987 and 1988 domestic demand growth exceeded GNP growth, compensating for declines in exports. The main elements of this domestic growth have been consumer spending, a housing boom, and increased plant and equipment investment expenditures. In 1987, housing starts, for example, increased by 18.4 percent which also induced an increase in spending on consumer durables. In 1988 rising wages increased workers' purchasing power, helping to boost consumer spending which contributed 2.8 points to the economy's 5.7 percent real growth. Further, increased consumption continued into 1989, fueled first by early spring purchases of durable goods prior to the introduction of the consumption tax, the abolition of luxury taxes which made expensive items more attractive, and increased cash due to a 7.17 percent rise in summer bonuses over the previous year, the largest in nine years. Imports also have grown between 1985 and 1988, increasing by over 50 percent during that three-year period, and, most noteworthy, half of imports are now composed of manufactured goods compared to 31 percent in 1985.

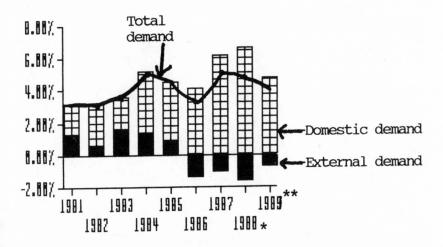

Figure 5–2. GNP Demand components: FY 1981–1989. *Source:* "FY 1989 Outlook for the Japanese Economy," *JEI Report* (Washington, D.C.: Japan Economic Institute, No. 9A, March 3, 1989), p. 9.

However, a more detailed look at recent economic trends casts some doubt on the role of consumption as the key driving force of the economy as publicized in the mass media. An analysis of table 5–2 reveals that consumer spending as a percent of GNP has, in fact, declined from higher levels in the late 1970s, and is now comparable to spending levels in the early 1970s. Furthermore, consumer spending's growth rate has generally been lower than the increase in GNP, exceeding it only during recessionary periods. Thus, it appears that consumer spending serves to prop up GNP during low growth periods, but its importance declines during economic expansions. Japan's savings rate also remains high, indicating that savings behavior is not changing and that the rate remains two to four times higher as a proportion of income than that of the United States. In 1988, for example, average savings of a Japanese worker household reached $69,665

TABLE 5–2.   Private real consumer spending and economic growth: 1970–1987

	Consumer spending as percent of GNP	Contribution of consumer spending to GNP growth	GNP growth rate	Consumer spending growth rate	Saving rate*
1970	57.6	4.1	9.5	6.9	17.9
1971	58.3	3.2	4.3	5.6	17.8
1972	58.7	5.4	8.5	9.3	18.2
1973	59.4	5.4	7.9	9.2	20.4
1974	60.1	−0.2	−1.4	−0.3	23.2
1975	61.1	2.6	2.7	4.4	22.8
1976	60.4	2.1	4.8	3.5	23.2
1977	59.7	2.6	5.3	4.2	21.8
1978	59.9	3.2	5.2	5.4	20.8
1979	60.5	3.9	5.3	6.5	18.2
1980	58.9	0.9	4.3	1.4	17.9
1981	57.5	0.8	3.7	1.3	18.3
1982	58.1	2.4	3.7	4.1	16.5
1983	58.1	1.9	3.2	3.2	16.3
1984	56.8	1.6	5.1	2.7	16.0
1985	55.6	1.6	4.9	2.7	16.0
1986	56.1	1.8	2.4	3.2	16.6
1987	55.8	2.2	4.3	3.9	16.6

*Household savings as a percent of current household disposable income. In contrast, consumer spending represents the real expenditures of households and nonprofit organizations.
    Source: "The Changing Japanese Consumer," *JEI Report* (Washington, D.C.: Japan Economic Institute, No. 45A, December 2, 1988), p. 3.

which came to 1.44 times average yearly income, an increase from the 1.35 figure in 1987. In 1988 the composition of saving also changed, with lower growth for time deposits, the traditional savings vehicle, and vastly higher growth for others such as life insurance which grew by 15 percent and holdings outside financial institutions which rose by 17 percent.

More recent quarterly data presented in table 5–3 paint a similar picture

TABLE 5-3.   Quarterly growth of real GNP and consumer spending: 1987–1988

	Real consumer spending	Real GNP
1987: I	2.0	1.5
II	0.7	0.0
III	1.0	2.0
IV	0.4	1.8
1988: I	2.5	2.7
II	0.6	−1.0
III*	1.3	1.9
IV*	1.2	1.1

*NRI & NCC Co., Ltd. November 1987 Forecast
Source: "The Changing Japanese Consumer," *JEI Report*, (Washington, D.C.: Japan Economic Institute, No. 45A, December 2, 1988), p. 5.

TABLE 5-4.   Indicators of consumer spending: 1981–1988

	Sales of large retail stores		Car registrations	Nominal private consumer spending
	Total	Department stores		
1981	8.0	6.6	0.5	5.7
1982	4.3	3.2	6.0	6.8
1983	3.0	2.2	3.2	5.1
1984	4.2	4.6	−1.3	4.9
1985	3.6	4.4	0.3	5.0
1986	4.6	5.4	1.4	3.7
1987	4.9	5.5	4.1	3.7
1988: I	6.6	7.5	14.7	5.2
II	7.2	7.8	17.4	4.6
III	n.a.	n.a.	11.2	n.a.

Source: "The Changing Japanese Consumer," *JEI Report*, (Washington D.C.: Japan Economic Institute, No. 45A, December 2, 1988), p. 6.

of consumer growth generally less robust than that of the economy as a whole. However, sales growth in the retail sector is more supportive of the publicized growth role of consumption. Table 5–4 shows that retail sales, after growing slower than consumer spending in the early 1980s, have exceeded consumer spending growth in the 1986 to 1988 period.

Thus, actual consumer spending data do not seem consistent with the many reports of a consumer "buying spree" in Japan. The reported examples of increased spending may be temporary or isolated to a relatively small group of consumers. For example, much of the growth in consumer durable goods purchases is attributable to the ten-year buying cycle for such products, and that cycle appears to have peaked so that consumer durable spending may not be sustainable. As far as the consumer groups are concerned, increased consumption appears to be confined to the richest 20 percent of the population composed of the self-employed and professionals. Table 5–5 provides comparisons of "wage-earning households" with "general households," the latter represented by the top income earners. As can be seen, wage-earners have displayed little growth in consumer spending while general households have increased their spending. Thus, it is chiefly the latter group that is buying more luxury goods and imports, and, therefore, at aggregate levels, consumer spending does not seem to have changed a great deal.

TABLE 5–5. Household expenditures: 1985–1987 (year-to-year percent change)

	Wage-earning households Consumer spending	general households Consumer spending
1985	2.4	3.4
1986	1.4	0.6
1987	0.8	4.1

Source: "The Changing Japanese Consumer," *JEI Report*, (Washington, D.C.: Japan Economic Institute, No. 45A, December 2, 1988), p. 7.

Aggregate consumption figures are only partially indicative of changes in purchasing psychology and motivations. The distribution of expenditures among broad product categories provides better insight into consumer behavior trends. In 1987–1988, the proportion spent on food declined, while spending on housing, transportation, education, and recreation increased as a percentage of total household expenditures. These 1987–1988 trends in the

various expenditure categories suggest some variance in consumer preferences, with particularly strong growth for recreation, housing, education,
and medical care, and below average growth for food. Even though these
trends suggest only moderate changes in consumer purchasing habits,
important changes in tastes or preferences may be occurring within
categories which have not yet fully shown up in the statistics.

A special characteristic of Japanese consumer spending is the gift-giving
periods during the year. The two major periods are the oseibo, year-end gift-
giving, and ochugen, mid-summer gift-giving. These two periods coincide
with the distribution of semi-annual corporate bonuses to employees. The
gift-giving is a reflection of Japanese culture, intended to demonstrate
gratitude and to confirm personal relationships. Major retailers estimated
that the 1989 ochugen would increase sales by 10 to 15 percent over the
previous year, spurred largely by higher summer bonuses in 1989. One
phenomenon associated with the gift-giving is the trade in gift certificates,
which are "near-money." Some 50 shops in Tokyo buy certificates at 6 to
8 percent below par value and then resell them. In addition to the traditional
oseibo and ochugen, other gift-giving occasions are also arising. Some of
these are simply borrowed from other nations, such as Christmas, Easter,
Mother's Day, and especially Valentine's Day. A more recent development,
termed the "Anniversary Syndrome," has people celebrating special
personal events such as a first date, acceptance into college, even getting
a driver's license. These anniversaries are seen as a way to put spice back
into life.

The changing consumer

The events leading to an increased consumer orientation derive from both
domestic and international economic policy decisions, particularly the
appreciation of the yen between 1985–1988 and the rise in stock and land
prices. They have given a segment of Japanese society a sense of increased
wealth which has led to increased consumption. Between September 1985
and January 1989, the yen appreciated from Y240 to Y126 against the
American dollar, a considerable increase in value. Japanese manufacturers,
initially fearful that the resulting higher prices would lead to declining
exports, cut costs and, thus, were able to continue serving the international
and also expand output for the domestic market. In this sense, on the
supply side, the yen appreciation generated increased capacity for the
domestic marketplace.

The yen appreciation's impact on the demand side is also noteworthy.

The slow decline in import prices had the two-fold effect of increasing imports and gradually lowering domestic product prices to achieve price competitiveness with foreign goods. As manufacturers increased imports of lower cost raw materials and consumers preferred imported luxury goods, such as BMW and Mercedes Benz automobiles, French perfume and wines, and gourmet foods, imports have risen by 50 percent in volume terms since 1985.

Another source of perceived wealth has been the rise in the value of the stock market and real estate. Japan's stock market has been on a continuous growth path since the 1960s, culminating in the boom of the 1980s, although the market was frequently moved more by speculation than by underlying economic forces. Land prices boomed between 1983 and 1987, increasing by more than 160 percent in Tokyo alone, and the percentage of households in 1988 in greater Tokyo with property worth more than 100 million yen ($769,000 at Y130 = $1.00) expanded from 3 percent to 13 percent of total homeowners. Recently, however, land prices have begun to stabilize due to a variety of government measures. Nonetheless, the growth in stock and real estate values has created the so-called *nyuu ritchi*—new rich, a class composed of property owners, self-employed businessmen, and high level corporate executive, who are freely engaging in conspicuous consumption such as the purchase of expensive jewelry, cars, and country club memberships. As a counterpoint to the *nyuu ritchi*, there are now the *nyuu puaa*—new poor, mostly salaried workers who lack assets and consume more modestly. Compared to the *nyuu ritchi*, whose spending increased by 4.3 percent in 1987, the *nyuu puaa* increased their spending by only 1 percent and their expenditures were for more mundane items such as low-priced imports from the Asian NICs.

Increased asset wealth was accompanied by an increase in real wages which in August 1988 were 4.3 percent higher than the year before. Because productivity growth exceeded wage increases, the potential for wage-push inflation was curtailed. However, the effect of the 3 percent consumption tax effective April 1, 1989, may be problematic in that it coincided with a reduction of commodity taxes on luxury goods, including a number of imports. The new consumption tax applies to the overwhelming majority of everyday purchases while the luxury tax reduction affects a smaller number of products. Therefore, the impact of the consumption tax on aggregate consumption is difficult to predict.

The consumption tax provoked controversy regarding its impact on consumers. Traditionally, the Japanese, while demanding as customers, seek to avoid conflict and have not either individually or as groups challenged businesses regarding pricing or other marketing practices. This lack of antagonism has inhibited the formation of consumer groups similar to those active in other developed countries. But consumer awareness of the marketing system was raised because of the potential effects of the tax. Concerns arose because 70 percent of all companies were exempted from collecting the tax, but these small firms could still raise their prices to the levels of large firms and, thus, earn wind-fall profits. The options for levying the tax, either as a 3 percent addition at the point of sale or as a portion of the selling price, also allows tax-exempt companies to disguise unwarranted price increases. Shortly after the consumption tax was implemented, government ministries warned numerous businesses, including barbers, restaurants, and other service establishments where price increases were said to be rampant to restrain themselves.

Consumer Behavior Changes

Consumers are affected by two developments, one of which is contrary to traditional Japanese values. The first is a tendency toward greater individualism, and the other is a growing sense of frustration. While these developments can be considered separately, they interact and have their origin in the changing wealth structure of the country.

The tendency toward individualism springs from the relatively affluent upbringing that people under 30 have experienced. They were not deprived of necessities during their youth and grew up in material comfort. As they age, unlike their parents, they are not motivated by the need to "keep up with the Joneses," that is, to achieve a lifestyle similar to associates and neighbors. Instead, they seek to develop an individual, personalized lifestyle. Not surprisingly, the older Japanese consider this younger generation as self-centered and overly intent on achieving pleasure because they spend freely not to accumulate things, but to possess unique products that express their individuality. They lack the motivation to save as well as the work ethic and social conscience that motivated their elders. In terms of products and services, this individualism translates into the purchase of sophisticated electronic equipment, entertainment and leisure activities, travel abroad, fashionable clothing, and preference for selective store-brand products that are distinct from name-brand items.

The wealth and individualism which promotes consumption is accompanied by a surprising sense of frustration. Such feelings are rooted in the widespread sentiment of being a "poor people in a rich country" which resulted in the emergence of the *akirame-ritchi*, the "given up rich," who compare themselves to the *nyuu puaa*. The *akirame-ritchi* have, by and large, surrendered their dreams of owning a home and, though not very prosperous, seem to compensate for unattainable dreams by spending lavishly on luxury imports and other expensive items as a means of affecting a wealthy lifestyle.

Individualized consumption, both as a general trend and as a characteristic of income groups, extends to three significant groups of consumers: women, *shinjinrui* (New Person), and the elderly. Each of these groups occupies a special place in the marketplace.

Women have always played an important role in controlling the household budget; currently, they control 80 percent of disposable income. But their changing role in society is also affecting their behavior as consumers. Japanese women are joining the labor force at a more rapid rate than men and, at present, more than 47 percent of all housewives now work at least part-time. This coincides with a changed attitude among younger women who no longer feel that their place is in the home. The rise in female employment has given women even more income, enhancing their importance as consumers while generating changes in expenditures. Their traditional shopping style is altered, and, to save time, convenience foods and dining out are often substituted for home-cooked meals. New appliances such as quieter washing machines and automatic bread makers are also much in demand. Nonworking housewives have also changed their behavior. Rather than sitting at home, they participate in outside leisure activities away from the home. Such women compose almost half the students at commercial "culture centers" where, for example, they play golf and tennis, or improve their cooking.

One interesting development is the increasing attention that insurance companies are paying to women. Because insurance is sold door-to-door to the housewife who controls the family budget, companies must direct their appeals to women. They rely on salesforces composed mostly of women who are expected to be more effective in dealing with housewives. The companies are also devising a variety of policies and investment programs that offer a better place for savings than low interest bank accounts.

Unmarried women are in a special position because 30,000 to 40,000 more boys than girls have been born in Japan since 1960. This surplus of men enables Japanese women to be more selective in choosing a mate, which leads men to be more conscious of women's preferences. Consequently, single Japanese women are in a position to dictate consumer fashions and trends, although their recent consumer behavior appears somewhat contradictory. On the one hand, they continue to live with their parents and save toward their wedding. On the other hand, they engage in "free-spending," and purchase large quantities of clothing, jewelry, and cosmetics. They also spend on exercise classes, travel abroad and ski vacations, and other leisure activities.

Shinjinrui—or "New Person"—is the term used to portray the behavior of the high-living, free-spending young people, both men and women. It refers to a lifestyle quite different from that of previous generations. These New Persons are often perceived in a critical manner because of their individualistic pursuit of pleasure, and lack of dedication and commitment. Their spending behavior indicates that they want to experience Japan's newfound affluence now, enjoying leisure time and buying whatever appeals to them.

The advent of such a lifestyle may signal the evolution of a consumer attitude that could eventually become dominant. Indeed, some marketing experts believe that Japan remained a producer society too long, thereby delaying improvements in the quality of life. They think that the switch to a domestic demand-led economy should have been made much sooner and that the shinjinrui phenomenon may be the initial reflection of a consumer attitude that might guide future generations. In contrast, others argue that whether the shinjinrui consumer lifestyle becomes permanent remains to be seen, especially since various cultural constraints such as marriage and family responsibilities may revive the controlled purchasing habits as they mature. They caution that the shinjinrui may simply be another passing fad in a notoriously faddish society, a product of media attention rather than the reflection of changing social values.

Japan's elderly are also the focus of extensive attention and concern nowadays. The growing size of this group suggests a market segment of increasing importance. In 1984, there were 12 million people over the age of 65 representing 9.8 percent of the population, but by the year 2000 there may be 20 million elderly, or 15.6 percent, and by 2020, the 28 million over 65 could account for almost 22 percent of the total population. Such trends may make the Japanese society the oldest in the world, with a market potential of $1 trillion by the year 2000. A report by the Ministry of Health and Welfare indicates three fundamental characteristics of the elderly that suggest their product and service needs: deteriorating physical performance, desire for a new purpose in life, and increased consciousness about physical and financial needs.[4] The elderly's growing disabilities require products such as hearing aids, reading glasses, wheelchairs, modified everyday products such as easier-to-use clothing, and home delivery services. The search for new life goals requires cultural and social organizations and special travel programs. The maintenance of physical and financial well-being involves a complex set of services because many elderly parents now live alone, and the children, while concerned, find it financially or otherwise impossible to care for them.

Another growing group is the single-member household. A 1985 census found that such households compose 20 percent of all households. This group is growing because of a reluctance among men and women to marry — more than half of the male population between the ages of 25 and 29 is unmarried. A rising divorce rate also is contributing to the growth of this group. Marketing directed at singles includes products and services appropriate to their lifestyles: compact clothes dryers and washing machines, take-home meals, and nighttime services such as freight delivery and laundry. There are also products intended to reduce the loneliness of living alone.

Consumer Credit and Services

Japan was always a pay-as-you-go cash society. Savings were and still are accumulated for emergencies, the children's education, retirement, and major household purchases. This preference for cash purchases, together with the lack of a credit information system, was one of the major obstacles to the development of consumer credit in the past. In 1981, for example, outstanding loans for consumer finance amounted to only 10 percent of disposable income compared to 17 percent in the United States. However, despite such shortcomings, total consumer financing began to grow at a rate of about 20 percent during the early 1980s and may have reached 17 percent of disposable income by 1988.

Over the years a variety of different institutions have offered consumer credit. In 1981, banks were responsible for 32 percent of new loans, retailers for 11 percent, public financial institutions for 11 percent, captive finance companies of major manufacturers for 10 percent, *shinpan* — credit companies — for 14 percent, and *sarakin* — cash loan companies — for 9 percent. In recent years, the *shinpan*, however, began to experience difficulties. While their loan portfolios increased by 20.8 percent in 1983, they grew by only 14.4 percent in 1984, 9.2 percent in 1985, and 7.6 percent in 1986.[5] This was due to heightened competition as a decline in demand for loans offered was accompanied by an increase in the number of financial institutions offering the loans.

Such problems have forced the *shinpan* to devise new strategies for growth. Because installment credit is restricted, they are beginning to offer credit cards as well as financing and leasing guarantees. They are also striving for improved efficiency with increased investments in credit-information systems. For example, Orient Finance has invested $125 million in a on-line system called "Orion" that began operating in January 1989, and Nippon Shinpan, a competitor, is planning a $80 to $125 million on-line system.

The *sarakin* have had an interesting, albeit somewhat notorious, history. They came into prominence in the 1970s by offering cash loans to high-risk borrowers at interest rates that often exceeded the legal maximum of 109 percent. Not surprisingly, the collection of such high interest loans often involved intimidation such as midnight visits, physical threats, and even pressure on delinquent borrowers through other means. Because banks during the 1970s were awash with surplus funds but were unfamiliar with consumer financing, they willingly provided funds to consumer finance companies. The *sarakin* benefited from bank financing, often attaining growth rates of over 200 percent in their lending activities.

However, the publicity given to the *sarakin*'s ruthless tactics eventually led to a series of regulatory actions. The maximum interest rate for loans was reduced to 73 percent in 1983 and 40 percent in 1988; restrictions were placed on the maximum amounts that families could borrow as well as on the collection methods; and companies were allowed to extend in-house loans to employees to prevent them from relying on *sarakin*. Such regulations plus repayment difficulties among borrowers created problems for *sarakin*. Many experienced financial difficulties, and a shakeout occurred in 1984. The number of *sarakin* registered with the government declined to about 44,000, a decrease of almost 50 percent in only a year's time.[6] However, the Ministry of Finance (MOF) appears committed to the survival of the top four *sarakin*, even though their prospects are shaky due to greater competition from financially stronger companies such as the *shinpan*.

Credit cards have become more accepted in recent years. By the end of 1988, there were 120 million such cards in circulation, meaning that the average Japanese consumer has one credit card, far fewer than the number held by the average American. The cards are issued by commercial banks, department stores, supermarket chains, and *shinpan*. Most banks are issuing cards linked to major international credit card companies such as Visa or MasterCard. Visa is associated with Diamond Credit and 24 other card issuers; in FY 1987, it had 9.5 million cardholders who spent $7.835 billion at 746,000 outlets. MasterCard's issuers in Japan include Union Credit, Million Credit Service Co., Kyodo Credit Service Co., and also Diamond Credit. Its holders spent $12.600 billion at 1,705,000 outlets during the same period. Japan's only international credit card company, Japan Credit Bureau (JCB), had 11.1 million cardholders who spent $10.394 billion at 896,000 member stores in 1987. Banks, however, are constrained because bank card purchases cannot be paid in monthly installments; new payment balances must be liquidated at the end of each month. Thus, banks want the relevant regulations changed, but such a change may be slow in coming. Of course the *shinpan* want to maintain the status quo.

Even as credit cards have become more widely used, this "plastic technology" was adapted to Japan's traditional cash preferences. One example of this is the "pre-paid" telephone card, a "pay-now-consume-later" card first introduced by Nippon Telephone and Telegraph (NTT) in 1982. Issued in denominations of 500 to 5,000 yen (about $4 to $40 in 1989), NTT's cards are inserted in pay telephones at the beginning of a call and then returned after the completion of the call, with the face value reduced according to the length of the conversation. NTT sold 9 million cards in 1984, 60 million in 1985, and 228 million in 1987, for a total of more than $2 billion. The cards often carry illustrations of scenery or pictures of teenage idols; and, because they have become ideal gifts, politicians print their photos on the cards and give them to voters, and businesses include messages directed at past or potential customers. Pre-paid card demand has also been promoted by the 1989 consumption tax, because deduction of purchases from the cards alleviates the need to carry small change to pay the tax. McDonald's, in fact, sells customers a Y1,030 card for Y1,000. thereby paying the 3 percent consumption tax as a service to its customers.

NTT's success prompted other firms to introduce their own pre-paid cards, thus increasing competition among card offerers. Nippon Card System (NiCS) issued its U-card in association with Coca Cola (Japan) for use in Coke vending machines in Tokyo. Separate U-cards were developed for purchases at McDonald's fast food and Baskin-Robbins ice cream outlets. NiCS's eventual goal is to issue a card that is widely accepted by, for example, taxis, supermarkets, bus companies, and game parlors, rather than having a separate card for each company. It anticipates annual card sales of $0.8 to $1.6 billion within five years. Other cards are being offered by the Japan Card Center Kaisha which is connected with the CSK information service company, Nihon-Card of the Sumitomo trading company, and the Prepaid Card System of JCB. Mitsubishi and several other companies established the Japan Leisure Card System which is intended for use in the *pachinko*—pinball—outlets. Japanese railways are also offering cards to pay train fares.

All of these card-issuing firms are attracted by the immediate availability of funds from card charges. Moreover, since cards are used over a prolonged period of time, the issuing companies have access to "free" money. In effect, the purchaser is extending credit to the seller. The growth of card usage, however, has attracted the attention of the MOF, which views the cards as an alternate form of currency. The ministry does not like the idea of private firms issuing "money," and the Bank of Japan is worried about a loss of control over the money supply. There is also a concern that consumers may suffer losses if a card company goes bankrupt. Thus, the use of pre-paid cards may eventually be restrained.

Recent Product Trends

The traditional Japanese fascination and readiness to experiment with innovative ideas leads to the continuous introduction of a wide variety of new products. This traditional attitude is complemented by recent economic and social trends that are driving consumption. To systematize the emerging product preferences, the well-known marketing analyst George Fields, who lives and works in Tokyo, has identified the following purchasing patterns:[7]

Preference for "soft" rather then "hard" ware: telephone cards, stationary products, rental VTRs, up front old age support insurance, coffee stands, compact discs, and Filo Fax pocket notebook. This category is service oriented.

Life-enriching durables: VTR cameras, Japanese word processors, imported cars—particularly BMW and Mercedes, television games, liquid crystal television, large screen color televisions. Electronic products predominant this group.

Food: spicy snacks, convenience foods, premium ice cream and candy, low calorie sweetener, confectionery products; imports are strong—beer (Asahi's Dry beer was prominent) and European wine.

Investment: memorial gold coins, the ARK Hills urban redevelopment project in Tokyo—one-third of office occupancy by foreign capital.

Fashions/Fads: Men's DC Brand Fashion, comic strips, stuffed toys, male fashion magazine Men's Non—No.

Personal Care Products: Hair nutrients for males, ear plugs.

Sports and Culture: ladies' golf equipment, party house rentals, health centers.

A great many products could be added to these categories. For example many consumers are ready to spend on luxury goods such as "life-enriching" durables, and the streak of individualism is evident in the auto market where people are buying not only expensive imports but also a variety of small and offbeat looking cars that resemble Land Rovers, Jeeps, or 20-year-old Russian models.

It is interesting to note that Nikkei Marketing Journal's 1988 list of hit products also included the Tokyo Dome, Japan's first dome stadium, overseas travel, imported beef, refrigerated food delivery, resort condominiums, accessories by Chanel, and laptop computers. This fascinating variety confounds judgment on consumer preferences. Thus, it is difficult to draw conclusions about the so-called new Japanese consumption style. It appears that anything may become a top-seller, and this is an indication of the emergence of highly individualized consumer purchasing preferences.

The Distribution System

The Japanese distribution system is the result of several hundred years of evolution. Thus, it reflects geographic and traditional social and cultural factors. Retailers are located throughout the country which is divided by islands, and this generated layers of wholesalers who can move products to numerous geographically dispersed, small retailing establishments. Because the country's size limits the storage space available to wholesalers, retailers, and consumers alike, the Japanese make frequent small purchases in stores located conveniently near home. Thus, wholesalers must be able to replenish quickly the small inventories of retailers and provide numerous additional services.

The distribution system also functions as a private-sector welfare service in that it employs retirees, elderly, or poorly educated people who need a job. These characteristics undoubtedly lowered the economic efficiency of the distribution system, but the ability to establish a small business enabled many people to earn a living and limited public welfare expenditures. In 1986, for example, employment in wholesaling and retailing rose by 210,000, offsetting the loss of 90,000 manufacturing jobs due to the sharply appreciating yen.[8]

Interactions among the various wholesalers and retailers are based on personal relations which are formed over a long period of time. The financially stronger members of the distribution chain extend credit to the weaker members, with payment terms longer than in the United States. Risk is shared between the manufacturer, wholesaler, and retailer, as the manufacturer must accept the return of unsold goods (*henpin*). Manufacturers also provide extensive services to wholesalers and retailers, and the retailers, in turn, charge the prices suggested by the manufactuer and do not stock products offered by competitors. Such supportive relationships clearly engender strong bonds among channel members which may present entry obstacles to new competitors, both Japanese and non-Japanese.

Almost 30 years ago, observers of the Japanese business scene predicted a "distribution revolution." They saw the appearance of small-scale discount retail chains, or *supah*, as signalling the emergence of large retail chains similar to those in the United States and predicted that the *sogo shosha* (trading companies) would extend their activities into retailing through networks of affiliated firms. Thus, marginal retailers would be driven out of business by large corporations which would have improved economic efficiency. However, such predictions proved to be premature, and as the economy grew, the unchanged distribution system expanded along with it. Although large retailers and wholesalers grew in importance, small and medium wholesalers and retailers also increased in number. Table 5–6 illustrates the retailing and wholesaling trends between 1954 and 1985.

The large number and complex interactions in the distribution system generate strong criticism abroad. Foreigners, particularly Americans, consider the system inefficient and costly, contributing to the relatively high prices of consumer goods as each channel member's profit margin drives up prices. Data in table 5–6 tend both to support and contradict such claims. Japan's wholesalers, for example, have lower sales per establishment and a higher wholesale/retail turnover ratio, and serve fewer people per employee than those in the United States. Annual sales per establishment are higher in the United States, but sales per employee are higher in Japan as are total

TABLE 5-6. Growth trends of wholesale and retail industries: 1954–1985

Wholesale Industries

Year	Total number of establishments (thousands)	Employees (thousands)	Employees per establishment	Annual sales (Y billion)	Sales per employee (Y million)
1954	174	1,130	6.50	9,015	7.98
1956	180	1,294	7.20	11,804	9.15
1958	193	1,551	8.10	13,986	9.02
1960	226	1,928	8.50	18,468	9.58
1962	223	2,129	9.50	27,474	12.91
1964	229	2,524	11.00	38,830	15.39
1966	287	3,042	10.60	52,082	17.12
1968	240	2,697	11.30	62,817	23.29
1970	256	2,861	11.20	88,331	30.88
1972	259	3,008	11.60	106,780	35.50
1974	292	3,290	11.30	173,113	52.62
1976	340	3,513	10.30	222,315	63.28
1979	369	3,673	10.00	274,545	74.75
1982	429	4,091	9.50	398,536	97.42
1985	413	3,997	9.70	426,506	106.71
1988	436	4,331	9.90	446,423	103.05

Retail Industries

Year	Total number of stores (thousands)	Employees (thousands)	Employees per store	Annual sales (Y billion)	Sales per employee (Y million)
1954	1,189	2,717	2.30	2,592	0.95
1956	1,201	3,003	2.50	2,999	1.00
1958	1,245	3,273	2.60	3,549	1.08
1960	1,288	3,489	2.70	4,315	1.24
1962	1,272	3,550	2.80	6,149	1.73
1964	1,305	3,811	2.90	8,350	2.45
1966	1,375	4,193	3.00	10,684	2.55
1968	1,432	4,646	3.20	16,507	3.55
1970	1,471	4,926	3.30	21,773	4.42
1972	1,496	5,141	3.40	28,293	5.50
1974	1,548	5,303	3.40	40,300	7.60
1976	1,614	5,580	3.50	56,029	10.04
1979	1,674	5,960	3.60	73,564	12.34
1982	1,721	6,369	3.70	93,971	14.75
1985	1,629	6,329	3.90	101,716	16.07
1988	1,619	6,850	4.20	114,829	16.76

Source: "The Japanese Distribution System," *JEI Report* (Washington, D.C.: Japan Economic Institute, No. 28A, July 24, 1987), pp. 5 and 7; and "Notes: Distribution System," *JEI Report* (Washington, D.C.: Japan Economic Institute, No. 14 B, April 7, 1989), pp. 12–14.

annual sales. This indicates the relatively greater involvement of middlemen whose added profits margins raise prices. The yen's appreciation may disguise some wholesaling inefficiencies since comparisons for 1982 showed higher total and per employee sales in the United States than in Japan. On the retail side, Japanese retailers have lower sales per store and per employee than their U.S. counterparts. Per capita retail sales are now higher in Japan, however, and the populations served by a retail employee are essentially equal between the two countries. But the yen's appreciation may also hide inefficiencies in Japanese retailing. Consequently, distribution data must be interpreted carefully.

The recently reported decline in small retailers led some Japanese marketing experts to conclude that the "distribution revolution" has finally arrived in the late 1980s.[9] As shown in table 5–6, the steady increases in the number of wholesalers and retailers reversed itself in 1985, with reductions in the number of both wholesalers and retailers. This reduction was accompanied by sales increases in both sectors, indicating that reorganization and consolidation were taking place. Large wholesalers absorbed numerous small and regional wholesalers and large retailers increased their number of stores. This put pressure on small retailers; thus, during the 1980s, many of these small stores closed or switched to offering services such as rental videos or take-home food shops. More recent 1988 data indicate a further, though less substantial drop in the numer of retailers by 0.2 percent as compared to 1985. However, behind the small percentage drop are major changes in distribution structure as the number of family-owned retail shops with only one or two employees decreased by 55 percent from the 1985 level, while convenience stores increased by 40.8 percent.[10] In contrast, changes in wholesaling do not suggest that it is becoming more efficient. Rather than reductions in the multiple tiers of intermediaries, there was a 5.7 percent increase in the number of wholesalers between 1985 and 1988. These recent trends cast doubt on predictions that the number of wholesalers may be reduced by 20 percent and the number of retailers by 30 percent in the near future.

Regulatory measures are also contributing to the changes. While major adjustments in the Large Scale Retail Stores Control Law are unlikely, MITI came to recognize that large stores can attract other businesses and serve as a magnet for local development. Thus, it is interpreting the law more flexibly so that large store floor space is growing more rapidly, increasing by 5 percent in 1988 and growing twice as fast in 1989. Large domestic retailers expect MITI to reduce the consultation period with small local retailers to eight months to be offset by restrictions on large retailers' floor space. An example of such consultations provided by the Daiei department store chain illustrates the effects of the law. Daiei began negotiations with small store owners in 1985, and it will be able to open its store in June 1990. Its agreement includes a reduction in floor space from 21,450 square meters to 11,900 square meters, a closing time of 7 p.m. rather than 8 p.m., 28 non-operating days rather than 12 during the year, and contributions of more than 100 million yen but less than 200 million yen for modernization of the small shopkeepers streets. The Fair Trade Commission (FTC) also intends to make the secrete rebate system more transparent. Distributors use this system to reward their best retailers, but smaller retailers are often discriminated against because they are not informed of products with rebates. Finally, manufacturers' use of suggested retail prices is also likely to be restrained in the future as is the restrictive sole-agent arrangement, which is already weakening. An interesting example of the impact Japan's mergers and acquisitions activities have on the distribution system is the 1989 case of the Shiperu Kobayashi's Shuwa Corp. Kobayashi has departed from the Japanese tradition by engaging in hostile takeovers, and his stock

TABLE 5-7.   Comparison of the wholesale and retail industries in Japan and the United States, selected years[a]

	Japan	United States
Wholesale industry		
Number of wholesale establishments	413,016 (1985)	415,800 (1982)
Number of employees	3,998,000 (1985)	4,985,000 (1982)
Number of employees per wholesaler	9.7 (1985)	12.0 (1982)
Population per wholesale employee	30.3 (1985)	46.6 (1982)
Annual sales (millions dollars[b])	$1,795,468 (1985)	$1,997,895 (1982)
	$3,502,154 (1988)	$2,729,000[c] (1988)
Annual sales per wholesaler[b]	$4,347,380 (1985)	$4,804,942 (1982)
Annual sales per employee[b]	$449,092 (1985)	$400,781 (1982)
Wholesale/retail turnover ratio	4.21 (1985)	2.08 (1982)
	3.93 (1988)	1.88 (1988)
Retail Industry[d]		
Number of retail outlets	1,628,644 (1985)	1,541,500 (1982)
Ratio of retailers to wholesalers	3.94 (1985)	3.71 (1982)
Number of employees	6,329,000 (1985)	9,802,000 (1985)
	n.a. (1988)	12,846,000 (1988)
Number of employees per retailer	3.9 (1985)	6.4 (1982)
Population per retail employee	19.1 (1985)	23.7 (1982)
	n.a. (1988)	19.2 (1988)
Annual sales (millions of dollars[b])	$426,423 (1985)	$961,325 (1982)
	$891,682 (1988)	$1,454,608 (1988)
Annual sales per retailer[b]	$261,827 (1985)	$623,630 (1982)
Annual sales per employee[b]	$67,376 (1985)	$98,074 (1982)
	n.a. (1988)	$148,399 (1988)
Per capita sales[b]	$3,523 (1985)	$4,134 (1982)
	$7,262 (1988)	$5,910 (1988)
Annual sales per square foot of selling space[b]	$600 (1985)	n.a. (1982)

[a] The 1988 data are not directly comparable with the figures for 1985 (Japan) and 1982 (United States), which are census years.

[b] The 1985 yen figures were converted at the year's average exchange rate of Y238.54 = $1.00; the comparable conversion factor for 1988 was Y128.15 = $1.00.

[c] Estimated using actual sales by merchant wholesalers in 1988 ($1,637.4 million) and the assumption that merchant wholesalers generate 60 percent of total wholesale turnover.

[d] Excludes eating and drinking establishments in both countries.

Source: "Japan's Distribution System: The Next Major Trade Confrontation?" *JEI Report* Washington, D.C.: Japan Economic Institute, No. 11A, March 17, 1989), pp. 5 and 6.

purchases in two mild-sized retailers, Inageya and Chujitsuya, provoked considerable opposition from the retailers' management. What is most intriguing about Kobayashi's stock purchases is his intention "to make the retail industry more efficient or to reorganize the industry . . .," lofty ambitions that would significantly alter the distribution system.

However, foreign governments are likely to increase pressure on the Japanese to introduce more changes in the distribution system. Particularly the United States can be expected to do so because American businesses have gained less from the rapid increase in imports than the Asians or Europeans. Table 5–8 shows the increases in Japanese imports from 1980 through 1988,

TABLE 5-8. Japan's imports of capital and consumer goods: 1980 and 1985–1988 (in millions of dollars, c.i.f. value, and percent market shares)

	1980	1985	1986	1987	January-November 1988
Capital goods	$9,096	$11,541	$13,229	$16,328	$20,332
United States	$4,888	$7,504	$7,785	$9,025	$11,203
Share of capital goods	53.7%	65.0%	58.8%	55.3%	55.1%
European Community	$2,247	$1,845	$2,763	$3,606	$4,091
Share of capital goods	24.7%	16.0%	20.9%	22.1%	20.1%
Southeast Asia	$790	$1,179	$1,473	$2,313	$3,294
Share of capital goods	8.7%	10.2%	11.1%	14.2%	16.2%
Consumer nondurables	$2,677	$3,319	$4,711	$7,718	$9,814
United States	$322	$314	$403	$857	$1,091
Share of nondurables	12.0%	9.5%	8.6%	11.1%	11.1%
European Community	$697	$692	$1,008	$1,400	$1,777
Share of nondurables	26.0%	20.8%	21.4%	18.1%	18.1%
Southeast Asia	$1,167	$1,574	$2,368	$4,093	$5,074
Share of nondurables	43.6%	47.4%	50.3%	53.0%	51.7%
Consumer durables	$2,395	$2,974	$4,601	$7,977	$10,725
United States	$561	$590	$740	$1,086	$1,522
Share of durables	23.4%	19.8%	16.1%	13.6%	14.2%
European Community	$855	$1,105	$1,949	$3,575	$4,774
Share of durables	35.7%	37.2%	42.4%	44.8%	44.5%
Southeast Asia	$672	$873	$1,393	$2,538	$3,440
Share of durables	28.1%	29.4%	30.3%	31.8%	32.1%

Source: "Japan's Distribution System: The Next Major Confrontation," *JEI Report* (Washington, D.C.: Japan Economic Institute, No. 11A, March 17, 1989), p. 3.

and, as can be seen, imports from the United States have experienced both a loss of market share and slower growth than other supplying countries, especially in the consumer product categories. To explore the possible reasons for this, in March 1989 a delegation from the U.S. Departments of State, Commerce, Agriculture, Justice, and the Trade Representative's Office sought information about the distribution system. The delegation was briefed on the retail store law, restrictions on direct marketing, mail advertising and, the MOF's policies on credit cards. However, even as the American government prepared itself to make new demands, representatives of the American Chamber of Commerce in Japan (ACCJ) expressed doubt about the need for the two governments to get involved. Chamber members do not believe that the distribution system discriminates against non-Japanese business only. In their opinion, entry problems are faced by all new firms, regardless of nationality. Nonetheless, on April 28, 1989, the American government cited the Japanese distribution system as an "unfair trade barrier" in its annual report on trade restrictions abroad.

Distribution Innovations

Most of the innovations in the Japanese distribution system are occurring at the retail level largely in response to changing consumer attitudes and lifestyles. Retailers are trying to achieve a level of distinctiveness that appeals to customers. Department stores, in particular, have remodeled and revamped their interiors, creating separate store areas that project impressions consistent with the self-images that individual Japanese are trying to achieve.

In large measure, these stores within-a-store are targeted at the *shinjinrui* and rely on multiple-appeals to reach the "New Person"'s sophisticated and diverse tastes from electronic equipment through clothing to sporting goods. Special house brands, distinctive from name brands, are offered so that customers can own more exclusive products. The Marui department store chain, for example, is particularly active in creating such multiple images. It sets aside store spaces for the products of individual designers but associates the "designer spaces" so that product images reinforce each other. Other department stores have followed suit: Seibu department store offers specially designed bicycles or climbing boots, its saleswomen promote new styles by wearing their own chic clothes during work rather that a typical department store uniform, and Isetan's design service offers "made-to-order" furniture, and several others market special food preparations.

The *conglo-merchant* is a distinctive type of Japanese retailing establishment that represents a corporate group composed of many types of retail stores. Conglo-merchants try to dominate the retail business in a given area by simultaneously operating different kinds of stores. The goal is to achieve an increasing market-share in an area on the basis of combining stores rather than relying on a single type of business. For example, convenience shops are located in residential districts, and department stores are established in urban centers, with specialty shops located nearby. The same merchandise is often sold at different stores in the same distribution group, and the stores share the same purchasing, physical distribution, and information systems. Daiei, the largest retail group in Japan, which includes the Printemps department store, Lawson convenience stores, Topos discount stores, and D-Mart (a joint venture with K-Mart of the United States) is a good example of this type of retailer. Ito-Yokado, Daiei's rival, is another conglo-merchant which includes in its group Daikuma discount stores, speciality shops, and the 7-Eleven convenience stores (a joint venture with Southland of the United States).

Increasing competition has caused some of the conglo-merchants to switch to another line of business in unprofitable retail stores so as to appear more distinctive. Called "development of a line of business," this shift often results in a new kind of retailing not seen before. These "new lines" are incorporated into the conglo-merchant group's activities as retailing innovations, thereby increasing diversification.

The appreciation of the yen also has spurred innovations. Small and medium-sized wholesalers are going directly to overseas suppliers to combat intensifying competition from giant importers and wholesalers. In the food industry, the "Cooperative Import Organization" was formed to purchase food products from abroad, first purchasing Canada Dry and five other soft drinks from a U.S. wholesaler. The "All Japan Wholesalers' Association for Living and Household Wares" and the "Japan Furniture Wholesalers Association" have both established direct channels for purchase of furniture from Southeast Asia. Discount stores are popular due to the sale of low-priced imports. They often use parallel imports, i.e., obtain products directly from the manufacturer at lower prices than if purchased through sole agents in Japan. Manufactured goods such as VCRs, color TVs, refrigerators, and other electric appliances from the NICs are particularly attractive, because such NIC products fit with discount stores' strategies of selling to the mass market at low prices. Sales of these low-priced NIC imports boomed in 1987 and 1988, but early in 1989 they came under increasing criticism because of poor quality, lack of after-sales service, absence of guarantees, and the failure of discounters to refund money for broken products. These shortcomings created a poor reputation among Japan's quality-conscious consumers, leading to the buildup of inventories of hard-to-sell products. Recognizing the problem, discounters and other importers of NIC products and the NIC manufacturers themselves have started to upgrade products and offer better service to halt the drop in sales.

Large retailers have also taken advantage of both the appreciation of the yen and the lower manufacturing costs in the NICs. They use a "develop-and-import" formula, giving NIC manufacturers instructions on how to manufacture products based on the retailer's specifications for the Japanese market. Moreover, they have established separate departments to merchandise less expensive imported products. An interesting example of using the yen appreciation for competitive purposes is a chain of 60 stores selling imported beef that is priced in dollars, though paid for in yen, that is pegged to the previous week's dollar exchange rate. This enables consumers to buy beef at prices substantially lower than those set by the Livestock Industry Promotion Board to protect domestic producers. Other interesting examples of unique approaches to import promotions are offered by the cities of Osaka and Shimonoseki. Both cities are planning to create large import centers to promote products from Southeast Asia. Osaka, for example, plans to offer membership to 300 exporters from the Asia-Pacific region to exhibit products ranging from cars to electrical machinery to clothing.

Computerization may prove to be the most significant innovation for reshaping the Japanese distribution system. Point-of-sale (POS) computer terminals perform the usual cash register functions of calculating and totaling customer purchases. However, the real benefit of POS is in the information that the terminals provide to monitor sales of specific items so as to detect fast-moving and slow-moving products, facilitate adjustments in store displays, and present products in a manner that maximizes sales. Analysis of POS information allows the development of "time segment displays," a type of revolving display that is altered throughout the day to present products that are expected to sell at particular times. For example, snacks may be displayed in the morning, which is replaced by pre-packaged foods in the daytime, and box lunches in the evening.

In addition to improved merchandising, POS data allows faster restocking. Retailers and suppliers can monitor sales and quickly arrange for the delivery of replacements stocks. POS systems also enable small shops to form groups to jointly order and deliver products at lower cost than through the traditional channels, thereby altering the structure of the distribution system.

The Changing Role of the Sogo Shosha

Japan's *Keiretsu* — corporate groups — have played an important role in the development of the Japanese economy. Each of these corporate groups includes a variety of enterprises in different industries such as banking, construction, textiles, chemicals, metals, and machinery that do business with each other, exchange personnel and information, and provide financial and other intragroup forms of support.

An important member of each group is its *sogo shosha*—the trading company that carries out the group's international transactions. In FY 1986, for instance, the *sogo shosha* of the six largest *keiretsu* handled 50.6 percent of all Japanese trade, 42.9 percent of exports, and 63.9 percent of imports.[11] But in recent times, the *sogo shosha*'s traditional functions, encompassing purchasing, marketing, and financing, have undergone considerable changes. From the 1950s into the 1970s, they were involved in purchasing raw materials such as oil, ores, and wood as inputs for heavy industries like steel and chemicals. They also took responsibility for marketing the output of these and other industries, both domestically and internationally. During this time period, there was also a shortage of funds, and so the *sogo shosha* became intermediaries between banks and manufacturers, providing credit for raw material purchases and inventory building. In all of these activities, their primary role was as an information intermediary—possessing information to link buyers and sellers of products and services.

In the late 1970s, however, economic developments reduced the need for the *sogo shosha* to perform all of these functions. The domestic economy shifted to the manufacture of high value-added technology-intensive products, leading to a decline in the importance of the basic heavy industries such as steel, chemicals, and heavy machinery. Raw material imports also declined as a result of decreased demand and higher fuel prices. Furthermore, the marketing role became less important because manufacturers set up their own marketing operations, and the financing function was also reduced because more firms were able to self-finance growth and banks became more active lenders. More recently, the yen's appreciation contributed to declining sales and profitability as contracts denominated in dollars translated into lower yen revenues and earnings.

These developments forced the *sogo shoshas* to alter their basic marketing and financing strategies during the 1980s. In some instances, they attempted to adjust to the changing economy by importing and exporting high technology products such as computers, terminals, and software even though they lacked the sales engineering skills needed. Their experience in bulk, low-margin commodities and plant and equipment were not suited to the new high tech products and, consequently, many of the diversification moves failed. Some have also moved into telecommunications, where their traditional information-processing capabilities could be a strength. For example, Mitsubishi in 1983 entered into a joint venture with IBM to market the latter's "Information Network," and Marubeni is cooperating with Timeshare group of the United States to market the "Time-Net" system. However, as they are all trying to implement similar information networks, none of these operations seems to be profitable at the present time.

The *sogo shoshas* appear to have had more success in other new business endeavors. For example, to restructure their financing activities, they entered merchant banking by establishing offshore banking facilities to raise funds for reinvestment in other projects. Marubeni established such a facility in London in 1984, Sumitomo set up a fund-investment company in Luxembourg also in 1984, and Mitsubishi formed a company in london in 1985. Other new international activities include assisting and facilitating foreign direct investment by Japanese firms and contracting with foreign producers to supply products such as apparel, food, consumer appliances, and industrial goods for the growing domestic marketplace. They have also become involved in funding joint R&D ventures with foreign firms in return for licenses in biotechnology, metals, and composite materials.

Examples of Successful Foreign Companies

Despite the complaints about the distribution system as a nontariff barrier, many foreign firms have succeeded in penetrating the Japanese market. While they made special efforts to overcome the obstacles posed by the distribution system, their strategies also entailed other elements, ranging from improved marketing research to more effective product innovations. One of the best examples is Kodak. While Kodak has been involved in Japan for several decades, it became serious in its commitment only during the last several years. It entered into a joint venture with the Nagase trading company to market and distribute Kodak photographic products, established research and development and technology centers, listed its stock on the Tokyo Stock Exchange (TSE), and obtained equity positions in several Japanese companies. It altered products to fit consumer preferences, offered its film in Japanese packages, and developed product innovations. One such innovation was its Gold Film which was especially designed for Japanese tastes as a replacement for its regular film which was criticized for making Japanese skin tones appear yellowish. Its purchase of a 50 percent equity stake in Kodak Nagase K.K., in effect, gave it business contacts that provides Kodak access to Japan's commercial and consumer markets, including 200,000 outlets that sell film products.

Michelin is another example of a company that demonstrated a commitment to the market. It has successfully capitalized on its prestigious name and quality reputation by appealing to the strong status orientation of the Japanese. Most significantly, it has established a distribution network second to none in its industry. Twenty-nine warehouses serve both manufacturers and the replacement tire aftermarket, permitting deliveries to most of the sales outlets in one day. Such arrangements proved effective in overcoming the traditional Japanese fear that foreign firms are unable to provide the necessary sales support over the long term.

Some of the most interesting examples of overcoming the distribution system's limitations are provided by foreign automobile manufacturers. Until recently, the Yanase & Co. Tokyo trading company controlled the import of foreign cars, but its share of the imported car market declined from 52.5 percent in 1980 to 42 percent in 1988. This happened because of the more aggressive marketing by the foreign manufacturers themselves. BMW, for example, increased its sales from 3,662 vehicles in 1981 to 26,826 in 1988 by establishing its own independent dealer network and by offering low-cost (6 percent) financing, the lowest in the industry. It also spent heavily on targeted advertising, cut prices to lure customers into showrooms, and used its snob appeal reputation. Other luxury foreign car makers have also increased their marketing efforts in Japan, and companies such as Mercedes-Benz, Volvo, Porsche, and Audi experienced sales growth of 30 to 45 percent in 1987.

Nippon Lever, the Japanese subsidiary of Unilever, has also achieved notable success. It accommodated its strategy to the Japanese marketplace by emphasizing strong service. Its products are sold through the traditional distribution channels, but its salesforce calls on all primary and secondary wholesalers, thereby providing sales support throughout the distribution chain. Heinz has followed a similar approach in selling its Ore-Ida frozen potatoes. It set up a subsidiary headed by a Japanese manager who selected ten wholesalers who already had strong ties with the leading supermarkets. After Ore-Ida potatoes were introduced in September 1984, the product captured a 30 percent share of the frozen food market within six months' time and reached $21.4 million in sales in 1987, a 30 percent increase from the previous year. The case of McIlhenny Co.'s Tabasco sauce is an interesting example of the acceptance of an unusual foreign food product. McIlhenny credits its success to its willingness to accept and work within the Japanese distribution system. The product is imported by PBI, a marketing firm in Tokyo that represents McIlhenny, and is then distributed through the traditional wholesaler-retailer arrangements.

The experiences of McIlhenny and other non-Japanese firms illustrate the strategy elements that companies wishing to enter the Japanese marketplace must consider. First, they must demonstrate a commitment to the market. This requires a patient development of the firm's image and of its relationships with customers as well as its Japanese managers and employees. Quick profits must be sacrificed in favor of strong long-term market positions. Second, products must be adapted because the Japanese are demanding consumers and do not tolerate products that do not meet their expectations. Third, products must be backed by reliable service, that is, on-time delivery and the maintenance of good working relationships with distributors. It is necessary to have convenient warehouse facilities to fill orders and to maintain a salesforce of adequate size that can support the product adequately. As the first few firms in an industry often develop an unassailable competitive advantage, so it is important to be among the early entrants, and to reduce costs continually so as to price aggressively.

The choice of the right partners is another important consideration for success, although this may involve conflicting elements. On the one hand, a foreign firm initially needs a Japanese partner who knows the market and has long-standing relationships with potential customers. On the other hand, it is potentially troublesome to distribute through a potential competitor who may not promote the product and willingly suffers losses to keep the foreign firm from eventually establishing itself fully. Sole agency arrangements may also involve conflicting considerations because either the agent may have the necessary contacts and effectively market the product or may overprice the product and offer only limited distribution. Finally, foreign firms, especially companies with well-known names, must develop and project a strong image in the market because the Japanese are very image conscious. A well-known and respected foreign firm must take advantage of its name recognition and establish its own distribution system.

The experiences of other firms point to a decline in several Japanese marketing myths that have long guided foreign producers. One myth that is losing ground is that imports must be priced high to succeed. Typically in the past, high prices were necessary to suggest high quality or exclusiveness, but low pricing is now seen as an option for succeeding in the mass market, particularly since yen appreciation has lowered the price of imports. The dissipation of the "homogeneous" market myth is allowing foreign producers to appeal to identifiable niches that represent distinct groups in the population. Foreign marketers are also finding that the requirement for product adaptation does not always hold. Often, unadapted products are accepted by consumers, which should not be surprising because the Japanese are ready to try new and innovative products.

Recently, however, several problems have also arisen for foreign firms, reducing their ability to compete. The appreciation of the yen was supposed to lower the price of imports, allowing foreign firms to sell more, but increased costs have accompanied the yen's appreciation. For instance, in 1988 it was twice as expensive to maintain expatriates in Japan as in 1985. Advertising and promotion costs also have risen, by 12 percent in 1988 alone. Furthermore, notwithstanding the gradual disappearance of the myth that imports must be high-priced to succeed, certain foreign products with established prestige images cannot be successfully marketed at lower prices. The lesson of these experiences is that there are no simple answers to succeeding in the Japanese market; only enlightened and committed efforts may lead to success.

Advertising

Japan spends less on advertising than other industrialized nations with comparable domestic markets. Table 5–9 illustrates international differences in advertising expenditures in 1984. The data indicate that as a ratio of GNP, Japan's advertising is less than that of other countries, but most striking is its far lower per capita ad expenditure.

TABLE 5–9. Advertising expenditures of industrialized countries: 1984

Country	Total ad expenditure (mil. U.S. $)	GNP (bil. U.S. $)	Ratio of total ad expenditure to GNP (%)	Per capita ad expenditure (U.S. $)
United States	87,820.0	3,678.2	2.39	371.02
Japan	12,213.6	1,251.4	0.98	20.47
United Kingdom	5,340.8	422.8	1.26	101.78
West Germany	5,283.7	613.0	0.86	86.05
Canada	4,030.8	321.3	1.25	160.59
France	2,963.5	486.8	0.61	53.98

Source: "Advertising Expenditures of 20 Countries (1984), *Dentsu Japan Marketing/ Advertising Yearbook, 1988* (Tokyo: Dentsu Incorporated, 1987), p. 235.

Recent trends in ad expenditures relative to GNP growth confirm the limited role of advertising in the Japanese economy during the past. In 1984, the economy grew by 6.4 percent and advertising by 4.8 percent; in 1985 GNP growth was 6.1 percent and ad growth 2.3 percent; in 1986 GNP growth was 4.4 percent and ad growth 4.1, although in 1987 GNP growth of 4.1 percent was exceeded by ad growth of 8.1 percent. For 1988, Dentsu, Japan's largest advertising agency, reported a 12 percent increase in ad expenditures to Y4.418 trillion ($34.88 billion), a growth far exceeding that of GNP.[12] This sharp increase was due to Japan's growing affluence and the increased presence of foreign companies. The privatization of former government monopolies, such as NTT and the former Japanese National Railway (JNR) system, also stimulated advertising in communication and transportation. However, whether this rapid growth can be sustained in the future is open to question.

The industries spending the most on advertising have shifted from time to time to reflect Japan's economic development stages. As the economy became more industrialized during the 1950s, electrical appliance manufacturers became the leading advertisers, outspending producers of basic consumer goods such as food and cosmetics. With increased growth during the 1960s, automobile firms joined consumer electronic manufacturers on the list of companies spending the most. By 1986 food and beverages advertising expanded and accounted for 17.2 percent of total ad expenditures, followed by services/entertainment with 11.2 percent, wholesalers/ department stores at 7.5 percent of the total, and cosmetics/ detergents, 7 percent.[13] But Dentsu's 1987 list of the top 20 advertisers showed little change from the years before. Automobile producers Toyota, Nissan, Honda, and Mazda continued to be in the top ten, along with the electrical equipment manufacturers Matsushita, NEC, and Hitachi, though Kao, a soap products/toiletries producer, was the leading advertiser for several years.

Television, newspapers, magazines, and radio are the dominant advertising media in Japan. As indicated in table 5–10, these four media accounted for more than three-quarters of total ad expenditures in 1986, and they remained dominant in 1988 as shown in table 5–11.

Television is the major media for several reasons. One-half of Japan's population is concentrated in the Tokyo and Osaka areas so it is cost-efficient to use television in these areas. What is not apparent in these media data, however, is that most Japanese advertising agencies include sales promotions such as exhibitions, trade fairs, or special events as part of a client's ad campaign. In 1987, for example, about 34 percent of total advertising spending was for such sales promotions. In other industrialized countries, advertising agencies normally are not involved with sales promotions, but this is not the case in Japan because of a growing shortage of both air time and ad space in publications. The need to overcome these shortages has forced Japanese ad agencies to devise alternatives to the mass media, so they even use travelling billboards, sound trucks, and in-store promotions.

TABLE 5-10. Ad expenditures by media: 1985–1986

Media	An expenditure (in billion yen)			As percent of total	
	1985	1986	Increment	1985	1986
Newspapers	855.0	878.4	23.4	28.7	28.8
Magazines	196.5	209.7	13.2	6.6	6.9
Radio	155.8	157.7	1.9	5.2	5.1
Television	1,050.3	1,077.1	26.8	35.2	35.3
Total of 4 media	2,257.6	2,322.9	65.3	75.7	76.1
Direct marketing, outdoor, other ads	644.1	661.5	17.4	21.6	21.7
Export ads	81.2	67.1	(14.1)	2.7	2.2
Total other than 4 media	725.3	728.6	3.3	24.3	23.9
Total of ad expenditure	2,982.9	3,051.5	68.6	100.0	100.0

Source: *Dentsu Japan Marketing/Advertising, 1988* (Tokyo: Dentsu Incorporated, 1987), p. 91.

TABLE 5-11. Ad expenditures by media: 1988

Media	1988 ad expenditures	Percent growth ad expenditures
Television	$10.5 billion	12
Newspapers	$ 9.1 billion	14
Magazines	$ 2.4 billion	15
Radio	$ 1.5 billion	9
Outdoor	Y 2.5 billion	11

Source: "Advertising Outlays in Japan Rose 12% to $34.88 Billion in '88," *The Asian Wall Street Journal Weekly* (March 6, 1988), p. 6.

A striking characteristic of Japanese advertising is that a few ad agencies dominate the business. The top ten firms account for 58 percent of agency billings, compared to America where the top ten have only 20 percent of the market. The largest, Dentsu, has 27 percent while Hokuhodo, the second largest, has 11 percent. This dominance is related to the agencies' traditional function as buyers of media time / space so that advertisers go to the agencies that control the most media time. Another reason for the dominance is the lack of concern about potential conflicts of interests; the same agency may maintain accounts with competing advertisers in the same industry.

This dominance makes it very difficult for non-Japanese ad agencies to enter the industry. For example, in 1988, Ogilvy & Mather decided to end its operations in Japan and to terminate its association with I&S Corp., Japan's fifth largest agency. Ogilvy & Mather found it too difficult to develop the name recognition and stature to compete successfully against the formidable domestic agencies. Nonetheless, other non-Japanese ad agencies have entered into joint ventures to take advantage of the growing domestic market. Thus, such agencies are following manufacturers to Japan, but they need ties with domestic ad agencies to succeed. Even as foreign ad agencies struggle to succeed in Japan, Japanese ad agencies are planning to expand their international operations, posing additional challenges for foreign agencies. For instance, Dentsu intends to increase its overseas sales from 7 percent of its revenues to 20 percent and Hakuhodo is targeting the European market, seeking to boost its current sales from 7 billion yen to 15 billion yen by 1992. Dentsu is expected to engage in an active M&A program to achieve its overseas goals, while Hakuhodo is already working to develop an independent network abroad.

Advertising Styles

In 1985, a top executive of the J. Walter Thompson Japan Group criticized Japan's advertising industry as being ineffective and underdeveloped. He pointed out that rather than creating advertising that is relevant and unexpected and, therefore, effective, Japanese advertising tends to be unexpected and irrelevent, though it is defended as creative under the guise of "Japan is different." The executive also identified several reasons for these conditions, including the Japanese ad agencies' traditional role as media buyers, and their unwillingness to pay attention to ad content. There is a follow-the-leader syndrome in that the ads of companies facing little competition use mostly image advertising that is imitated by other firms. Moreover, because television advertising is relatively inexpensive—the executive argued—it has not received enough management attention to insure that TV ads achieve a strong impact on viewers.

These observations summarize most of the criticisms that non-Japanese industry experts typically express about Japanese advertising. This is interesting because Japanese ads frequently win awards at international advertising competitions, although these same ads are seldom seen in Japan. The ads that are seen most frequently are criticized by non-Japanese observers as emotional with little product information.

However, such ads are effective because they are consistent with Japanese preferences that include vague, indirect forms of communication, and reject hard-sell informative ads. Japanese ads also use famous celebrities or humor which is intended to build a bond with the audience, an intention that appeals to the Japanese concern for developing and maintaining trusting personal relationships. A similar approach is used in ads which, rather than promoting a particular product, evoke a trustful image of already well-regarded companies. This latter approach appeals to the Japanese belief that if they can trust a company, they can trust its products.[14]

Emerging Forms of Advertising and Promotion

Several new forms of advertising and promotion are evolving in Japan at the present time. These new forms are associated with recent innovations in communications technologies. One of these is the expansion of cable television which, while available for more than 30 years, has developed slowly. But the launching of a broadcasting satellite in 1988 increased the popularity of cable TV, making it a more viable advertising medium. Another new form is the Character and Pattern Telephone Access Information Network (CAPTAIN) which is a visual two-way communication system. It allows retrieval of stored information via telephone, but this system is also slow in exanding due to limited information and long delays in processing requests.

Direct mail promotion is also increasing. In 1987, the Ministry of Posts and Telecommunications (MPT) allowed special discounts of up to 30 percent off first class mail rates for marketers' bulk mailings of 3,000 or more pieces. The introduction of these special discounts ended one of the main obstacles to direct mail promotions and sales; consequently, direct mail sales recently have grown by 10 percent per year, exceeding regular retail sales growth. Direct mail appeals to working women because they are time-savers. But this development may also prove beneficial to non-Japanese firms as a means to avoid the distribution system and to reach consumers more effectively. Even as direct mail is becoming more popular, however, negative reactions are arising. Recent surveys indicate that 30 to 40 percent of respondents feel that their privacy is invaded by the use of direct mail and telephone solicitation.

A related development is the availability of the International Catalog Media (ICM) in the Seibu department stores. ICM has set up consoles in Seibu stores where shoppers can browse through American catalogs and place orders immediately. Although purchasing through catalogs involves a 20 percent surcharge as well as import duties, catalog prices are still 30 to 40 percent lower than comparable Japanese retail prices. Another retailer, Dai-Ichi Katei has entered into an agreement with Sears to sell refrigerators on a mail order basis and has plans to set up a "Sears Corner" in its sales outlets.

Foreign Direct Investment in Japan

Foreign direct investment represents an inflow of capital: thus, it is not one of the policy options recommended by the Maekawa Commission to reduce the current account surpluses. Nonetheless, it needs to be reviewed because by enhancing the international division of labor, such investments aid the integration of Japan into the global-economy.

Japan's historically restrictive policies toward foreign direct investment were loosened somewhat following World War II. Beginning in 1949 foreign interests could either make a "validated" investment under the Foreign Investment Law or establish a yen-based company. The so-called validated investments were officially approved, and this guaranteed access to foreign exchange for repatriation of dividends or capital. Such approvals were usually given to projects involving technology that could not be obtained through licensing. However, foreign ownership was limited to a maximum of 50 percent, and the Japanese joint-venture partners were always in control.

A yen-based investment could be made without formal government approval, but a yen company had no guaranteed access to foreign exchange. Full ownership of such a firm was possible, and this alternative was usually chosen by foreign investors who possessed a valuable product and/or technology but did not want to license it or accept a 50 percent joint venture arrangement.

During the early 1960s Japan decided to joint the Organization for Economic Cooperation and Development (OECD) and, to do so, agreed to liberalize foreign direct investment by providing foreign exchange privileges to all foreign affiliated companies. Simultaneously, it did away with the yen-based companies.

Beginning in 1963 the government began a gradual liberalization of all other aspects of foreign direct investment through a series of Liberalization Steps which culminated in the reform of the Foreign Exchange and Foreign Trade Control Law in 1980, thereby formalizing the various changes introduced during the previous 17 years.

The 1980 reform changed the basis of the foreign direct investment system from approval to prior notification and allowed foreign investors to acquire stock in existing companies up to 100 percent, or full ownership. Certain industries, however, were exempted (agriculture, fishery and forestry, mining up to 50 percent foreign ownership permitted, petroleum refining, and leather manufacturing) in accordance with the OECD rules which allow for a stricter screening of investments in these indudstries. The major financial services industries and telecommunications are also subject to special provisions which are contained in legislation specific to these industries.

Moreover, the Japanese government retained the right to prohibit foreign investment if such investments have a negative impact on national security, public safety, the performance of the national economy, if the investment is believed to be an attempt to evade controls in case of a national emergency, or if the government wants to maintain reciprocity with a nation's foreign direct investment policies affecting Japanese interests.

The procedures involved in establishing a foreign direct investment project have also been simplified. Notification is done through the submission of certain forms to the Bank of Japan, and if the Ministry of Finance or the relevant industrial ministry does not object, the project could commence the following day. If the MOF or the ministries decide to investigate the project for any of the above-mentioned reasons, it might mean a delay of up to five months.

Foreign direct investment in industries regulated by specific legislation, however, may involve a more complicated procedure. In such cases a different system of approvals applies. For example, industry-specific legislation in financial services and telecommunications differentiates between foreign and domestic investors and may, thus, create more problems for the foreign investor.

From the beginning, the number of direct investment projects initiated annually showed a fluctuating but generally upward trend. In FY 1976, for example, a total of only 196 such projects were started whereas a little less than 10 years later in FY 1985, the total reached 780. By the end of FY 1987, the accumulated number of such projects was 27, 124, with the United States accounting for most of the investments (23 percent). Table 5–12 shows the accumulated totals by country as of the end of FY 1987. According to MOF data, total foreign direct investment in Japan in 1988 was $3.24 billion up from $2.21 billion in 1987 and $940 million in 1986. About 55 percent of the 1988 investments came from the United States, followed by the Federal Republic of Germany and Switzerland. The majority of projects were in manufacturing.

The sharp increase in foreign direct investment in recent years is the result of the growing recognition abroad that not only does Japan provide excellent sales and profit opportunities but that to become a global competitor major corporations must have a presence in one of the world's most important

TABLE 5-12.   Cummulative foreign direct investment in Japan by country: March 31, 1988

	No. of firms
USA	6,245
UK	2,281
Switzerland	1,555
Germany, FR	1,422
Netherlands	1,031
France	1,376
Canada	490
Hong Kong	3,170
Other Europe	1,404
Foreign affiliated	2,647
Japanese	5,503
Other	—
Total	27,124

Source: *Ministry of Finance* (Tokyo, 1988).

economies. Nonetheless, the overall level of such investment is still relatively low when compared to that in the European Community or the United States. A joint 1987 study by the American Chamber of Commerce in Japan (ACCJ) and the Council of the European Business Community (EBC) conducted by Booz, Allen & Hamilton, for example, found that in 1987 foreign companies present in Japan accounted for less than 2 percent of total sales and employed less than 1 percent of the total laborforce. But they are quite profitable; according to a 1987 MITI survey of over 1000 foreign companies, they reported an average profits to sales ratio of 6.1 percent while the average of the Japanese companies was only 2.5 percent. At the same time, American companies have invested ten times more in Western Europe than Japan, and Japanese direct investment in America and Western Europe is four times as large as that of U.S. and European firms in Japan.

The reasons for this are historical, as past restrictions on direct investment and market access have negatively influenced potential investors abroad. The highly competitive nature of the domestic marketplace, the difficulty of finding good executives in a society where most managers are still reluctant to change jobs, the close long-term business relations, the complex distribution system, and the sharply increased cost of doing business as a result of the yen appreciation have all combined into a formidable hurdle which only foreign investors with commitment and patience as well as adequate financing can overcome.

The situation, however, is rapidly changing. The ACCJ and EBC study concluded that the majority of the almost 400 foreign executives working in Japan who participated in the study acknowledged that while Japan is a very difficult place to do business, this difficulty affects both domestic and foreign companies and is not the result of government restrictions. Moreover, they pointed out, these factors must not restrain a major coporation from investing in Japan which is quickly becoming not only an important marketplace but, in a number of industries, also a leading source of new research and development ideas.

As for the methods of investment, until a few years ago most of them involved the establishment of start-up operations or joint-ventures and, eventually, the buyout of the joint-venture partners. However, foreign investors now prefer the establishment of wholly owned subsidiaries or equity investments in Japanese companies. But acquisitions are still rare because Japanese companies are still viewed as "communal organizations", that is, a collection of people and not of assets that can readily be sold. Other reasons include cross-shareholding and the high debt-equity ratios which make it difficult for stockholders owning only a small percentage of the company to gain control. Moreover, in many companies, nonshareholders or holders of only a few shares in the organization can still maintain control through well-established personal relations. In addition to these practices, the acquisition of Japanese companies by foreign investors was also made difficult by the rule which required that the bids of foreigners had to be made through domestic security companies which had to give the Ministry of Finance ten days advanced notice of their intentions. If the potential foreign investor cleared this hurdle, he had only about 20–30 days following the notification to complete the deal, a short time even under the best of circumstances. Furthermore, Japanese companies were not subject to these rules.

Recognizing the restrictive nature of the rule, the Ministry of Finance in the fall of 1989 announced that it would relax its requirements and thus make it easier for foreign companies to acquire Japanese firms. A Tokyo district court ruling in August of the same year removed another barrier against takeovers; it ruled that Japanese firms subject to a takeover bid can no longer sell shares at reduced prices to dilute the potential investor's equity below the 33 percent level above which the investor has a right to call a shareholders meeting.

With respect to the industrial sectors, in the past, most foreign direct investment went into distribution, particularly wholesaling. This reflected the strategy of foreign companies to set up a strong sales organization to establish themselves in the Japanese marketplace. Next came the service sector, with financial and information technology business services leading the way. Manufacturing, in third place over the years, was represented chiefly by high-technology companies, particularly in the field of electronics, although investments were also made in the more traditional nonelectronic machinery, transportation, communication, and fabricated metal products industries.

By the second half of the 1980s this pattern, however, was beginning to change. More foreign companies decided that the only way to stay in the highly competitive Japanese marketplace was to establish a manufacturing and a research and development base. They concluded that investments in distribution facilities alone would not be sufficient in the future because not only does a production and research base enhance competitive abilities but its also makes the acquisition of the increasingly significant Japanese research findings much easier. Thus, the share of manufacturing investments in total investments reached 52.7 percent in FY 1986 and 64.6 percent in FY 1987. Within manufacturing, the machinery sector received more than half of all new foreign direct investments.

A case in point is the Eastman Kodak Corporation of Rochester, New York. Although the first Kodak products were sold in Japan almost 100 years ago, for many years the company's direct representation was limited to a small office staffed by a few Americans. Independent Japanese firms distributed the Kodak products, and handled all marketing decisions, including promotion and pricing. It was not before 1984 that the company increased its expatriate staff to more than 20 and acquired some distribution channels of its own. Moreover, it entered a joint venture with another distributor, and took a 10 percent minority position in Chinon Industries, a Japanese camera manufacturer.

In October 1988 Kodak opened its $74 million research laboratory in Japan which represents the company's single largest research investment outside the United States. Kodak made this investment not only because it intends to market its products more aggressively in Japan but also to learn from domestic companies about electronics and other high technology areas in which these firms are world leaders. Kodak wants to follow technology developments from directly from inception to implementation, instead of finding out about Japanese technological advancements after they are embodied in new products marketed throughout the world.

To underline its new commitment to the Japanese marketplace, Kodak also changed its marketing strategy in 1986. For the first time, it began selling its film in boxes labeled in Japanese, and supported its marketing effort through extensive promotional campaigns. Moreover, to meet the expectations of Japanese amateur photographers, who are the most demanding in the world, Kodak introduced a new, highly sensitive color film. Thus, after taking the Japanese market for granted for nearly 100 years, Kodak made the kind of commitment that is necessary for long-term success in the Japanese marketplace.

By late 1988 Kodak had also announced the opening of its first manufacturing plant in Yokohama designed to cut and package film shipped from Rochester in the United States. Its intention was to become more efficient in making graphic arts products that come in sizes unique to the Japanese market. Thus Kodak's decision was another indication of its commitment to provide high quality products and services to the Japanese consumers. It is interesting to note that the Kodak announcement came only a few days after Fuji Photo Film Co., its major Japanese competitor, held groundbreaking ceremonies for its first manufacturing plant in America.

Other U.S. companies followed Kodak's example. General Electric, Du Pont Co., Motorola, Procter and Gamble, and W.R. Grace are just a few selected examples of major U.S. corporations that have recently made significant investments in Japan ranging from manufacturing to research facilities. As a matter of fact, a 1988 U.S. Department of Commerce survey had indicated that capital spending by American corporations in Japan is going to reach $2.3 billion in 1989, up 51 percent over 1988 and more than twice the amount invested in 1985. However, not only U.S. corporations are investing in Japan. Imperial Chemical Industries of the United Kingdom, Bayer A.G. of the Federal Republic of Germany, Rhone-Poulenc S.A. of France, and Ciba-Geigy of Switzerland are just a few of the growing number of major European corporations that have also established manufacturing and research subsidiaries. A number of these American and European companies, particularly in the pharmaceutical industry, have made these investments as part of their strategy to separate themselves from Japanese joint-venture partners who have now become rivals and, consequently, can no longer be expected to promote American or European products. But while some U.S. companies are investing more in Japan, others companies began selling off assets such as real estate in 1989. They do so to use their highly valued Japanese assets to improve financial structures in the short run. This does not bode well for America's investment position in Japan in the long run because the exorbitant land and very high stock prices may make it difficult to purchase new assets in the future.

The importance of maintaining a manufacturing operation in the high technology industries is well illustrated by the case of the American semiconductor producers. Subject of a drawn-out trade conflict based on the U.S. demand that American companies obtain a 20 percent market-share by 1991, major U.S. chipmakers are actually doing quite well in Japan. Although their share of Japan's $20 billion chip market went up from 5 percent in 1987 to only 5.8 percent in 1988, Intel, Motorola, and Texas Instruments are breaking into the market in a convincing manner. Intel Corporation's sales were up by 72 percent in 1988 over 1987, and its profits rose by 41 percent; Motorola's yen-based sales rose by 60 percent, and Texas Instruments' sales jumped by 47 percent during the same time period. Japanese computer manufacturers as, for example, Fujitsu Ltd., consumer electronics producers such as Matsushita, and even car manufacturers (Nissan) are beginning to buy large quantities of American chips. The reason for this impressive performance of the three major American producers is their presence in Japan. They closely follow technological developments in the user industries, provide high quality chips, cooperate in long-term design undertakings, deliver on time, and, in general, offer whatever service and support the users need. While even such "design-in" deals may not achieve the 20 percent market-share the U.S. government demands by 1991, the trend implies that through a direct presence and a dedicated commitment to customer needs and requirements, American chip manufacturers can compete with the best the Japanese have to offer in their own market.

Thus, the increasing willingness of major American and European corporations to invest in Japan is the result of a well-understood self-interest. Free of government restrictions, supported by internationalizing capital markets, and, most of all, forced by competitive considerations, more and more foreign companies can be expected to establish a direct presence in Japan. However, although the overall investment climate has improved in recent years and the global competitive forces are compelling, evidence indicates that they will still have to grapple with a problem that no official measure can alleviate, let alone eliminate.

According to a 1988 Ministry of Labor survey on labor and management problems in foreign companies, these companies suffer from a relatively high labor turnover. At the 990 firms the ministry surveyed, 16,500 employees were hired in one year while 9,000 left during the same time period. The average length of employment was 10.2 years; only one in six companies had a labor union, and only a very few offered employment contracts. About 77 percent of the companies hired new employees during the year, 56 percent of whom were taken on outside the regular job-hunting season for college graduates, indicating that more than half of the new employees were changing jobs.

The working conditions at the foreign companies were considerably better than in domestic corporations. On the average, they paid Y10,000 ($80 in 1988) more a month, and offered substantial annual bonuses; almost 80 percent of them maintained a less than 40-hour workweek while 95 percent used a five-day workweek in some form, and 40 percent of the foreign companies allowed more than 120 days off annually. Thus, the Ministry of Labor concluded, the high turnover of Japanese employees can be explained only by their sense of insecurity generated by the scarcity of employment contracts and the widely held belief that foreign companies are not committed to the building of a loyal, long-term laborforce. Whether this is true or not is immaterial. What matters is that foreign investors do everything possible to change such beliefs and to provide the expected security to their Japanese employees by whatever means necessary.

Notes

1. Kenichi Ohmae, *Triad Power: The Coming Shape of Global Competition* (New York: Free Press, 1985); also Michael E. Porter, ed., *Competition in Global Industries* (Boston: Harvard Business School Press, 1986).

2. MOF officials estimated that each Y1 trillion ($6.5 billion) increase in domestic demand would generate less than Y77 billion ($500 million) in additional imports.

3. Bela Balassa and Marcus Noland, *Japan in the World Economy* (Washington, D.C.: Institute for International Economics, 1988), p. 4.

4. *The Japanese Market* (Tokyo: Japan External Trade Organization, 1987), p. 21.

5. "Credit Industry: Fight for Survival," *Tokyo Business Today* (December 1986), p. 56.

6. Peter J. Morgan, "Japan's Consumer Finance Industry," *The Journal of the ACCJU* (February 1985), p. 43.

7. George Fields, "The Year of the 'Shinjinrui' and 'Kokusaika,'" in *Dentsu JAPAN Marketing/Advertising Yearbook, 1988* (Tokyo: Dentsu Incorporated, 1987), pp. 64–68.

8. Randall S. Jones, "The Japanese Distribution System," *JEI Report*, No. 28 A (July 24, 1987), p. 10.

9. *Sumitomo Quarterly* (Autumn 1988), pp. 13–14.

10. *The Japan Economic Journal* (February 25, 1989), p. 19.

11. *Tokyo Business Today* (January 1989), pp. 14–16; and *JEI Report*, No. 34A (September 2, 1988), p. 2.

12. *The Japan Economic Journal* (December 24, 1988), p. 25; and *The Asian Wall Street Journal Weekly* (March 6, 1988), p. 6.

13. *Dentsu Japan Marketing/Advertising Yearbook 1988* (Tokyo: Dentsu Incorporated, 1987), p. 93.

14. *Dentsu Japan Marketing/Advertising Yearbook, 1988* (Tokyo: Dentsu Incorporated, 1987), pp. 51–57.

6 DEREGULATION OF THE FINANCIAL SECTOR

On May 24, 1984, then-finance Minister Noboru Takeshita and Secretary of the Treasury Donald Regan jointly announced a report prepared by the U.S.–Japan Ad Hoc Group on The Yen/Dollar Exchange Rates, Financial and Capital Market Issues. The group was formed in 1983 and took a year to develop its conclusions and recommendations which called for the internationalization of the yen, the institutional restructuring of the financial markets, and the decontrol of interest rates. This process became known as the deregulation or liberalization of the Japanese financial markets. (For a chronological listing of the financial deregulation measures, see Appendix B.)

The 1985 Action Program and the original 1986, as well as follow-up 1987, Maekawa Commission reports continued to emphasize the liberalization process that was initiated in 1984 and eventually fundamentally changed Japan's financial markets. The deregulation embraced the market processes, financial instruments, and institutions. Step by step, new types of financial instruments were introduced; for the most part, interest rates were deregulated, and the roles of the different financial institutions were modified. Hence, by 1989, investors and borrowers had a much broader range of options available to them than in the past, and, inundated with liquidity, Tokyo had emerged as a major international financial center.

Shortly after the Ad Hoc report was made public in 1984, the Ministry of finance (MOF) published a report entitled "Current Status and Future Prospects for the Liberalization of Financial Markets and Internationalization of the Yen" which contained a schedule for the deregulation process. Ever since, with some exceptions, this schedule has been followed by the MOF. Foreign banks were admitted to the trust banking industry, foreign securities houses became members of the Tokyo Stock Exchange (TSE), small-lot Certificates of Deposits (CDs) were introduced, long-term interest rates were deregulated, and Money Market Certificates (MMCs) linked to short-term market interest rates were approved. Further deregulation took place in the form of internationalizing the yen through the establishment of an off-shore market and the deregulation of the euroyen. The major exception was the delayed liberalization of interest rates on small deposits.

Thus, by 1989 the deregulation process had reached a point where no more major changes should be expected during the 1990s. The MOF is now treading cautiously to avoid the pitfalls experienced by other countries during the liberalization of their financial markets, as, for example, the insolvency of numerous savings and loan institutions in America or the aftermath of the "Big Bang" in London. As a consequence, concerns were expressed abroad that Japan may revert back to a slower pace in any future restructuring designed to bring Tokyo in line with the other major financial markets of the world. Critics pointed out, for example, that the MOF is already promoting securitization more slowly then desired abroad, particularly by the United States.[1]

Policy Considerations

The Japanese government's deregulation policy reflects a risk-averse strategy that dictates a gradual implementation of changes. The liberalization measures are generated through a broad-bases consensus-seeking approach and are designed to distribute as equally as possible both the costs and benefits of the process.

To deregulate the financial markets the MOF has slowly and systematically weakened existing polices and laws. This is altering the very philosophy and structure of the nation's financial institutions and traditional processes. For example, the prerogative to float convertible bonds traditionally held by the long-term credit banks is slowly being eroded by the MOF decision to permit nationwide commercial banks to engage in this practice. Similarly, the MOF has decided to allow *sogo* (mutual loans and savings) banks to become commercial banks.

It is the MOF's philosophy to apply new regulations and standards as it believes the financial industry needs them. It prefers to deal with problems as they arise rather than to anticipate them and thereby run the risk of imposing changes prematurely. This deliberate approach has been demonstrated time and again in the MOF's cautious regulation of the financial advisory industry and in its careful premeditated crack-downs on insider trading. However, one should not mistake this approach as excessively slow, ineffective, or tardy, as the MOF's willingness to take quick action when needed has been demonstrated in its swift implementation of new accounting and capital ratio standards. Such speedy measures provide ample proof that the MOF is capable of timely intervention.

Many of the non-Japanese financial firms, especially the securities houses, have repeatedly expressed their frustration at not being able to rapidly introduce products and services that they offer in other international financial centers. These securities houses are convinced that Japanese investors are at a disadvantage due to the absence of some financial instruments and services. But the MOF is equally convinced that by carefully reviewing the risks of such instruments it is meeting its responsibilities to the Japanese investors.

Promoting a restructuring program that is balanced between the various types of banks and financial institutions on the one hand, and between the securities houses on the other hand, is a formidable task. When deregulation is underway, insolvencies are likely to occur. The MOF, however, retains a strong sense of responsibility toward investors and society as a whole as it seeks to prevent bankruptcies. Thus, a conflict between the liberalization process itself and the priorities of the MOF may emerge. Eventually, as the process advances, this may lead to an increased number of mergers and acquisitions to circumvent these problems. However, unlike the mergers and acquisitions that take place on Wall Street, the Japanese variants are expected to be more "friendly" and less potentially destructive.

The MOF has to deal not only with financial institutions and public opinion but also with the internal conflicts within its own bureaucracy. Its four bureaus that oversee the financial markets—Banking, Securities, Insurance, and International Finance—compete for influence on a daily basis. The two major divisions are between the banking and securities bureaus and between the internationalists and the domestically oriented officials. The bureaus are more or less self-governing bodies, and it is the career finance Vice-Minister who is responsible for the resolution of policy conflicts. This, in effect, makes him one of the most powerful economic policy-formulators in the country. Although the bureaus do not openly oppose the financial industry nor does the industry openly challenge the MOF, in the end the ministry usually gets its way because it issues the licenses and is responsible for the interpretation of the rules. However, because the introduction of changes in the financial markets affects the other sectors of the economy, the MOF must carefully consider and balance the complex economic, social, and political interrelationships involved.

The deregulation process is also overseen by the Bank of Japan (BOJ). But in the fast-changing financial environment the BOJ is finding it difficult to maintain firm control over monetary policy, because its main channel for controlling credit and interest rates is the domestic bill discount market. Thus, to enable the BOJ to maintain control, changes were introduced in the money markets, particularly the overnight and short-term funds markets on November 1, 1988. The changes included the introduction of discount bills with shorter maturities and unsecured call money transactions with longer maturities.[2]

These changes were necessary because there was a transfer of funds from the domestic bill discount market into the euroyen market. By the end of August 1988, the interest rate gap between the most popular three-month bills in the interbank market and the three-month CDs in the open market had widened to approximately 1 percent, leading to the rapid transfer of funds between these two markets. But in addition to these changes, more restructuring is still required in the short-term government securities market which is less developed than, for example, in the United States.

The Japanese government's commitment to create an internationally competitive and efficient financial market through deregulation has put Tokyo in contention for becoming the world's most important and influential financial center. However, this role calls for a fully liberalized market that is characterized by high risk, a prospect the Japanese government does not cherish. In addition, as deregulation is slowly reducing the MOF's influence over the market and the yen, so the powerful ministry is quietly resisting. Thus, it seems that Tokyo, in addition to New York and London, is going to become a third major center in the international financial triangle rather than the focal point of global finance.[3]

The Internationalization of the Yen

Underlying the liberalization of Japan's financial markets is the increasing international role of the yen. According to International Monetary Fund (IMF) data, the yen's share of the world's foreign-currency reserves skyrocketed from 0.5 percent in 1975 to 6.9 percent in 1986 while the dollar dropped its share from 79.4 percent to 66.6 percent during the same period. Moreover, Bank of International Settlements' (BIS) data show that the yen's ratio in the total of major industrialized nations' bank assets jumped from

13.0 percent in 1986 to 20.3 percent during the first nine months of 1987 alone. Many countries now consider the yen as an integral part of their foreign currency reserve assets. Undoubtedly, the introduction of euroyen loans was an important factor in triggering this trend.

Trade between Japan and the rest of the world is now also increasingly denominated in yen. As a result of this trend, which began in 1985, the ratio of Japan's imports settled in yen reached a record high of 10.6 percent in 1987, and by February 1988 it had surged to 12.4 percent, on a monthly basis. However, the ratio of Japan's exports settled in yen dropped from 36.5 percent in 1986 to 33.4 percent in 1987 due to the sharp appreciation of the yen which made it unprofitable for foreigners to settle their import accounts in the yen. Nonetheless, unless the value of the yen is subject to wild fluctuations in the international currency markets, the share of yen-settled imports and exports is likely to grow throughout the world in the near future. In conjunction with these developments, the use of the yen in capital markets has also increased dramatically over the last eight years. According to MOF data shown in table 6–1, for example, the ratio of yen-denominated international bonds to total issuances jumped from 1.5 percent in 1980 to 14.1 percent in 1987.

TABLE 6–1.   Growing international use of the yen (in percentages)

			1980	1986	1987
Ratio of nation's currency used in merchandise trade:	JAPAN (Y)	exports	29.4	36.5	33.4
		imports	2.4	9.6	10.6
Currency components of international bond issues:	U.S.$		66.5	62.7	35.8
	Y		1.5	10.0	14.1
	DM		17.5	9.0	8.1
Currency components of world's foreign exchange reserves:	U.S.$		69.0	66.6	—
	Y		4.5	6.9	—
	DM		15.6	14.8	—

Source: *Japan Economic Journal* (Tokyo, May 14, 1988), p. 1.

Some financial experts predict that the dollar's depreciation is going to continue into the year 2000, thus increasing the aversion to holding the U.S. currency, while the yen is likely to strengthen even more, perhaps reaching the Y100: US$1 exchange rate during the early 1990s. Others predict that by the twenty-first century Tokyo may become the largest international financial market and Japan the second largest import market after America. Such predictions are likely to make the yen an evermore attractive currency to hold and use.[4]

The Japanese government supports the increasing international role of the yen. At the September 1988 IMF meeting in West Berlin, Bank of Japan governor Satoshi Sumita announced that the yen is going to become a major international reserve currency. The statement was intended to make Japan's position on the internationalization of the currency unequivocally clear to the rest of the world. However, because American monetary authorities expressed some concern about this intention, the Japanese explained that they do not want to replace but to complement the dollar as the leading international currency.

Japan has made great strides in making the yen internationally more stable, attractive, and convenient. It has done so by liberalizing the yen markets, improving market efficiency, and maintaining a growing but noninflationary economy. Moreover, it deregulated capital markets, that is, provided easier access to the stock market and revised the long-term government bond market through the introduction of major changes in the auction system in 1989. In the short-term markets, deposit interest rates were deregulated by the fall of the same year as were interbank markets. All measures have been introduced in a manner that would still allow the BOJ the degree of monetary control it needs to keep the economy on an even level.

Although, in the past, Japan's efforts to internationalize the yen were mainly due to foreign, in particular American, pressure, it is now doing so to facilitate its own economic progress. The increased global use of the yen reduces foreign exchange risks as most of Japan's foreign assets and exports are still dollar-denominated.

Of course, there are risks associated with the yen's becoming a major international currency. If it achieves real international status and is used for international settlements, then nations are going to accumulate considerable quantities of the currency which they may, on occasion, also sell in large amounts. As a result, the yen could "nose-dive," affecting Japanese economic and monetary policy. However, those who argue for the internationalization of the yen say that it is Japan's responsibility to become a capital-exporting country and, thereby, to contribute to the world economy regardless of the risks involved.[5]

The Tokyo Stock Exchange

Japan has been trading in stocks since 1878. Ten years after the 1868 Meiji Restoration, the Stock Exchange Ordinance was enacted, leading to the establishment of the Tokyo and Osaka Stock Exchanges. The Tokyo Stock Exchange (TSE) is Japan's leading stock market. It accounts for 95 percent of all the shares listed and of all the shareholder equity. Institutional investors hold 60–70 percent of the shares listed on the TSE and, because they are long-term oriented, rarely sell the shares for short-term profit. This leaves only 30–40 percent of listed shares available for trading. In general, on the surface the TSE may look like the other leading stock markets of the world, but this is misleading because it is governed by uniquely Japanese rules that often frustrate and confuse non-Japanese investors as they try to interpret its movements through standard analytical measures. Most foreign securities firms, for example, complain that all the basic assumptions they use in trading on the world's other stock exchanges do not apply to the TSE.

Worldwide interest in the Tokyo market is largely due to its growing capitalization. It has not only become larger than the U.S. market but has also outperformed it. However, foreign financial experts and even some Japanese experts argue that the market is overvalued and could be headed for an eventual crash that may drive the rest of the global markets to follow suit. In particular, they are worried about the rising stock prices, the inflated price-earning ratios, and the numerous investments collateralized by exorbitantly priced land. Ironically, the New York market collapsed about the time that these speculations first gained currency in the United States.

The TSE is not only Japan's dominant stock exchange but it has also become the world's most valuable stock exchange in dollar terms. This is the result of the yen's appreciation against the dollar and the sharp increase of stock prices. According to Morgan Stanley, at the end of October 1988 the New York Stock Exchange was capitalized at $2.254 trillion, while Tokyo was worth $2.677 trillion at the prevailing exchange rate. Figure 6–1

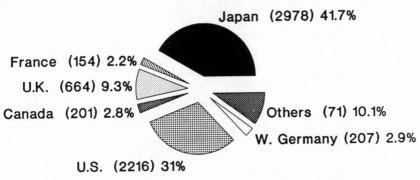

Japan (2978) 41.7%

France (154) 2.2%

U.K. (664) 9.3%

Canada (201) 2.8%

Others (71) 10.1%

W. Germany (207) 2.9%

U.S. (2216) 31%

Figure 6–1. Percentage Distribution of the Value of the World's Major Stock Markets: End of December 1987. *Source:* "Tokyo Stock Market Emerges as World Leader," *Tokyo Business Today* (Tokyo: May 1988), p. 46.

illustrates the stock-value relationships among the world's major stock markets.

A prime example of the TSE's unique nature was the global stock market crash of October 1987 and its aftermath. During the crash the price levels of the world's leading stock markets fell by 30 percent, while Tokyo prices fell by only 15 percent from the October 14 high of 26,646.43 as measured by the Nikkei index of 225 stocks. The Japanese prices should have fallen a lot lower than they did because they were "stratospheric," that is, many times higher to begin with than the price of stocks listed in New York or London at the time. Figure 6-2 shows the trend of the Nikkei Stock Exchange average between 1978 to 1988.

Although "Black Monday" triggered a worldwide decline in stock prices, it took the TSE only 176 days to recover from the losses it suffered in October

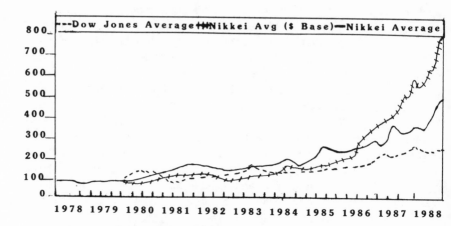

Figure 6-2.   Nikkei Stock Average Trend: 1978–1988 (July 1978 = 100). *Source: The Japan Economic Journal* (Tokyo: July 23, 1988), p. 4.

1987. This was a remarkable achievement, as other international markets are still struggling to recover their losses. The TSE average reached a new high of Y27,123 on April 14, 1988, which topped the previous high of Y26,646 that was recorded on October 14, 1987—just before the crash. Black Monday did not shake the Japanese investors' confidence in their stock market. They did not engage in panic selling; the records show that the only stocks that were sold were those held by non-Japanese investors.

The world's investors were surprised at the speed at which the TSE recovered from the October shock and quickly became convinced that Tokyo was now a leading market. Many non-Japanese institutional investors who were primarily net sellers of Japanese stocks before the October crash have now became major investors on the TSE. In view of the 1987–1988 developments they now believe that the Tokyo market moves on its own, independent of Wall Street.

The speedy recovery of the TSE can largely be attributed to Japan's favorable economic growth rates as compared to the other industrialized nations. Moreover, inflation is under control and interest rates are low. The economic expansion has left Japanese corporations with record profits during 1988. A survey of corporate performance conducted by the *Tokyo Business Today* magazine of 581 Japanese companies in FY 1988 found that current profits increased 9.5 percent over FY year 1987. In addition to the solid performance of the economy, the MOF's decision to allow institutional investors not to revalue their stocks to the low market price has also aided in the stock price recovery, as investors did not need to sell to avoid losses.

The crash of October 1987 failed to deter the entry applications of non-Japanese firms wishing to trade on the TSE. In fact, the sturdiness of the TSE during and after the crash provided more incentives to apply for an exchange seat. Moreover, while after the crash hundreds of high-paid jobs were lost on Wall Street, neither Japanese nor non-Japanese securities firms carried out such layoffs in Tokyo. In fact, most non-Japanese securities companies are planning staff increases in Tokyo: in 1980, they employed only 400 people; this number reached 3,000 by 1986 and approximately 3,500 in 1987. Industry experts predict that non-Japanese securities companies are likely to have a combined staff of over 5,000 in the Tokyo market by 1991. Figure 6–3 shows the increase in the number of the foreign securities companies and their employees between 1980 and 1991.

Such predictions are based on the expansion plans of non-Japanese securities firms—Merrill Lynch, Morgan Stanley, Goldman Sachs, Shearson Lehman Brothers, S.G. Warburg & Co., and First Boston. They are expanding their activities beyond an exclusive reliance on foreign financial products to include Japanese investments, such as securities underwritings and stock dealings. To do so, they must maintain a company staff of approximately 400. However, the only non-Japanese securities firms that are currently capable of maintaining such a large staff are Merrill Lynch and Morgan Stanley.[6]

The TSE defies conventional wisdom for reasons that can best be illustrated in comparing the *Kabutocho*, the TSE district in Tokyo, with Wall Street. To begin with, Japanese measures to evaluate stocks differ from those used in the United States. To appreciate the differences, it is important

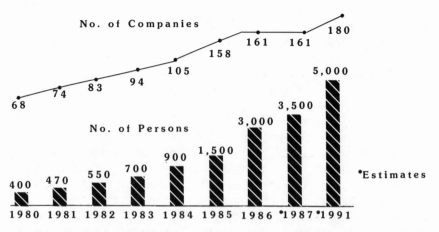

No. of Companies

180
161 161
158
105
94
83
74
68

No. of Persons

5,000

3,500

3,000

1,500
900
700
550
470
400

•Estimates

1980 1981 1982 1983 1984 1985 1986 •1987 •1991

Figure 6-3. Number of Foreign Securities Companies and Employees, 1980–1991 (estimated). *Source*: "Tokyo Stock Market Emerges as World Leader," *Tokyo Business Today* (Tokyo: May 1988), p. 46.

to understand that Japan's two-year stock market boom occurred during a period when the Japanese economy was slowing down due to the appreciating yen. As a result, most Japanese companies invested in the stock market for a profit (*zaitech*) rather than investing in equipment or new factories, and the funds they used to buy stocks were either spare cash, excess liquidity, profits, or, in many cases, borrowed money. As land prices increased, they also began accumulating real estate and, thus, investors actively sought companies that owned valuable and appreciating land which, naturally, drove up the value of their stocks. Thus, land ownership became a major consideration in stock valuation.

The TSE is also virtually free of hostile takeovers. This is in sharp contrast to Wall Street where such practices abound. Moreover, shareholders' rights are deemed far less important in Japan than those of employees, and there is also a closer working relationship between regulators and the regulated than in London or in New York. This practice is frowned on in international circles because it allows for possible stock manipulation. On the other hand, it is this closeness that, among other things, moderated the decline on the TSE during the October 1987 crash.

The TSE maintains a number of safety measures. If a stock's price rises or falls more than a set percentage or if the buy orders exceed ten times the amount of sell orders, the exchange suspends trading in that stock. Furthermore, the TSE does not use computer-programmed trades, which induced the 1987 Wall Street plunge, and while futures trading began on July

2, 1988, and there is no limit on margin trades (buying stock on credit), the rules require a set minimum payment which is adjustable to market conditions. The sturdiness of the exchange is enhanced by a handful of institutions that have a great deal of influence over the direction of the market. Statistics show that about a quarter of the shares are owned by individual investors; the rest are held by financial institutions that heed the advice of the four leading securities companies—Nomura, Daiwa, Nikko, and Yamaichi. As compared to the large brokerage houses of London or New York, these four securities companies play a much larger role on the exchange.

The 'Big Four'

Currently stock shares held by small investors account for approximately 25 percent of the total shares traded on the TSE as opposed to nearly 70 percent held in the 1950s. This drastic drop in private holdings was primarily due to the rapid increase in the number of shares listed and the number of cross-holdings by corporations. However, of the remaining stock listed on the TSE, the "Big Four"—the four largest securities firms of Nomura, Daiwa, Nikko, and Yamaichi—account for approximately 67 percent of the total turnover. By virtue of their size alone, the Big Four exert a very significant impact on the Japanese capital markets.

As part of the deregulation process the MOF has explored the possibility of dismantling the near-monopoly of the Big Four. An example of this was the February 1988 investigation of the convertible bonds market. After the initial probe, Nomura, Daiwa, Nikko, and Yamaichi voluntarily reduced their hold on the underwriting of Japanese corporate bonds, although only by 0.1–0.2 of a percentage point. But in spite of such measures, capital and influence are still concentrated in a handful of securities houses, banks, and corporations. Thus, most non-Japanese firms find it difficult to do business in this system, although they make an effort to understand it. In fact, it even takes new Japanese companies years to function effectively in a concentrated setting that combines honor and loyalty with profit and balance sheet considerations.

The Big Four securities firms together are responsible for over 50 percent of all stock transactions in Japan, and this percentage would be considerably higher if their affiliated securities firms were also taken into account. Their pretax profits accounted for 68.3 percent of the total profits of all securities houses for the half year ending in March 1988, and their entrusted assets accounted for 67.6 percent of the total. Their ability to maintain high priced yet stable stocks for newly listed companies is only one example of their influence and strength. However, amidst the deregulation the Big Four securities firms are expected to lose some market share to other Japanese and non-Japanese securities houses. At the same time, it is noteworthy that although they often incur heavy losses while underwriting issues, they nonetheless do it because of the close relationships with the issuing companies. This relationship is also well illustrated by the fact that if a company plans to raise funds on the capital market, its stock price almost always rises, reflecting the combined profits of the issuing company and the securities houses.[7]

Price Earnings Ratios

Since 1983, the Japanese stock market has been continuously bullish. The Nikkei Stock Average climbed from around 8,000 points at the end of 1982 to the 28,000 level in June 1988. Many observers attribute this rise to market manipulation by the MOF and the Big Four securities firms, and are uneasy about the high price levels of stocks which they believe are seriously overvalued. Particularly non-Japanese TSE analysts are quick to point out the high average price earnings ratios (PER) as evidence of overvaluation.

Dissimilarities in corporate accounting methods and interest rate differentials can partly explain the wide differences in the PER levels of Wall Street and of the TSE. For example, most U.S. financial analysts roughly double Japanese net profit figures when comparing the two countries PER levels. They claim that the doubling is necessary to adjust for differences in earnings between parent companies and their consolidated subsidiaries, differences in taxation, depreciation, and depreciation methods. However, even with the doubling, most non-Japanese analysts still find the Tokyo PERs too high.

In an attempt to explain the high PER level, a joint study was conducted by Takasugi Wakasugi, an economics professor at the University of Tokyo, and Fumiko Konya, a senior economist of the Japanese Securities Research Institute.[8] They found that the price level of the Japanese stocks reflects two factors: the value of corporate assets held by firms that have increased enormously due to soaring land prices in the big cities, and the domestic optimism about the successful restructuring of Japanese companies and the national economy.

Wakasugi and Konya arrived at their conclusions by estimating the value of assets held by all the companies listed on the TSE (excluding banks, securities houses, and insurance firms). Then they revalued these assets (including land, securities, and inventories) in current prices and calculated the ratio of the aggregate market value of these stocks to net assets. The results showed that the ratio was at 0.270 in March 1978, and it gradually rose over the next eight years, reaching 0.453 in March 1986. Even though there had been a significant increase in stock prices since March 1986, this ratio is still estimated to be well below 1 due to the expansion in asset values resulting from rising land and securities prices. This implies that land value is one of the most important components of the high asset values of these companies, many of which are old and well established and own large amounts of land in metropolitan areas that is usually valued at original cost. As a matter of fact, the Wakasugi-Konya study shows that the current value of land is approximately 25 times that of the book value as of March 1986 and that the land accounts for 44 percent of these companies' total assets in current prices, compared to only 4 percent in book value. Therefore, the net assets of companies may exceed their total market capitalization.

In most industrialized economies where mergers and acquisitions are common, companies with market capitalization less than half of net asset values are ideal takeover targets. However, in Japan hostile takeovers aiming at the liquidation of assets are rare due to cultural reasons and widespread cross-shareholdings. Many publicly traded companies belong to a specific *keiretsu* or a group of companies, and usually more than half of their shares are held by other companies of the same *keiretsu*, thus making "greenmail" or stock "cornering" almost impossible. However, this "safe" environment may change in the future because of increased corporate equity financing and a growing need for more efficient asset management. Takeovers may become more common, resulting in domestic stock prices which could better approximate corporate asset values.

Some critics of the Wakasugi-Konya study argue that land prices in the Tokyo metropolitan area are so overvalued that any analysis of the Japanese stock prices based on them is meaningless. However, it can be argued that these high land prices are justified insofar as they reflect the potential "use" value of the land as a great deal of the land is currently held by stagnant industries. There is, therefore, an urgent need for a more efficient land use policy, which Wakasugi and Konya believe is going to happen in the near future. This could, in effect, raise the profits and stock prices of the concerned companies to a level that matches their asset values.

It should, however, be noted that if land prices declined due to, for instance, decentralization or other government measures, it would make it easier to redistribute land among the various industries, and this would promote the restructuring of the economy. This, in turn, could push up profits and stock prices so that even if the Nikkei average fell 10 or 20 percent at some future date due to economic adversity, it may still stay at a much higher level than currently because the PER level reflects the belief that the Japanese economy and its corporations have the capability to deal with adversity.

Another factor influencing stock prices is that supply is limited because many of the shares on the TSE are simply never traded. In addition to the cross-shareholders, such shares are held by groups of friendly shareholders, whose stock ownership in the company cements business relations; thus the selling of this stock would be a betrayal of trust and is, therefore, frowned upon. Many non-Japanese brokers also believe that there is another reason why the market is short: to insure the profitable stock offerings of former government monopolies such as Nippon Telegraph and Telephone (NTT). Indeed, Japanese investors rushed to buy the first offering of the NTT stock in February 1987 at the staggering price of Y1.19 million per share ($7,758 at U.S. $1:Y153). The share's second offering in November 9–12, 1987, went for Y2.55 million ($19,000 at U.S. $1:Y134)—a price earning ratio of 270. Many investors bought the stock in this uncertain market solely on the belief that the goverment would not let the price fall, although the MOF repeatedly argued that such beliefs were mistaken. Despite the investors' belief that the second offering would go through a sharp rise, after hitting Y2.75 million ($22,000) on November 13, 1987, the share price edged down to Y2.38 million ($19,040) on December 11 of the same year. Although most analysts thought that the shares would not break the Y2.55 million offer price level, most investors still expected NTT prices to stay high for a period of time. Thus, the amount of margin buying (50 percent deposit) increased; it rose by 20,000 shares within a week in November. By December the total number of NTT shares bought on margin rose to over 120,000, amounting to an estimated total value of Y350 billion ($2.8 billion). Eventually, most securities firms became hesitant to recommend NTT shares to investors, and quite a few were no longer responding to NTT buy orders from individual investors.

As the NTT stocks did not product instant capital gains for investors during the second round of offerings, market observers believed that most securities firms had agreed to maintain NTT prices. A decline, so the argument went, could have adversely affected the third release and with it the government's overall privatization policy. In October 1988, the MOF reduced the third offering of NTT shares; it had initially planned to release 1.95 million shares but instead offered only 1.5 million. This, and the spring 1989 arrest of former NTT chairman Hisashi Shinto in connection with the Recruit-insider trading affair, could adversely affect future NTT stock offerings.[9] In fact, on September 13, 1989 the government announced that it has cancelled its plans to offer any of the 1.95 million shares of NTT stock during 1989 as originally planned. The government currently holds 67.4 percent of the 15.6 million shares outstanding.

Insider Trading

What is understood as insider trading abroad has long been part of the TSE scene. Many foreign and domestic brokers believe that nearly every market participant, from small groups of investors through corporate fund managers to securities firms, is somehow involved in insider trading, especially since, in the past, most accused companies have been cleared of insider trading charges.

Japanese-style insider trading is a time-honored tradition that exists to cement the relationship between brokers and their big clients. In fact, most Japanese are well aware that their system encourages leaks on big transactions. For example, just before Nippon Steel bought 18 percent of Sankyo Seiki, one of the world's largest music box manufacturers, Sankyo's stock rose 10 percent, probably based on leaks. This incident was not pursued because the Insider Trading Law of 1989 had not come into effect. Many market experts were not surprised at the probable leak because most large brokerage houses have a special preferred list of customers who are alerted to the recommended stocks of the day before the rest of their customers. Furthermore, if a broker's advice sours, he would typically give his client a chance to recoup his losses in a *kyusai* or rescue stock.

The most noticeable difference between the United States and Japan in the buying and selling of shares based on advance information is that most Japanese do it for their companies and not for personal profit. Equal access to information is a foreign concept because "information always belongs to someone." Moreover, in considering the 1988–1989 TSE insider scandals, it is important to understand that the exchange has characteristics that have often been compared to those of a private club. The circulation of advance information is considered a good way to lessen the risk in the volatile market.

However, by the second half of 1988, the Recruit-insider trading scandal put a new light on the matter. International headlines carried stories of suspected involvement by high ranking politicians and government officials and in time public disapproval escalated as more and more information came to light. The case involved one of Japan's fastest growing new firms which sold unlisted shares to influential people just before it went public in October 1986 when the stock quadrupled in value.

The Japanese and American media compared the Tokyo scandals to those on Wall Street. This, however, is an oversimplification because in the American market, the investment bankers and the floor traders are segregated so that profits cannot be obtained so easily by insider knowledge, while in Japan, until recently a company's investment banker was very often also its portfolio manager. Thus, he was privy to information on which he probably traded or which he passed along to colleagues before it became public. The Tateho Chemical Industries case is an illustration. Hours before Tateho Chemical reported its $210 million loss in the bonds future market in September 1988, Hashin Sogo Bank, one of the company's lead banks, sold all its holdings in the company. Although the Osaka Securities Exchange (OSE) declared the sale suspicious and the bank admitted that it had an idea that Tateho was about to make an important statement, it could not be proved that the bank knew the details of the announcement.

To protect themselves against further insider trading charges Japanese financial institutions began to erect the so-called "fire" or "Chinese" walls in September 1988. Nomura Securities Co., Ltd. lead the way by announcing in July 1988 that it was going to separate its corporate finance and trading departments. All major brokers and many large corporations followed suit. Thus, for the first time, investment bankers were separated from the traders. The Japanese believe that this, in conjunction with the possible dismissal of violators, is an effective method to stop insider trading because in a country where lifetime employment is still important, dismissal would not only bring about shame but would also reduce the chance of finding another job. However, non-Japanese brokers are very skeptical of this change. Many believe that the ties within the securities houses are too close to allow for effective separation of functions. They point out that securities house employees work together since they graduated from school and that swapping information has always been a way of life for them.

In response to the various TSE scandals new insider trading regulations were approved by the Diet in May 1988. These regulations were to have gone into effect April 1, 1989, however, due to the rash of cases and the mounting criticism the MOF implemented parts of the legislation sooner than planned. The Ministry received stronger surveillance powers beginning August 23, 1988 (Article 154 of the Securities and Exchange Law) and introduced specific regulations governing insider trading (Article 188 and 189) on October 1, 1988. Additional and more extensive insider trading regulations were introduced on the original planned date of April 1, 1989 (see Appendix C). These rules, for the first time, clearly specified what kind of information can be made public before the shares are traded. Under the new regulations securities subject to insider trading are company bonds, stocks, and warrant bonds issued by domestic and non-Japanese companies listed on the TSE.

In addition, there are now guidelines concerning the type of advance information which is not allowed for trading purposes such as advance knowledge of mergers, earnings reports, new products or technology, and new stock or bond offerings. Company employees cannot trade on internal information until it has appeared in two or more public fora as, for example, newspapers, television, or radio. The new regulations also carry stricter fines; for instance, anyone found leaking merger plans can face up to six months' imprisonment or fines up to 500,000 yen (approximately $3,900 in early 1989).

The regulations also enable the government to investigate companies and individual investors directly. Previously, the MOF could only request information from securities houses or ask the stock exchanges to start an investigation. But it is interesting to note that the inside information, i.e., recommendations offered by the Big Four that are so influential in determining stock prices, is not covered by the rules. Thus, the Big Four (Nomura, Daiwa, Nikko, and Yamaichi) may continue to recommend stocks to their customers, thereby affecting stock prices.

It is also noteworthy that as a consequence of the Recruit scandal, the tax reform package introduced on April 1,1989 includes a capital gains tax (see Appendix D). The taxpayer has a choice of calculating tax liability either on the basis of 20 percent of the profits or 1 percent of the total value of the transaction. This feature is accompanied by the lowering of the securities transaction tax from 0.55 percent to 0.3 percent of the transacted value for stocks and from 0.26 percent to 0.16 percent for bonds. Tax experts estimate that this may bring the government an added revenue of Y600 billion ($4.8 billion at US $1:Y125) by FY 1990.

MOF and BOJ Guidance

The MOF and the BOJ monitor the stock market. Neither wants a situation that could lead to a crash since it would result in huge asset losses for financial institutions and possibly precipitate an economic crisis. In particular, the MOF exercises "administrative guidance" indirectly through contacts with the top executives of the Big Four securities houses.

Thus, the market power of the major securities houses is not without restrictions for they must ultimately answer to the MOF which approves their licenses. Although there are frequent meetings between the MOF, the top executives of the securities houses, and other major market participants, the contents of these meetings are not made public and are surrounded by considerable controversy, often raising global interest. On numerous occasions MOF officials have insisted that these meetings are not called to dictate the direction of the market but to discuss its trends and future outlook. It is, however, not unreasonable to assume that even though the MOF does not outright tell the market movers what to do, it may from time to time offer guidance that is accepted.

Non-Japanese Participants

The original Article 8 of the TSE charter prohibited non-Japanese securities firms from becoming members of the exchange. Although the article was amended in 1982, it was not until February 1986 that the TSE allowed the first six non-Japanese firms to join the 99-member exchange. They included Merrill Lynch Japan Inc., Goldman Sachs Japan Corp. and Morgan Stanley International Ltd. of the United States, and Vickers da Costa Ltd., Jardine Fleming (Securities) Ltd., and S.G. Warburg Securities (Japan) Inc., of the United Kingdom. Following these admissions, the TSE granted 16 more of the 22 newly offered memberships to non-Japanese securities houses effective May 1988. The 16 new members included six U.S. and four British firms, and two each from W. Germany, Switzerland, and France. Thus, currently the total number of non-Japanese TSE members is 22, representing less than half of the 46 non-Japanese firms registered with the Japanese Securities Dealers Association by early 1988. Membership is expensive; each seat on the exchange is worth Y1.2 billion ($9.6 million at U.S. $1:Y125 in 1988). Of this, the membership fee accounts for Y500 million and the remainder covers admission expenses. (See Appendix E for the complete list of foreign securities companies operating in Japan.)

In a press conference announcing the new members, the TSE president stated that they were chosen on the basis of "business scale, performance and history of operations in Japan and financial conditions." Although it was expected abroad that additional non-Japanese firms would gain entry, the sixteen admissions in May 1988 were, nonetheless, a big jump from the previously selected six. They were a reflection of the growing importance of non-Japanese firms on the TSE, although of the 16 new firms only eight were prepared to start trading immediately following admission. The others still had to train their floor traders and install the necessary computer systems.

The initial client-base of the non-Japanese securities houses, particularly of the first six admittees, was almost 100 percent international. The current ratio of international to domestic clients in the non-Japanese securities houses is 4:1, however, the more aggressive and more optimistic houses would like a 1:1 ratio by 1991. But most fear the higher costs of updating computer systems and of the strengthening of the sales and trading operations. Such concerns may restrain their plans, at least in the short run.[10]

Unfortunately for the new TSE members, the October 1987 crash had reduced the volume of trading. About one-third of the 22 non-Japanese brokerage companies suffered a drop in net profits in 1987, and of the 15 companies that opened offices in Tokyo during 1987, all incurred heavy losses caused by rising costs, i.e., salaries and office rent as well as the increasing competition by other non-Japanese securities houses. The price of an exchange seat has also sharply increased due to measures that reduced the commission rates on large transactions and lowered the fee payable by non-member firms to members for handling transactions. While these changes have made it less expensive for non-member firms to trade, it has led to an increase in the cost of holding a seat on the exchange by the same percentage. Not surprisingly, many of the new TSE members find the Y1.2 billion ($9.6 million) membership fee very high, and this has been a source of concern for the TSE president who had requested that they maintain membership for at least three years. Many TSE experts believe that the exchange cannot continue to grow at the 1988 rate and maintain its global position unless more non-Japanese securities houses are admitted. In fact, in November 1989 the TSE's special stock exchange committee announced that it had proposed creating new seats on the 114-member exchange. As the new seats will also be open to non-Japanese securities houses this will be the third wave of new memberships for new non-Japanese securities houses.

As discussed before, the securities industry in Japan is currently dominated by four large domestic houses. However, many traders speculate that the Big Four will soon become the Big Five with the addition of Solomon Brothers. This American securities house has an impressive trading team and has made a name for itself in the government bond markets. It is also an active participant in bidding for the limited volume of Japanese government securities that are offered for tender. Moreover, in 1988 the company obtained the advisory services of a former high level MITI official, a rather rare feat, and, thus, seems well prepared to play a major role on the TSE.[11]

Speculation on the TSE

The TSE has never been exposed to the ruthless tactics of professional speculators as Wall Street has. However, many Japanese financial experts now believe that *Kabuchoto* is beginning to look and act more like New York's financial district. Professional speculators or *shite-suji* groups are buying shares in some of the TSE listed companies and, as their activities increase, many firms are witnessing a rapid decrease in the number of shareholders or shares available for trading. As a consequence, some face the danger of losing their listing because TSE rules require that a firm with more than 120 million shares must have at least 2,000 shareholders to be listed on the exchange. The main goal of the *shite-suji* is to obtain capital gains by buying the shares of particular companies so as to sell them at a higher price at a later date or to force the firms to buy back the shares under the threat of a possible takeover. Although few speculator groups have actually gone so far as to obtain majority holdings, some firms still find it difficult to raise new funds because of the speculators' heavy buying of their stock and the resulting price surge.[12]

The New TSE and Financial Center

May 1988 was a significant month for the Japanese financial community as it represented not only the formal entry of the 16 new non-Japanese securities firms but also the opening of the new TSE building in Tokyo's *Kasumigaseki* district. In addition to the exchange itself, this 15-story building houses the administration and executive offices and serves as the new landmark of the *Kabutocho*, Japan's Wall Street.[13] While the new TSE building is impressive, Tokyo needs an international financial complex to take its rightful place as one of the three top financial centers of the world alongside New Yorks's Wall Street and London's City—particularly since, according to recent projections, the approximately 30,000 people currently employed by the financial community are going to grow to 60,000 by 1992 and expand to 75,000 by 1997.

Based on such predictions the financial community formed a study group in the fall of 1987 to find an appropriate location. The ten member private-sector group led by the Bank of Tokyo and Mitsubishi Corp. identified four potential sites for the proposed new Tokyo International Finance Center (TIFIC). The location they selected is the 440-hectares Harbor waterfront site which the Metropolitan Government wants to develop into Tokyo's seventh major subcity. The subcity, dubbed *rinkai bu fukutoshin* (seaside metropolitan sub-center), is expected to be a focal point for business, fashion, and high technology, and also include residences. The financial center itself is planned to have a total of 105 dealing rooms: 15 large with 3,000 square meters, 40 medium-sized with 1,500 square meters, and 50 small with 1,000 square meters.

However, the proposed site raised concerns about rapid transportation to and from the Ohtemachi-Marunouchi area where most financial institutions and their major clients are located near the triangle formed by the MOF, the BOJ, and the TSE. To overcome such concerns, the TIFIC plan includes the construction of a direct highway or tunnel linking the two areas as a condition of building the TIFIC on the waterfront site. Officials would like to see the project completed by late 1993 or early 1994, but given the concerns expressed, this time frame may be too optimistic.

Futures Market

Although in general the deregulation of the financial markets has progressed relatively fast, the introduction of the financial futures market has proven to be a difficult task. Under pressure from the Chicago Board of Trade and the Chicago Mercantile Exchange to establish a financial futures market, Japan introduced long-term government bond futures which were listed on the TSE in October 1985. Moreover, on June 9, 1987, the *Kabusaki* 50 (Stock Futures 50) was listed on the Osaka Stock Exchange (OSE) as the first step toward establishing a futures market. The *Kabusaki* 50 is unique in that issues are selected and traded as a single package of 50 stocks whose price is determined by the average price of the stocks included. Trading is done on a margin and involves cross-trading which is similar to futures trading.

The *Kabusaki* 50's quick success was due primarily to the reduction of the securities transaction tax in September 1987 (which reduced trading costs) and to the risk-hedging made possible by its use. As a consequence, the number of daily contracts increased from a previous average of 500 to 3,024 by the end of December 1987. Although at the beginning of 1988, trading was sluggish, record highs were reached at 3,500 daily contracts toward the end of February, and by March 1, 1988, the number of daily contracts reached 5,532. This was the largest volume traded on a daily basis since the introduction of the stock futures. Figure 6–4 shows futures contract trading volume between June 1987 to March 1988.

The non-Japanese participants in the *Kabusaki* 50 market tend to be mainly European because they are not limited by regulations. American investors are not permitted to participate unless they receive a "no-action" letter from the U.S. Commodity Futures Trade Commission (CFTC). Such letters are provided to investors trading on the SIMEX (Singapore International Monetary Exchange) but not to investors on the OSE's *Kabusaki* 50 because the delivery procedures used are in conflict with CFTC regulations.

The *Kabusaki* 50 did not fully satisfy the risk-hedging needs of institutional investors. Therefore, responding to the changing market needs and pressures from abroad, Japanese banks and securities houses drew up their respective plans for the creation of a Japanese financial futures market. Since the Securities and Exchange Law permits only the securities firms to

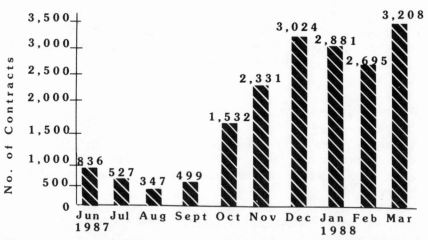

Figure 6–4.   Daily Trading Volume Averages of Future Contracts (Kabusaki 50): 6/1987–3/1988. *Source*: "Kabusaki 50 — One Year Later" *Tokyo Business Today* (Tokyo: May 1988), p. 44.

trade cash securities, such firms claim that security-related futures should be listed on the stock exchange and not be traded by banks. On the other hand, the banking industry, although acknowledging the close ties between cash and futures trades, argued that these two forms of trading are distinct. The bankers claimed that in Europe and America the financial futures are traded not only by securities houses but also by banks; therefore, if Japan wants to create an internationally acceptable futures market it must adhere to global practices. Thus, the banking industry suggested that both the securities houses and the banks should become full participants in this new market. The opposing views thrust the MOF into the role of arbitrator and, not surprisingly, it came up with a compromise plan.[14]

The MOF disclosed its much-awaited compromise plan developed by the banking, securities, and the international finance bureaus on January 20, 1988. It called for a revision of the Securities and Exchange Law and a new Financial Futures Trading Law as well as for stock and bond futures to be listed on the TSE and other stock exchanges, while the currency and interest rate futures would be listed on Tokyo International Financial Futures Exchange (TIFFE). Following the announcement of the MOF's plan, the Diet passed the "Revised Securities and Exchange Law" and the "Financial Futures Trading Law" on May 25, 1988. Shortly thereafter, the TSE and the OSE announced that they were going to begin trading stock price indexes on

July 2 of the same year. Thus, as of July 1988 the TSE began the trading of the "Tokyo Stock Exchange Price Index" (TOPIX) and the OSE, the trading of the "Tokyo Stock Exchange Price Averages" futures. The Tokyo International Financial Futures Exchange (TIFFE) opened on June 30, 1989. The 263 Japanese and non-Japanese member firms conduct trade in three instruments on the Tokyo Futures Exchange—three-month Euroyen and Eurodollar interest rate futures and yen futures. TIFFE has 96 clearing members including 11 foreign firms.[15] Both banks and securities houses could trade freely on either exchange and, with a few exceptions, they could both deal in most instruments such as stocks, bonds, currencies, and interest futures. Non-Japanese firms dealing exclusively in futures would not be subject to any restrictions; the new system would be reviewed by 1990. The creation of TIFFE closes an important gap in the global financial futures market as the exchange's trading hours will essentially fill most of hours between closing of the Chicago exchanges and the opening of the London International Financial Futures Exchange in London.

However, both the banking and the securities industry are far from satisfied. The banks complain that the plan called for the MOF to shelve its design for a single law to establish an integrated financial futures market. In addition, they claim that dividing the financial instruments between two kinds of exchanges hampers the introduction of new instruments on the financial futures exchange. In contrast, the securities firms believe that the MOF allowed the banking industry to encroach on their territory as banks can now engage in the brokering of securities futures. They complain that the MOF favored the banking industry in designing the plan. However, this is an exaggeration because overall the MOF's plan is well balanced and meets its long-term objective of having both industries become equal participants in the expanding financial markets.

Since Tokyo started trading in stock futures in September 1988, the market has outperformed all expectations. But although the volume has steadily increased, the market is still immature because Japanese investors are not yet fully confident and tend to invest in futures with the shortest terms. Moreover, the bulk of the futures trading has been done by securities firms on an arbitrage basis, and the volume of trading between the two futures indices, the TSE TOPIX and OSE Nikkei 225, as well as domestic and international indices, is small in comparison to the sophisticated futures markets in New York or London.[16]

On an additional note; the OSE began trading stock index options on June 12, 1989. The index is based on the Nikkei Stock Average of 225 selected stocks. Additionally, on March 10, 1989 Japan precious metals futures market permitted foreign firms to trade on the Tokyo Commodity Exchange for Industry (TDCOM). However, these foreign firms are only associate members of the exchange and must still place their trade orders through Japanese traders and are only allowed to trade for there own accounts.

The Bond Market

Japan's primary (public) bond market is made up of mostly 10-year government bonds. Approximately Y18 trillion (or $144 billion at the exchange rate of $1:Y125) worth of such long-term government bonds were issued in 1987. In general, this instrument accounts for more than 80 percent of the outstanding government debt. While the MOF intends to limit long-term bond issues, it wants to double the issue of short-term bonds, i.e., Treasury bills. In accordance with its fiscal reform plan, the Japanese government also wants to terminate deficit-covering government bonds by FY 1990.

Non-Japanese firms—in particular, U.S. firms—have for a long time complained about the nature of the Japanese bond market. During the U.S.-Japan Yen-Dollar Committee talks on April 20, 1988, the Japanese side promised that it would remove "unfair," i.e., restrictive, elements from this market if the U.S. side could show that such elements existed. In response the Americans pointed to the Japanese government bond underwriting practices which the U.S. Congress singled out in the Omnibus Trade and Competitiveness Act of 1988 by enabling the U.S. monetary authorities to revoke, if they wished, the primary dealerships awarded to Nomura, Daiwa, and Nikko in the United States. It was such American pressure that eventually led to the full auctioning of the ten-year Japanese government bonds of which previously only 20 percent were sold at auctions.

But even after the long-awaited introduction of the fully auctionable ten-year government bond, non-Japanese securities companies still found it difficult to underwrite other bonds such as convertible and warrant bonds. To increase their market participation, the MOF introduced a more price competitive auction system in April 1989 for the issuance of government bonds. Under the new system the underwriting syndicates conduct a price-competitive auction for 40 percent of the value of ten-year bonds issued each month while the remainder is distributed in predetermined quantities on the basis of the average price of successfully traded auction bids. In addition, four non-Japanese securities companies were allowed to become syndicated lead managers.[17] Figure 6–5 shows the movements of long-term interest rates (ten-year government bonds between February and September 1988).

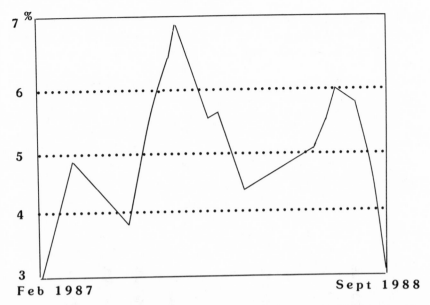

Figure 6-5.   Movement of Long-Term Interest Rates: 2/1987–9/1988. (Ten Year
Government Bonds). *Source*: *Tokyo Business Today* (Tokyo: compiled from
various issues in 1987 and 1988).

Secondary Bond Market

The MOF and the securities industry have made a commitment to modernize
the secondary market for ordinary bonds such as government-guaranteed,
regional, and yen-denominated bonds issued by non-Japanese institutions.
A new trading system was introduced in July 1988 when the MOF simplified
procedures and terminated the registration mark requirement.

In introducing the changes, the MOF wanted to lessen price fluctuations
and to increase liquidity. Previously the settling of bond transactions made
it difficult for investors to hold short positions due to market price
fluctuations as investors settled transactions every five trading days. Through
the changes the MOF allowed investors to borrow from institutional
investors (trust and insurance companies) to settle accounts so that the
investors would not have to hold the bonds and could engage in trading
scarce bonds. This opened up a new kind of purchase market with bond
lenders earning premiums on the transactions.[18]

Traditionally Japanese corporations did not use corporate bonds as a major borrowing mechanism because of limits on interest rates, the eligibility to issue such instruments, and the collateral required. To the extent that corporate bonds were used, the issues were bought chiefly by banks, which in turn used them as lending instruments. It was not until Japanese companies started issuing bonds overseas in foreign currencies that the situation began to change. Nonetheless, the corporate bond market is still characterized by a great deal of issuance abroad which amounted to only 25 percent in 1976 but grew to 56 percent by 1985, indicating that Japanese companies were raising more money in foreign capital markets than at home. Figure 6-6 shows domestic and overseas corporate bond issue trends between 1976 and 1985.

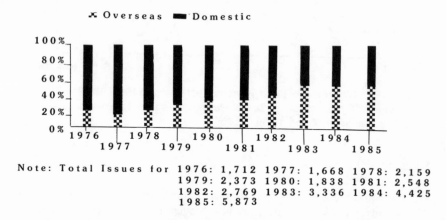

Note: Total Issues for 1976: 1,712 1977: 1,668 1978: 2,159
1979: 2,373 1980: 1,838 1981: 2,548
1982: 2,769 1983: 3,336 1984: 4,425
1985: 5,873

Figure 6-6.   Corporate Bonds Issued Abroad: 1976–1985. *Source*: Selected Publications (Tokyo: Ministry of Finance, 1984–1988).

The 1984 Economic Planning Agency (EPA) "Economic White Paper" confirmed the popularity of bonds issued abroad and this eventually lead to the relaxation of the decade-old restrictions during the 1980s. The 1933 regulation requiring collateral was first bent when Sears, Roebuck and Company was allowed to issue an unsecured yen-denominated bond in 1978. This was not only the first uncollateralized issue but also the first foreign corporate issue, for previously only foreign governments could issue such *samurai* bonds (foreign issues of yen-denominated bonds). In April 1979, Matsushita Corporation followed suit by also issuing unsecured convertible bonds, and between 1979 and 1984, 21 other companies joined in. In 1984 a new set of rules further relaxed the issuance of unsecured corporate bonds, and by the end of the same year about 100 companies were active participants in this market led by the TDK Corporation. After numerous studies and committee reports in 1986, the MOF announced that it would further ease the eligibility requirements and, thus, by February 1987, the number of corporations participating in the bonds market reached 360.

Japanese banks submitted a plan to the MOF in 1988 to deregulate the large issues of privately placed corporate bonds. According to the plan, banks would be placed on a more balanced footing with securities companies by raising the ceiling of a single, privately placed issue from Y5 billion ($40 million at Y125 = $1.00) to Y10 billion ($80 million) and by shortening the maturity period of bonds from two years to six months. These changes would provide the banks with greater flexibility to meet customer demand for large-scale financing and simultaneously expand the secondary bond market. Securities companies are, of course, opposed to these changes; they want to keep banks out of these markets and believe that if banks are permitted to make large private placements, they would next turn their attention to the primary bond market.[19]

The bond futures market opened in October 1985 prompted by the desire of the Japanese government to find an instrument that would provide a hedge against interest rate fluctuations due to the deregulation of deposit interest rates. In addition, the opening of bond futures market in Singapore coupled with certain stipulations in the 1984 Yen-Dollar agreement with the United States further encouraged the Japanese government to create such an instrument. The new market was extremely successful and, one year after its opening, its trading volume was almost at par with the call market. The trading of yen bond futures began on June 1987 on the London International Financial Futures Exchange (LIFFE), and a modified interchangeable contract was introduced on the Chicago Board of Trade in 1988. The 20-year government bond futures became available on the TSE in June 1988. Furthermore, the TSE began trading U.S. Treasury bond futures in December 1, 1989. In addition, there are plans to introduce long-term government bond futures options during the following years.

Liberalization of the secondary bond market was further enhanced by the deregulation of the euroyen market which began in June 1983 and focused on the deregulation of euroyen bonds and the creation of the Euroyen Certificate of Deposits. The deregulation of this market lead to an increase by approximately 19 percent of euroyen bond issues because Japanese companies appreciate the low funding costs and simplified issuance procedures. Japanese securities houses and banks can freely compete in the underwriting of the euroyen bond market.[20]

Short-Term Markets

The majority of financial innovations in the short-term markets during the 1970s and mid-1980s were aimed at institutions, that is, financial and non-financial corporations, rather than individuals. The new short-term money market instruments were immediately successful as their introduction drew funds from other markets. However, by the mid-1980s Japan was still lacking several forms of short-term financial instruments—in particular, treasury bills. The MOF was also slow to develop the commercial paper (CP) market.

There were good reasons for the Japanese government's slow progress. It wanted to hold down the cost of the huge government debt by resisting the increase in the quantity of treasury bills floated at market rates. In addition, it wanted to protect city banks that specialize in short-term loans to large corporations because the development of the short-term market could have resulted in the loss of depositors as investments could have been transferred to treasury bills. Although most of the financial instruments introduced in the mid-1980s (Certificates of Deposits [CDs], Bankers Acceptances [BAs], and Money Market Certificates [MMCs]) were short-term instruments that actually helped the banks' position, a threat also existed from the securities firms' involvement in the *gensaki* (trading of bonds with market-determined interest rates) and the BA market. Figures 6–7a and 6–7b show the structure, in yen, of the money market in terms of the various instruments in 1985 and 1987.

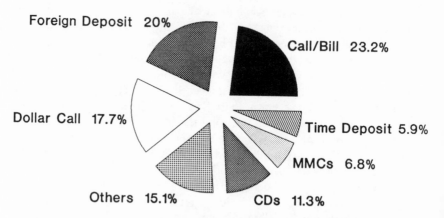

Figure 6–7a.   Distribution of Yen-Dominated Money Market Instruments: 1985.
Source: Selected Publications (Tokyo: Ministry of Finance, 1986).

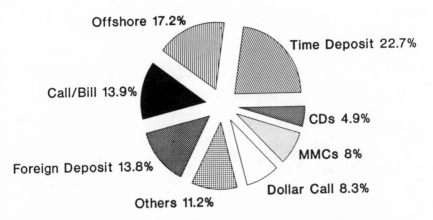

Figure 6-7b.   Distribution of Yen-Dominated Money Market Instruments: 1987.
Source: Selected Publications (Tokyo: Ministry of Finance, 1988).

With the introduction of the various short-term instruments the call-market has outgrown its usefulness. Nonetheless, it has been updated by the removal of collateral requirements in June 1985. This allowed non-Japanese banks to raise funds more freely, demonstrating, yet again, the growing influence of such banks in the Tokyo market.

The 1979 introduction of CDs was very successful, albeit slow and gradual. The instruments' use grew at an average annual rate of 32 percent as the MOF reduced the minimum denomination and increased the maximum amount of issues step by step. This again demonstrated the MOF's desire to avoid sweeping changes although it had realized that change was inevitable. Such a gradual pace can best be understood in the context of the domestic banks' concern over the increasing losses of large corporate deposits due to the growth of the *gensaki* market beginning in 1976. IN 1978, for instance, nonfinancial corporations invested Y2.5 trillion ($11.9 billion at $1:Y210) in the *gensaki* market, but banks received only 22 percent of this investment while 65 percent went to securities companies. The MOF's concern about maintaining a balanced market lead to the creation of the CD market in order for banks to regain the lost deposits. The plan worked because after 1979 the *gensaki* market's growth leveled off. Figure 6-8 shows the year-end distribution of CD holdings, by type of issuer, from 1981 to 1987.

One of the provisions of the May 1984 Yen-Dollar Accord was the creation of yen-denominated bankers acceptances (BAs), to enable a larger percentage of Japan's trade to be yen-denominated and the yen to

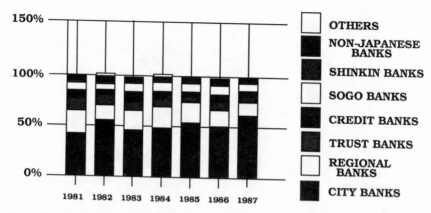

Figure 6-8.   Yearend Distribution of CD Holdings by Type of Issuer: 1981–1987.
Source: Selected Publications (Tokyo: Ministry of Finance, 1988).

appreciate. This was done by June 1985, but the BA's introduction presented a problem for the MOF, for it had to assign a role to the securities firms in trading such instruments. Amidst the escalating rivalry between the securities firms and the banks, the MOF again decided on a middle-of-the-road solution. The banks were given a ten-month lead over the securities firms and started trading in June 1985. The securities firms began trading in BAs only in April 1986. However, this lead did not benefit the banks too much because the instrument was not popular among corporate borrowers due to a tax levied on transactions. This tax was coupled with bureaucratic red tape and, because corporations could borrow tax-free through other market instruments (straight short-term loans or commercial loans), the BA market did not develop as fully as the CD market.

In spite of high stamp and transaction costs and unattractive lender rates, Japan's commercial paper market has been an enormous success. Its outstanding balance reached approximately Y6 trillion ($48 billion) ten months after the market opened in November 1987. Nonetheless the Japan Foreign Trade Council, an association of the *sogo shosha* (large general trading companies), asked the MOF to reform the market. The association has asked for a reduction of the minimum CP issue to Y10 million ($80,000) from Y100 million ($800,000), the elimination of the ranking requirement each time a company issues a CP, and the commencement of CP futures trading. Although the MOF is willing to drop the 0.1 percent stamp tax and lower its rating standards to increase the number of issuers, it stands firm in requiring companies to state their outstanding balance whenever new issues are introduced so that investor confidence can be maintained.[21]

The creation of Money Market Certificates (MMCs) was also agreed on in the 1984 U.S.–Japan Yen-Dollar Accord. One year after the introduction of MMCs on March 1, 1985, they represented 16 percent (Y6.3 trillion or $50.4 billion at $1:Y125) of all short-term financial assets. Japanese MMCs differ from those in the United States in that they represent smaller-denominated CDs used by smaller institutions, such as *sogo* banks, credit cooperatives, agricultural cooperatives, and labor associations. Maturities are set between one and six months, with a Y50 million minimum denomination ($209,600 at the 1985 exchange rate) and with the total issue of CDs and MMCs not to equal more than a 150 percent of the banks' net worth. Since city banks were already close to their limit on CD issues (100 percent of net worth), this allowed the smaller institutions to expand into this new market. The smaller institutions were also given a month's lead (March 1) for issuing this instrument, while city and regional banks had to wait till April 1, 1988. In the long run, the one-month lead is not likely to have any effect on the market shares held by the two types of institutions.

Initially the MMC interest rates were set at 0.75 percent below the CD rate. As CD rates are set every week, the MMC rate is "flexible." This rigid pricing formula represents the MOF's position that larger denomination issues (CDs) must have higher interest rates than less denominated issues (MMCs). This explains why the MOF does not want the MMC interest rates to be market-determined as market forces might narrow the interest rate gap between the two instruments.[22]

Deregulation of Interest Rates

The deregulation of interest rates has been a sensitive topic in Japan. Banks have planned for some time to free short-term prime rates from the BOJ's official discount rate so as to be able to provide competitive instruments to depositors and raise equity ratios. This move, which increases the cost of borrowing, has caused strained relations between banks and corporations. Thus, large corporations are now resorting to other markets such as the commercial paper market to borrow money. MOF's progress in deregulating the interest rates on small savings was also hampered by bureaucratic infighting because while interest rate deregulation has begun, the main problem of how to include the giant postal saving system in the deregulation process still remains. The Ministry of Post and Telecommunications (MPT) wants to retain its privileges, but its competitors, commercial banks, want liberalization.

In dealing with the problem, the MOF declared that free-market rates should apply to MMCs offered by both banks and the postal service. The rate is pegged to the current CD rate and is paid semiannually. The MMC has a minimum amount of Y3 million ($24,000 at US $1:Y125) and a maximum maturity of ten years. The MPT wants the MOF to increase the single postal savings account from Y5 million ($40,000) to Y10 million ($80,000) in exchange for favoring the MMC and, thus, having to drop the *teigaku* deposits or postal savings deposits with high fixed interest rates and ten-year maturity. This, in effect, would place postal accounts on equal footing with commercial bank accounts.

The MOF has received counterproposals from both the MPT and commercial banks. These counterproposals include rasing the postal account ceiling to only Y7 million ($56,000) and cutting the time period on which to pay interest from five years to three and a half years. However, there seems little chance for a compromise between the MOF and the MPT, and the MOF's attempt to modify the Teigaku-deposit certification system may not be achievable in the near future.

The MOF is also considering several other options such as having ten-year and three-year maturities on postal-system MMCs and permitting the MPT to pre-approve credit lines via magnetic cards. Most of these options do not have a chance because they do not equally favor the postal system and the commercial banks. The MOF is under great pressure by the commercial banks and the MPT to deregulate and expand both areas but to do so on "equal footing."

The Abolishment of the Maruyu System

On April 1, 1988, the tax exemptions on interest earned on small saving accounts (*Maruyu*) was abolished, and this resulted in another area of common concern for the MOF and MPT. This measure moved large amounts of funds from bank time deposits and Teigaku-Deposit Certificates to high interest-yielding instruments of life insurance and securities companies, and to money trust funds of trust banks. This has created a major problem for both the banks and the MPT as they must now find new ways to compete against the high interest-bearing instruments.

If the Teigaku-Deposit Certificates were allowed to remain and small-account MMCs were established, the MPT would come out on top. However, if the new Teigaku-Deposit Certificates were abolished and post office deposits and small-account MMCs were unified, the MOF would emerge the victor. Both of these outcomes are unlikely. The MOF is concerned that if the deregulation of small deposits were achieved simultaneously with rising interest rates, then a major restructuring of the financial markets would take place. This would probably set off a trend of large financial institutions taking over small and medium-sized banks.

One still unanswered question is the problem of the complete deregulation of interest rates on, particularly, small deposits (less than Y10 million or $80,000 at US $1:Y125). (See Appendix F for the interest rate liberalization process through 1988.) This issue is important because it effects not only the private financial institutions but also the postal savings system; therefore, the MPT is encouraging deregulation but would like to do so on its own terms. However, the MOF and private financial institutions find the MPT's position too extreme, as MPT wants to offer MMCs in units as small as Y100,000 ($800) to make MMCs accessible to small savers. But this would drastically increase the costs of deposits as banks would be obliged to offer a similar instrument. The situation is complicated by the postal savings system's emergence as a major competitor of banks and securities firms. To reach an agreement, the MOF is attempting to reduce gradually the minimum denomination size and to set interest rates that are pegged below the return on larger certificates and other market-rate instruments. The outcome of this conflict between ministries is likely to end in a compromise: the postal system achieving freedom but at a much slower pace than the MPT would like, and the MOF making quick changes rather than its preferred gradual changes.[23] On June 5, 1989 banks began the offering of "Super MMCs" and the post offices began the offering of "Posts". The new financial instruments are floating interest-rate, six-month or one year MMCs. They can be purchased for a minimum of Y3 million as oppose to the previous Y10 million.

Another issue that is playing an increasingly significant role in the financial markets is Article 65 of the Japanese Securities and Transaction Law which is synonymous with the U.S. Securities and Exchange Law. The MOF wants to see this article, which separates commercial banking and securities operations, amended. Its goal is to essentially eliminate barriers between these two industries, but both are strongly resisting changes in their own sector while exerting even stronger pressure to have access to the other's markets. Not surprisingly, the banks are more interested in opening brokerage firms and the securities houses are more concerned with protecting their market. This is understandable because deregulation and a stock market boom has resulted in record profits for the securities industry. The MOF is following its usual step-by-step strategy by providing both sectors "equal or equivalent access" to all new markets. It is also waiting for the outcome of the debate over the Glass-Steagall Act in America before it considers amending the law.

In addition, the MOF has established a special subcommittee, the

THE INTERNATIONALIZATION OF THE JAPANESE ECONOMY

Financial System Research Council, to resolve the issue of how to permit commercial banks and securities houses to compete in each other's market. However, Japanese banks and brokers are beginning to behave more and more aggressively as they are allowed to participate freely in Europe's securities operations. The Industrial Bank of Japan (IBJ), being the most aggressive, has, through its European Subsidiary, IBJ International Ltd., obtained a seat on the London stock exchange and has publicized its intention to not only trade in foreign equities but also in 10 Japanese stocks. This move further illustrates the split within the MOF bureaus as the commercial banking bureau approved the move and did not inform the securities bureau. No action was taken as IBJ later assured the MOF that it would not trade in Japanese stocks with Japanese residents through its London subsidiary. Currently the MOF has submitted 5 proposals to the subcommittee of which 3 are under serious consideration.

The 5 proposals are as follows: (1) a universal banking system similar to the European model; (2) a system similar to the U.S. model which permits firms to create "umbrella organizations" whose subsidiaries conduct securities and banking operations independent of each other; (3) a system modeled after the Canadian system in which banks and securities houses compete in each other's market through wholly owned operations; (4) a system under which banks and brokers create a wholly owned investment bank subsidiary which engages in commercial and investment services with the large institutional clients only; and (5) minimum modifications to the current system which specifies and limits the banks and securities houses involvement in each other's market. So far (1) and (5) have been ruled out as undesirable options by the subcommittee.[24]

The Banking System

By the end of 1988, in terms of assets, the world's five top banks were Japanese, and of the top ten positions, the Japanese banks held seven. This was primarily the result of the appreciation of the yen which helped magnify the banks' assets in dollars, the resurgence of the Japanese economy combined with low inflation and the gradual interest rate deregulation which led to higher net income, and of the U.S. banks' large "write-downs" and even bigger loss reserves for developing country loans.

On December 1987, the Bank of International Settlements (BIS) set new capital adequacy ratios to be met by 1990 (see Appendix G for details). Although these standards were designed to balance global banking and ensure the soundness of banks everywhere, they were aimed at the Japanese.

The European and American banks wanted to curb the overwhelming presence of Japanese banks in the London Euromarket where until the 1980s they have dominated. According to a 1988 Bank of England survey, the total asset shares in the London Euromarket at the end of 1980 were distributed among the United Kingdom (42.5 percent), United States (19.8 percent), and Japan (13.5 percent). However, by March 1987 the distribution changed to United Kingdom (36.9 percent), Japan (26.3 percent), and the United States (10.8 percent). This happened because the capital requirements of Japanese banks were lower than those placed on the American or British banks; thus the Japanese banks could increase their loans without reserves and still meet their capital to asset ratio requirements.

The Japanese, of course, resisted the new BIS standards by arguing that while some American banks had folded, Japan has not had a single bank failure since 1942 because safety margins are satisfactory. Nonetheless, they accepted the new requirements and began curbing poorly performing loans and the issue of large amounts of new shares to meet the standards. Following such measures, the activities of the Japanese banks on the London Euromarket were somewhat reduced by late 1988. However, concerned international banking experts quickly declared that the Japanese banks might withdraw from the Euromarket, thus upsetting the global financial balance and triggering a financial crisis. But the BOJ rejected such arguments and took the position that the new BIS standards were no handicap and may even serve as a "springboard to make the Japanese banks stronger" by helping to improve their financial management.

The introduction of the BIS standards requires Japanese city banks and long-term credit banks to carry out large-scale capital expansions and to change lending policies.[25] To bolster their capital base while keeping assets, including loan contracts, at a constant, they are raising lending rates. The higher profits caused by higher interest rates expand the banks' internal reserves, thus increasing their capital adequacy ratios. However, this new emphasis on profits has upset the delicate balance between the banks and their borrowers who have long been accustomed to easy access to funds. Consequently, city banks raised loan interest rates only to small businesses and new types of borrowers because they do not want to lose their traditional, large clients. On the whole, however, the city banks are tightening their loan requirements to large borrowers as well.

The introduction of the new BIS standards has lead to a "shakedown" of bank loans. Although many Japanese believe that the standards were introduced to undermine Japan's low interest rate structure, among others reasons, most also believe that the standards provide a good opportunity to review the Japanese financial system. In contrast, some critics argue that many banks are using the BIS standards as an excuse to cut back on loans and to move into other, more profitable fields because their main goal now is a higher return on assets.

In response to the new BIS standards, banks are also increasing shareholders' equity by issuing new stock and/or convertible debt instruments. Dai-Ichi Kangyo Bank, Ltd., for example, issued 40 million shares in September 1987, a record broken by the Bank of Tokyo, Ltd. in April 1988 when it offered 60 million shares and Y60 billion ($480 million at Y125 = $1.00) worth of convertible bonds at one time. In fact, the majority of large banks planned significant increases in market offerings during the 1989–1990 time period.

Banks are also slowing the growth of total lending relative to the growth of capital. One of the main reasons that capital-to-asset ratios of Japanese banks are lower than those of American or European competitors is that Japanese asset growth has averaged 10 to 12 percent annually for the past 10 years. In contrast, most non-Japanese banks keep asset growth below 10 percent a year, usually in the range of 7 to 8 percent. If the asset growth of Japanese banks is kept to 10 percent or less (7 to 8 percent, for example) annually they need to raise Y7–Y8 trillion ($56–$64 billion at U.S. $1:Y125) before 1992. If asset growth is not limited to 10 percent or less, capital needs would be about Y9–Y10 trillion or $72–$80 billion.

Finally, Japanese banks are also raising their return on assets to build equity. They are reviewing low-yield loans (low rates and easy payments), hoping to renegotiate them because it has been a tradition for Japanese banks to carry clients through hard times. In an effort to improve returns, banks also cut back loans to large corporations at low rates or easy conditions while they promote small loans with higher interest rates.

These strategies have had considerable effect on the Japanese financial markets. For instance, they provided a favorable atmosphere for new stock issues whose prices have been on a steady increase during 1987–1988. But there is concern that the number of new issues is so large that the market may become saturated. Hence, the MOF plans to monitor the issue schedules of the major banks so as to space them at even intervals. Securities firms are preparing for the flood of stocks in the market by forming new investment trusts based on bank stocks and debt instruments, and this may help the less known, smaller Japanese banks to float their stocks.[26]

In an effort to help the banks meet the new BIS standards the MOF is examining rule changes that would permit banks greater flexibility that would in turn increase their earnings potential. Restrictions were eased on overseas holdings by Japanese banks at the beginning of 1989. MOF is considering letting the foreign subsidiaries of Japanese banks underwrite overseas issues by Japanese firms of foreign currency-denominated bonds. Under considerations is also the raising of the ceiling on reserves backing poorly performing Third World loans from 10 percent to 15 percent of the outstanding amount. In addition, the MOF is approving instruments with four-year maturities, such as mandatory and plain convertible bonds, preferred stock, and various types of subordinated-term debt. Moreover, banks may now sell or securitize their housing loan portfolios and are allowed to charge 1 to 3 points more on consumer loans than they can on large commercial loans. However, to benefit from this, banks have to increase the number of branches throughout the country. This may force smaller institutions to merge or find alternative market niches.

The Japanese banks are also trying to improve the quality of their investment portfolios. Many banks, particularly after the October 1987 crash, are decreasing their stock holdings and are instead investing in long-term government and government-guaranteed bonds. These bonds are considered to be virtually risk-free and, thus, can be counted at full value toward capital. In fact, the bond market's increased activity has pushed down the yields on long-term government bonds to the level of short-term notes. This trend is expected to continue at least through 1992.

Considering the response of the Japanese banks to the BIS standards, it is ironic that the very rules that were introduced mainly to curb their increasing influence in the London Euromarket are turning these banks into even stronger competitors. But industry experts are quick to point out that the rules are forcing Japanese banks and their clients also to adopt new business practices which lead to the reduction of the close ties among Japanese companies and, thereby, eventually help weaken the *Keiretsu* or industrial groups traditionally managed by major banks.[27]

Sogo Banks

In December 1987, the MOF Financial System Research Committee recommended to allow *sogo* (mutual loan and savings) banks to become commercial banks. As a result, if they are capitalized at Y1 billion ($8 million in 1988) or more, the MOF now permits *sogo* banks to convert to commercial status. Most *sogo* banks have decided to do so, and while many of them had already changed their names by February 1989, others followed suit in April of the same year.

The MOF made this decision to equalize competition because the transition from *sogo* status to commercial status enables the current *sogo* banks to overcome financial regulations that previously barred them from financing large companies. Until December 1987, the Mutual Loan and Savings Bank Law restricted *sogo* bank activities to small and medium-sized companies employing less than 300 people and capitalized at Y800 million ($6.4 million) or less. Because *sogo* banks have a less positive public image than commercial banks, their newly won ability to turn commercial not only revitalizes the financial markets but also enhances the confidence of the public in these markets.[28]

Funds Market

In an effort to segment the financial markets of the 1950s, the MOF used administrative guidance to encourage city banks (since no specific legislation existed) to let their trust departments become independent banks. The newly formed trust banks fulfilled their role as long-term lenders, but problems began to arise in the 1970s as other forms of financial institutions wanted to participate in the rapid growth of pension funds that they managed.

The topic of pension funds was raised in the 1984 U.S.–Japan Yen-Dollar Agreement as corporations had expanded such funds when the average age of the labor force started going up during the 1970s. Today this market is made up of two types of funds: those managed by outsiders and the self-managed funds. Approximately two-thirds of the pension funds managed by outsiders are run by seven trust banks, while the remaining business is spread over 23 life insurance companies.

The self-managed funds are the *tekinen,* or the tax-qualified retirement pension fund run by the tax authorities, and the *chonen,* or adjusted pension fund managed by the Ministry of Health and Labor. The *tekinen* system is used by corporations with over 1,000 employees and the *chonen* system is used by companies employing between 20 and 999 employees. There was a rapid growth in the two outside-managed pension funds market from only Y462 billion in 1971 ($1.3 billion at the average 1971 exchange rate) to Y19.5 trillion by 1986 ($115.7 billion)—an average annual increase of 28 percent. This compares with the total growth of Japan's financial assets by 14.1 percent over the same period. The self-managed pension funds do not qualify for tax benefits; hence they represent a minor portion of pension fund assets and are mostly used by small companies that account for only 10 percent of all companies maintaining pension funds.

Beginning in the 1980s, Japanese securities companies together with U.S. banks pressured the MOF to deregulate this market. The collaboration of these two types of institutions was essential because foreign pressure increased the probability of change and the involvement of Japanese securities companies encouraged the MOF to pay attention to the demands.

However, the opposition from the banking and insurance sector was so strong that nothing substantial was proposed in the 1984 Yen-Dollar Accord. The banks and insurance companies argued that it was an issue of "general agreement versus specific objections" and that safety and obligation were the key elements of this special financial service that must not be endangered.

Thus, only after substantial pressure from abroad did the MOF eventually allow the admission of nine, mostly American and European, foreign banks either alone or together with Japanese trust banks. Not to be left out, securities firms and other foreign institutions created investment advisory companies to interact with the pension fund market. For example, Prudential Investment Corporation of America formed a joint venture advisory firm with the Mitsui Trust and Banking Company, and, as a resut of such developments, by mid-1985 most of the major financial companies were in some form connected to the pension fund business. Eventually the MOF further liberalized this market by requiring the trust banks to report the overseas investments of pension funds ex post facto rather than through advance notification as it had previously required. In addition, the MOF has announced that it is preparing guidelines for the admission of new companies, including foreign groups, into the investment trust industry by the end of 1989 and intends to grant licenses from early 1990. This and other related moves of deregulation are expected to increase the value of private pension funds from the current $200 billion-plus to about $700 billion by the year 2000.

Tokkin Funds

The development of the *tokutei kinsen shintaku (Tokkin)* funds has been closely associated with the development of the pension fund market. Tokkins are basically a portfolio management contract in which a corporation opens a trust account with a trust bank and enters into an agreement with an investment advisory firm for the management of that account. By 1986 Tokkin funds accounted for approximately 10 percent of the total of corporate financial asset portfolios. They are attractive because they benefit from the capital gains tax and provide anonymity. In both, pension and Tokkin funds, securities firms have gained a substantial advantage as large portions of these funds are invested in corporate equities purchased in the stock market.

Trust Banks

Since the October 1987 crash the popularity of *zaitech,* the sophisticated money-management techniques, has dropped. This has left the non-Japanese trust banks trying to diversify trust assets while at the same time trying to maintain profitability. While on the *zaitech bandwagon,* the Japanese trust banks and the six U.S. and three European trust banks experienced a sharp growth in trust assets. The Japanese banks capitalized on their long-standing corporate relationships while most non-Japanese trust banks considered the *zaitech* to be "a boom that was a *kamikaze* (sudden divine wind), bringing fat profits to foreign-owned trust banks, at least for a while."

In 1987, numerous Japanese companies began investing in Tokkin funds and *kingaishin* (non-money trust) fund trusts because holding securities in these two types of trust could be separated from those held in portfolios. This provided companies that traded on the stock market with a method to avoid the tax on capital gains on long-held noninvestment shares. The nine non-Japanese trust banks also took advantage of this method. Their total trust assets went from under Y890 billion ($7.12 billion) in March 1987 to nearly Y2000 billion ($16 billion) in March 1988. This so-called boom was enhanced by the fact that foreign-currency denominated assets were popular with Japanese corporate investors.

However, large amounts of corporate funds are no longer pouring into Tokkin and fund trusts. The reduction in asset volume among the non-Japanese trust banks is expected to continue, and these banks are investigating other areas of possible diversification such as the housing-loan credit trusts, the real-estate business, and the pension fund accounts market. For example, Manufacturers Hanovers Trust, Credit Swiss, Citibank and Banking Corp., and Japan Bankers Trust were awarded the pension contracts by Tokyo Electric Power Co., totaling Y1 billion ($8 million). But because there is a long-standing relationship between the Japanese trust banks and their pension clients it is not going to be easy for the non-Japanese trust banks to diversify into this area.[29] Figure 6–9 shows the trusts banks' main sources of income from 1981 to 1988, and 6–10 shows the corporate pension fund assets from 1975 through 1988.

Notes

1. *JEI Report,* No. 6A (Washington, D.C.: Japan Economic Institute, February 12, 1988).
2. *The Economist* (December 10, 1988), pp. 1–36.
3. *Japan Economic Journal* (November 26, 1988), p. 10.
4. *Japan Economic Journal* (May 14, 1988), pp. 1, 7.
5. *Tokyo Business Today* (November 1988), p. 64.

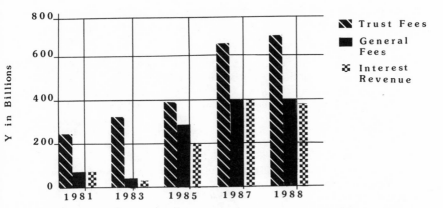

Figure 6-9.   Trust Banks' Main Source of Income: 1981–1988. *Source*: Selected
Publications (Tokyo: Ministry of Finance 1989).

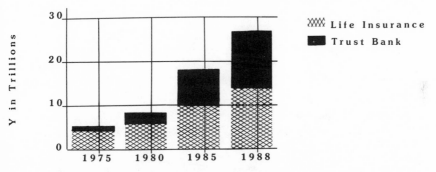

Figure 6-10.   Corporate Pension Fund Assets: 1975–1988. *Source*: Selected
Publications (Tokyo: Ministry of Finance, 1989).

6. *Tokyo Business Today* (May 1988), pp. 46–47.
7. Japan's six major banks are part of an extended family of corporations (*keiretsu*) which
are diversified into different sectors of the economy. The affiliated companies hold each other's
shares and are mutually supportive. This system of interlocking-shareholdings provides for low-
risk financing and constitutes a defense against hostile takeovers.
8. *Japan Economic Journal* (July 23, 1988), p. 4.
9. *JEI Report,* No. 36B (Washington, D.C.: Japan Economic Institute, September 25, 1988);
Japan Economic Journal (December 19, 1987), p. 6.
10. *Wall street Journal* (March 14, 1988), p. 12.
11. *Japan Economic Journal* (January 1988), p. 2; *Asahi Evening News* (December, 1987).
12. *Japan Economic Journal* (July 23, 1988), p. 3.
13. It is interesting to note that *Kabutocho* means "helmet town" and refers to an eleventh

272   THE INTERNATIONALIZATION OF THE JAPANESE ECONOMY

century legend according to which a samurai warrior placed his helmet on the ground where the new TSE stands, to rest and to savor the defeat of his enemies.

14. *Japan Economic Journal* (July 16, 1988), p. 3; *Tokyo Business Today* (May 1988), pp. 44–45.

15. There are 11 non-Japanese clearing members and eight non-Japanese regular members on the TIFFE. The foreign clearing members are: Societe General, Credit Lyonnais, Citicorp Futures, J.P. Morgan Futures, Chase Manhattan Futures, Continental First Option, First Boston (Asia), Goldman Sachs (Japan), Solomon Brothers Asia, Shearson Lehman Hutton, and Morgan Stanley International. The eight foreign financial institutions that are regular members are: BT Asia Securities, Banque Indosuez, Barclays de Zoete Wedd Japan, Korea Exchange Bank, Banque Nationale de Paris, Banque Paribas, Midland bank, and Chemical New York Capital Market.

16. *JEI Report*, No. 42b (Washington, D.C.: Japan Economic Institute, November 4, 1988).

17. *Japan Economic Journal* (April 30, 1988), p. 3.

18. *Japan Economic Journal* (April 30, 1988), p. 4.

19. *JEI Report*, No. 42B. (Washington, D.C.: Japan Economic Institute, November 4, 1988).

20. *Japan Economic Journal* (February 11, 1988), p. 10.

21. *JEI Report*, No. 42B. (Washington, D.C.: Japan Economic Institute, November 4, 1988).

22. *Ibid.*

23. *Tokyo Business Today* (October 1988), pp. 44–45.

24. *JEI Report*, No. 33A. (Washington D.C.: Japan Economic Institute, August 25, 1989).

25. Commerical banks in Japan are classified by the BOJ into three distinct types: citibanks, regional banks, and foreign banks. The citibanks are big money center banks based in major cities and have traditionally functioned as the primary source of funds for Japanese industrial development.

26. *Asahi Evening News* (July 21, 1988), p. 5.

27. *JEI Report*, No. 25B. (Washington, D.C.: Japan Economic Institute, July 1, 1988).

28. *Tokyo Business Today* (November 1988), p. 8; *Mainichi Daily News* (February 14, 1988).

29. *Japan Economic Journal* (June 11, 1988), p. 1.

7 THE DOMESTIC POLICY OPTIONS

By 1986, the Japanese government was committed to the gradual implementation of the Maekawa Commission recommendations to internationalize the economy. Prime Minister Nakasone, banking on his influence generated by the overwhelming July 1986 electoral victory, forged ahead with his plans. Moreover, the underlying trends in the economy were setting the stage for the implementation of the recommendations. At the same time, the government had no illusions about the difficulties that lay ahead. Its outlook was clouded by social and cultural traditions, economic policies based on narrow interests, its own fiscal austerity and the unclear impact of the yen's rapid appreciation on the economy as a whole, at least in the short run.

The domestic policy options chosen to internationalize the economy in included personal and corporate income tax reform, increased infrastructure and housing investments, the continuing promotion of private sector vitality through privatization, deregulation and increased basic research, as well as the reduction of working hours to increase leisure time.

The Tax Reform

Dissatisfaction with the tax system is not new in Japan. Over the years people referred to it as the *ku-ro-yon* (nine-six-four) system, meaning that salaried employees paid 90 percent of their tax obligations, businesses 60 percent, and farmers only 40 percent. By the fall of 1985, the concern among ordinary citizens and even corporate managers was so high that the government had to act; thus, Prime Minister Nakasone appointed a Tax System Advisory Council comprised of government officials and business executives. The advisory body was instructed to review the tax system in light of the fiscal austerity policy and the internationalization of the economy. More specifically, the Council was told to consider the equity of taxation, the fairness of tax rates, economic growth, and the economic opportunities for individuals and businesses in its deliberations. Concurrent to the Council's deliberations, the LDP's Tax System Research Commission also began its discussions, and in early 1986, both bodies made interim recommendations. These included personal and corporate income tax cuts, particularly for middle-aged salaried workers, and an emphasis of the need for simplification of the 15–bracket progressive structure.

The underlying economic scenario for the proposed tax reforms was developed by the Ministry of Finance in October 1986. According to MOF's estimates, the overhaul of the system incorporating total tax cuts of about $28 billion would boost GNP in real terms by about 0.1 percent and capital spending also by 0.1 percent during the first year of the reform. Moreover, people in almost all brackets would benefit, despite the elimination of the tax exemption on the *maruyu* or small, tax-free savings interest and the introduction of a new indirect tax.

All of this was based on the assumptions that personal income and residential taxes would be cut by $17 billion, corporate income taxes by approximately $11 billion, and that a new indirect tax together with a tax on the interest of *maruyu* savings, would generate about $28 billion, thus making the reform revenue-neutral. MOF also estimated that while overall consumer spending would be unaffected in the short run, the eventual expansion of domestic demand could reduce the current account surplus by about $500 million a year.

The proposed changes in the personal income tax system were designed to shift the burden so that salaried employees would pay slightly higher taxes during the first few years of their career and after they turn 60 years old. However, they would pay substantially less during their forties and fifties, when the progressive tax structure was most punishing under the old system. To maintain the "revenue neutrality" of the reform, the Council proposed eight different versions of a new indirect tax without, however, identifying which was most appropriate.

In its report the Council also recommended lowering the effective corporate income tax rate from 52.92 percent to 49.99 percent. It emphasized that the corporate tax rate should be reduced gradually together with the personal income tax rates, and it supported its recommendation with the argument that the 52.92 percent effective tax rate was higher than in the United States, the United Kingdom, and France, and lower only than that of West Germany which had a 56.52 percent effective rate.[1].

The reduction of corporate income taxes was supported by MITI's advisory group, the Research Council on Corporate Vitality and Taxation, which argued that Japan's effective corporate tax burden was the "heaviest among all Western economies" and that this began to seriously affect the nation's international competitiveness. The group called for a substantial reduction in corporate taxes, more policy-based corporate tax breaks, and changes in the statutory depreciation schedules. In addition, it also proposed special tax cuts to facilitate research and development, acquisition of resources and energy, improvements of social infrastructure, and the promotion of medium and small businesses. These arguments and recommendations were also supported by the Keidanren which in the spring of 1986 released its own tax reform plans.

On the basis of MOF's assumptions and these considerations, the Tax System Advisory Council submitted its final recommendations to Prime Minister Nakasone in late October 1986. The recommendations included a reduction of personal income and residential taxes through a change of the tax brackets so that a basic tax rate of 15 percent would apply to the incomes of most of the Japanese wage earners. However, taxes would be progressively increased by 10 percent for each higher income bracket, with the maximum rate set at 50 percent. The minimum rate would be set at 10 percent for the lowest earners, and the *maruyu* system would be abolished.

The centerpiece of the proposed corporate income tax reform was a reduction of such taxes through a change of the effective tax rate from 52.92 percent to 49.99 percent as put forth by the Council. As expected, Prime Minister Nakasone sent the entire tax recommendations package to the LDP's Tax System Research Commission to develop the final version of the plan so that it could be submitted for Diet approval in early 1987.

By the first week in December 1986, the Commission reviewed the proposals and issued its final recommendations. It supported a total tax cut of $27.7 billion a year comprised of a reduction in personal income taxes by $11.8 billion, personal residential taxes by $4.7 billion, and total corporate income taxes by $11.2 billion. More specifically, the Commission reduced the number of income brackets from 15 to 6, cut the maximum rate from 70 percent to 50 percent, set the minimum rate at 10 percent and the basic rate at 15 percent. It also agreed to reduce the effective corporate income tax rate from 52.92 percent to 49.99 percent.

At the same time, however, the Commission also recommended the introduction of a maximum 5 percent value-added-tax (VAT) and the imposition of a 20 percent tax on interest earned on *maruyu* savings. These measures were expected to raise $18 billion and $10 billion, respectively, thus generating a total of $28 billion in new revenue.[2] Moreover, the Commission recommended the exemption of firms earning less than $625,000 annually and of certain basics such as medical care and food from the VAT. Elderly people, the handicapped, and single-parent families were also allowed to retain the tax-exempt status of their *maruyu* savings.

The Commission decided to carry out the personal income tax cuts beginning in FY 1987 over a period of two years and the planned corporate income tax reduction over a period of three years. The tax exempt status of the *maruyu* would be repealed in October 1987, and the new VAT would be introduced in January 1988. However, the income tax cuts would be phased in gradually so that tax reductions would equal the modest expansion of some lesser levies such as the property ownership transfer and license tax. In this fashion the tax reductions and increases beginning in FY 1987 would be balanced throughout the year, insuring the revenue neutrality of the reform. According to critics, had the tax cuts been fully implemented in the beginning of 1987, the Japanese would have enjoyed an approximate $18.5 billion tax reduction in real terms during the first year. Nonetheless, some Japanese economists predicted that there could be a short spur in spending before the introduction of the VAT, giving the economy a much-needed boost.

Thus, by early 1987 the first major tax reform in 36 years was in sight. This was a considerable achievement, because although the LDP discussed tax reform several times before, previous governments could not carry it off. Even this time it took lengthy and often heated negotiations to reach consensus. Resistance was particularly strong from the postal-savings *zoku* which opposed abolishing the tax exempt status of the *maruyu*. It took the three top LDP leaders, Secretary General Takeshita, Executive Board Chairman Abe, and Policy Affairs Research Council Chairman Ito, to develop a plan which the postal savings *zoku* and its bureaucratic ally the Ministry of Posts and Telecommunications (MPT) was willing to accept. The compromise plan consisted of expanding post office financial services and easing restrictions on MPT's management of funds collected through postal savings. The key role of the LDP Tax Systems Research Commission and of the top LDP leadership in reaching the necessary consensus on the reform was another illustration of how policy formulation power has shifted from the bureaucrats to the politicians.

Expectedly, critics immediately objected to the plan. Prime Minister Nakasone's opponents claimed that the reform broke a pledge made by the Prime Minister prior to the July 1986 elections when he declared that no large-scale indirect tax would be introduced which the Japanese people and the LDP could not support. Others objected to the regressive nature of the VAT which puts the same burden on the rich as on people with more modest means. Particularly strong concern was expressed about the ease with which the VAT could be raised in the future, because taxpayers would not feel the change directly. Critics pointed to the Federal Republic of Germany where the initial 10 percent VAT rate was raised to 14 percent, and to the United Kingdom which increased its original rate from 10 to 15 percent. The European experience was relevant, they argued, because in 1986 Japan's tax and social security contributions accounted for only 36.1 percent in comparison to major Western European nations where the same ratio stood at well over 50 percent. Thus, the critics claimed, as soon as the government finds it necessary to raise additional revenues, it could point to the relatively low tax-social security burden in Japan and increase the VAT.

In response, supporters of the reform pointed out that the maximum 5 percent VAT was not large scale and that the LDP had agreed to its introduction. Moreover, the exemption of small firms and of certain basic goods from the VAT minimized the regressive features. Most importantly, they emphasized, any proposition to increase the VAT in the future would have to go through the same lengthy and complicated consensus seeking process as the tax reform had to.

The proposed VAT was widely unpopular, but what eventually killed it — and with it the entire tax reform — was the specific opposition of the retail business community comprised of both the large-scale chain stores and small proprietors who represent an important political base for the LDP. When the LDP suffered losses in the April 12, 1987, local elections, tax reform had to be withdrawn by what many considered to be an overconfident LDP leadership still basking in the overwhelming dual electoral victory of 1986. Thus, another attempt at the long overdue tax reform failed, destroying any hope Prime Minister Nakasone may have had for a third term at the helm of the government. The only part of the reform that the government salvaged was the abolition of the *maruyu* system; beginning April 1, 1988, savers had to pay a 20 percent tax on the interest earned on small deposits.

When Nakasone selected Takeshita as the new prime minister in the fall of 1987, the latter declared that he firmly believed in the necessity of tax reform and that he would put such a reform at the top of his domestic policy agenda. Takeshita understood that Japan needed new sources of revenue to keep its pledge to increase domestic demand through public spending without borrowing. The nation also needed to prepare for the day when its aging population put pressure on the budget for more health and welfare benefits, a prospect only a decade or so away from becoming reality. However, because an indirect tax, now called consumption tax, again had to be the centerpiece of the new reform proposal, political observers declared that Takeshita's survival depended on his ability to pull off the reform.

After months of detailed discussions and negotiations, the LDP's Tax System Research Council revealed its new reform plan on June 15, 1988. The proposal envisioned a $44.8 billion (at Y125 = $1) tax reduction by FY 1990 generated through the reduction of corporate and personal income tax rates as of April 1, 1989; the reduction of local personal income (residence) taxes also as of April 1, 1989; reduction of corporate income taxes in two steps to be completed by FY 1990; and the reduction of inheritance and gift taxes retroactive to April 1, 1988. In exchange for these reductions, the proposal called for the raising of $25.6 billion by FY 1990 through the introduction of a capital gains tax, the elimination of some corporate tax exemptions, and a new, 3 percent general consumption tax. Firms with sales less than a specified amount would not pay such taxes or would be subject to lower rates. Moreover, certain transactions involving, for example, medical fees paid by public insurance companies, would be exempted.

To move the proposal through the legislative fora, an extraordinary Diet session was convened on June 22, 1988. After some initial clashes with the opposition the LDP agreed to first pass the Y1.27 trillion ($12.7 billion) FY 1988 tax reduction bill which was done on July 29, thus opening the way for a full-fledged discussion of the proposed reform. However, the Recruit-insider trading scandal, which exploded in the summer of 1988, and the continued rejection of the consumption tax by the opposition parties created a difficult environment for Prime Minister Takeshita and the LDP. Lengthy debates, criticism, political manuevering by the opposition, and the extensive discussion of the Recruit case in the mass media prompted some political observers to doubt the Prime Minister's ability to carry the bill through the Diet.

But through astute political manuevering, Takeshita, backed by the large LDP majority, pushed the six bills containing the reform proposals through the Special Committee on Tax Reform of the Lower House on November 10, and gained the Lower House's approval in a plenary session six days later, on November 16, 1988. Sharply criticized for his aggressive strategy and in spite of the last-minute delaying tactics of the opposition, the Prime Minister also managed to get the six bills approved in the Upper House on December 24, thereby clearing the way for the nation's first major tax reform in 40 years.

More specifically, beginning April 1, 1989, individual income taxes were cut to benefit, in particular, salaried employees. An average family of four earning Y5 million ($40,000) annually pays 27 percent less in national taxes. Tax brackets were reduced from 12 to five, the top rate from 60 to 50 percent, and the bottom rate from 10.5 to 10 percent. Local tax brackets were cut from seven to three, with the top rate declining to 15 from 16 percent while the lowest rate remained unchanged at 5 percent.

The effective top rate of corporate income taxes was cut to 49.98 percent from 51.55 percent beginning with FY 1990. The basic tax rate declines from 42 percent to 37.5 percent, and the preferential rate of small companies from 30 to 28 percent also as of FY 1990.

As the centerpiece of the tax reform, the new 3 percent consumption tax became effective April 1, 1989. This tax is collected as 3 percent of the value added to the product at each stage of its manufacture and distribution, as well as at the time of purchase by the consumer. While similar to the EC's VAT (value-added tax), the new tax differs from it in that for book-keeping purposes the manufacturers, wholesalers, and retailers do not have to use invoices to prove the value of the transactions; they only have to show the value of the transactions on their books. Smaller companies receive preferential treatment. Those with less than Y30 million in annual sales ($240,000) are exempt from the tax, while those with annual sales of Y500 million, or $4 million, and less (over 96 percent of all businesses) are allowed to use simplified procedures to report to the tax authorities. Such businesses may consider 80 percent of their sales — 90 percent if they are wholesalers — as the cost of purchasing and then pay 0.6 percent on these sales as the consumption tax. Exempt from the new tax are interest payments, insurance premiums, land and securities transactions, medical and health services, and educational and certain welfare expenditures. To enable businesses and the public to understand the procedures better, the new consumption tax was first collected on an experimental basis until September 1989, when it took full effect.

To address the widely held concern of tax inequity, particularly in light of the summer 1988 Recruit scandal, the new tax code contains heavier taxes on profits from the sale of capital assets. Beginning April 1, 1989, investors have to pay an effective tax rate of 26 percent on the gain from the sale of equities; 20 percent of this represents a national tax and 6 percent a local tax. If investors hold the equities for more than three years before the initial public offering, only a 13 percent tax rate applies. Moreover, investors may choose to pay a 1 percent withholding tax on the value of the equity sale which amounts to a 20 percent tax on 5 percent of the value of the transfer. The securities transaction tax was also cut from 0.5 to 0.3 percent of the value of the shares sold and from 0.26 to 0.16 of the value of convertible bonds and bonds with equity-purchase warrants.

Finally a number of indirect taxes applied to a variety of goods and services were either eliminated or changed. Of the 29 such taxes, five national and three local taxes were abolished because they were replaced by the new 3 percent consumption tax. These include the 30 percent national commodity tax applied to 85 items in the luxury products category as, for example, furs, carpets, TV sets, cameras, furniture, and automobiles. However, passenger cars are subject to a temporary rate of 6 percent until 1992. Liquor and tobacco are subject to former and new indirect taxes, but the tax rates have been reduced. In particular, premium spirits and wines, mostly imported, are subject to the new lower taxes, a demand that American and European exporters have long upheld. Moreover, to equalize prices between domestic and imported spirits, the tax on low grade domestic products was sharply increased.

In general, the reform changed Japan's heavy reliance on direct income taxes which in the past put great pressure on individuals and corporations. The introduction of the consumption tax reduces this pressure, enables the government to develop sound financial plans for the support of the aging population, and promotes equality among taxpayers in that the self-employed, who until the reform did not pay their share of taxes, can no longer escape the tax collector's net. Of course, the measures are not welcomed by all Japanese; the reforms are resented and criticized by many for a variety of reasons. Some are concerned about the current land tax system and wanted major changes in it, while others believe that the basic inequities of the old system was not altered apart from the introduction of the capital gains tax on the sale of assets. Critics also point out that the new 3 percent consumption tax is confusing and that allowing businesses to record only transactions without the proof of invoices is going to lead to large-scale tax evasions and/or price gouging of consumers. To address the last concerns, MITI decided to conduct monthly nationwide surveys to check if products are being sold at the proper prices following the introduction of the 3 percent consumption tax. Moreover, MITI also intends to see if prices have dropped as a consequence of the abolition of the commodity taxes.

Overall, government and most private sector economists predicted that the tax reductions outweigh the new 3 percent consumption tax and some other increases by approximately Y2.6 trillion ($20.8 billion at Y125 = $1) in FY 1989. Inflation-adjusted GNP is likely to be enhanced by about 0.2

percent during FY 1990–FY 1993, and as a result of increased imports the current account surplus is expected to be reduced by $5 billion annually during FY 1988–FY 1991. Furthermore, the share of total revenue obtained from direct taxes is projected to decline from 73 percent in FY 1987 to approximately 67 percent by the end of FY 1989, thereby realizing one of the major objectives of the reform. At the same time, in response to the new consumption tax, prices may rise by a little over 1 percent over the next couple of years. This, in conjunction with the diminishing trend of the year-to-year decline in labor costs in manufacturing that became noticeable in early 1989, raised some concern among economists about price movements in the years to come.

However, by the summer of 1989 it became clear that the consumption tax, while economically justified, turned into a major political problem. Millions of people were incensed that expensive cars, whiskey, gold, diamond and platinum jewelry became approximately 12 percent less expensive while vegetables, milk and rent went up by 3 percent. Many businesses with less than 30 million yen annual sales which were exempted from the new tax have nevertheless imposed the tax on their customers in the form of higher prices and pocketed it. Where the new tax resulted in tax savings i.e. lower taxes, few of the businesses passed on the savings to consumers in the form of lower prices. In general, price rises were applied unevenly by retailers and other businesses with some ignoring the tax while others raising prices by as much as 20 percent. Furthermore, many of the small firms could not cope with the adjustment of price registers and of price tags and simply "rounded off" the prices usually to the disadvantage of consumers. Most of all, the necessity of the consumption tax and its structure was never fully explained to the Japanese people who paid more attention to the increase in the price of a bowl of noodles by 50 yen than to the government's claims that overall the reform reduced everybody's tax burden.

The opposition parties took advantage of the angry mood of the public and supported by a media-campaign made the 3 percent tax a cornerstone of their Upper House election strategy in June of 1989. They argued that the consumption tax was a symbol of the arrogance of the LDP politicians and the Ministry of Finance bureaucrats who have become unaccountable to the public. Irritated by the Recruit scandal and its aftermath as well as by the widening income distribution the public responded and dealt the LDP its first loss in a national election in 34 years.

Following the election, the opposition and other critics of the consumption tax demanded its elimination. However, the government resisted such attempts and agreed only to a review of the tax application process and of its effects. The government's Tax System Commission established a subcommittee to review the tax and the Ministry of Finance also began a study of possible changes. Some of these included the renaming of the tax, its application to social welfare programs, the requirement to include it in the displayed price rather than to charge it separately at the cashier, stricter protection against cheating and overcharging and even the reduction of the rate. By December 1, 1989 the LDP's Research Commission on the Tax Systems developed a set of changes in the consumption tax which it planned to submit to the Diet in the form of a bill. The changes included, among other minor adjustments, the abolishment of the 3 percent tax on food at the retail level and the reduction of it to 1.5 percent at the producer and wholesale level. The compromise was reached after a bitter intra-party struggle.

Infrastructure Investments

As reported by the Economic Planning Agency, by the end of March 1986 (FY 1985), Japan had an estimated $2 trillion in social infrastructure assets stated in 1980 prices.[3] Moreover, the EPA pointed out, in FY 1982 (the only year for which breakdowns are available), of the $1.4 trillion total in that year approximately 31.7 percent represented sewage systems, parks, schools, and other environmental facilities. About 44.6 percent represented transportation and communication facilities such as roads and railways, 9.8 percent national land, and about 11.7 percent agriculture, fishery, and forestry infrastructures.

An alarming set of statistics was reported by the Environmental Agency in late 1988 concerning the decline of the untouched forest areas of the nation by 23 percent during the last ten years. Compared to the first such census data reported in 1973, the total of Japanese beech forests was reduced by 423,500 hectares on the Japan Sea side and by 17,600 hectares on the Pacific Ocean side for a total of 441,100 hectares. This is more than twice the area of Tokyo, which covers 214,400 hectares. As a consequence, the natural Japanese beech forests now account for 3.9 percent of total land area and 5.8 percent of total forests, much less than in the past.

The FY 1985 social infrastructure of $2 trillion is high by international comparison. However, a more detailed breakdown reveals that the diffusion level of social infrastructure in Japan is lower than in most industrialized countries. For example, the diffusion of sewages was 72 percent in the United State and 97 percent in the United Kingdom in the late 1970s, but only 33 percent in Japan in 1983. In 1983, only slightly over 53 percent of Japan's roads were paved as opposed to West Germany's (99 percent), the United Kingdom's (96.4 percent), and France's (95 percent). Furthermore, during the early 1980s, Tokyo had the lowest per capita park space, 2.1 square meters, among the world's major capital cities, while Washington, D.C., had 45.7, Bonn 37.4, London 30.4, Paris 12.2, and Stockholm and impressive 80.3 square meters.

The major reason for the discrepancy between the reported value of social infrastructure and its diffusion rate is due to the high cost of construction in Japan relative to other industrialized nations. These higher costs do not include land prices; consequently, the decisive factor may be the topography, which is characterized by mountainous regions. Moreover, most of the social infrastructure in Japan was built after the 1960s whereas in Western Europe or the United States, the infrastructures were built over longer periods of time and were, therefore, less costly.

Japan's urban infrastructure in particular leaves much to be desired. This is borne out by a May 1986 report on Japan's urban policies published by the Organization for Economic Cooperation and Development (OECD) at the request of the Japanese government.[4] The report emphasized that while Japan was once a rural nation, by the early 1980s around 77 percent of its population lived in cities, thus making it the most urbanized of all 24 OECD member countries. Therefore, the government should now give priority to urban policies, in particular to the improvement of urban social infrastructures, not only to increase domestic demand but most importantly, to improve the quality of life for its citizens. As for funding, the OECD suggested that this could be obtained through the use of private savings for the national budget's infrastructure investment and loan programs.

In addition, the report also chided the Japanese authorities for their apparent lack of interest in making Japanese cities more pleasant for their inhabitants. At the same time, it counseled caution concerning the plans for the deregulation of the various current controls to stimulate private sector activities in urban redevelopment. In view of the OECD urban experts, Japan's current regulations still leave enough room for improvements without a possibly overhastened deregulation which could disregard traditional concerns and, thus, cause problems in the long run.

Public efforts to improve the social infrastructure are already under way.[5] By mid-1986, the Ministry of Construction proposed 51 projects, the Ministry of Transport 18, and MITI 98; once possible duplications are eliminated, probably more than 100 projects will remain on the list. Moreover, if joint projects between the private sector and local governments as well as independent local initiatives are also included, the total may rise to 150. All of these projects will be financed with public funds complemented by substantial private sector investments which are expected to have a multiplier effect throughout the economy.

One of the largest building projects, the Kansai Cultural and Scientific

Research City, is a Ministry of Construction project in the Kinki area, the western Japan counterpart of Tsukuba Academic City in Ibaraki Prefecture near Tokyo. The new planned city will include not only public research institutes but also universities, private research institutes, recreational facilities, housing and parks in a bid to create a pilot model city for the twenty-first century and an international center of research and culture. It will be built in an area that reaches into three prefectures—Nara, Osaka, and Kyoto—covers approximately 25 million hectares, and will house a population of about 120,000 people when completed. Total investment is expected to reach about $30 billion of which $22 billion is expected to be provided by the private sector. The construction is already under way.

Another major construction project in the same area is the new Kansai International Airport. The $8 billion project is due to be completed in 1993, and will service about 18 million passengers and 660,000 metric tons of cargo annually. In addition, the Osaka Prefectural Government tentatively calculated that the new airport will require additional services such as food and communications, thereby creating new demands of perhaps $32 billion over the next few years. The airport is unique in that it is built on an artificial island of about 1,260 acres. Kansai will be Japan's first 24–hour airport, and it will be connected to the mainland by a 2.4 mile-long bridge. The Kansai International Airport Co. was established to oversee construction; the company is capitalized at $500 million of which over 60 percent is borne by the Japanese government, and the rest by local authorities and the private sector. This is the first time that local authorities and private firms have participated in building an airport; until 1986, such projects were undertaken only by the government.

The major infrastructure project under construction in the Tokyo area is the Trans-Tokyo Bay Highway, to be completed by 1996. The highway will run across the central part of Tokyo Bay and will be linked with the Tokyo Bay Shore Highway and other roads to form a major beltway system. The four-lane expressway (two additional lanes will be built sometime in the future) will cross one of the most crowded sea areas of the bay; consequently, it will consist partially of roads, tunnels, and one bridge connecting two man-made islands. Total costs are estimated to reach $10 billion, but total spending, including all the necessary additional investments, is predicted to reach $16 billion. The multiplier effect of the project is also expected to be substantial as the Ministry of Transportation, for example, is already planning to build hotels a yacht harbor, and housing facilities on the two artifical islands.

In addition to such major national undertakings, local governments also intend to develop regional projects envisioning the creation of industrial and urban areas around high-technology and information-oriented corporations and the expansion of urban facilities in general. In greater Tokyo, which includes the prefectures Chiba, Kanagawa, and Saitama, for example, projects to build new business zones, telecommunications networks, and residential areas are getting underway. The major goal of these projects is to reduce the pressure on Tokyo as the nation's political, business, and cultural center, and to establish a new global financial complex comparable to New York or London.

The largest project in Tokyo, built under the jurisdicition of the municipal government, is the construction of a new metropolitan district on the waterfront of Tokyo Bay. Included are a 24-hour telecommunications center called Tokyo-Teleport, a number of intelligence buildings equipped with in-house information networks, an international convention hall and hotels, as well as apartment buildings. Other projects, such as a huge exhibition hall and high-tech business center in Chiba, high class office buildings, exhibition halls, hotels and telecommunications facilities in Kanagawa, and the construction of up-to-date industrial and commercial zones similar to those planned in Tokyo, Chiba, and Kanagawa, are planned for the southern part of Saitama. Although most people view these projects with enthusiasm, some remain concerned that they will draw more people into an already badly congested area. The critics point to the government's recent decision that the number of people in the region should be held down to less than 33 million by 1995 (up by only 3 million from 1985), a target difficult to achieve with the massive developments planned. The potential problems were underlined by a 1989 survey of the Tokyo Metropolitan Government which showed that the overwhelming majority of the region's residents believe that the influx of people has already made life very difficult and that the movement of more people to the capital area should be curtailed. Such concerns are rooted in statistics revealing that while greater Tokyo has a total area that represents only 3.6 percent of the total land available, a little over 30 million people or more than 25 percent of the country's population live there.

Not surprisingly, the debate about building a new capital away from Tokyo or, at least, to decentralize some of the governmental functions to some other areas began again in the spring of 1988. Referred to as *sento-ron,* the debate quickly evolved into what can best be called "Tokyo-bashing": politicians, the mass media, and other opinion-makers reinforced by a large number of official and unofficial committees argued over the merits of various possible locations and the steps necessary to do away with congestion in Tokyo. By January 1988, the Takeshita cabinet decided to relocate 31 agencies, representing at least one from every ministry, and increased this number to 79, involving approximately 20,000 people in the summer of the same year. Moreover, an LDP committee headed by the influential senior politician Shin Kanemaru in 1988 began to prepare a relocation report to be submitted in final form by 1991. The entire decentralization project is expected to take 10 years or so and is likely to spark intensive interministerial rivalry, because while all bureaucrats agree that decentralization is necessary, none of them wants to leave Tokyo if he/she can help it.

Former Prime Minister Takeshita was very much interested in the decentralization project because it fit into his grand domestic policy design to make Japan a better place in which to live. Early in his administration he promoted the idea of *furusato*, or the building of "hometowns," by moving industries and people into the less developed regions of the country and by creating a network of neighborly communities where people would have a sense of belonging and could enjoy their lives. The concept is to be implemented by the Furusato Foundation and funded primarily by local governments and private enterprise, although the national government would also provide assistance. In January 1989, for example, it announced the allocation of Y100 million ($800,000) to each of the nation's 3,056 cities, towns, and villages between 1989 and 1991, to be spent any way they wanted. It should be pointed out that the funds come from the local allocation tax, which was originally designated for local governments to use at their discretion. While the local governments understandably welcome the plan and the allocation of funds, some critics are concerned that it might just be a short-term project and that it could suffer the same fate as former Prime Minister Tanaka's Japanese Archipelago Reconstruction plan of the early 1970s which touched off land speculation and was only marginally successful. Others point out that the creation of the Furusato Foundation is likely to set off an interministerial turf battle that could seriously constrain the project. The resignation of Takeshita in the spring of 1989 fueled such speculations even more.

While the stimulating effects of such mammoth infrastructure projects on domestic demand is generally acknowledged, there is concern about the extent to which such undertakings can increase imports. A case in point is the building of the Kansai International Airrport which gradually developed into another U.S.–Japan trade conflict. Washington was lobbying vigorously to obtain a share of the $8 billion project through an open bidding system. While the airport was the immediate focus of this effort, the broader goal of the United States was to get a foothold so that American companies could bid for the estimated total of $191 billion public construction projects as they become available in the future.

However, under Japanese construction laws, foreign firms need permission from either the Ministry of Construction, the governor of the prefecture, or the local authorities concerned to engage in construction activities. Moreover, the traditional Japanese "designated" bidding system is quite different from the open bidding system that American and other foreign companies are used to. Under the designated bidding system, the organization in charge of a project selects about a dozen or so firms from the list of registered contractors on the basis of their established capabilities. These so-called "designated companies" then submit bids, and the lowest bidder is awarded the contract. Officials justify this restriction on eligibility as a means to prevent below-standard or unscrupulous firms from getting involved with projects and conceivably causing major problems.

While such considerations undoubtedly play a role, the major reason for the restrictions is the saturation of the Japanese construction market. The main characteristics of the industry are intense competition involving more than 500,000 firms, most of which are small-sized, with those capitalized at Y100 million or less ($770,000 at Y135 = $1) accounting for 99 percent of the total. Small contractors are incapable of undertaking large projects on their own and normally survive by doing civil engineering work, such as road paving and repair. They also depend heavily on subcontracts from large construction companies.

The designated bidding system, under which only certain approved contractor can bid on a public works project, is used by the national and local governments to assure that a certain percentage of the work is obtained by the small firms. Interested companies are first rated by the jobs completed, equity capital, number of employees, liquidity ratio, ratio of capital to fixed assets, ratio of net profits to total capital, and the length of operating. The Ministry of Construction also evaluates the bidders with respect to quality of workmanship, safety record, and employee compensation. Furthermore, until the 1988 U.S.–Japan construction agreement, actual construction experience in Japan was also a consideration so that non-Japanese companies could not even submit bids; of course, without winning a bid they could not obtain Japanese construction experience in the first place.

Construction companies sometimes also obtain the support of politicians who recommend them to the Ministry of Construction, and they also employ former government bureaucrats through the traditional *amakudari* retirement system. Moreover, because the industry is a key supporter of the LDP, the construction-*zoku* of the LDP in the Diet looks after the interests of the industry. At the same time, the industry receives only split support in its controversies with other nations. The Ministry of Foreign Affairs, for example, is always more interested in maintaining good relations with other countries rather than in defending the narrowly defined interests of an industry under pressure from abroad. Japan's Fair Trade Commission (FTC) has, over a number of years, investigated certain industry practices which it identified as anti-competitive and, therefore, illegal, much to the chagrin of the industry and the delight of the foreign companies seeking access to the construction market.

The focal point of these investigations is the so-called pre-bidding or *dango* consultation system. This is a procedure used in most public works projects that involves the designation of the contract works projects that involves the designation of the contract winner prior to actual bidding. The decisions are made by consensus on the basis of legitimate technical and business considerations, but once the winner is agreed upon, the other companies adjust their bids accordingly. In a sense, a *dango* is what is known in the United States and Europe as a "gentlemen's agreement" concerning the allocation of business in a very competitive industry. The practice preserves profit margins and provides each company a "fair share" of business as they take turns in getting contracts.

Dango is, of course, illegal, and the FTC series of hearings in 1981 and 1982 revealed many of the intricacies of the process. It was denounced by the FTC as unfairly limiting competition and was prohibited by a special order. As a result, in 1982 the representatives of major construction companies met to discuss how the practice was used by the Japanese Association of Civil Engineers which allocated trillions of yen for public works projects every year. A committee of "elders" and other arrangements were identified as the major instruments of *dango* and were disbanded.

However, this does not mean that the practice has been completely eliminated. In December 1988, for example, the FTC ordered 70 construction companies to pay fines for rigging bids for orders they received from the U.S. Navy, and it also warned another 140 companies about their involvement. The order, the first of its kind since 1981, came at the urging of the United States which wanted to expose the rigging as the kind of *dango* practice that it claims is still widely used in Japan. In the early fall of 1989 the FTC ordered another six Japanese construction companies involved in the Kansai International Airport project to disband their sand price-fixing cartel. The firms were expected to pay $2.2 million in surcharges which amounted to 1.5 percent of the total value of the sand supplied under the agreement.

During the aftermath of the 1981–1982 FTC hearings and in response to the increasing pressure from the United States, particularly between

1986 and 1988, the issue of allowing foreign companies to enter the construction market became very divisive. It led to confrontation among ministries, public authorities, politicians, and businessmen as they searched for a compromise that would satisfy demands from abroad, especially America, yet, at the same time, protect the legitimate interests of the domestic industry.

American pressure sharply increased when it turned out that by February 4, 1986, a few weeks before the original bidding deadline, the Kansai International Airport Company, which is in charge of construction, had already reached an agreement with six Japanese consulting firms to develop a master plan for the airport terminal. Furthermore, by early 1986, planning for the construction of the artificial island was also well advanced; this included the geological survey of the site and the development of the project ship, which had been awarded to domestic private and public organizations 10 years earlier. In a response to the outcry from abroad, both the Ministry of Transportation and the Ministry of Construction pointed out that while they cannot reconsider the contracts already awarded, foreign companies will be able to compete for contracts in the various other stages of the project, such as the construction of air terminal facilities and buildings and the provision of navigational assistance. Officials also pointed out that while there were more than 30 American companies among the large number of firms from abroad which had registered for the project, none of them expressed official interest in the first stage. Only firms from the Republic of Korea expressed a desire to participate in this stage.

Nonetheless, by the spring of 1986, the U.S. government and the American construction industry were highly critical of the Japanese handling of the project. The U.S. side claimed that as early as 1985, they asked the Ministry of Transportation to use an open bidding system for the project. While the ministry was noncommittal, the U.S. argued, the 1985 Action Program promised that the Japanese government would liberalize the bidding procedures on all public projects. Moreover, the Americans pointed out, while U.S. companies are virtually excluded from the Kansai project, Japanese construction companies have obtained contracts in excess of $1.7 billion in the United States in 1985 alone. The Japanese argument, that the Kansai construction is being handled by a "quasi-governmental" corporation (Tokusku Kaisha) and is thus a private project, was refuted by the U.S. side, which insisted that the government owned two-thirds of the Kansai International Airport Company, and that more than 100 of the company's 150 employees came from the public sector.

The handling of the Kansai project and the imbalance in bilateral construction-trade angered Congress, and in June 1986 Japan was harshly criticized during the hearings on trade in construction services. Senate Republicans even asked the USTR to investigate whether Japan is violating international agreements by refusing to allow foreign companies to bid on the first stage of the Kansai project and by not allowing open bidding in general. In the end, through extended bilateral negotiations, the Americans obtained a commitment that U.S. companies and other construction companies would be able to bid on the future stages of the project, albeit, under the traditional Japanese designated bidding system.

The president of the Kansai International Airport Company argued that the system is rooted in the traditions of the Japanese construction industry, and that he would not accept demands to replace it. He pointed out that changes would create great confusion, inefficiency, and bankruptcy in the industry. His arguments were of course supported by the more than 6,700 domestic companies that had expressed interest in the airport project. The Japanese, however, agreed to designate foreign companies for phases two and three of the project if they can offer appropriate technology and demonstrate their ability to carry out the contract. Moreover, they agreed to hold a seminar on the Japanese designated bidding process in September 1986 to familiarize foreign companies with the special characteristics of the system. Prime Minister Nakasone personally instructed his transportation and construction ministries to assure that the traditional system be applied in a "reasonable manner" so that foreign companies are not discriminated against. It is noteworthy that the majority of American companies represented at the seminar were manufacturers of construction and electronic machinery; less than ten were construction companies. Of these, by the end of November, only two companies expressed the wish to participate in the first-stage construction project. At the same time, it must also be pointed out that the Japanese construction companies that received the first-stage contracts are reluctant to consider the possibility of subcontracting work to qualified foreign companies because they "saw no benefits in such arrangements."

At the conclusion of this special seminar, the U.S. side decided to drop its demand for a switch from the designated to the open bidding system as long as the Japanese guarantee "fair access" to the upcoming projects for all foreign firms. This contrasted with previous U.S. Administration demands that the Japanese eliminate the traditional arrangements. However, while the official U.S. attitude was conciliatory, representatives of the American construction industry expressed great dissatisfaction with the outcome of the seminar, and promised to lobby the new Congress, controlled by a Democratic majority in both the House and the Senate, for retaliatory action.

By the middle of December, the industry's dissatisfaction apparently has had some effect. In a reversal of its position following the special seminar, the U.S. Administration declared that despite the intervention by President Reagan and Prime Minister Nakasone, only "extremely limited" progress has been made in efforts to enable U.S. companies to compete for contracts of the Kansai airport project. The Administration raised the possibility of formal actions, although it did not specify what those would be. Some Washington observers believed that the new stance was an attempt to preempt harsh actions by the protectionist-minded new Congress controlled by the Democrats.

However, this was not the case. Beginning in 1986 the Reagan Administration intensified the pressure on Japan which resulted in two years of contentious negotiations. The United States wanted open access to all public and eventually private-sector works projects even if it involved changes in the traditional designated-bidding system and in other industry practices. The Japanese were willing to discuss the participation of foreign firms but were reluctant to introduce major changes into a system that served the construction industry well in the past.

Nonetheless, after the cabinet-level U.S. Economic Policy Council warned in the spring of 1988 that if no agreement were reached before the end of March it would recommend an investigation of the Japanese public works bidding procedures under Section 301 (unfair trade practices) of the 1974 Trade Act, an agreement was reached on March 29. Despite heavy pressure from the domestic construction industry and the powerful construction-*zoku*, Prime Minister Takeshita wanted to resolve the dispute which could have erupted into a full-fledged trade conflict.

The breakthrough came when Japan agreed to open the so-called third sector contracts (funded by the government but administered by private-sector companies) to foreign bidding as well. This was a very important concession because the government has no legal authority to force private companies to abide by government-to-government contracts. Thus, the government put itself into a very delicate position.

The agreement provides foreign firms with access to 14 major construction projects planned for the next 10 to 15 years. With these projects and the special procedures agreed upon, foreign firms should be able to obtain the experience required to do construction work in Japan in general. Moreover, the agreement clarifies the requirements for licensing, for bid qualification, and for the submission of bids on the 14 major projects.

The procedural agreement involves bidding on the Kansai Airport project (referred to as the K-1 procedures), the Tokyo Bay Bridge, and the new Nippon Telephone and Telegraph (NTT) building. The K-2 procedures are known as the special measures, and they are virtually the same as the K-1 procedures except that the time between designation and bidding is 40 days rather than 60 days and there are no special provisions for International Chamber of Commerce arbitration measures in case of disputes. The projects include the government-commissioned work on the Haneda Airport expansion, the new Hiroshima Airport, the Tokyo Port Redevelopment, and the Kansai Science City, among others.

The parts of the total of seven projects that are commissioned by private and third-sector-funded entities are covered by the K-3 procedures. To insure foreign participation in these projects, the Japanese government states in the agreement that it expects the private and mixed funding entities to follow nondiscriminatory procurement practices, including the establisment of arrangements that would promote foreign participation. The construction projects affected include the building of airport terminals at Haneda and Narita. The agreement is monitored by the Ministry of Foreign Affairs, the Ministry of Construction, the Ministry of Transportation, and the American Embassy in Tokyo. It is noteworthy that while the agreement was limited to U.S. firms only, shortly after it was signed the Western European countries, the Republic of Korea, and the People's Republic of China were asking for similar privileges. By early June, five American and Western European companies were selected as designated bidders on the $8 billion Kansai Airport terminal building project. However, the Koreans and Chinese were not accorded the same privileges.

While the agreement settled a major U.S.–Japan disagreement, it did not guarantee business for American companies. As a matter of fact, American construction company executives who have managed to do business in Japan before the agreement emphasized in the summer of 1988 that U.S. contractors must try harder if they are serious about entering the Japanese construction market. They pointed out that U.S. firms should not expect to get business without at least setting up offices in Japan and hiring local engineers who can read and understand building codes in Japanese. Furthermore, they stated that the Japanese designated-bidding system is not much different from the American "short list" system in which potential bidders are screened before they actually submit a bid. Others remarked that the construction talks were so politicized that U.S. negotiators were no longer representing the interests of the construction industry which were in the high technology, engineering, and equipment sectors. Instead, Washington negotiators wanted complete access to all Japanese projects such as heavy construction, building roads, and digging ditches, activities in which American firms are not competitive. This is a particularly interesting point because most of the $17 billion worth of projects covered under the 1988 agreement involves heavy construction work. Not surprisingly, American architectural engineering and high-tech equipment manufacturing companies already present in the Japanese market expect only limited benefits from the agreement reached after hard and prolonged negotiations.

By early 1989 a number of U.S. construction companies have not only been appointed as designated bidders on a number of public works projects, but several have even received contracts, mostly through joint-venture arrangements with Japanese companies. Schal Associates of Chicago, for example, obtained a contract on a $138 million project in Yokohama in association with Toda Construction Company. Others, such as Tishman Construction and Turner Construction, teamed up with Aoki Construction and Kumagai Gumi, respectively, to build a hotel and office building. Other deals are in the offing.

But, even before these joint-venture contracts were announced, the Office of the United States Trade Representative (USTR) in late 1988 began an investigation of the Japanese construction industry's methods of awarding contracts for signs of discrimination against American companies. The investigation was required under the Omnibus Trade and Competitiveness Act of 1988 and as such it enabled the American construction industry to pressure the Bush Administration to retaliate against Japan if not enough contracts were forthcoming. During the hearings the director of the Japanese Institute of Architects testified that the *dango* problem has not yet been resolved and that more needs to be done to open the construction market fully to foreign companies. His testimony was supported by the Association of General Contractors of America and the International Engineering and Construction Industries Council who maintained that "subtle, pervasive and very effective barriers" still keep American companies out of the market and that the U.S. government must demand access on the same terms and to the same extent as Japanese construction companies enjoy in the United States. They claimed that the barriers deny American companies up to $2 billion worth of construction work annually. In addition, in March 1989 the representatives of these two organizations also testified that in spite of the 1988 agreement, American companies managed to become only minor partners in Japanese building consortia and did not win any major contracts by themselves. Thus, it appeared that the construction issue could again develop into a major disagreement between the two nations.

Increased Housing Investments

According to the 1986 OECD report on Japanese urban policies, the nation enjoys an excess supply of housing units in relation to the number of households, but if other factors are also taken into account, the total housing situation is much less satisfactory.[6] There are large numbers of vacant housing units comprised mainly of substandard, small wooden constructions in metropolitan areas. Moreover, when compared with other OECD nations, Japan has far fewer (320) housing units per 1,000 inhabitants than the others (around 400), and the floor area available per person (26 sq.m.) is also smaller than in most OECD countries (35–40 sq.m.). Size is a particular problem in the large metropolitan areas such as Tokyo, where, according to Japan's Construction Ministry, over 30 percent of the people live in homes with less than 39 sq.m. of space. This is the result of too many people moving to metropolitan areas to seek employment and of the dramatic increase in land prices. Table 6–1 shows an international comparison of housing provisions during the first half of the 1980s.

As the data show, in comparison to a select group of OECD countries, Japan with the largest average number of persons per household (3.3) has the second fewest (323) number of houses per 1,000 inhabitants. This, combined with the small scale of the units, illustrates why housing investments are especially important for the improvement of the quality of life. Haruo Maekawa, chairman of the Maekawa Commission, stated, "The most urgent tasks at present are housing policy and urban renewal. . . . From the viewpoint of improving the quality of the people's living, we are more inferior to other nations in housing than in any other areas."[7]

While such views are frequently heard in Japan, it is interesting to note that according to a late 1985 survey by the Prime Minister's Office, 71.2 percent of the Japanese people were "more or less" satisfied with current housing conditions, and only 28 percent indicated that they were dissatisfied. Moreover, officials point out, the percentage of satisfied repsondents has increased with each successive survey on the topic. However, some observers suggested that such results were possible only because most of the respondents compared the present housing situation to the immediate post-World War II years, and not to the American or Western European standards which should be applied to the Japan of the 1980s. This is in line with official views expressed in the Construction Ministry's latest housing plan, which envisions the matching of Japan's housing conditions with those of the United States and Western Europe by the twenty-first century.

But comparisons of Japanese housing with that in other developed countries as, for example, the United States, may be misleading. The

TABLE 7-1   International comparison of housing provisions

	Number of houses per 1,000 persons	Average number of persons per household
Japan	323 (1983)	3.3 (1983)
Denmark	427 (1982)	2.5 (1981)
France	444 (1983)	2.8 (1982)
Germany	438 (1984)	2.4 (1981)
Netherlands	367 (1984)	2.8 (1985)
New Zealand	322 (1983)	3.1 (1981)
Sweden	441 (1980)	2.3 (1980)
United Kingdom	391 (1983)	2.7 (1981)
United States	398 (1981)	2.7 (1980)

Source: *Urban Policies in Japan* (Paris: Organization for Economic Cooperation and Development, 1986), p. 77.

Japanese assign different functions to the same rooms, their construction techniques differ and although many Japanese nowadays build Western style homes, the traditional style continues to be more popular than the non-Japanese designs, particularly among the young, well-to-do.

Japan's specific housing goals are usually announced in five-year construction plans prepared by the Construction Ministry on the basis of the Housing Construction Program Act of 1966. The plans spell out the number of units to be built, and set the guidelines concerning minimum, average, and residential environmental standards. During the 1981–85 period, the plan called for the construction of 7.7 million units, which was a decline from the 8.6 and 9.6 million units of the two previous planning periods. Typically around 40–45 percent of the units are publicly financed, and the achievement rate is about 85–90 percent. The total amount spent on housing is around 6 percent of GDP, which is the highest among all OECD countries.

The most recent five-year housing plan for the FY 1986–FY 1990 period calls for the construction of 6.7 million units, 1 million units fewer than the previous FY 1981–85 plan. The total investment is projected to be more than $500 billion at 1980 prices.[8] Of these, 2.25 million units will be financed through loans from the governmental Housing Loan Corporation, 280,000 will be built and owned by the public sector, and 130,000 units will be constructed by the Urban Development Public Corporation. About 3.3 million units will be built through public funds, which will be about 200,000 units fewer than during the previous five-year housing plan.

The Construction Ministry noted in its plan that because slightly more than 10 percent of Japanese households are made up of married couples with two children who are living in units which are smaller than the minimum size set by government standards, the newly constructed homes will have more floor space; the total space will also be expanded to accommodate aged family members. Furthermore, the' ratio of owned to rented houses will change from 7:3 in the past to 6:4, indicating that more people will be renting houses instead of owning them. The reason for this is the increase in land prices, particularly in major metropolitan areas where most people want to live.

To promote new housing development, the government also intends to reduce the various regulatory requirements which in the past have seriously hampered private-sector investment. In 1983, Prime Minister Nakasone specifically instructed the Construction Ministry to develop ways to change zoning laws under which local governments promote and at the same time control urbanization to prevent disorderly development. Not surprisingly, such laws made it difficult to increase the supply of housing; consequently, the cabinet issued a directive to the Construction Ministry in 1985 to advise local authorities to be more flexible about zoning changes from "urbanization control areas" to "urbanization promotion areas." As a result, by 1985 a number of prefectures, among them Hokkaido, Kyoto, and Kanagawa, reassessed their zoning policies and freed some 39,000 hectares for housing developments. Moreover, around 1,100 cities, towns, and villages have also established new development guidelines which will ease the regulation of new constructions. While progress was made, zoning requirements still pose a problem throughout most of the country and are likely to continue to hamper private-sector housing investments in the future.

In addition to zoning rules, new housing investments are also affected by the high cost of housing relative to disposable household income. According to the 1986 OECD report, based on recent construction costs and income data, the rate of increase in both is about the same in Japan as in other OECD nations. However, the housing cost-income ratio is much less favorable in Japan due to the scarcity of land and the resulting high land prices. In 1987, for example, average land prices throughout the country rose by 21.7 percent, with commercial areas experiencing the largest increases. Not surprisingly, land prices went up most in the metropolitan areas; within one year (1986) in Tokyo, for instance, commercial land prices increased by 34.4 percent and residential land prices by 18.8 percent. In the fashionable Tokyo areas such as Ota and Setagaya wards, residential land prices jumped by more than 90 percent in 1986–1987.

According to statistics released by the Economic Planning Agency (EPA) in late 1988, the value of land in Japan is now more than 100 times as high as that of the United States, although America is nearly 25 times larger than Japan. This stunning development was fueled primarily by the large price increases in the Tokyo metropolitan area during the 1986–1987 period. The EPA data also showed that Japan's land and buildings together were worth 20.2 percent more by 1988 from a year earlier. This was the highest increase since FY 1973, when this measure rose by 26.3 percent due to the speculation unleashed by the Archipelago Reconstruction Plan of Former Prime Minister Tanaka.

To address the controversial issue of rising land prices, Prime Minister Takeshita in 1987 established a special cabinet council with himself at the helm. By August of the same year, the government implemented a set of measures to restrain speculative land deals. One of these measures was the revision of the National Land Use Planning Act to enable local governments to monitor land transactions more closely and to demand price reductions, if necessary. The government also asked financial institutions to refrain from lending money to parties who intend to speculate in land. Moreover, it introduced a maximum 96 percent capital gains tax to be applied when land is resold less than two years after buying it. As a result of these and other related measures, land prices in the Tokyo metropolitan area started to subside in late 1987, a development that continued through all of 1988 and into 1989. In 1988, for example, land prices rose an average of 8.3 percent, although prefectural land prices were rising faster with such cities as Osaka and Nogoya reporting 32.1 and 16.4 percent increases, respectively. According to real estate industry experts, this was the result of the delayed Tokyo price increase impact, the possibility of government decentralization away from the capital, and the rapid growth of resort areas in the outlying regions of the nation. By July 1, 1989, nationwide land prices were up by 6.8 percent in residential and 7.5 percent in commercial areas over July 1, 1988. However, for the first time since 1975, Tokyo residential real estate prices were down by 4.4 percent in comparison to the previous year. This compared favorably with the increase of 8.1 percent in 1988.

While such sharp land price increases in conjuntion with the booming stock market created a "wealth-effect," i.e., promoted consumption and, thus, economic growth, it also has created a class of Japanese who have given up their dream of owning a home. Not surprisingly, by the second half of 1988 housing starts were down by 8 percent relative to 1987, indicating a general softening of demand for new homes in the years to come, unless the government comes forth with a new program to stimulate demand.

According to the National Land Agency, the explosion of land prices could be partially attributed to the influx of foreign business as, the growing demand for office buildings in metropolitan areas, especially Tokyo, and the growing number of luxury homes purchased in the suburbs by individuals who were selling their centrally located real estate holdings. Moreover, the agency claimed that prior to the 1987 and 1988 government measures, it was the easy money policy of the Bank of Japan in combination with the continually high savings rates and the reduced demand for credit from the business sector that had made the price explosion possible.

By late 1988, however, a number of domestic and foreign economic analysts identified additional reasons for the land price explosion. Balassa and Noland in their previously cited study, for example, argue that while the high price of land in Japan is undoubtedly due to a number of different reasons, it is in particular caused by the nation's inefficient land use policies shaped by the tax system and the zoning requirements. They argue that only a fundamental reform of the land tax and zoning rules, in conjunction with other measures, would reduce land prices and, thus, make housing affordable to more people than just the wealthy. It is interesting to note that Balassa and Noland also argue that the high land prices are a major reason for the continually high household savings rates which, in turn, play a major role in maintaining Japan's huge current account surpluses.

Privatization

Both the government's financial and administrative reform plans and the Maekawa Commission's recommendations emphasize the need to reduce the size of the public sector. Traditionally, the government owned and operated a large number of corporations. These played a major role in the economic development of the nation, particularly during the post-World War II years when rapid growth provided a financial cushion to protect even the most inefficient public corporations as long as they offered a socially necessary service.

Nippon Telegraph and Telephone (NTT), the Japanese National Railways (JNR), Japan Air Lines (JAL), and the Japan Tobacco and Salt Public Corporation (JTS) were among the largest of the public corporations. Demand for their services was rapidly growing during the 1950s and 1960s; therefore, most of them did reasonably well. However, increasing energy costs, economic slowdowns, and declining demand during the 1970s turned a number of them into money losers, contributing to the growing fiscal deficits which the government could not afford. Moreover, the emergence of new technologies such as telecommunications required more flexible and dynamic organizations than the unwieldy giants that were mired in bureaucratic red tape. At its peak, for example, the Ministry of

Transportation, in charge of JNR and JAL before privatization, was known as the "Ministry of Rules and Permissions."

In 1983, the special Commission on Administrative Reform concluded that NTT, JTS, and JNR should be privatized, although the government would continue to own their stock, for a while at least. Prime Minister Nakasone, who initiated the current reform drive before he took office, was personally committed to privatization as a means of bringing government deflicits under control. He also viewed privatization as a way to revitalize the private sector and, in the case of NTT and JTS, to reduce bilateral trade conflicts with the United States. The Prime Minister's expectations were supported by a 1986 Bank of Japan study which concluded that privatization together with private sector investments would generate enough domestic demand to boost GNP by 1.1 percent over the next year or two. The study emphasized that the privatization of NTT alone would generate $20 billion worth of domestic demand through new investments over the next five years. Moreover, investments by financial institutions in computerized and other related services as a result of liberalization of the financial markets would also generate $15 billion worth of demand over the same period. Significantly, the study reported, part of this demand would have to be satisfied through imports, particularly from the United States whose telecommunication and information systems industries are very competitive internationally.

The first major public corporation to be priviatized was NTT which changed its status as of April 1, 1985. The Diet passed the necessary legislation in December 1984 after long negotiations between Prime Minister Nakasone (supported by MITI), the telecommunications *zoku* and the Ministry of Posts and Telecommunications (MPT). At first, the *zoku* and MPT proposed a bill that would have enabled the ministry to retain much of its regulatory power and thus moderate competition in the industry. Competition, however, was important, because during the late 1970s and early 1980s, the procurement practices of NTT, which obtained almost everything from its "family" of about 1,000 domestic firms, was one of the centerpieces of the U.S.–Japan trade conflict that dragged on for some time and left bitter feeling on both sides.

The Prime Minister and his supporters eventually overcame the telecommunication *zoku's* resistance, and NTT became the largest public corporation to be turned into a private company since 1934, when the state-owned Yawata Steel Company went private and was reorganized into Nippon Steel Corporation. Today, with some 320,000 employees, NTT is Japan's largest private company, organized around dozens of wholly owned subsidiaries and joint venture partnerships. Expected to be innovative and competitive, the new subsidiaries have enough authority and are small enough to fulfill their role.

Although the legislation was passed and the organizational arrangements were made by 1985, the new private NTT still faced a number of problems. It had a difficult time with the foreign companies that wanted a share of the newly competitive telecommunications market. The problems centered on the ministerial ordinances which implemented the privatization legislation because historically, such ordinances were always drafted behind closed doors by the relevant ministries together with industry advisory councils. This tradition was in sharp contrast to the American practice of holding open hearings to shape the operational details of comprehensive legislative actions. The resulting U.S.–Japan tensions were heightened by the spring 1985 "Japan-bashing" exercise in Congress and the generally anti-Japanese mood that prevailed throughout most of Washington. However, after some additional discussions, the matter was settled, and foreign business representatives, including Americans, were invited to participate in the advisory councils.

At the end of its first year as a private company, NTT showed impressive results.[9] The company's pre-tax profits for FY 1985 were 56 percent higher than projected. While no year-to-date performance comparisons were possible because NTT used different accounting methods as a public corporation, informal estimates indicated that the FY 1985 pre-tax profits increased by 50 percent from the previous year. This placed NTT in third place behind Toyota Motor Corporation and Tokyo Electric Power as Japan's top performers. This was naturally welcomed by the government which began selling NTT shares to 1.65 million investors chosen through a national lottery in the fall of 1986. When the shares were first traded on the floor of the Tokyo Stock Exchange (TSE) in February 1987, exchange officials had to put together a special set of rules to prevent demand for stocks from getting out of hand. Although subsequent offerings had a mixed reception, the government's goal continues to be the sale of stock so as to bring the government's share down to 50 prcent, with 30 percent ownership as the long-range target.

Following NTT's privatization, the telecommunications market became more competitive, although the degree of liberalization depends on the nature of the business. Common carriers are divided in the Category I and Category II companies according to their ownership of telecommunications circuits. Because the Category I field is public in nature, the Ministry of Posts and Telecommunications (MPT) regulates entry into the market in line with the supply and demand of services. The new telecommunications companies that have entered into competition with NTT, however, are small and weak in comparison to the giant corporation. The three most recent entrants, for example, set themselves the modest goal of a 6 percent joint market-share by 1990. The Category II firms provide Value-Added-Networks (VANs), for enhanced data communication through leased lines. This market is easier to enter; by 1988 more than 500 companies have already done so. Data base services, particularly commercial data bases, are already very much in demand. Between 1988 and the year 2000, MPT estimates that the market is going to grow at an average rate of 7.9 percent annually.

However, in spite of the deregulation of the telecommunications market, pressures have mounted in Japan to split the giant corporation into several firms. The Telecommunications Council, an advisory body to the Minister of Posts and Telecommunications, for example, in 1988 expressed strong misgivings about the firm's size and its continuing near-monopoly of the telecommunications market. The VAN-operators recommended that NTT's data communications department be split off and established as an independent company. The influential *Keidanren* (Federation of Economic Organizations) suggested in an 1988 report that NTT should be broken up because it does not compete fairly with the new industry entrants.

While such recommendations are controversial, MPT concluded that changes may be necessary and that the NTT law should be revised so as to allow a possible reorganization. Under the law that deregulated the industry in 1985, NTT's corporate structure has to be reviewed by 1990; therefore MPT established a task force to consider the issues involved and asked the Telecommunications Council for recommendations. The March 1989 arrest of Hisashi Shinto, the former chariman of the corporation, on charges of accepting bribes in the Recruit affair, is likely to make it much easier for the supporters of the breakup to reorganize the corporation. Shinto's departure left NTT with no one to step into his shoes and to defend the status quo. Shinto became president of the former NTT public corporation before deregulation and privatization in 1981 and has been fighting off schemes to break up NTT into several companies ever since.

Already during 1988, but particularly in the spring of 1989, the United States renewed its complaints about the difficulty of selling American telecommunications products in Japan. To vent its anger, Congress specifically referred to the telecommunications industry in the Omnibus Trade and Competitiveness Act of 1988 and required the Administration to report regularly on the competitive status of American firms in Japan. In the April 1989 USTR report on foreign trade barriers, the Japanese telecommunications market was identified as protected by "unfair trade barriers" in response to Motorola's complaints about the problems of selling cellular telephones. This opened the way for possible American retaliation under the Super 301 section of the 1988 Trade Act.

The other major privatization move involved the 80-year-old Japan

Tobacco and Salt Public Corporation which became the Japan Tobacco, Inc., on April 1, 1985. As a result, beginning on that date, foreign tobacco products could be imported, ending the government monopoly which had existed since 1904. However, the new firm remained the sole domestic producer and processor of leaf tobacco, and became a "special corporation" under the government's jurisdiction. This placed limits on how it could act; its operating plans, for example, must be approved by MOF. Nonetheless, the corporation's board of directors is free to set the budget, and MOF does not get involved with any of the operational details.

According to the original privatization plans developed during the early 1980s, the entire monopoly was to be dismantled, including tobacco processing. However, vehement opposition from the tobacco *zoku* made this impossible, and thus Prime Minister Nakasone had to be satisfied with a partial restructuring of the industry. The new company did not have an easy start; by 1986 it faced stagnant demand, increased competition from abroad, and a surplus of workers. To resolve the problems, Japan Tobacco tried to diversify into new lines of business.

The third major privatization project was the denationalization of the Japan National Railroads (JNR) as of April 1, 1987, which also turned out to be a difficult undertaking. Long admired by the rest of the world for its advanced technology and excellent customer service, JNR was a debtridden, 227-line railroad system operating over 14,500 miles of track and employing approximately 330,000 people. Only a few of the lines, the *Shinkansen* (bullet trains) among them, earned a profit; the others incurred a daily operating loss estimated at over $40 million in 1986. The total FY 1985 losses were a record $9 billion up 12 percent from the FY 1984, although total revenue was up 5 percent during the same time period. The major reasons for such a dismal performance were the sudden jump in retirement allowance payments, and the heavy interest payments on the staggering $150 billion long-term debt.

To keep the virtually bankrupt system functioning over the years, the government had to provide a $4 billion annual subsidy with the remainder of the deficit financed through loans from the postal savings and insurance accounts, and by special bonds. In spite of such burdens, JNR's revenue increase of 5 percent in FY 1985 indicated that the railroad system had certain strengths. Through streamlining efforts by management and employees, some lines were doing reasonably well, whereas others were quite profitable. Revenues form the *Shinkansen* bullet-train services, for instance, reached about $10 billion in FY 1985, up 14 percent form FY 1984. Even the non-*Shinkansen* passenger lines increased their revenues by 2 percent in FY 1985 over the previous year.

Critics charged that JNR's financial troubles began with the pressures to expand the system in the 1960s, and 1970s, when politicians used the project contracts to expand their influence among the voters. The contractors, the politicians, and the public benefitted from the expansion, but the JNR had to pay more than 30 percent of its revenues for the massive debt accumulated through the construction. Thus, critics argue, to divert attention from the real culprits, management and workers were accused of inefficiency and had to pay the price for past political patronage through loss of employment, early retirements, retraining, and transfers. Such charges were especially vocalized by *Kokuro* (the National Railway Workers Union), which with 220,000 members was the militant vanguard of the divided Japanese trade union movement. Although a 1948 law prohibited strikes in the public sector, the *Kokuro* mobilized its supporters on the extreme left who engaged in a series of sabotage acts against the railroad in 1986, and threatened violence if the privatization bill moved ahead in the Diet. Furthermore, at the union's extraordinary convention in October 1986, *Kokuro's* newly elected chairman stated that he would fight privatization and that he would never agree to the plan of the former union head who wanted to sign a labor-management agreement with JNR to save jobs. This split the union, and after the convention, 13 *Kokuro* chapters that had supported the former leadership, established a new organization to compromise with the JNR so that some jobs could be saved. The demise of the once powerful union was further accelerated by the resignation of more than 10,000 JNR workers every month during 1986.

The privatization of JNR was contained in eight bills submitted to the Diet. They called for the establishment of six regional passenger and one freight company; other measures included increased management flexibility and the ability to enter nontraditional lines of business, the erasing of JNR's massive debt through the sale of assets such as land, the redemption of bonds by the government, and most of all, the reemployment of redundant workers.

Since time was of the essence in the fall of 1986, the government incorporated only the major privatization measures into the bills and left the details to ministerial ordinances to be issued later. Nonetheless, to deal with the drastic labor cuts expected, the JNR established Human Resource Centers throughout the country in 1986 to employ redundant workers in various revenue-saving and cost-saving activities on a temporary basis. It also provided for the early retirement of some 20,000 workers, and promised to help those displaced and looking for jobs. Prime Minister Nakasone personally appealed to other public sector companies to employ 30,000 of the discharged employees, to JNR-affiliated enterprises to provide jobs for 21,000, and to the private sector to accept another 10,000.

The privatization of JNR and its division into several regional companies was not seen by the government as an immediate cure for the financial deterioration that took place over decades.

Therefore, it came as a pleasant surprise when the seven JR group firms reported unexpectedly large, Y151.6 billion ($1.3 billion) unconsolidated pretax earnings for FY 1988. Backed by favorable external business conditions, rationalization, and aggressive marketing, the best performance was shown by the East Japan Railway Co. headquartered in Tokyo, followed by Central Japan Railway Co. based in Nagoya and the West Japan Railway Co. operating out of Osaka. The Hokkaido, Shikoku, and Kyushu Railway companies, as well as the Japan Freight Railway Co., obtained more modest earnings, but even they did better than generally expected.

While doing well, the newly privatized railroads continue to be burdened by the huge debts accumulated during the past. As a matter of fact, due to rising interest payments and unexpectedly low revenues from land sales, the total debt that amounted to about $214 billion at the beginning of FY 1987 rose to almost $230 billion by the end of the fiscal year or March 31, 1988. Land sales did not do well because they were virtually frozen beginning in the fall of 1987 due to the government's concern about land speculation and its inflationary impact. However, based on a continually strong economy, the sale of new stock, and more land sales, the government expects the debt to begin to decline by 1990.

In the meanwhile, after lengthy debates and delays due to the government's fiscal and administrative reform plans, the Takeshita cabinet began to discuss again the building of new *Shinkansen lines* in December 1987. In spite of several major problems such as financing, Takeshita went ahead because a number of LDP members were asked by their constituents to get construction approval and to start the projects. As a result, construction on the new bullet-train between Takasaki and Karuizawa in the Hokuriku area is set to begin during FY 1989. Construction costs, the most important problem that had to be overcome, are to be split equally between the government and the privatized JR groups.

With the repeal of the Japan Air Lines Law in November of 1987, the road was set free to the privatization of Japan Air Lines (JAL) after 34 years of government ownership. The government released its share of 34.5 percent 48.1 million shares) which it had obtained under the former Japan Air Lines Law. To insure that no private organization could obtain a 51 percent majority, the privatization law included certain procedural safeguards. While the new JAL no longer has access to low-interest, government-guaranteed financing, previous restrictions on capital increases, long-term borrowing, diversified investments, and the issuance of corporate bonds were removed.

To improve the carrier's financial structure following its privatization,

JAL announced in the fall of 1988 that it intended to issue 7 million shares for public subscription at the market price as well as issue gratis shares equivalent to 7 percent of its capital to stockholders of record by the end of September 1988. The new issue was expected to raise the company's net worth ratio to about 23 percent from the past 16 percent. Of the Y100 billion ($850 million) raised through public subscription, the company expected to offer 50 percent as a premium to stockholders and to use the other half for new capital investments, including new planes and ground facilities.

In addition to the privatized JAL, All Nippon Airways (ANA) and the former Toa Domestic Airways (TDA), now called Japan Air Systems Co. (JAS), are currently the most important Japanese airlines. They are expected to compete in both the domestic and international markets, but rapid expansion of their activities is limited by airport capacity which is not likely to increase before the early 1990s when the offshore expansion of Haneda airport is completed and the new, 24-hour Kaisai International Airport begins operations.

Nonetheless, in the spring of 1989 ANA announced that it would buy a 3.5 percent stake in Austrian Airlines which was going through a privatization process. ANA management also indicated that it wants to boost its equity position to 5 percent by 1990 or 1991 to underline its commitment to a joint-venture flight scheme which, in July 1989, linked Tokyo with Vienna through twice weekly Austrian Air flights. The two airlines share costs, revenues, and marketing of the service. As part of its international expansion, ANA was also about to conclude a marketing cooperation agreement with the Scandinavian Airlines System (SAS) in the spring of 1989.

Research and Development

Japan is a prime example of a country whose economic progress is partially a result of the effective use of technology developed by other nations. It is estimated that since the early 1970s about 50 percent of the Japanese GNP growth was generated by scientific and technological advances as opposed to 15 to 20 percent in America during the same time period. Now the Japanese believe that the key to future economic success lies in the rapid development of basic technology at home. This sudden urgency to expand basic research was sparked by two timely incidents: the development of the high-temperature superconductors in 1987 and the winning of the Nobel price for medicine by Dr. Susumu Tonegawa, a MIT-based Japanese scientist. The fact that Dr. Tonegawa did most of his immunology research in an American laboratory, the so-called "Tonegawa shock," caused the Japanese to examine their basic research system. They quickly realized that the rigid structure of Japanese universities coupled with poor facilities and low levels of funding have forced talented Japanese scientists to go abroad.

In their past drive for rapid economic success, the Japanese have avoided scientific activities that required lengthy investigations; hence, they are as weak in basic research as they are strong in the practical execution of ideas developed mainly in the United States during the last 40 years. As a consequence, and because Japanese researchers tend to concentrate on the same topics, there is a severe shortage of Japanese who are experienced in investigating the "unexplored domains." They have excelled in improving the existing automobile, household appliance, and semiconductor manufacturing technology, to name only a few major product categories. But American and European politicians, government officials, and scientists are now determined to stop the easy one-way flow of basic research to Japan. Thus, Japanese companies may no longer be able to dominate selected global markets in the future by relying on the improvement of imported technology, products, and on superior manufacturing know-how. This sentiment is also reflected among Japanese technology executives who believe that they should contribute to global basic research. Moreover, they realize that to become a "technological superpower," a balance between basic and applied research must be established as soon as possible. Such a balance would also reduce Japan's technological dependence on and trade frictions with other nations, particularly America.[10]

The Japanese government has tried to improve basic research by way of its Japan Key Technology Center (JKT). Moves such as the JKT Center joint-venture with 14 private companies, led by Mitsubishi Chemical Industries Ltd. and Kyowa Hakko Kogyo Co., to form a consortium called the Protein Engineering Research Institute (PERI) are examples of this attempt. PERI's research center in Osaka began operations in the summer of 1988. The goal of this institute is to pioneer basic research in the field of artificial synthesis of proteins for application in new pharmaceuticals and bio-computers. In an effort to gain international support for this program and the institute itself, PERI has invited several foreign companies to join in this high-tech research project.[11]

Although the expansion and internationalization of Japan's research capabilities is under way, certain culturally conditioned practices continue to differentiate its scientific community from that of other nations. For example, in Japan, it is customary to obtain the consensus of all the researchers who are associated with a particular project before reaching decisions. In the United States and Europe researchers need only a majority to agree. Moreover, while abroad, the success or failure of a project affects the career of individual researchers, in Japan, both honor and risk affect all the members of the research group. Most non-Japanese scientist view competition within the research group as creative and constructive, while in Japan competition within a group is synonymous with "destructive confusion." It is not unusual for individual researchers to slow down their work so that less gifted members of the group can catch up.[12]

Close cooperation between universities and industries is also commonplace abroad as many university researchers hold second jobs in industrial firms as consultants or even executives. Moreover, in the United States, for example, many prestigious institutions (MIT or Stanford) interact with industry through research support programs that are mutually beneficial.

In contrast, such cooperation is a rarity in Japan. While there is no law that forbids university professors from holding second jobs as researchers in the private sector, most of them observe tradition and abstain. However, the Japanese are now trying to establish cooperative relationships between universities and industrial firms. A case in point is the Tokyo University of Agriculture & Technology (TUAT) that holds special exhibitions to publicize academic research to the agricultural industry and to the general public.

Japanese industrial firms are also changing their attitudes toward universities. While in the past they cooperated only with well-known American universities, they are now considering collaboration with domestic academic institutions. For example, a professor of the University of Tokyo heads the ceramic superconductor group that is composed of ten corporate researchers. Other major companies such as NTT and NEC are donating funds to develop relevant technical courses at the University of Tokyo.

These changes reflect the desire of the Japanese to reduce their dependence on American and European basic research. To promote this trend, the Diet on May 20, 1988, passed Law No. 57 "To Promote Research Exchange." The law calls for cooperation between the private sector and foreign research institutes and is also expected to further overall research efforts in both the private and public sectors at home.[13]

However, in spite of the extensive promotion of basic research by the Japanese government, academe, and corporate leadership, the Japanese do not believe that they are going to surpass the Americans and the Europeans as the source of new inventions, at least within the next decade. As figure 7–1 shows, Japanese researchers by a 2:1 margin expect the Europeans and Americans to continue to lead the world in research and development output.

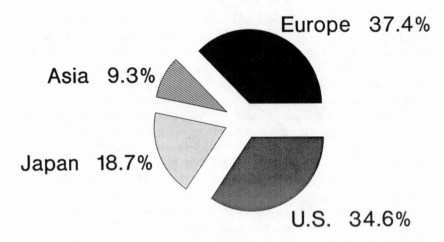

Figure 7-1. Expected Source of Major Research and Development Contributions as Seen by Japanese Researchers (in percentages). *Source: The Japan Economic Journal* (Tokyo: March 11, 1989), p. 1.

'Science Center' Cities

Tsukuba, the "Science City," is a government-sponsored research center. Created in 1963, it is intended as a "high-tech stronghold" focusing on basic research. The Center's main objectives are to serve as a channel of research communication among government, industry, and academe, to promote and aid the internationalization of Japan, and to advance regional development. It helps private firms to gain access to national research institutes, promotes horizontal relations among firms, and serves as a backup scientific information service. It contains 46 national research institutes (including Tsukuba University) and over 100 private-sector research centers. It is staffed by 7,000 researchers, with one-third holding Ph.Ds. Even though the Japanese are famous for their ability to work in groups, there are reports of strained relations in Tsukuba among the government, industry, and academic representatives. In an effort to counter this situation, the Tsukuba Research Support Center, composed of 55 major private firms, was set up in 1989. According to plans, Tsukuba is not going to be the only science center of the nation. Currently, 19 other future "technopolis" communities are designated to focus on basic research and to enhance regional developments throughout the country.

The internationalization of the science centers is not going to be an easy task. The traditional practice of assigning research projects on the basis of personal contacts with the different ministries hinders competition among research groups. In addition, there are other obstacles to internationalization such as the language problem and the traditional flow of information chiefly from and to government agencies, selected firms, and industry organizations. Such practices hinder the widespread dissemination of technical information so necessary for scientific advances. To help enhance the flow of information, Tsukuba University is now connected through personal computers with research institutions so as to create an information-pool readily accessible to qualified investigators.[14]

The Japanese realize that to develop their basic and applied science capabilities fully, they must change many currently used research practices at the institutional and corporate level. The government-run research institutions are pressed to put aside traditional customs and to set up new systems, while high-tech companies are beginning to spend more on R&D than on equipment. A 1989 survey conducted by the Nomura Research Institute of 68 manufacturing companies, for example, found that in 1987 the firms' capital investment amounted to approximately Y1.9 trillion ($15 billion), while R&D investments reach Y2.1 trillion ($17.2 billion) as compared to Y2.1 trillion ($16.8 billion) and Y2 trillion ($16 billion), respectively, in 1986; and Y2.4 trillion ($19.3 billion), Y1.8 trillion ($14.6 billion) in 1985.[15]

The recent growth in R&D investments is mostly attributed to the surge in long-term projects. As such investments affecting the future growth of firms are increasing, the traditional "production"-oriented corporate structures are changing into "thinking" structures. This process brings with it new staffing patterns. More and more corporate managers believe today that an R&D section composed of only Japanese researchers would probably not come up with unique ideas because they tend to think in similar ways. Thus, firms are now on the hunt for researchers of varying backgrounds to join their teams. Major industrial companies have started to place want ads in American and European magazines for researchers to work in Japan. The firms include Sumitomo Electric Industries Ltd., Matsushita Electric Industrial Co., Furukawa Electric Co., Meiji Milk Product Co., and Honda Research and Development Co. (a Honda Motor Co. unit). Japanese managers are beginning to realize the importance and the benefits of the internationalization of research activities.

Japanese firms are also beginning to open R&D facilities abroad. Several advantages of doing so include, for example, proximity to markets benefiting product design and development, and access to R&D data that may not be available in Japan. An example of this is the European Design Center of Sony in Stuttgart, Federal Republic of Germany, an R&D arm of Sony Corp. and Ricoh Co.

The establishment of more American and European corporate R&D divisions in Japan has lead to a search for local research team leaders. Thus, Japanese scientists who are currently working for the Japanese government or domestic companies are much in demand. An example is Imperial Chemical Industries, Britain's largest chemical firm, which set up the ICI Japan Technical Center in Tsukuba and recruited a former director-general of the research institution of the Agency of Industrial Science and Technology of MITI. Most of the researchers employed by foreign companies specialize in the fermentation and magnetic materials fields, areas in which the Japanese are world leaders. Large Japanese companies are also recruiting more engineers and are now providing various benefits to college engineering graduates to maintain company loyalty.

There is a shortage of systems engineers in Japan, currently numbering about 20,000. Thus, "brain drain" has hit the mid-size and small Japanese software developer-producers the hardest as their engineers are being enticed by stronger rivals, foreign and Japanese. Software houses are taking steps to keep their employees by enhancing their company image, for example, by applying to be listed on the stock exchange.

Non-Japanese companies are also recruiting from the large *kaisha*, a rather new practice. Du Pont Japan Ltd., for example, established its central technological institute, Du Pont Japan Technical Center, in October 1986. Its current director previously worked on the magnetic tape development project at Sony Corp. Other examples are the research directors of Kodak Japan's Research and Development Center which opened in August 1988. All in all, as a result of aggressive recruitment, 240 Japanese researchers switched to foreign capital-affiliated firms in 1986 alone.[16]

In the past, Japanese high-tech exports such as semiconductors, robots, and VCRs were the product of American inventions. However, nowadays technology is also flowing from Japan to America in a number of industries. This technology transfer is occurring in various ways such as licensing as in the chemical and pharmaceuticals industries, whereas joint product developments are more common in the semiconductor and robotics industries. In the steel industry, the Japanese are sharing their technology through joint-ventures to produce at lower costs in the United States.

Not only is there a reversal in the technology pipeline but many U.S. companies are now even trying to "tap Japanese ideas at the source." Rockwell International, for example, opened an office in Tokyo in 1986, solely for the purpose of monitoring and obtaining Japanese technology.

Today there are over 20 major U.S. multinationals corporations that have established R&D centers in Japan. Aware of this reversal, the Japanese are now inviting foreign firms into government-organized research consortia. For instance, Dupont has joined the consortium for superconductors.

Unfortunately, there are no reliable data on the quality or value of Japanese technology exported to America. The American government does not keep separate records of such activities and relies only on the balance of payments figures that lump together technical fees with royalties. According to Japanese data, as late as 1975 they paid the United States 16 times the amount for technology bought as they had received for technology sold. This figure declined to only three to four times as much by the mid-1980s, and the Japanese today claim that the value of their technology transfer to America is probably higher than what the official U.S. data show. Many Japanese firms engage in technology transfer through strategic corporate alliances such as the Toyota venture, NUMMI with General Motors, and this is not accounted for in the balance of payment figures. However, the accuracy of Japanese claims is also questioned by American analysts who believe that the Japanese export figures are exaggerated because, although Japan is a net exporter of technology, 60 percent of that technology goes to developing countries.[17]

U.S.–Japan Technology Controversies

As Japan has gradually closed the technology gap in a number of industries, science and technology became another major controversy between the United States and Japan. In fact, the Japanese were so effective in applying technology invented abroad that they have taken the lead in the manufacture and improvement of semiconductors, automobiles, and other key industries. This caused the Americans to become more concerned about technology transfer to Japan just as the historic reliance of the Japanese on imported basic research is beginning to decline.

The U.S. government and business circles firmly believe that the Japanese "economic miracle" is to a large extent the result of past American basic research and technology development efforts. They point to the approximately 16,000 Japanese researchers and engineers who even now visit the United States each year as opposed to the only 2,000 American researchers who travel to Japan. Many of the Japanese stay at American research institutions for up to two years while their American counterparts keep their visits short, mostly to lecture.

U.S.–Japan science and technology cooperation was formalized through the U.S.–Japan Science and Technology Agreement signed by Prime Minister Ohira and President Carter in May 1980. This little known umbrella agreement with no real political significance was vague. It allowed Japan to partake in U.S. university R&D programs (especially in leading-edge technologies), but it permitted only limited American access to Japanese industrial R&D. This was in step with the traditional one-way flow of scientific ideas between the two countries. Thus, not surprisingly, shortly before its expiration in April 1985, the original agreement was thrust into the political limelight. The head of the Reagan Administration's Office of Science and Technology Policy called for greater reciprocity in U.S.–Japan science and technology relations.

The United States was aggressively arguing its case by pointing out that because of Japan's economic and technological success since 1980 and the one-way flow of scientific ideas, the original agreement needed to be amended. The American side called for procedures to solve bilateral technological disagreements; the balancing of the "currently lopsided" flow of scientist and scientific information; the protection of defense-related technology; the establishment of common standards for protecting intellectual property rights; and an increased involvement by American researchers in projects jointly funded by the private sector and the Japanese government. Other demands included the overall promotion of joint efforts, easier access to Japanese government-funded projects, and an increase in the number of large-scale bilateral R&D projects in leading-edge technologies such as superconductors.

The American drive for renegotiation was fueled by the Toshiba Machine Co., Ltd. incident. This incident, which violated COCOM rules, heightened American concerns about the national security implications of technology transfers.[18] America wanted tighter controls on technologies with potential military applications and asked for guarantees concerning intellectual property rights. In particular, the Americans demanded a more consistent enforcement of Japan's 1956 Patent Secrecy Law which was never effectively applied. The United States' Invention Secrecy Act of 1951 prohibits companies from registering patents with Defense Department classification in countries that cannot guarantee their secrecy. Thus, Tokyo's past policies have effectively blocked U.S. patent application for certain sophisticated technologies. Some American R&D experts speculated that this could affect future U.S.–Japan cooperation in Strategic Defence Initiative research, the development of the next-generation fighter support plane (FSX), and other prospective joint defense projects.

However, the Japanese did not believe that it was necessary to rush into another agreement simply because the current one was running out. They took the position that in the absence of an agreement, most project-based joint efforts could still continue uninterrupted as the pact was based on the spirit of mutual friendship. They pointed out that an agreement to keep military technology patents secret contradicts the basic philosophy of the Japanese patent system which is based on the open disclosure of information. The American concern for national security also generated protests among Japanese electronic manufacturers, who represent a key high-tech industry that is internationally very competitive. They argued that information that cannot be disclosed should not be given patents, because the changes proposed by the Americans could endanger the competitiveness of their industry.

There were concerns that the renegotiated accord might undermine bilateral cooperation since it called for restrictions on exchanging certain research findings between the two nations. These concerns were demonstrated by the Japanese government's repeated stance against restrictions on technology transfers with military potential as it believed that this would retard global high-technology developments. Moreover, restrictions would hamper communications between researchers, obstruct the exchange of information, and, in general, would drastically change the free and open research climate in Japan. Domestic political factors also played a role as the opposition parties were resisting any restrictions on high-tech patents. They claimed that restrictions would lead to an increased military buildup which would conflict with the "peaceful purpose" of the May 1980 scientific cooperation agreement.

While the debates went on, the Japanese were concerned that if the two sides could not come up with an acceptable solution, America would retaliate by enforcing a potentially damaging provision of the U.S. Technology Transfer Act of 1986. This provision authorizes directors of federal laboratories to exclude foreign researchers from their programs if their governments do not offer American scientists or engineers similar opportunities. Eventually, however, President Reagan and Japanese Prime Minister Takeshita signed the revised agreement at the economic summit in Toronto on June 20, 1988. (For the key points of the U.S.–Japan Science and Technological Agreement, see Appendix H.) The agreement symbolizes Japan's commitment to share the burdens of doing basic research and development with the United States. It runs for five years, and it focuses on the achievement of a more balanced intergovernmental research program, calls for more controls on the outflow of technological information with military applications from America, and provides better American access to

Japanese research activities and findings. In addition, the agreement covers joint government work in the fields of superconductivity, manufacturing technology, life sciences, and information systems. Thus, the agreement enables the United States to shift its R&D relationships with Japan from "equal access" to "symmetrical access," meaning that instead of past technology exchanges on a private-to-private or public-to-public sector basis, there would now be an overall balance in the exchanges involving both the private and public sectors. However, to what extent such an overall balance can be developed and maintained in practice, only time can tell.

The new 1988 agreement gives the Japanese access to American classified military technology with the understanding that the Japanese government guarantees its secrecy. This was made possible by the United States' agreeing to submit all confidential patent applications to the Japan Defense Agency (JDA) rather than the Patent Office of MITI. JDA is expected to act as a "confidential repository" of all classified patent applications until such time that the U.S. Defense Department declassifies them. Thus, the accord not only enhances national security but also benefits American high-technology companies which, until the agreement, were losing potential licensing fees and other payments made by companies for the "commercial spin-offs" of their classified research and development efforts.[19]

Intellectual Property Rights

Japan and America also disagree on the question of intellectual property rights. But, while the Japanese want to discuss the protection of intellectual property rights in a multilateral GATT setting, the United States wants to include the issue in a comprehensive science and technology policy agreement.

The American side is particularly concerned about the delays in the Japanese patent system which takes approximately three years to grant a patent. As a result, by the time the patent is issued inventions could lose their originality. The major reason for the long delays is the shortage of staff in the Japanese Patent Office (JPO) which cannot handle the volume of paperwork required to process applications. In FY 1987, for example, 34,000 general patent applications were filed for large inventions, accounting for 40 percent of the world's total. In addition, 200,000 applications were filed for utility patents, that is, for small inventions. To examine these and other applications, the JPO employed 856 staff members during FY 1987.

The Japanese patent system also requires the disclosure of patent applications 18 months after filing, which is usually before a patent is granted. This is in sharp contrast to the United States where patent applications remain confidential until they have been examined. Thus, most non-Japanese believe that the patent system is biased against foreign companies. The JPO, however, defends the system by arguing that disclosure keeps researchers informed about new technological developments and that patents, trademarks, and copyrights are common goods rather than an exclusive possession.

As a result of continuous pressure from abroad, the patent application and examinations system is currently undergoing major changes. MITI and its affiliate JPO announced the ten-year "paperless plan" which calls for the elimination of patent-related paperwork and the introduction of a computer filing system. To decrease the time between patent application and issuance to approximately two years, as in most developed countries, the plan also calls for the employment of private companies to examine applications.

In spite of such developments, the United States continues to criticize the Japanese system of protecting intellectual property rights. The American government claims that deficiencies in the Japanese system have cost American firms an estimated $192 million in 1986 alone. The inadequacy of copyright laws, their poor enforcement, as well as the patent granting and trademark registration procedures were mentioned as major reasons. But American complaints notwithstanding, it seems that a concrete solution to these problems may have to wait for the conclusion of the current GATT Uruguay Round talks. The agenda includes the discussion of intellectual property rights and other related matters.[20]

Reduction of Working Hours

One of the more controversial policy options to increase domestic demand and, thus, to promote the internationalization of the economy is the reduction of working hours to increase leisure time. This option is based on the proposition that the Japanese have lived under the threat of economic deprivation for such a long time that even today when they are well off, they do not know how to relax and enjoy life. Critics of the Japanese lifestyle point out that the word for leisure, *yoka*, means "excess time" which implies the misuse of time. Moreover, they argue that *reja*, as the English word "leisure" is pronounced, does not fit the experience of most Japanese, and thus is not understood. Most of all, they claim, many Japanese still do not feel confident that the nation's prosperity can be preserved without continued sacrifice and diligence, and believe that the free time they already have is enough.

There is evidence to support such views. In a 1986 survey by the Office of the Prime Minister, 56 percent of the respondents stated that they are satisfied with the leisure time currently available to them.[15] Although 41 percent wanted more free time, the percentage of those who were satisfied with the present arrangements increased by 3 percent over the last poll taken in 1982. Expectedly, more than half of those who wanted more free time were under 30 years of age, representing the new generation.

A 1986 study by the Ministry of Labor confirms that young Japanese "salarymen" differ from their parents in that they are increasingly disenchanted with work.[16] According to the findings, about 33 percent of the workers under the age of 30 have already changed jobs, and about the same percentage plan to do so in the future. Moreover, 75 percent consider work simply as a means of making a living; work as a means to fulfill the purpose of life and as a civic duty was cited by only 10 percent of the respondents.

At the same time, views on the general importance of leisure activity appears to be undergoing a change among both the younger and older generations. A 1986 survey by the Office of the Prime Minister showed that in contrast to past years, when the procurement of housing was ahead of leisure, by 1985, 28 percent of the Japanese considered leisure activities more important than the provision of housing (25 percent) and securing food (15 percent).[17] Thus, leisure is seen as a more important activity than the procurement of basic necessities of life by over a quarter of the population regardless of age. This seems to contradict the results of the 1986 poll concerning satisfaction with available leisure time, in which the younger and older generations expressed differing opinions. The discrepancy, however, is not a contradiction because the 1986 findings probably reflect a short-time response to the deflationary effects of the appreciation of the yen, whereas the 1985 results imply that a slow but steady society-wide change in basic attitudes is under way. A 1987 survey by the Prime Minister's Office confirmed this conclusion.

Meanwhile, international comparisons still show that of all industrialized nations, the Japanese work the hardest. A historical overview shows that Japanese diligence reached its peak in 1960 with 2,432 annual working hours, declined to 2,064 hours as a result of the first oil crisis in 1973, and then gradually rose again from 1974 through 1985. By 1985, the average annual working hours in Japan reached to 2,110 hours, whereas in the United States and Great Britain, workers spent 1,850 hours on the job, and in France only 1,650.[18] Between 1985 and the end of FY 1987, Japanese workers continued to put in the same number of average annual working hours and, thus, maintain their international position.

Not surprisingly, the Japanese also put in the longest workweeks during the first half of the 1980s. Although only 22.1 percent of all companies employing 30 or more people maintained a six-day week and 77.1 percent some type of five-day work week, only 27 percent offered a real, two-day weekend on a continual basis. About 16.7 percent provided five-day weeks twice a month, 14.7 percent once a month, 10.9 percent every other weekend, 7.7 percent three times per month.[19] In comparison, the overwhelming majority of American and Western European workers enjoy real five-day workweeks on a continual basis.

Moreover the data indicate that during the early 1980s, Japanese workers also received fewer paid annual holidays (10) than Americans (19), British (23), and French (26). Of all Japanese employees with 20 or more years of service, 91 percent received 20 days or less annual vacation, only 5.1 percent received 21 to 26 days, that is, the average for all British and French workers, regardless of the number of years of service.

Although a basic societywide change in attitudes toward leisure is under way, the pace of change is slow. In 1986, for example, the average number of vacation days taken by workers in the manufacturing industries was 7.6 days, in other industries (mainly white-collar) only 5.1 days, amounting to an increase of 0.5 and 0.7 days, respectively, over 1985. This confirms the Labor Ministry's claim that only about 40–45 percent of all Japanese workers take all their annual paid leave entitlement, and that the majority continue to go back to work before they are required.

The Maekawa Commission recommended a reduction of the average annual working hours, and promoted the idea of longer vacations and a five-day workweek as a means of increasing leisure time, and thereby domestic demand for products and services. Such efforts are not new; in 1980, the Labor Ministry developed a Plan to Promote the Reduction of Working Hours which called for a decrease of average annual working hours to 2,000 by 1985. The plan was predicated primarily on the demographic changes engulfing Japan, that is, the evolution of the "aging society," and a projected increase in the workforce from 60 to 65 million between 1985 and 2000. It also considered the necessity to increase domestic demand to reduce international trade conflicts and to improve the quality of life. However, the plan failed because beginning with the 1973 energy crisis, labor productivity began to level off; 3 million redundant workers were carried by firms which instead of hiring new employees increased overtime when economic conditions improved. However, undaunted by its failure, the Ministry developed a second plan in 1985 which called for a reduction of average annual working hours to 2,000 by 1990. The plan envisioned a revision of the 1947 Labor Standards Act which was based on an 8-hour day and a

48-hour workweek, because to achieve the 1990 goal, weekly work hours had to be reduced from 48 to 45. Moreover, annual vacation days needed to be increased from the 6–20 to a 10–20 day range.

Revision of the 1947 Act was necessary because Labor Ministry officials found that a decline in overtime did not significantly contribute to increased consumption. Only a shortening of the scheduled hours worked as mandated by the Act would significantly increase consumption expenditures because a permanent five-day workweek would trigger far more leisure activity than an uncertain and temporary reduction in overtime.

The Labor Ministry's plan could provide a significant demand boost because leisure activity goods and services represent a major part of Japan's growing service market. According to MITI's Leisure Development Center, a government entity unique to Japan, a general 40-hour or 5-day workweek could increase this market by a minimum of $20 billion or 6.6 percent annually.

In light of such expansive estimates, it is not surprising that in June 1986 the government termed the realization of reduced working hours and increased leisure time a "national task." Prime Minister Nakasone was also actively promoting the reduction of working hours, the introduction of the five-day workweek, and an increase in annual vacation time. To set a good example, he and Deputy Prime Minister Kanemaru took relatively long summer vacations. The Prime Minister took 20 days in four installments, and the Deputy Prime Minister vacationed for just over 20 days. Moreover, for the first time, there were no scheduled cabinet meetings between August 16 and 25, so that all other ministers could take some time off. This made it possible for government workers to take longer vacations than usual as well.

In addition, the government decided to adopt a five-day workweek for its employees during alternate weeks on an experimental basis for one year, beginning November 30, 1986. This was significant because for many years, the government maintained that it could not adopt a five-day workweek until other public service institutions such as banks did. Following the banks' first move in 1981, government employees got one Saturday a month off; when banks added another Saturday during the summer of 1986, the government followed, thereby sending a clear signal to the private sector that it meant what it said. To expedite matters, the Labor Ministry asked one of its advisory councils to develop a set of recommendations concerning the reduction of working hours.

The council concluded its discussions by early December 1986, and proposed a revision of the Labor Standards Act so that statutory working hours would be reduced from the current 48 hours to 40 hours in three stages. During these stages, working hours would be cut first to 46, then to 44, and ultimately to 40 hours per week. Companies would, however, be allowed to exceed the legal limit occasionally as long as they maintain an average of 40 hours per week over three-month periods. Moreover, the council recommended that small-sized and medium-sized firms with less than 300 employees be given a grace period of three years to switch to the new system, and that the minimum number of holidays be increased from the current 6 to 10 days in all organizations.

The government accepted the recommendations and, after clearing it with the LDP policy formulation apparatus, forwarded it to the Diet which approved the legislation. Thus, as of April 1, 1988, the Labor Standards Act was revised to allow the reduction of the average annual working hours from over 2,000 in 1988 to 1,800 hours by 1993, bringing Japan more in line with the other industrialized nations. Both business and labor supported the new legislation; *Nikkeiren*, the Japan Federation of Employers' Association, for example, proposed in early 1988 that management and trade unions work together to implement the reductions.

As the first step of the reduction process, the legal working hours were reduced from 48 to 46 beginning in 1988. This is going to be followed by another two-hour cut to 44 hours three years later. The first stage also included an increase of the annual paid holidays for newly hired employees from six to ten. To promote the process, the government began a bimonthly five-day workweek, and financial institutions such as banks as well as the postal service, also have started to close their doors on every Saturday in the spring of 1989. To provide basic services, the banks, however, have decided to keep their cash-dispenser and automatic-teller machines open until 2 P.M. so that money can be withdrawn.

The government and the financial services industry is in the vanguard of the working-hour-reduction process, but most other industries are lagging behind. Although the term *yutori* (elbowroom) became very popular as an expression of the desire to have more leisure time, serious obstacles remain. One of them is the still widespread notion that productivity is tied to long working hours; thus, any reduction could endanger the economic performance of the nation and of the firms. Many corporate managers and employees over 40 years of age are so convinced of the validity of this relationship that they are reluctant to enjoy longer holidays and shorter working hours. But the greatest resistance to work-hour reductions is shown by the managers and workers of small to medium-sized companies which employ less than 300 workers. While by 1989, about half the firms with more than 1,000 employees already were on a five-day workweek, of the firms employing between 33 and 99 workers, only 3.5 percent closed down every Saturday. In the even smaller firms, i.e., those employing less than 33 people, the five-day workweek is not even considered a possibility. Because firms employing less than 300 workers constitute the majority of Japanese firms, their unwillingness to go along with the proposed changes, together with the reluctance of others, are creating problems for the plan calling for a more leisurely national life-style.

A 1989 study of the Japan Productivity Center underlines this possibility. The Center, which conducts research in labor matters, found that 47.7 percent of the 3,630 firms studied believed that 2,000 to 2,100 annual working hours were just right for their employees. Asked about the current working hours, 71.1 percent of the companies responded that their employees still worked at a rate of more than 2,000 hours a year. Only 38, or 2 percent, of the companies had established a five-day workweek. It is interesting to note that of the 980 company trade unions that participated in the study, 88.5 percent replied that 2,000 annual working hours are too many and that working hours should be reduced according to plan to 1,800 by 1993.

Thus, it seems that during the next few years the reduction of annual working hours is going to remain a controversial issue. While the government, a few industries, and the large firms are trying to show the way and encourage others to follow, the small- to medium-sized companies are showing great reluctance to do so. The final outcome of the controversy is probably going to depend a great deal on how the global and domestic economies fare between 1989 and 1993. If growth is continuous and relatively smooth, most of the small to medium-sized companies are likely to come around and reduce working hours. However, if the global and domestic economies slow down, it is possible that even some of the large corporations already committed to the five-day workweek may reconsider to maintain their international competitiveness. In spite of what is being said about the changing work ethic, it appears that the *yamato damashii* or the Japanese spirit is still alive and well, even among the younger generation. The May 1989 report of the Ministry of Labor showing that the Japanese worked an average of 2,100 hours during FY 1988 (ending March 31, 1989), a drop of 0.8 percent or 20 hours from a year earlier, supports this argument.

To promote the idea of a more leisurely national life-style, Prime Minister Takeshita's advisory committee on social policy in April 1989 recommended legislation to require management to provide employees with seven days of consecutive annual holidays. The committee also indicated that the introduction of daylight savings time may provide more opportunities for leisure and should, therefore, be considered.

Notes

1. The effective tax rate which includes both national and local taxes was calculated on the assumption that corporations reserve 30 percent of their pre-tax profits for dividend payments.
2. Because of rounding, the tax cut and increase do not add up to the same total.
3. All statistics are reported from *40 Years Since the End of World War II: On The Threshold of the Age of Maturity* (Tokyo: Economic Planning Agency, 1986), pp. 192–193.
4. *Urban Policies in Japan* (Paris: Organization for Economic Cooperation and Development, 1986).
5. Of the $23 billion reflationary package announced in September 19, 1986, about $13 billion were spent on public works in FY 1986.
6. OECD, *Urban Policies, op. cit.*, p. 75.
7. *The Journal of Commerce* (July 7, 1986), p. 4A.
8. Of the $23 billion reflationary package announced on September 19, 1986, about $4.5 billion were spent on the improvement of home financing schemes.
9. *The Japan Economic Journal* (June 7, 1986), p. 23.
10. *The Japan Economic Journal* (November 28, 1987), p. 31.
11. *The Japan Economic Journal* (September 10, 1988), p. 21.
12. *Asahi Evening News*, editorial (December 25, 1987).
13. *Look Japan* (August 10, 1986), p. 14.
14. *Tokyo Business Today* (April 1988), pp. 48–49; *The Japan Economic Journal* (March 26, 1988), p. 27.
15. *The Japan Economic Journal* (June 4, 1988), p. 26.
16. *The Japan Economic Journal* (July 23, 1988), p. A1.; (September 10, 1988), p. 10.
17. *The Japan Economic Journal* (July 16, 1988), p. A1.
18. COCOM: Coordinating Committee for Exports to Communist Countries.
19. *The Washington Post* (June 21, 1988), p. A15; *Asahi Evening News* (February 1, 1988), p. 3; *The Japan Economic Journal* (January 16, 1988), p. 2; *JEI Report*, No. 16B (Washington, D.C., April 21, 1988), p. 8.
20. *The Japan Economic Journal* (October 22, 1988), p. 23; (March 2, 1988).

8 THE INTERNATIONAL POLICY OPTIONS

Prime Minister Nakasone's blue-ribbon Economic Council recommended that Japan's record 1985 current account/GNP ratio of 3.7 percent, and the expected more than 4 percent 1986 ratio be reduced to around 1.5 to 2 percent by FY 1992. Subsequently, the Maekawa Commission in both its 1986 and 1987 reports suggested this objective. While this can partially be achieved through the implementation of the domestic policy options to increase demand, and thus imports, other measures such as increased foreign direct investment and foreign aid are also needed. To illustrate the point, the elimination of the 1986 current account surplus of $86 billion alone would have required a 33 percent domestic economic growth rate.

Overall Foreign Direct Investment[1]

In view of this, the Maekawa Commission recommended that Japan more than double its foreign direct investment as a percentage of Gross Domestic Product (GDP) by 1992, which would require an average annual growth rate of about 10 percent, a realistic expectation considering that during the first half of the 1980s, such investments were growing at an annual rate of about

14 percent. This, the Commission emphasized, would increase employment abroad and contribute to the economic growth of the developing nations. Moreover, in the long run, expanded foreign direct investment would be a more effective way to moderate the trade conflicts caused by the huge current and trade account surpluses than the various earlier market access measures. To this end, the Commission suggested that the government develop new tax, financial, and insurance incentives to encourage and protect Japanese direct investments throughout the developing world.

The Maekawa Commission's recommendations were supported by a report of the Mitsubishi Bank released in the fall of 1986. The report pointed out that Japanese corporations have already stepped up their direct investments abroad as a result of the rapid erosion of their export competitiveness due to the sharp appreciation of the yen. If this continues at the same pace as during the previous five years ending in FY 1985 (March 31, 1986), the accumulated total of such investments by 1990 may be twice as much as that by the end of FY 1985, or about $168 billion. As it turned out, these forecasts were too low, and Japanese foreign direct investment exceeded the projected figures already by the end of FY 1988, or March 31, 1989. Of course, part of the dramatic increase in value can be explained by the appreciation of the yen. Nonetheless, the rapid pace of foreign direct investment during the second half of the 1980s reflected a major change in Japan's involvement in the world economy.

During the first 20 years after World War II, Japan's accumulated foreign direct investment amounted to a paltry $6.7 billion, an annual average of about $330 million. By 1984, the sum increased to $72.2 billion and during the 1970s, the annual average ranged from over $2 billion in 1974 to almost $5 billion in 1979. Beginning in the early 1980s, the annual averages grew to $8–10 billion, reflecting Japan's newly acquired economic power. During the second half of the 1980s, due to the appreciation of the yen as well as other factors, foreign direct investment increased at a feverish pace, climbing to $22.3 billion in FY 1986, $33.4 billion in FY 1987, and to an astonishing $45.8 billion in FY 1988, ending March 31, 1989. As a consequence, the FY 1984 cummulative total grew from $72.2 billion to $106.7 billion by FY 1986, $140.7 billion by FY 1987, and $185.9 billion by FY 1988, more than a 100 percent increase over the short period of five years. Table 7–1 provides a summary overview of these developments.

According to the prediction of a private advisory panel to the Economic Planning Agency, Japan's direct foreign investment is expected to rival that of the United States, which currently is still in first place with well over $200 billion accumulated foreign direct investments, and the United Kingdom by the year 2000, with Japan's accumulated total estimated to reach

$300 billion. This would represent about 20 percent of total Japanese manufacturing capacity as against the current capacity abroad of only 2.4 percent, and assumes an average annual increase of almost 14 percent, the average growth rate in foreign direct investment achieved between 1978–1984. The post-1986 trends indicate that this is a realistic prediction likely to be realized.

TABLE 7-1. Japan's foreign direct investments: FY 1951–1988 (in billions of U.S. dollars)

Fiscal year	Worldwide annual	Worldwide cumulative
1951–1979	n.a.	32.6
1980	4.7	37.3
1981	8.9	46.2
1982	7.7	53.9
1983	8.1	62.0
1984	10.2	72.2
1985	12.2	84.4
1986	22.3	106.7
1987	33.4	140.7
1988	45.8	185.9

Source: Industrial Bank of Japan (Tokyo, 1989). Subsequently published Ministry of Finance data show FY 1988 investments amounting to $47.0 billion and the total accumulated investments to be $186.3 billion on March 31, 1989.

The reasons for the sharp increase in foreign direct investments between 1985 and 1988 are by now well understood. Japan's huge current account surpluses and the relatively limited domestic investment opportunities, the sharp appreciation of the yen and the competitive requirement to establish offshore production bases, the threat of increasing protectionism in the United States and the European Community, particularly after 1992, the relatively low price of foreign investment projects when compared to similar investments in Japan, and the "globalization" of major industries are probably the most appropriate explanations. Because most of these causal trends are likely to continue into the 1990s, it is reasonable to argue that Japanese foreign direct investment is going to be a major factor in the world economy for years to come.

In the past, particularly during the 1960s and 1970s, slightly over 70 percent of all Japanese foreign direct investments were made in Latin

America and Asia. Moreover, because during these years of rapid economic growth a stable supply of natural resources was important, the majority of investments were resource-related. To the extent that manufacturing investments were made, the motives for such investments were the protectionist import substitution policies of a number of countries, and in the case of the NICs of the Asian-Pacific region, the relatively high productivity and low wages of the labor force.

Beginning in the late 1970s, most investments in the developing nations went into manufacturing. The systematic resource and energy conservation efforts were successful, and thus, a stable supply of resources was no longer a dominant concern. At the same time, starting in the early 1980s, more manufacturing and service industry investments, such as in finance, were also made in the industrialized nations. This was partially due to the reduction in the relative wage differentials between Japan and these nations, and in the case of the United States and Western Europe, to the increasing protectionist attitudes and trade conflicts generated by the bilateral trade imbalances. Other reasons included the high rate of economic growth in America, particularly in the Southern and Western states which began around 1983, as well as the pre-1987 tax incentives such as the investment credits and Accelerated Cost Recovery System introduced by the Reagan Administration in 1981. As a consequence, by the mid-1980s, over one-third of total annual foreign direct investment was made in the United States. Table 7-2 illustrates the regional distribution of accumulated Japanese foreign direct investment as of the end of FY 1986.

Industrial patterns of foreign direct investment also began to change during the second half of the 1970s. Earlier, the textile and machinery industries, including machine tools, electric appliances, and transportation machinery, accounted for more than 20 percent of the total. By the early 1980s, however, the machinery industry alone increased its share to around 40 percent whereas the textile industry's share declined to less than 5 percent of the total.

Due to the sharp appreciation of the yen and the general expansion of international finance, Japanese foreign direct investment underwent additional changes during 1985–1986. As part of the total increase of 20.3 percent over FY 1984, investments by financial and insurance companies jumped by 82.5 percent, and those by trading houses, channel of distribution intermediaries and advertising agencies by 28.9 percent. According to Ministry of Finance officials, this was mostly due to the revised Australian banking law which allowed foreign banks to establish subsidiaries, thus opening the way for the Bank of Tokyo and four other Japanese banks to move abroad. Another reason for the surge was the establishment of finance

TABLE 7-2. Japan's foreign direct investments by country and region: as of March 31, 1987

	No. of Cases	Amount[a] (US$ million)		No. of Cases	Amount[a] (US$ million)
U.S.A.	13,757	35,455	Taiwan	1,631	1,051
Canada	766	1,951	Philippines	633	913
North America, total	14,523	37,406	Thailand	1,111	884
U.K.	1,190	4,125	China	296	513
Netherlands	354	2,337	**Asia, total**	12,349	21,790
Luxembourg	99	2,308	Australia	1,313	4,502
Germany, F.R.	817	1,552	**Oceania, total**	1,966	5,234
France	742	970	Saudi Arabia/Kuwait	4	1,309
Spain	163	601	**Middle East, total**	321	3,016
Italy	156	203	Panama	2,747	8,841
Europe, total	432,4	14,471	Brazil	1,326	4,857
Indonesia	1,427	8,673	Mexico	243	1,556
Hong Kong	2,568	3,433	**South America, total**	5,480	20,373
Singapore	1,860	2,571	Liberia	679	2,744
Korea, Rep. of	1,393	2,118	**Africa, total**	1,160	3,678
Malaysia	1,009	1,283	**Total**	40,123	105,970

[a] Figures are the accumulated value of approvals and notification.

Source: Japan 1988, *An International Comparison* (Tokyo: Keizai Koho Center, 1987), p. 56.

and insurance operations by manufacturers and trading companies that wanted to provide better services to their foreign marketing organizations. In contrast, investments by manufacturing companies declined by 6.1 percent during 1985–1986, the second successive annual decrease caused chiefly by the retrenchment of textile, chemical, and metal firms, although investments by transportation equipment and electric appliance manufacturers, particularly in Europe and North America, increased. According to MITI officials, most manufacturers were uncertain about the unstable exchange rates, and wanted to wait until the dollar—yen relationship became more predictable.

The pressures on Japanese manufacturers to invest abroad increased throughout 1986, particularly as the yen appreciated to below 180 against the U.S. dollar, and it became clear that the trend would not be reversed. Moreover, nations resisting Japanese exports, particularly in the European Community, demanded local manufacture instead of exports. The capture of Congress by the Democrats in the fall 1986 elections also indicated that some form of protectionist legislation may be on its way in the United States by 1987. Thus, foreign direct invesment gradually became not only economically but also politically feasible and necessary. According to MOF statistics, Japanese investments in the North American region (U.S. and Canada) showed a dramatic increase by 45.4 percent during FY 1988. This area was followed by Western Europe and Asian investments growing by 38.7 and 14.4 percent respectively. Investments in America alone represented 46.2 percent of the total, a 2.1 percent increase over FY 1987. But investments in Asia grew the most rapidly in recent years. Japanese companies stepped up investments, particularly in Malaysia, Indonesia, and the People's Republic of China. In contrast, investments in the Southeast Asian NICs (South Korea, Taiwan, Singapore) were slowing due to higher labor costs and unfavorable exchange rates. Investments in the European Community (EC) and Europe in general increased by 90 percent, reflecting the desire of Japanese companies to prepare for the aftermath of the EC's 1992 market integration plan.

The share of manufacturing investments in Japan's total foreign direct investment in FY 1987 rose to 23.5 from 17.1 percent the year before. Investments in, for example, the electronics and chemical industries reached the highest amount ever, increasing by 100 percent in the one-year period. At the same time, the overseas production ratio, which is the ratio of sales of products manufactured overseas to the sales of domestically manufactured goods, has not kept pace with the investments. According to MITI figures, the overseas production ratio was 4.3 percent in FY 1984, 3 percent in FY 1985, and 3.2 percent in FY 1986, and 3.7 percent in FY 1987.[2]

Japan's overseas production ratio, therefore, was still considerably below the 18.1 percent of the United States in 1985, and the Federal Republic of Germany's ratio of 19.2 percent in the same year. It is, however, noteworthy that the sales of good manufactured by Japanese companies overseas have been steadily increasing from $54 billion in 1984, to $56 billion in 1985, $71 billion in 1986, and $86 billion in 1987.

The nonmanufacturing sector also experienced sharp increases in foreign direct investments in the financial services and insurance industries as well as in real estate during FY 1987. Financial and insurance investments rose by 47 percent while those in real estate went up by 36 percent from the previous year. Most of these investments went to the United States, although real estate investments rose by 81.7 percent in Australia as opposed to a more modest increase of 50.7 percent in the United States from the year before. However, due to the sharp increase in manufacturing from 17.1 percent of the total in FY 1986 to 23.5 percent of the total in FY 1987, the share of nonmanufacturing investments in the total declined from 80.4 percent in FY 1986 to 75.2 percent in FY 1987. It is noteworthy that real estate investments, which became a focal point of controversy particularly in America, made up less than 1 percent of the total foreign direct investment in FY 1987.

The current wave of Japanese foreign direct investment is not limited to medium- to large-sized firms. Investments by small to medium companies (less than 300 employees) amount to about 20–25 percent of the annual total. They are undertaken to either reduce their comparative disadvantage in labor-intensive production or to continue the subcontracting relationships with the large corporations that have moved abroad. Most of the small to medium companies are interested in investing in Korea, Taiwan, Singapore, and Thailand to take advantage of the lower labor costs. About one-fifth of these firms want to invest in the United States to continue subcontracting relationships.

These trends have raised concerns about the "hollowing" of Japanese industry. According to MITI estimates, increased foreign direct investment may reduce domestic employment by about 560,000 jobs while generating more than 2 million new positions abroad by the year 2000. Of the new jobs, about 1,026,000 could be created in Indonesia, 840,000 in the United States, and 86,000 in the Republic of Korea. Some private sector economists, however, disagree with such estimates and believe that if the current investment trends continue, job losses could exceed the projected 560,000 and that more than 2.5 million new jobs may be generated abroad by the turn of the century. According to nonpublished estimates by the staff of a major private research organization by the fall of 1986, of the slightly more than 14 million people employed in the manufacturing sector, about 900,000 were surplus workers. In its 1987 annual "White Paper on Labor," the Ministry of Labor estimated that approximately 450,000 jobs could be lost between 1986 and 1995 as a result of the "hollowing" process. Others, however, disagree with such projections and do not believe that the Japanese economy is undergoing a hollowing. They point to the low overseas production ratio which reached 3.7 percent in FY 1987, but was still four to five times less than that of the United States and the Federal Republic of Germany. The dissenters argue that as long as the ratio is less than 10 percent, any claim of hollowing is an exaggeration, particularly since to stay competitive, Japanese companies must invest and manufacture abroad.

Most of Japan's industrial captains believe that the boom to expand abroad is a lasting phenomenon. In a 1986 survey conducted by *The Japan Economic Journal*, 38 percent of the corporate heads surveyed believed that foreign direct investments will continue to grow over a long period of time even if the yen weakens somewhat.[3] Almost 60 percent believed that the boom will continue over the long run, although it may be subject to exchange rate swings. Thus, well over 90 percent of Japan's corporate leaders expect the trend to continue and only a very small minority thinks that it will end as soon as the yen exchange rate is "corrected," whatever that may mean.

With respect to the domestic impact of increased foreign direct investment, 71 percent of the industrial leaders believed that some hollowing of certain industries may occur; 5 percent argued that entire industries will be subject to such adverse effects whereas only 20 percent expected no hollowing at all. The industries most affected will be the automobile and electronic industries, textiles, and nonferrous metals and metal products, in this order. It is interesting to note that both the automobile and electronics industries have been among Japan's internationally most competitive industries since the mid-1970s, and they were the mainstay of the export drive of those years.

About 40 percent of the corporate leaders believed that the hollowing process will start during 1987–1990 while 10 percent did not expect it before 1990–1991. When queried about what the government should do to prevent the process, most argued for income, housing, and investment tax reductions, but only a few believed that additional interest rate reductions would be helpful. A number of respondents, however, wanted the government to promote investments in up-to-date manufacturing and information industries rather than in traditional public construction projects such as roads and bridges.

Members of the Maekawa Commission were not concerned about the possible hollowing of the Japanese economy.[4] They see the appreciation of the yen and the resulting foreign direct investment drive as an opportunity for the large Japanese *kaisha* to develop into multinational corporations, and thus, to take advantage of the international division of labor. They want to see increased investments not only in the United States and Western Europe but also in the developing countries and in the NICs of the Pacific-Asian region. Capital outflows, they argue, promote the transfer of technology and management to the areas that need it, thereby contributing to Japan's official development assistance (ODA) program.

Concerned by the fairly widespread views that the Japanese economy is about to be hollowed out through foreign direct investment, MITI officials in the fall of 1986 released a report that contradicts most of the doomsday prediction. The report rejects the view that the increase of such investment would result in major macroeconomic and microeconomic changes. With respect to the macroeffects, MITI argues that the economy is not going to be hollowed out. As a matter of fact, despite the growth in foreign direct investment, the ratio of manufactuered output in Japan's real GNP increased to 32.9 percent during 1980–1984, compared with 29.6 percent during 1970–1974. Moreover, MITI officials pointed out that in spite of increased American foreign direct investment in manufacturing over the years, the ratio of manufacturing output to GNP in America remained about 20 percent for the last two decades.

Concerning the microeffects, MITI officials cited evidence that the job losses in the United States as well as in the Federal Republic of Germany over the years were mostly due to improvements in productivity rather than increased foreign direct investments. They also argued that over the five years between 1980–85, the Japanese economy generated 750,000 new jobs and that the high-tech and service industries are constantly creating new employment opportunities.

Projections by the EPA support MITI's conclusions.[5] Based on a multi-sectoral model of the economy designed to forecast industrial structures and employment trends by the year 2000, the EPA concluded that Japanese industry is going to shift from the production of large volumes of a limited number of mass-marketed products to a low-volume of a limited number of mass-marketed products to a low-volume production of a wide variety high quality, that is, higher value-added products. At the same time, the EPA conceded while in 1980 employment in the secondary sector was 34.8 percent of the total, by the year 2000, this may be reduced to 30.1 percent. However, concurrently, employment in the tertiary sector will grow from 54.5 percent in 1980 to 65 percent by the turn of the century. Along with the employment growth in the teritary sector in general, the trend toward service rather than production employment by firms in the secondary sectors will also continue. The noticeably strong growth in business services is evidence of this, the EPA concluded.

In spite of such optimistic official views, unionized workers were very concerned about the potential job losses. In the summer of 1986, unemployment reached a record high of 2.9 percent and while it declined slightly to 2.8 percent by the fall of the same year, a trend was under way which was greatly disturbing in an economy where until recently, unemployment was not an issue. The Trade Union Council for Multinational Companies, a joint organization of trade unions in the automobile, textile, and steel industries, warned that the sharp appreciation of the yen will result in increased foreign direct investments with a corresponding loss in domestic employment. Deeply concerned, the 600,000-member influential Confederation of Japanese Automobile Workers' Union, is also trying to find ways to cope with the possible hollowing out of its industry. Encouraged by this, the labor unions of the major electrical and electronics manufacturers have also begun exploring possible counter-measures against shifting production operations abroad.

Thus, while the appreciated yen has set in motion an increase in foreign direct investment, there is no consensus on what such an outflow of capital and jobs could mean in the long run. Views and predictions clash, and only time will tell whether hollowing will occur, what industries may be affected, and to what extent more foreign direct investment might raise a new set of domestic socioeconomic problems.

While there is disagreement about the domestic effects of the rapidly growing foreign direct investment, Japanese corporate management agrees that for a variety of competitive reasons the trend is going to continue. Moreover, they believe that instead of the uncoordinated investments of the past, foreign direct investments are now planned and managed with the "global integration" concept as the strategic focal point. Management wants to manufacture products and perform other corporate functions such as R&D in the most cost-efficient locations, where skilled labor and research facilities are available and which are close to key markets. While the development of such comprehensive strategies in most corporations is still in its early stage, a number of companies have started its full-fledged implementation. From Toyota to Nissan and Sanyo to Honda, Hitachi and NEC, the giant *kaisha* are "integrating." The NEC Corporation, for example, is planning to manufacture and export from its American plants high value-added products such as facsimile machines and telecommunications modems to Japan, Western Europe, and other markets. NEC's top priority is to coordinate transactions outside Japan so that its subsidiaries in

America, Europe, and Asia do not have to go through Tokyo headquarters when transferring parts and products within the corporate system.

As part of the global integration process Japanese corporations are also increasing participation in *teikei*, or strategic coalitions with foreign partners. According to a study done by faculty members of Hitotsubashi University, a respected private institution in Tokyo, Japanese companies formed more than 6,000 such coalitions over the five-year period between 1982 and 1986.[6] The researchers found that of this total, 22 percent were joint ventures while 75 involved other arrangements such as joint R&D, subcontracting, or brand-name licensing, while the remaining 3 percent involved equity participation.

Of the foreign partners, 43 percent were American; 6 percent French, West German, and English; 4 percent South Korean; 3 percent Taiwanese and Italian; and 2 percent Swiss and Australian. The majority of *teikei* partners were electrical equipment, machinery, transportation equipment, and precision machinery manufacturers; but the so-called high technology industries as, for example, information technology and biotechnology, were also well represented as were financial services and fast-food franchises.

The numer of coalitions abroad (2,484) and those taking place in Japan (2,768) were approximately the same, while in slightly over 800 arrangements the coalitions were set up jointly in Japan and abroad. Most of the arrangements involved marketing (30 percent), manufacturing (26 percent), and R&D (20 percent). Because the study covered the period only up to 1986, it is reasonable to assume that during the three years leading up to 1989 a substantial number of similar coalitions were set up involving essentially the same nationalities and industries, and the same kind of functional areas.

Although globalization proceeds through a variety of arrangements, foreign direct investments raise some troubling questions. During FY 1986, MITI compared 1,043 Japanese corporations and their subsidiaries abroad with 1,052 non-Japanese companies in Japan in terms of selected management practices. The results were published in late 1988 and revealed that Japanese corporations were creating more jobs abroad in FY 1986 (897,000) than in FY 1983 (658,000), an increase of more than 200,000. But, at the same time, 45.4 percent of top managers in the subsidiaries abroad were transferred from the Japanese parent companies against only 17.3 percent of such transfers in foreign corporations operating in Japan. At the middle-management level (department heads and section chiefs) the respective percentages were 17.4 and 1.6. Moreover, MITI reported, while foreign companies in Japan sourced long-term capital primarily from Japanese banks (69.3 percent), the Japanese companies abroad obtained 34.7 percent from Japanese investors, 31.2 percent from Japanese banks abroad, and only 26.5 percent from non-Japanese banks. "Local content" was also negatively affected since the proportion of manufactured intracorporate exports in total Japanese-manufactured exports rose from 29.9 percent in 1983 to 39.2 percent during FY 1986. At the same time, the MITI report showed that Japanese corporations were not as profitable during FY 1986 as is generally believed. The ratio of pre-tax profits to sales was 0.7 percent in contrast to the 5.3 percent ratio of the foreign companies operating in Japan. Thus, it is possible that the tendency of Japanese companies to rely more on their managers and Japanese supply sources is, at least, partially caused by the necessity to exert tight control over foreign subsidiaries to improve financial performance. While this may very well be the case, the broader implication of this strategy raises a lot of questions in the host countries and is probably one of the reasons for the growing criticism of Japanese foreign direct investment in some parts of the world.

The increased globalization moves of Japanese corporations in conjunction with their tight management control abroad and the resentment this generates in the host countries have created a dilema for MITI. Due to the internationalization of the economy in general and the increased participation of Japanese companies in the international division of labor though a variety of means in particular, the ministry has lost its traditional *raison d'etre*. MITI officials understand that they have to redefine the ministry's role and that such a redefinition means more loss of influence over Japanese firms than they have already experienced in recent years both at home and abroad. To address the issue, MITI in 1988 created a special advisory committee comprised of industry leaders, academicians, and economists who were asked to prepare a set of recommendations that would allow the ministry to recast itself in light of the domestic and international challenges of the 1990s and beyond. One of the questions the committee was asked to consider is how MITI could nudge Japanese companies abroad toward "good corporate citizenship" as understood in the host countries. This is a thorny problem because, in an era of domestic liberalization, no new regulations are possible and host countries would resent any attempts by MITI to influence what they consider to be domestic companies. Officials also know that the time-honored practice of "administrative guidance" cannot be applied abroad, particularly in light of the 1988 GATT ruling that found its use in enforcing the 1986 U.S.–Japan semiconductor agreement in violation of international trading rules. Formal of informal curbs on the foreign direct investment activities of Japanese companies could also contradict efforts by the GATT and OECD to promote cross-border capital transfers, an activity that MITI supports.

Investments in the United States

The United States has long been a major target for Japanese foreign direct investment. In FY 1979, for example, 26.9 percent of all investments were made in the United States, which increased to 33.1 percent in FY 1984 and then declined to just over 30 percent in FY 1985.[7] By comparison, in FY 1984 Asia received 16 percent, Europe 19.1 percent, Latin America 22.6 percent, and the Middle East and Africa 2.7 and 3.2 percent, respectively. This trend not only continued but sharply accelerated in FY 1986 when, according to Industrial Bank of Japan data, approximately 46 percent of Japanese foreign direct investment went to the United States, increasing from an annual total of $5.4 billion in FY 1985 to $10.2 billion in FY 1986. In the following year, FY 1987, of the annual total foreign direct investment 44 percent was placed in America, increasing the annual total from $10.2 in the previous year to $14.7. This was followed by $22.8 billion of investments in FY 1988, accounting for almost 50 percent of total Japanese foreign direct investments in that year. This raised the cumulative total in America from $12.6 billion in FY 1984 to $65.7 billion, more than a five-fold increase over a period of five years. By the end of FY 1988 (March 31, 1989), the $65.7 billion stake in the United States represented 35.3 percent of the total $185.9 billion worldwide accumulated Japanese foreign direct investment.

As far as the distribution of direct investment in America is concerned, about 75 percent of it is in the "commerce-services" category, which includes marketing organizations, financial services, and real estate, among other things. Manufacturing investment represents a little over 20 percent, although these types of investments were the most rapidly growing category in calendar year 1988 and 1989. According to a 1988 Japan Economic Institute report, by the end of 1987, Japanese corporate investors had a stake of 50 percent or more in 628 U.S.-based manufacturing operations, up from 489 the year before.

During the late 1980s Japanese foreign direct investors still preferred to start from the ground. In 1987, for example, the ratio of new investments to acquisitions remained 2 to 1, although the number of acquisitions was up from the year before. Moreover, the majority of acquisitions was small, involving less than $20 million. Dainippon Ink & Chemicals, Inc.'s $540 million purchase of Reichhold Chemicals and the Sony Corporation's acquisition of CBS Records for $2 billion also in 1987 were large-scale deals representing an exception rather than the rule, at least so far. The majority of investments involved wholly owned operations, although joint-ventures showed a slight increase during the late 1980s while hostile takeovers remained an anathema to the Japanese. According to a 1988 General Accounting Office (GAO) report, of the 16 hostile takeovers either attempted or completed by foreign companies during 1987 and the first half of 1988, only one was undertaken and completed by a Japanese company (Dainippon). Of course, this does not mean that as they gain international experience, Japanese companies may not become more active in the hostile M&A field in the future—particularly if the yen continues to be strong and Japanese interest rates as well as U.S. stock prices remain relatively low.

Japan's growing direct investment in the United States was hardly noticed until the second half of the 1980s. Following the sharp rise in such investments beginning in 1986, however, the issue became one of major concern. A variety of politicians, academicians, mass-media commentators, and business interests summarized the concerns, many of which are legitimate, under the heading of "the selling of America." While the United States, just like any other sovereign nation, should be concerned about the impact of foreign direct investment on the economy and society in general, and on national security in particular, the mixture of well-informed and reasoned arguments and of ill-informed and irrationally presented views created a divisive situation.

The arguments over foreign direct investments were particularly trouble-some to the Japanese investors who, while not always singled out, understood that most of the criticism was directed at them. Undoubtedly, some of the criticism was justified because—as pointed out in the previously cited MITI report—the Japanese are slow in adapting to local circum-stances. They want to maintain tight control and, consequently, provide few opportunities to Americans to move into top management positions. They are also slow to hire minorities and do not understand that under the Federal Contract Compliance Program they must establish certain minority hiring goals and quotas if they want to do business with the U.S. government. The argument that the Japanese as well as other foreign investors do not use enough local content also seems to be borne out by statistics. The imports of foreign-affiliated companies in the United States rose from $18 billion in 1981 to $74 billion in 1986, a period in which the total trade deficit increased by $27 billion. In some instances Japanese investors also try to keep labor unions at bay, and many still do not fully appreciate the importance Americans attach to "good corporate citizenship." They do not always understand the nuances of America's heterogeneous society and are not very good in developing community relations. Many Japanese are also slow in integrating themselves and their families into the communities in which they live.

Undoubtedly, these and other related concerns of thoughtful Americans need to be addressed by the Japanese investors. In fact, many are already doing so. Japanese car makers and the United Auto Workers union, for example, are gradually coming to terms; other investors are reviewing their minority-hiring policies, and there is talk in Japan of making financial donations tax deductible so that Japanese companies in America can improve their community relations. There is, however, another dimension to the foreign investment controversy in the United States that the Japanese do not understand and appreciate and that must be resolved by the Americans themselves.

Just as the "Arab oil-sheiks" were charged with "buying up" America with their petro-dollars during the 1970s, so foreign investors in general and the Japanese in particular are now suspected of "taking over" the United States with their "trade-deficit dollars" during the late 1980s and early 1990s. To make their points, the proponents of these views cite a variety of statistics showing how serious the situation already is. However, once put in context and interpreted properly, the scary statistics to which the American public is exposed on an almost daily basis indicate that the foreign investment trend is considerably less menacing than the users of the fragmented data would have the public believe. While official statistics about the foreign ownership of American assets are not comprehensive and up-to-date enough to provide a reliable accounting of the situation, approximate estimates based on such data show that by 1988 less than 2 percent of commercial real estate was owned by foreigners and that, of this percentage, the Japanese share was less than 1 percent.[8] Moreover, only 4 percent of U.S. corporate stocks was in foreign hands, and the 1988 foreign acquisitions represented less than 2 percent of America's business assets. The 8 percent assumed control of U.S. manufacturing capacity (officially defined as at least 10 percent interest) includes newly established facilities which are a net addition to industrial capacity that would not have been realized without foreign investors.

The point has been made many times before that due to the high fiscal deficits and the unwillingness of elected officials to make some hard choices as, for example, to raise taxes, America cannot do without the continuous inflow of foreign investment funds. Suffice it to say that as long as there is no political will to make the necessary choices, arguments to restrict such investments amount to a potentially self-fulfilling prophecy that emotionally may be very satisfying but that economically America can ill afford. The demands for restrictions become even more questionable if current U.S. foreign direct investment trends are considered. According to Department of Commerce data, the book value of American investments overseas grew by $84.4 billion between 1984 and 1987. This trend was continued into 1988, particularly in Europe, where U.S. corporations are heavily investing to prepare themselves for the post-1992 integrated EC market. Such moves have sharply increased the American stock of foreign direct investments which, according to the Department of Commerce, stood at $259.9 billion (at book value) in 1986, followed by the United Kingdom ($133.9 billion) and Japan ($58.1 billion), also at book value. It is noteworthy that while in 1987 U.K. investors owned about 1 percent of U.S. manufacturing capacity, American ownership of U.K. manufacturing amounted to about 15 percent. Thus, America's foreign direct investment presence throughout the world by far outweighs that of other nations' investment in the United States.

The increasing support for restrictive legislation such as the Bryant Foreign Ownership Disclosure Act during the late 1980s took place in conjunction with the increasing presence of Japanese investors in America. This, combined with the various mass media features during 1988, raise the possibility that the real concern is not so much with foreign direct investment in general, but with Japanese foreign direct investment in particular. The statistics of foreign direct investment in America underscore this concern. According to Department of Commerce data, of the $25 billion in direct investment (defined as at least 10 percent ownership involvement) in 1987, $20 billion came from Europe and only $5 billion from Japan. Moreover, the British invested almost twice as much ($7.8 billion) as the Japanese ($4.1 billion) who were surpassed by Dutch ($5.9 billion) as well. True, according to the preliminary figures of the Bureau of Economic Analysis released in April 1989, Japan's share in foreign direct investment in 1989 may increase to $15 billion, thereby surpassing the British; but its accumulated direct investment in America still stood at only $50 billion, well below the $90 billion accumulated by U.K. investors by 1988. A 1989 report by the *British-American Deal Review*, a quarterly published by an international investment banking firm, moreover, showed that in 1988 British investors completed 398 acquisition deals valued at $32.5 billion as against $12 billion spent on acquisitions by the Japanese in the same year. Putting it a different way, the study concluded that British investors spent an amount equivalent to 4.5 percent of the U.K.'s GDP on U.S. acquisitions. In contrast, Japan whose economy is more than three times larger than that of the United Kingdom invested 0.5 percent of its GDP in American acquisitions. In addition, Japanese investors stay away from hostile takeovers while British investors have no reservations about such corporate acquisitions.

Thus, it seems that in spite of the larger presence and the more aggressive acquisition methods of European, particularly British, investors, the American critics of foreign investment are less concerned about them. This may be explained by the cultural kinship that Americans feel toward the

Europeans in general and the British in particular as well as by the ability of the Europeans to integrate more quickly and effectively than the Japanese. However, all of these considerations put together do not justify the often emotional and irrational criticism directed only at Japanese investors. Of course, the Japanese are making mistakes, but most of them are chiefly due to the lack of international investment experience and not to inherent characteristics that make them less desirable investors. As a matter of fact, a 1989 study of the Operations Center of the Graduate School of Business at Columbia University found that Japanese-owned firms in the United States were outperforming their American counterparts and continued to grow both in terms of net fixed assets and size at the time when the U.S. firms were retrenching.[9] Moreover, the Japanese have outperformed their competitors in terms of employee absenteeism, management turnover, production-management methods, product quality, and customer service. The study also reported that the Japanese spend three times as much on R&D, employee training, and high technology as the European firms in America, including the British, the Dutch, and the Germans. Thus, the Japanese investors are making contributions to the improvement of the international competitiveness of selected U.S. industries.

Japanese business circles are aware of the foreign direct investment concerns in the United States as well as of the legitimate criticism directed at their investment and management practices. To address these problems, the *Keidanran* in the spring of 1988 established the Council for Better Investment in the U.S. which in the same year carried out a survey of over 300 firms either involved or interested in direct investments in the United States. The results showed that the majority of Japanese companies are now aware of the necessity to adjust certain management practices and to integrate themselves better within the local communities. In December 1989 The Japan Association of Corporate Executives published a set of guidelines for Japanese direct investors in the United States. The guidelines address most of the previously discussed problems and urge Japanese companies to eliminate controversial practices and to globalize their management. In the meanwhile, proposed legislation, such as the Bryant bill that would require foreign investors to register and to divulge various kinds of information depending on the size of their investment, could do irreparable damage to the U.S. economy, Demanding that foreign investors file financial statements in Washington while private American investors face no such requirements would be blatant discrimination. The notion that such information should be made public would scare potential investors away and would make America one of the least desirable industrial countries in which to invest. Such narrow-minded and inward-looking ideas do not address the real economic problems of the nation. The problems could be solved with more political will than currently exists in Washington where the easy solutions, however potentially destructive, are always more popular than the tough choices such as raising taxes.

Although the Bryant bill was not passed by the end of 1989, the "Committee on Foreign Investment in the U.S." (CFIUS) began to affect foreign direct investments soon following the passage of the 1988 Trade Act. The so-called Exxon-Florio Amendment to the act gave the President the authority to reject foreign takeovers on national security grounds and CFIUS is the interagency committee that makes recommendations whenever question are raised about an investment project. CFIUS represents eight agencies and offices, including the Treasury and Defense Departments, thus yielding considerable clout. It has 30 days to decide whether to investigate a proposed investment and 45 days to develop recommendations. The President then must decide within 15 days. A number of projects, including several Japanese ones were rejected by CFIUS during 1988 and 1989, thus indicating that the United States intends to defend selected industries and firms from foreign takeovers.

Investments in Western Europe

While modest in the 1960s and 1970s, Japanese foreign direct investment in Western Europe has continually increased during the early 1980s. According to MOF data, Japanese direct investment in Western Europe rose from $1 billion in FY 1984 to $6.6 billion in FY 1988 and is expected to surpass $9 billion in FY 1989, a nine-fold increase over a period of five years. As reported by the Japan External Trade Organization (JETRO), the number of Japanese-owned plants in one year alone surged from 282 in 1987 to over 400 in 1988.

JETRO reported in early 1989 that there were 411 Japanese-affiliated (at least 10 percent ownership) manufacturing companies in Europe, more than twice the 157 firms is 1983. Employing over 100,000 people, these firms are distributed over 16 countries, although most of them are located in the United Kingdom (92), France (85), the Federal Republic of Germany (67), and Spain (41). Other preferred investment sites are the Netherlands (27), Luxembourg (23), Italy (24), and Belgium (22). If the Republic of Ireland, Greece, and Protugal are included, 404 or 98 percent of the 411 plants are located in the EC member countries. The firms manufacture and market various types of products such as cars, trucks, chemicals, electronics, and pharmaceuticals.

The major objectives of the Japanese investors include the desire to reduce trade frictions by supplying the local market directly rather than through exports, to provide more local content, and to prepare for the post-1992 EC market integration, which calls for new competitive strategies. Most Japanese firms are in favor of the market integration because they expect a lowering of manufacturing and marketing and, in particular, distribution costs. Those already present in the EC seem to do well in the host economies. JETRO reports that more than 80 percent of the companies experienced no strikes, and the local content of the products was up from 47.3 percent at the start of operation to 62.8 percent by 1988.

Nonetheless, Japanese direct investors already present in the EC or planning to make investments in the near future have reservations about several aspects of the investment climate. They are concerned about the mixed signals emanating from some of the countries. On the one hand, the British, for example, are actively promoting Japanese investments while, on the other hand, there is growing concern in the mass media about a Japanese "takeover" of certain British industries. The French objected to the export of Nissan cars manufactured in the United Kingdom to the continent, arguing that the cars did not contain enough local content to qualify as European-made. Although it was eventually resolved, this issue was of particular concern because "local-content" laws remain on the EC nations' agenda. Up until 1989, for example, a chip was considered European-made even if only its final packaging was done in the EC; now a very sophisticated chip-manufacturing process, the so-called wafer fabrication, must also take place for chips to be an EC product. Work habits and employee relations also vary from country to country and they are all quite different from what the Japanese are used to at home. Furthermore, although in April 1989 the EC reversed its position and is no longer demanding "reciprocity" but "national treatment" to allow foreign banks to operate in the community, the Japanese are still concerned that other restrictions directed specifically at them may be on the way. In light of this, MITI is encouraging companies to set up "antenna offices" at the EC headquarters in Brussels to follow the various developments more closely. Fujitsu, Ltd., for example, has done so in late 1988 and now collects all available information on the unification of product standards, the application of competition policies, and the protection of intellectual property rights.

At the same time, MITI is advising Japanese companies to proceed with caution and to do everything possible to "localize" new investment as soon as possible. MITI also emphasizes that it is important that new Japanese investors, particularly in the car, home appliance, and precision machinery-building industries, do not aggressively confront European and American companies and, thereby, inflame the already tenuous trade relations with Brussels, Washington, and the other European capitals.

Investments in the Asian Pacific Region

Japanese direct investment in the region grew at a rapid pace during the early 1980s, increasing from 16 percent of the total in FY 1983 to 25.2 percent in FY 1984.[10] On a value basis, Indonesia received the most, followed by Hong Kong and Singapore. On the basis of the number of projects, Hong Kong led the list and was followed by Singapore and Taiwan.

On a value basis, the Association of Southeast Asian Nations (ASEAN) nations as a group received 31.1 percent of the total going into the region in FY 1981 and 18 percent in FY 1984. Analyzed by industry, more than half of the accumulated total investments throughout the region were in the nonmanufacturing sector, primarily in mining and financial services, whereas only a little over one-third were in the manufacturing sector, mainly iron and nonferrous metal, chemicals, and textile ventures. This pattern reflected past Japanese investment strategies which focused on serving local markets or producing for exports to third countries and the securing of raw material supplies.

However, while growing during the early 1980s, Japanese investments in the region declined 23 percent of the global total by the end of FY 1985. The ASEAN nations were particularly hard-hit; in FY 1985 they received only 7.7 percent of all investments going into the Asian Pacific region, less than half of the FY 1984 amount. The overall decline was due chiefly to the economic uncertainty caused by the sharp decline of oil rubber and tin exports, increasing protectionism in the target markets and the growing external debt. To deal with the uncertainty, governments introduced a series of investment performance requirements which had an unfavorable effect on the investment climate.

During FY 1986, direct investment in the Asian region continued its relative decline, accounting for 20.5 percent of the global total of Japanese direct investments by March 31, 1987. Some of the ASEAN nations were particularly affected as most Japanese investments bypassed them and went to the United States and Western Europe. Political uncertainty, economic instability, and the continuation of restrictive measures held back Japanese firms. However, during the second half of 1987 and throughout 1988, the situation changed for the better, especially as the appreciated yen began to take its toll on the international competitivenss of Japanese exporters in

1987. Searching for low-cost production bases and spurred on by the improving investment climate in countries whose governments realized that they need Japanese investments and therefore gradually began to remove restrictions, the Asian-Pacific region in general and the ASEAN nations in particular became preferred investment targets. According to MOF data, direct investments in the ASEAN nations rose from $855 million in FY 1987 to $1,524 billion in FY 1988, an increase of 78 percent. Most of these investments went to Indonesia and Thailand, both of whom experienced a more than 100 percent increase; but Malaysia, the Philippines, and Singapore also benefited as did the Republic of Korea, one of the region's leading NIC. Such trends, however, did not change the overall distributions of investments in the region. By the end of 1988, Indonesia was still in first place, followed by Hong Kong, Sinapore, and the Republic of Korea, while the People's Republic of china stayed in last place. Overall, the region's importance to Japanese investors can best be illustrated by the results of a 1988 survey done by the Industrial Bank of Japan which in early 1989 reported that 42 percent of the companies polled identified Asia as the most important region for future direct investments. This compared with 48 percent for North America and 5.9 percent for Western Europe.

During the second half of the 1980s the structure of Japanese direct investments was undergoing a change. Although in terms of the accumulated total, by late 1988 the nonmanufacturing sector was still ahead (52 percent) of the manufacturing sector (48 percent), most of the new investments were made in manufacturing. On a value basis, the mining industry still was in first place with the majority of investments (over $6 billion), followed by the iron and nonferrous metals and chemicals manufacturing industries and the "commerce" or distribution industry, each with investments slightly over $1 billion. On a case basis, the "commerce" or distribution industry was ahead of the electrical machinery-manufacturing industry which grew very rapidly during the second half of the 1980s and reached prominence by 1988. By the summer of 1989 it became apparent that a number of companies have decided to move R&D units into a select group of NICs, particularly Taiwan. Matsushita, for example, established the Matsushita Electric Institute of Technology, Taipei, Corp. which the Taiwanese view as a model of future cooperative arrangements with Japanese corporations. The reason for Matsushita's move is that the local R&D facilities allow a quicker and more effective response to changes in the maturing NIC markets. This trend is welcomed by the NICs because the establishment of R&D units may help reduce the brain-drain to the United States and Western Europe.

By late 1988, Japanese direct investment in the Asian-Pacific region took another turn. Due to the soaring wages and sharp currency appreciations in the Republic of Korea, Taiwan, Singapore, and Hong Kong (the "Four Tigers"), most new investments were beginning to bypass these nations and a number of existing plants closed down. During 1987–1988, for example, the Taiwan dollar had appreciated by 40 percent against the U.S. dollar, and average wages on the island nation were considerably higher than in Thailand or Malaysia. However, the new low-wage target nations are not restricted to Thailand and Malaysia, but also include the Philippines, Indonesia, the People's Republic of China, and India. While a number of these countries as, for example, Indonesia, Thailand, and Malaysia (all members of ASEAN), have long been favorite investment destinations, others such as the People's Republic of China and India were of no particular interest in the past. Today, India, for example, is viewed by Japanese investors as a large, low-wage country that is rich in natural resources and that could serve as a good base for exports to the Middle East. Not surprisingly, a joint MITI-MOFA (Ministry of Foreign Affairs) delegation to India in 1988 included representatives of such well-known companies as Sumitomo Corporation, NEC, Fujitsu, Honda, and the Bank of Tokyo.

The majority of investments going into these countries is in the manufacturing sector, and a number of them involve the transfer of plants from one of the Four Tiger nations. Examples include the 1988 transfer by Kyocera Corporation of its compact camera assembly operation from Taiwan to the People's Republic of China, and the move by Hitachi and Sanyo from Taiwan to Malaysia. Major Japanese banks are also in the process of establishing a foothold in Indonesia, Malaysia, and Thailand. Lured by rapid economic growth, the prospect of profits, the increasing deregulation of the financial sectors, and the presence of Japanese companies, the banks are rushing to set up either joint ventures or branches in Bangkok, Kuala Lumpur, and Jakarta. As of April 1989, there are 14 representative bank offices in Indonesia, 13 in Malaysia, and 10 in Thailand, with more expected in the near future.

Although in 1986 and 1987, the Asian-Pacific countries in general and the ASEAN nations in particular improved their investment climates to lure Japanese investors, such investments are not without problems. Just as in the United States and Western Europe, the tight control Japanese executives exert over subsidiary operations, together with other management practices, cause tensions. Such tensions are often reinforced by the memories of World War II and, thus, although the official government policy is to promote and welcome Japanese investments, resentment is widespread. In Thailand, for instance, Japanese companies are causing an upheaval in the labor market as local employees frequently leave domestic companies owned and operated by Thais to work for Japanese firms that offer better pay and working conditions. The better pay increases the average wage level, creating problems for domestic entrepreneurs. Local content is another source of friction. While most Japanese manufacturing companies are trying to increase such content, it is not always easy to do, particularly if the content-level is set by law and, thus, must immediately be met. Because the infrastructure of most countries in the region is not well developed, sudden increases in Japanese direct investment also put great strain on existing facilities. Bangkok's port, for instance, is frequently backed up with cargo waiting for unloading and loading. Some nations such as Singapore resent low-skill investments and want to focus on the quality of incoming projects. The city-state's Economic Development Board (EDB), for example, declared in late 1988 that it is moving toward greater automation in manufacturing, bio-technology, and, in general, investments that would provide its citizens with better quality jobs. Thus, the "screwdriver" type of assembly plant operations, using little local content, are no longer welcome.

Located within the Pacific region, Australians also expressed reservations about the influx of Japanese direct investment. In a 1988 poll commissioned by the Ministry of Foreign Affairs, the majority of Australians identified Japan as the country with the greatest economic importance to their nation. However, more than two-thirds stated that the 1988 level of Japanese direct investment was "sufficient" and that more would not be acceptable. In New South Wales and Queensland, where Japanese investments have grown the most rapidly, over 80 percent expressed negative attitudes.

Japan and the People's Republic of China are two of the most important countries in the region. Trade between the two countries is brisk. Japan is China's second most important trading partner after Hong Kong and ahead of the United States with an annual volume exceeding $16 billion in 1988. But Japanese direct investment is far more limited, amounting to approximately $1.2 billion in FY 1987, up from $230 million in FY 1986. This accounted for only 9 percent of total foreign direct investment in China, much less than that of Hong Kong and the United States. Even the dramatic increase in FY 1987 was misleading in that $1 billion of the investments involved a single oil development scheme and only the remaining $200 million were earmarked for various other projects. Without the major oil project Japan's investments in FY 1987 would have been stagnating at best.

A large-scale expansion of investments was not possible because the Japanese had major concerns about China's investment climate. In the fall of 1986 and in early 1987, MITI and MOF officials, for example, reported that potential Japanese investors were reluctant because they did not believe that the Chinese observed international trade customs and did not appreciate the technologies offered. Japanese business circles were particularly concerned about the Chinese practice of considering technology just another commodity, not paying internationally accepted prices and demanding the most advanced technology regardless of their ability to effectively absorb and apply it. Moreover, they objected to the short duration of joint-venture contracts, the problems of getting the necessary information for feasibility studies, the lengthy approvals, the difficulties in procuring local materials for plant construction, the often vague wage and related labor standards, and the uncertainties about being able to sell the goods produced in China's domestic market as well as the repatriation of earnings. Although in the fall of 1986 the Chinese government announced new measures which included lower taxes, reduced labor, land, and raw material charges, as well as greater freedom for the hiring and firing of labor, the questions of domestic sales and earnings repatriation were not addressed. The Japanese were also critical of the 1979 joint-venture law as it was applied to the special economic zones. Management and personnel policies were restricted, the rules governing the distribution of profits were unclear, and the protection of intellectual property rights was limited. Although Prime Minister Nakasone in 1986 tried to promote direct investment in China through improvements in insurance coverage and other related measures, Japanese investors continued to remain cool.

Prime Minister Takeshita's visit to China in August 1988 came at an important juncture. The two nations had just celebrated the tenth anniversary of the Sino-Japanese peace treaty signed in 1978, and the Chinese were very anxious to obtain Japanese capital to finance their sagging economic development and reform plans. Takeshita brought with him a Y810 billion ($6.5 billion) concessionary loan for 42 modernization projects covering FY 1990 through FY 1995. The yen-based loan was the third of its kind and represeented a 50 percent increase over the loan agreement in force at the time of the visit. The Japanese Prime Minister also offered assistance for environmental projects and the protection of Buddhist antiquities.

One of the highlights of the visit was the signing of the Japan-China Direct Investment Protection Agreement which was negotiated over a number of years and insured Japanese investors of "national treatment." Under the agreement Japanese companies are treated like their Chinese counterparts in matters of procuring materials, employing workers, and other related operational matters. Moreover, the agreement also stipulates procedures to be followed in the case of nationalization, outbreak of war, and possible investment disputes. However, the two sides agreed that national treatment is not applicable if, in order to promote public order, to guard national security, or to insure the sound development of the national economy, the Chinese decide to make an exception. To settle disputes over the interpretation of the those potential exceptions, a joint dispute settlement panel was authorized. It is noteworthy that while China has investment protection agreements with 20 nations, including France and Thailand, it has not granted the privilege of national treatment to any of them. The decision to do so for the Japanese was due to the recognition that the measures were necessary to motivate Japanese investors.

The specifics of the agreement and the timing of its announcement prompted a number of Japanese companies, particularly in the small to medium-sized category producing foods, toys, and miscellaneous goods, to consider possible investments. The guarantee that they would no longer be charged higher prices for materials and labor, and that their equity interests would be protected, eliminated a number of concerns. The need to shift production from the increasingly more high-wage countries of the region as, for example, Taiwan, to low-cost locations introduced economic considerations that were new. Thus, motivated by the assurance of better treatment and by cost considerations, even some of the large *kaisha* expressed an interest in China. By the late summer of 1988, Matsushita Electrical Corporation, Citizen Watch Company, and Mita Industrial Company, a leading copier manufacturer, and others had investment plans for the mainland.

However, the October 1988 decision of the Chinse to put brakes on the economic reform process renewed concerns about the future of foreign direct investments. The Chinese announced that for future investments they will give priority to foreign companies who want to take a 100 percent ownership position as opposed to a joint-venture with local partners. Moreover, potential foreign investors were urged to consider restructuring existing plants rather than constructing new ones. Although officials tried to assure the Japanese as well as others that the retrenchment would not directly limit foreign investments, the decision reinforced the long-held belief of foreigners that China's economic reform policy is characterized by uncertainties.

The Japanese, in particular, had not forgotten the upheaval that resulted from the unilateral Chinese decision to cancel large-scale joint projects due to foreign exchange problems in 1980. Thus, the far-reaching investment cuts ordered in October 1988 and the specter of double-digit inflation combined with widespread corruption reduced the positive effects of the investment protection treaty signed only a couple of months earlier.

The uncertainty was further increased when in November 1988 the Beijing based Foreign Enterprise Service Corporation (FESCO) announced that beginning January 1, 1989, foreign companies would have to pay the salaries of Chinese workers supplied by FESCO in U.S. dollars. In making the decision, the agency was trying to protect itself against the devaluation of the *renminbi*, and also wanted to obtain more convertible currency at a time when the country experienced severe shortages. Although the proposal would have exempted joint-ventures, American and European companies immediately issued a joint protest (the first of its kind), but the Japanese remained silent. Concerned about offending their Chinese hosts, the Japanese delayed action as long as they could but eventually joined the Americans and Europeans. Ultimately, more than 400 companies protested, including 280 from Japan. In the face of such a united opposition, FESCO reacted quickly and, on December 29, 1988, announced that the implementation of the new policy would be "postponed." While foreign investors in general and Japanese investors in particular viewed FESCO's initial decision as an expression of lack of faith in the domestic economy, they considered the scrapping of the proposal an indication of Beijing's weakened bargaining position with foreign investors.

During his visit to Japan in April 1989 Chinese Prime Minister Li Peng tried to convince the Japanese government and business circles that despite the austerity program China is going to continue its reform process. His message, however, did not seem to convince the Japanese business community, because the visit was preceded by reports that some joint-ventures have already come to a standstill due to high costs, shortages of materials, and electricity. Moreover, some Japanese investors reported that following the October 1988 announcement of the reform slowdown, the Chinese withdrew the national treatment from Japanese companies which they received only last fall under the bilateral investment protection treaty. Although Prime Ministers Li and Takeshita agreed to set up a bilateral committee to explore ways to increase Japanese direct investment in China, the 1988 slowdown was only a forerunner of worse to come.

The tragic events of June 1989 had a strong impact on the business links between the two countries. Although the Japanese were more reluctant and slower than other nations to condemn the Chinese leadership for the cruel suppression of the pro-democracy movement, eventually they also imposed sanctions, including the suspension of the $6.5 billion loan program. True, by August 1989 most of the sanctions were lifted and many Japanese business representatives returned to China to protect their investments. However, inspite of critical Western news reports that the Japanese have ignored the tragedy and returned to China ahead of everybody else, they continue to be just as cautious as Americans or Europeans. Japanese banks, for example, have pulled back and in the fall of 1989 were still not granting new loans. The government intends to continue negotiations only after the World Bank lifts its sanctions on new loans. New investments are not forthcoming because Japanese businessmen saw their worst fears confirmed by the sudden faceabout of the Chinese government. After witnessing the suppression and then hearing officials deny that it has ever happened, most of them are reluctant to resume business as usual and commit new funds. As a matter of fact, according to an August 1989 report of the "Wall Street Journal," it was the South Koreans who returned ahead of everybody else. They attended the Beijing trade fair in the summer of 1989 in large numbers as if nothing had happened and signed new contracts.

Official Development Assistance

Japan's foreign aid program, known as Official Development Assistance (ODA), is about 30 years old and has its origins in postwar reparations to the Southeast Asian countries.[11] Indonesia and the Philippines were among the first to receive substantial payments in the late 1950s, lasting until about 1965 when the formal aid programs began.

Throughout the second half of the 1960s, ODA programs provided primarily tied-aid which had to be spent on the purchase of Japanese goods. Later, in the aftermath of the 1973 oil crisis, financial aid was given primarily to resource-rich developing countries and nations situated on important shipping routes. Beginning in the early 1980s, the focus of aid programs changed again, and more emphasis was put on the reduction of poverty and the support of those developing countries which are important to the worldwide strategic concerns of the Western alliance. During the second half of the 1980s ODA was focused on rural and agricultural development, the creation of new and renewable energy sources, human resources, and the promotion of small- and medium-sized businesses.

In comparison to other industrialized nations, after a relatively slow start in the early 1970s, Japanese foreign aid grew at an average rate of 10.5 percent between 1978 and 1984, increasing the share of such aid in GNP from 0.24 percent during the mid-1970s to 0.34 percent in 1984. To strengthen foreign aid programs, the Japanese government called for an increase from $1.4 billion in 1977 to $2.8 billion in 1981, and then decided to again double ODA during the 1981–1985 period. The first time it achieved the goal, however, the second time funding fell short of the objective set; the amount spent was 16 percent less than targeted. As a consequence, ODA accounted for only 0.29 percent of GNP in 1985 as opposed to the high of 0.34 in 1984, and so Japan was still far off the 0.7 percent which the United Nations recommends as a target ratio.

The reason for the shortfall during the 1981–1985 period was that in 1985 alone, ODA was down by 12 percent from the previous year due chiefly to a sharp drop in contributions to multilateral agencies which reflected the cyclical nature of such contributions rather than a change in policy. The funding of mulitateral institutions declined by 34.4 percent in 1985 because Japan made special contributions to the International Development Agency (IDA), and subscribed to a special replenishment of the World Bank in 1984. Additional reasons for the shortfall of ODA included the average decline in the value of the yen of about 15 percent beginning in 1981 and lasting through the fall of 1985, and the deteriorating economies of the developing countries that delayed the implementation of several aid projects.

Of all ODA during 1981–1985, about two-thirds of it went to the Asian Pacific region, in particular the ASEAN countries of Indonesia, Thailand, Malaysia, and the Philippines. On an individual country basis, at first Indonesia led the way, but was replaced by the People's Republic of China in 1982. The ASEAN member nations have alternated in the second, third, and fourth positions over the years, never falling lower than fifth place. The distribution of ODA reflected Japan's desire to maintain satisfactory political relations throughout the region, and recently, to complement long-term Western strategic interests as illustrated by the aid given to the People's Republic of China.

By FY 1986 Japanese ODA increased to $5.6 billion which was a modest 4.8 percent increase in yen terms over the previous year. The ODA/GNP ratio which stood at 0.29 in FY 1985 was maintained. The FY 1987 ODA budget allocation increased by a respectable 13.5 percent in yen terms to $7.5 billion but due to the recovery of the economy the ODA/GNP ratio did not improve and stayed at 0.29 percent. In FY 1988, Japan increased its ODA disbursement by 22.5 percent to $9.1 billion over the previous year. However, it still remained second to the United States which disbursed $9.8 billion, exclusive of military aid. Moreover, inspite of the ODA increase, Japan's ODA/GNP ratio rose only slightly from 0.31 in FY 1987 to 0.32 in FY 1988, still well below the average of 0.35 of the industrialized (DAC) nations. On the other hand, Japan's ODA/GNP ratio tied for 12th place with the United Kingdom among the 18 DAC countries while America came in last together with Ireland.

In FY 1989, Japan intends to disburse $10 billion and, thus, finally become the world's largest foreign aid donor surpassing the United States, a move that was predicted several times in previous years.

While second in the provision of overall aid, by FY 1988 Japan was already the No. 1 bilateral aid donor in 25 countries, including the Philippines, Thailand, Indonesia, Burma, Bangladesh, India and the People's Republic of China. Combined with the huge private investments and the extensive trade relations throughout the Asian-Pacific region, Japan is rapidly becoming the major economic force in the region, a prospect that still unsettles some nations in the area.

The geographical distribution of ODA during FY 1986 and FY 1987 was essentially the same as during the years before concentrating on Asia and the ASEAN countries. In FY 1986 the People's Republic of China received most of the assistance, followed by the Philippines, Thailand, and Bangladesh. In FY 1987 Indonesia was the major recipient, followed by the People's Republic of China, the Philippines, and Bangladesh. Much of the aid (about 45 percent) each year was spent on capital-intensive programs such as improvements of public utilities and in industrial, mining, and construction projects, although the development of human resources remained a major objective.

Japan's relatively low ODA/GNP ratio is continually criticized by other nations. Some DAC nations point out that for a country that continues to accumulate huge current account surpluses, the 0.32 ratio achieved in FY 1988 is unacceptably low. In response, the Japanese argue that although they have consistently increased the ODA amount disbursed, the continued strong growth of their economy makes it very difficult to raise the ratio. Moreover, they emphasize, the third version of the current account recycling plan, announced in July 1989, brought Japan's commitment to recycle its surplus to $65 billion over the FY 1987–1991 period. Some of these funds will be spent, among others, on the environment, a cause emphasized at the 1989 Paris summit of the industrialized nations, the so-called Brady plan to ease the burden of the indebted nations and the long suffering sub-Sahara region of Africa.

At the 1988 Toronto summit of the industrialized nations, Prime Minister Takeshita announced that Japan intends to increase its ODA to $50 billion over the 1988–1992 period. This pledge replaced an earlier commitment made by Prime Minister Nakasone in 1985 concerning the raising of ODA to $40 billion between 1986 and 1992. Takeshita's pledge was well received throughout the world, although it was noted in Washington and European capitals that he did not say that such increased spending would exceed the average DAC/OECD foreign aid to GNP ratio of 0.34 or 0.35. Some members of the U.S. Congress expected Takeshita to commit Japan to reaching the 0.7 percent level specified by the United Nations as the desirable target for industrialized nations. However, a number of American and

Japanese foreign aid experts were not convinced that the developing world could effectively absorb an 0.7 percent Japanese ODA/GNP contribution, nor did they think that the Japanese ODA bureaucracy would be able to administer efficiently the funds that would become available if the ratio reached such a high level.

The FY 1989 ODA budget was eventually increased to $11 billion. To underline this position, the Ministry of Foreign Affairs announced that Japan intends to raise the ODA/GNP ratio to 0.4 percent by 1992, thus exceeding the DAC/OECD average. Not surprisingly, this statement was not well received by the MOF which continues to be concerned about the fiscal health of the nation and pointed out that the achievement of this target would mean an annual ODA budget increase of at least 10 percent through 1992. Nonetheless, to emphasize Japan's new role as a major source of foreign aid to the developing world, on January 5, 1989, the government announced that in addition to all of its previous commitments, it would also expand its concessionary yen loan program to cover middle-income countries such as Mexico which would become eligible if their debt/service ratio (percentage of annual export earnings spent on servicing debt) exceeded 30 percent. Until this announcement such credits were offered only to low-income countries with a per capita income of under $1,636 annually.

Japanese ODA has been criticized by the recipient countries for a number of reasons. Objections were expressed to the perceived strategy of using foreign aid to promote Japanese business interest. Recipients complained that the policy of granting aid on a request basis only, allows Japanese business firms to lobby governments for project requests which only they can fulfill. The large average yen loan share of aid packages, the relatively high interest rates, and tough repayment schedules have also been criticized. This developed into a particularly bitter complaint on the part of the ASEAN nations when the yen suddenly appreciated in 1985–1988, thereby dramatically increasing the repayment burden.

In spite of Japan's increasing ODA budget, criticism of its foreign aid activities grew during the 1985–1988 period. Aid experts pointed out that the approximately 60 percent grant component of Japanese foreign aid was too low in comparison to the 80 percent average of the DAC/OECD nations. Others suggested that due to the appreciation of the yen, the loan repayment burden of the recipient nations has increased so dramatically that Japan should consider forgiving that portion of the repayment that is due to the appreciation. ASEAN member nations wanted interest rates lowered on their loans, while DAC member nations criticized Tokyo's aid efforts because too many of the projects were capital intensive and, thus, led to the informal "tying" of aid to exports. Other critics argued that Japan should develop a global aid program and give up its concernation of the Asian-Pacific region in general and the ASEAN nations in particular.

The Japanese response to this criticism emphasizes that they want developing countries to become self-sufficient as soon as possible. Thus, Japan prefers loans to grants; it does not want to create an "aid-dependency" among the recipient countries. Furthermore, the Japanese argued, most of their projects are no longer tied to Japanese exports but only to certain services as, for example, pre-project consulting which is the only way to insure that the projects are done properly. In 1988, Japan reduced the interest rates on new loans to ASEAN nations, but it responded that the Asian-Pacific region is vitally important to Japan's national interests; therefore, any major re-orientation of the program is an unreasonable expectation.

The administration of the ODA program was criticized both abroad and at home. Japan, unlike most major donor nations, has no single government agency in charge of foreign aid. Currently ODA is administered under the guidance of several ministries and agencies. The Ministry of Foreign Affairs (MOFA) and the Ministry of Finance (MOF) are the two most important; MITI is involved through its Overseas Economic Cooperation Fund (OECF), while the Economic Planning Agency (EPA) is the fourth and least important of the policy-formulating and managing bodies. Of the two most influential ministries the MOFA is more interested in achieving foreign policy objectives such as goodwill and cooperation, while the MOF wants to maintain fiscal control over spending. In addition, others such as the Ministry of Agriculture, Forestry and Fisheries, and agencies as, for example, the Japan International Cooperation Agency (JICA) affiliated with MOFA, also participate in the administration of ODA. Although a number of ministries and agencies are involved, program administration is woefully understaffed. The number of officials in charge of ODA in 1977, for example, was 1,326. Ten years later, at the time when ODA spending increased more than five-fold, there were only 1,503 ODA officials. Thus, the foreign aid program is caught is a bureaucratic maze with considerable funds to allocate but with unclear, undefined administrative procedures, unstated objectives, and inadequate manpower.

In a 1988 report titled "Administrative Inspection of ODA Programs" the government's Management and Coordination Agency concluded that the ODA program has been "ineffective and must be sharply revised." The report described a foreign aid program which is entangled in red tape and where many requests for assistance have been poorly investigated and

THE INTERNATIONALIZATION OF THE JAPANESE ECONOMY

delayed. The agency investigators criticized the grant programs as "inflexible and ineffective" in offering emergency aid to developing countries. Even minor grant request must go through a long bureaucratic process, including Cabinet approval, and their approval depends on the circulation of a variety of official and properly signed memoranda. In conclusion, the investigators emphasized that the entire aid approval process should be reviewed, simplified, and restructured in such a way as to speed up the process of implementation and follow-up.

On top of such administrative problems, Japan's ODA also lacks a philosophical underpinning. Unlike other major donor countries, Japan does not have any foreign aid legislation. Its program is torn between U.S. demands that in lieu of more Japanese military spending it be used to support American strategic interests and the growing Japanese self-confidence that it can fashion an aid agenda of its own. With the evolution of the various trading blocs in the late 1980s, many Japanese politicians and officials believe that ODA funds should be used to strengthen ties with the Asian-Pacific region so as to guard against American and European trade protectionism. To promote the development of a comprehensive foreign aid program contributing to the needy nations of the world yet in line with Japan's national interests, a committee of 14 ministers and key politicians was set up in 1988. Thus, it seems that the politicians want to gain control over ODA from the bureaucracy that did not manage to overcome many of the problems previously discussed.

Not unlike the extensive U.S. foreign-aid programs which during the 1960s generated the phrase the "Ugly American," Japansee ODA programs are also beginning to have overall image problems. In Thailand, which received two-thirds of its assistance from Japan in 1988, the influx of Japanese money, for example, is changing the skyline of Bangkok and is creating a very dominant and visible Japanese presence. While the Japanese businessmen have adapted to the Thai environment and no longer insulate themselves from the locals the way they used to in the past, their increasing grip on certain industries as, for example, construction, is watched by the Thais with great concern. Now that in real terms, Japan is about to become the world's largest donor nation, such overall image problems and their potential implications represent an additional consideration in the restructuring of the ODA programs for the 1990s.

Notes

1. The *Ministry of Finance (MOF)* defines foreign direct investment as the purchases of foreign securities, loans, and remittances to establish subsidiaries abroad.

2. As reported by MITI.

3. *The Japan Economic Journal* (June 7, 1986), p. 1.

4. Shoichi Akazawa, Chairman of the Japanese External Trade Organization (JETRO); Tokyo, March 1986.

5. Internal documents, Economic Planning Agency (Tokyo, May 1986). The primary sector includes agriculture, forestry, and fisheries; the secondary sector is manufacturing, mining, and construction, while the tertiary sector is comprised of the service industries, government, and utilities.

6. As reported in *The Japan Economic Journal* (May 7, 1988), p. 22.

7. Ministry of Finance source (Tokyo, March 1986).

8. *The New York Times* (January 27, 1989), p. 27.

9. *The Performance of Foreign Affiliated Firms in America* (New York: Graduate School of Business, Columbia University, (1989).

10. In addition to Japan, the region includes the NICs of Southeast Asia (Hong Kong, Taiwan, Korea, and Singapore, also known as the "Four Tigers") as well as Indonesia, Malaysia, the Philippines, Thailand, and the People's Republic of China. The former four together with Singapore and Brunei are members of the Association of Southeast Asian Nations (ASEAN).

11. William L. Brooks and Robert M. Orr, Jr., "Japan's Foreign Economic Assistance," *Asian Survey* (March 1985), pp. 322–340.

9 LOOKING AHEAD

Although from the outside the process may seem slow and uncertain at times, the internationalization of the Japanese economy, i.e., the shift from export-led to domestic demand-led growth, is underway. The sharp appreciation of the yen unleashed a set of market forces that cannot be turned back. In unison with these market forces, the step-by-step, albeit occasionally cautious, implementation of the Maekawa Commission policy recommendations are changing Japan's domestic economic landscape and global role.

The Economy and Trade

Following the deflationary impact of the yen appreciation in 1986 and during the first half of 1987, the Japanese economy came back roaring in 1988 and achieved an inflation-adjusted growth rate of 5.7 percent, up from a respectable 4.5 percent the year before.[1] This was the highest growth rate since 1973 and put Japan ahead of the United States (3.8 percent in 1988) as well as of the other industrialized nations. Japan also had the highest per capita GNP among the seven largest industrial nations, reaching $23,400 at the current exchange rate in 1988, as compared to America's $19,800. However, using purchasing power parity estimates, the United States was still ahead of Japan.

It was significant that for the third year in a row, economic growth was achieved without net exports. Although inflation-adjusted exports grew 7.9 percent in 1988, imports rose at a 21.1 percent rate, by far surpassing the increase in exports, and so the external trade sector reduced overall economic growth by 1.9 percent. Consumer spending, one of the main engines of the economy, accounted for 55 percent of GNP, although it stood almost still at 0.1 percent during the last three months of the year due to a slowdown in asset appreciation (land and stocks) as well as the late emperor's illness.

FY 1989 promised another solid year of economic growth, although in April the Bank of Japan expressed concern about a possible increase in inflation due to rising oil prices, the weakening of the yen against the dollar, and the price impact of the 3 percent consumption tax introduced on April 1, 1989. Such a concern, however, has to be seen in the context of a scant 0.1 percent price rise in 1987 and almost no increase at all in 1988. As a result of the spring 1989 *shunto* or wage offensive which resulted in an average 5.1 percent increase, consumer spending is expected to increase by 6.5 percent, thus continuing to fuel an economic growth expected to be around 4.8 to 5 percent.

While the FY 1988 current account surplus dipped to just below $77 billion ($84.4 billion in 1987), the emerging foreign trade trends during the second half of 1988 caused concern in Tokyo and all over the world. True, the merchandise trade surplus also declined by 1.7 percent in 1988, the first reduction in six years, but the December 1988 data showed that exports were up on a monthly basis by 11.5 percent over a year ago. This expansion was due particularly to increased sales of semiconductors, office equipment, and steel products. It is noteworthy that this rise in exports took place despite strong domestic demand and was not the result of dollar-denominated price increases but of volume growth.

The bilateral trade surplus with the United States, the politically most sensitive aspect of trade, declined from the 1987 high of $59.8 billion to $55.4 billion in 1988. This was a welcome development, although not as convincing as was hoped for. America's overall trade deficit of $171.2 billion in 1987 declined to $137.4 billion in 1988, a 20 percent shrinkage of which more than 30 percent reflected a sharp improvement of the trade balance with the European Community (EC). The balance with other nations as, for example, Taiwan, the Republic of Korea, Hong Kong, and Singapore, also improved more than the trade balance with Japan. At the same time, America's exports to Japan increased by 33.6 percent to $37.7 billion over 1987, led primarily by agricultural and manufactured products which accounted for over 50 percent of total exports for the second year in a row.

It is, however, noteworthy that United States-Japan trade relations look differently if measured in yen terms. According to MOF data, between 1985 and 1988 Japanese exports to the United States declined by 26 percent from Y 15.5 trillion in 1985 to Y13.6 trillion in 1986, Y12.1 trillion in 1987, and Y11.5 trillion in 1988. Over the same three-year period the bilateral trade surplus of Japan declined 35 percent from Y9.37 trillion in 1985 to Y6.1 trillion in 1986. The difference between the dollar and the yen bilateral trade relations trends are the result of the weakening of the U.S. dollar during these years.

But, regardless of how the bilateral trade imbalances are denominated, the late 1988 and early 1989 developments caused concern in both Tokyo and Washington. The Japanese *kaisha* have clearly overcome the restraining effects of the sharply appreciated yen through a variety of measures including the shift to higher value-added exports that face less competition from the increasingly more aggressive NIC producers. This happened at a time when due to worldwide expansion the global demand for Japanese products ranging from capital goods to consumer products was on the rise.

Under such circumstances the reduction of Japan's large current account surpluses can be achieved only through increased imports fueled by a strong domestic economy or through a worldwide economic slowdown, not an appealing alternative. Measured in dollar terms, Japan's import perform-ance improved sharply between 1986 and 1988 as imports grew by slightly over 18 percent between 1986 and 1987 and by 25.3 percent between 1987 and 1988. Moreover, the share of manufactured goods in total imports rose to an all-time high of 49 percent in 1988 compared to a 44 percent share during the year before. This ratio as well as the per capita import level of Japan, however, remain below those of other industrialized nations; consequently, there is room for improvement. In particular, the Japanese must see to it that more of the yen appreciation is passed on to consumers in the form of lower import prices.

The most disturbing import trend is the stagnating or even declining share of the United States. According to MOF data, America's share of capital goods imports declined from 65 percent in 1985 to 55 percent in 1987; and, while it slightly improved in 1988, the increase was not convincing. The decline in consumer durables was even more steep: America's share fell from 19.8 percent in 1985 to 13.6 percent in 1987, and its 1988 share, while up, did not indicate a strong recovery. These trends, however, can no longer be explained by the "closed" nature of the market. While Japan's agricultural sector is still protected and the distribution system creates problems for new domestic or foreign entrants, the sharp import share gains by European or Southeast Asian producers are ample evidence that the "closed market" argument no longer holds. As reported by the MOF, the capital goods import share of the Southeast Asian producers, for example, increased form 10.2 percent in 1985 to 16.2 Percent in 1988; that of the EC from 16 to 20 percent during the same years. Furthermore, the Southeast Asian nations' import share of consumer durables grew from 29 to 32 percent between 1985 and 1988; that of the EC producers increased from 37.2 percent in 1985 to 44.5 percent in 1988. The sharp import share increases of the Southeast Asian nations was achieved through lower prices, while the EC producers offered well-designed quality products for which the Japanese consumers were willing to pay higher prices.

Although the economy continued to expand at a robust rate in the fall of 1989, growing labor shortages and increasing inflationary pressures began to send mixed signals. The boom, caused primarily by strong consumer spending and record high private sector capital investments, promised a FY 1989 growth rate of 5 percent.

To what extent Japan can maintain the strong domestic economic growth that it needs to sustain increasing imports beyond FY 1989 is not entirely clear. While consumer spending and private sector investments, two of the mainstays of the 1988 expansion, looked strong in the spring of 1989, the third component, new housing starts, appeared to be declining. This, combined with the increasing concern over inflation, the unclear impact of the 3 percent consumption tax, and the effects of the Recruit-insider trading scandal introduced some uncertainties. It should also be noted that while the Japanese government has control over macroeconomic policies, it cannot restrain its "leaner and meaner" *kaisha* from exporting, particularly if domestic demand softens. Thus, one of the objectives of the shift from export-led to domestic demand-led growth, namely the reduction of the current account surplus to GNP ratio from over 3 percent in 1988 to a more acceptable 2.0 to 2.1 percent in 1992, may not be achievable. The realization of this goal calls for a concerted effort by all the major industrialized nations of the world, particularly by the United States and the EC nations which have to come up with better ideas than "managed trade" or the unilateral application of domestic trade laws such as the Super 301 section of America's Omnibus Trade and Competitiveness Act of 1988.

The road to the aggressive and punitive use of the Super 301 section was cleared by the April 28, 1989, decision of the Bush Administration to name Japan, the Republic of Korea, Brazil, Canada, the EC, and India as the nations maintaining "unfair trade barriers" against American companies. Japan was cited for restricting American sales in the $9 billion annual telecommunications market and its complex distribution system in the

214-page report used eventually to identify the Super 301 target countries. According to the United States' Trade Representative (USTR), Japan was violating the Market Oriented Sector Specific agreement (MOSS) on telecommunications that the two nations signed in 1985, and did not undertake any efforts to "open up" its distribution system. Thus, the stage was set for a probably endless and fruitless bickering about industry-specific issues not only with Japan but with the other nations at the expense of the larger international trade interests of America and the global community. The EC's reaction to the April 28 report that the United States itself maintains 42 trade barriers and that the Community "would explain its position concerning the American charges but not negotiate" was an indication of things to come. America is going to have a difficult time trying to show the relationship between the "unfair barriers" of the nations cited and the $126.5 billion 1988 trade deficit which was caused mostly by the interaction of macro-economic factors and policy decisions made by various governments, including that of the United States, over a number of years. This is not to argue that American companies do not have legitimate complaints about market access in various countries; they undoubtedly do. However, the road taken by the United States in the spring of 1989 is not going to provide easier access for them. It is more likely to generate additional confrontations with other nations.

As is the case whenever a new government comes into office, former Prime Minister Takeshita announced a new five-year plan under the title "Japan Living Together with the World," in the summer of 1988, just in time for the Toronto summit of the industrialized nations. The plan was developed by the Economic Policy Council, a government advisory body consisting of leading business executives, academicians, and retired top-level bureaucrats and working staff made up primarily of Economic Planning Agency (EPA) officials. While such plans represent little more than intentions, they provide useful insight into how the nation's leading economic experts see the future.

Covering the period from FY 1988 through FY 1992, the plan envisions a rather modest real annual economic growth rate of 3.75 percent, a 4.1 percent growth contribution by domestic demand, and unemployment rate of around 2 percent by 1992 and stable prices. Moreover, it calls for the realization of an economy in which the Japanese people can enjoy a better quality of life, a reduction in the nation's global current account surpluses, greater contributions to the world at large, a smooth restructuring of industries, and a balanced development of local economies. To achieve all this, the plan emphasizes the need for more efficient land use so that sufficient good quality housing can be provided, a reduction of the current annual working hours from more than 2,000 to 1,800 hours by 1992, and a five-day work and study week in government offices and schools. To rectify the trade imbalances, it proposes an increase of imports in general and the easing of restrictions on agricultural imports in particular. Furthermore, it recommends the decentralization of key government administrative functions from Tokyo to other locations, the deregulation of selected inudstries such as distribution, and the continued improvement of the nation's infrastructure. Although the plan does not contain any prediction concerning the effect of all of this on the ratio of the current account surplus to GNP, EPA officials indicated that they expect this figure to be about 2 percent by the end of FY 1992.

As mentioned before, such plans are not considered blueprints for action and, thereofre, are usually not subject to detailed ciriticism. However, this plan was immediately castigated for its vagueness, even by some Council members. Others were concerned about the modest growth projections and argued that the nations should aim at a 4 percent 4.5 percent real growth rate, particularly since the reduction of the current account surplus to GNP ratio to 2 percent by FY 1992 could not possibly be achieved with the projected growth rates. Such low growth also makes it impossible to bring down the unemployment rate to 2.0 to 2.5 percent by the final year of the plan because it is predicated on the continuation of fiscal austerity marked by restraints on public works projects. Such excessive caution, the critics emphasize, could hinder the realization of the full potential of the Japanese economy and could fail to reduce the conflicts with trading partners in general and the United States in particular.

In contrast to the government's five-year plan, private sector research institutions offered a more expansive economic outlook. In its 1988 forecast for the FY 1988–FY 1993 time period, the Japan Center for Economic Research, for example, predicted a 4.2 percent real average annual growth rate led by a 4.7 percent rise in domestic demand. Furthermore, the institute forecast an increase in government spending by an annual average of 4.8 percent and emphasized that the revenues lost from the 1989 corporate and personal income tax reform would be offset by the new 3 percent consumption tax and the abolition of the tax exemption on interest earned on small savings accounts (*maruyu*). Most important, the institute predicted that the current account surplus is likely to stay above 70 billion by FY 1993, thus raising the specter of major disagreements with the nation's trading partners.

Unresolved Domestic Concerns

Over the next few years, Japan has to address a number of domestic issues to promote the internationalization of the economy. Foremost among these is the development of more efficient land-use policies. Government measures such as those introduced in 1987 and 1988 already had a salutary effect in that land prices increased by only 8.3 percent in 1988 as opposed to the 21.7 percent rise in 1987. Tax changes, such as the 1989 measure allowing higher deduction for capital gains on land offered for public expropriation, are steps in the right direction. The increase of tax deductions on capital gains obtained through the sale of urban farmland for residential use is also likely to alleviate the housing and land shortage in metropolitan areas. Such moves together with the gradual decentralization of selected government agencies from Tokyo to other locations are a good beginning. However, more needs to be done in terms of changing tax rules and zoning regulations to allow for a more efficient use of scarce land in the long run. As Balassa and Noland have argued, such moves could lower the cost of land which, in turn, would change Japanese savings behavior, because under current conditions 65 percent of household wealth is in the form of illiquid housing as compared to the United States where only 31 percent of the wealth is held in such a form.[2] Reduced savings would reduce the savings-investment imbalance, and this would remove a major cause of the sustained current account surpluses. It is, however, important to point out that land-use policies cannot be changed too suddenly or too extensively within the foreseeable future. The real estate holdings which have so dramatically appreciated in recent years represent hidden assets or *fukumi* which were extensively collateralized, particularly for stock purchases. If the real estate *fukumi* values were suddenly deflated, it could create a major crisis on the Tokyo Stock Exchange, affecting the entire economy, and conceivably spreading to America and the rest of the world.

Another unfinished domestic agenda item is the quality of life. Although the major objective of the internationalization of the economy is to establish more balanced global economic relations through a reduction of the current account surpluses, this objective is going to be accepted and supported by the Japanese people only if their quality of life is improved in the process. The "rich country, poor people" self-description of the majority of Japanese is not just a catch phrase, but a reflection of a real concern about the distribution of income and wealth during the boom years of 1986 and 1989. It is true that rapid economic growth and new avenues of accumulating wealth always distort such distributions, at least for a while. It can also be argued that such is the price of economic progress. However, in the egalitarian post-World War II society of Japan, where until 1987–1988 the majority of Japanese saw themselves as middle class, the socioeconomic distortions of the last two years are viewed with great unease. The events surrounding the Recruit-insider dealing scandal, involving leading politicians, government officials, and businessmen, reinforced these concerns.

The vast infrastructure investments of recent years, together with the 1989 tax reform, the reduction of working hours, and the generally increased emphasis on leisure, are moves in the direction of improving the quality of life. but as long as land prices are high, a large portion of the funds earmarked for infrastructure investments goes for the price of land. Many Japanese also believe that the April 1, 1989, tax reform has not eliminated past inequities, particularly in view of the 3 percent consumption tax. Others argue that the working-hour legislation exemptions given to small to medium-sized companies together with the continuing tendency of management to hold employee vacations to a minimum, slow down the progress toward a more leisurely national lifestyle. of course, these are issues about which reasonable people can disagree; thus, only time can tell to what extent the combined effect of the domestic policy changes introduced in 1986–1989 improve the quality of life in the long run.

One of the most critical domestic issues confronting Japan in the near future is the aging of its population. In 1988 there were 13.7 million people over the age of 65 representing 11.2 percent of the total population. At current rates, it would take Japanese society only 26 years to double its over-65 population; in contrast, it would take America 70 years to do so. Demographers predict that people over 65 are likely to represent 16 percent of the population by the year 2000 and 25 percent, or nearly 32 million, by the year 2020. These potential trends raise a number of questions about how society is going to care for its elderly in the future.

Economists argue that workers' pension contributions may have to increase from 12.6 percent of annual income in 1988 to 29 percent by 2010 to meet the nation's pension obligations. Such projections raise even more concern when the projected dependency rates of the nonworkers are considered. In 1988, for example, seven active workers supported every nonworking person; due to demographic trends this number is expected to decline to three by 2020.

To address these issues the government proposed and already implemented a number of changes in the retirement and pension systems. The 1985 revision of the pension law set an informal target of 65 as the retirement age, a rise from the previous retirement age of 55. The revision also included a reduction in pension payouts from 83 to 68 percent of a worker's annual pay. To formalize these policies, a government panel recommended in late 1988 that 65 be phased in as the initial age for collecting pensions. By delaying such payments, demands on the pension funds could be reduced and people would be encouraged to remain in the workforce rather than retire. The Ministry of Health and Welfare (MHW) also sought an increase in the premium-base for pensions by requiring everyone between the ages of 20 and 60 to be enrolled in the national pension system.

The aging of Japanese society is also likely to affect the labor force. By the year 2000, workers 55 and over may be in excess by 1.3 million, while those aged 15 to 54 may be in short supply. It is also possible that due to demographic and educational trends, the supply of professional and technical people may be deficient by 3 million people, also by 2000. The age supply gap between the older and younger generation may lead to work-sharing, and this process is likely to accelerated by the widespread tendency of those over 55 to take on another job even nowadays. Retirees often work to supplement their income and to be more financially secure but also to maintain their physical and mental health.

Japan's health care system is also affected by the aging population. There are a number of health care programs that cover portions of medical expenses, but the participants in these plans are not concerned about their share in medical costs. They frequently visit doctors, particularly the elderly whose costs are even lower than those of the rest of the plan memberships. Health care economists see major financial problems in the future; the cost of care for people 65 and over is expected to increase six-fold from $142 billion in 1987 to $856 billion in 2025. The IMF projects that Japan's social expenditures for health care, pensions, education, and other related areas may rise from 15.4 percent of Gross Domestic Product (GDP) in 1980 to 27.7 percent by 2025. In contrast, the IMF predicts that similar expenditures in America are likely to increase from 17.7 percent in 1980 to 19.4 percent in 2025.

Such projections have already led to the formulation of several policies to address upcoming problems. One of these calls for the merging of the various health systems into a single one by 1990. The plan is to combine National Health Insurance that serves many of the elderly and poor with the financially stronger salary-based systems. The government and society at large are aware of the current demographic trends and the issues this raises. But much more needs to be done in the near future to prepare the Japanese for the time when they will not only have one of the world's strongest economies but may also have one of its oldest populations.

Japan's International Role

As reported by the MOF in the summer of 1989, total Japanese assets at the beginning of 1988 reached $43.7 trillion, or 20.7 percent higher than the assets of the United States which amounted to $36.2 trillion. These figures represent the value of domestic land, plant, equipment, housing as well as of financial and other assets.

However, these figures are misleading because they were based on the exchange rate in force on December 31, 1987, a time when the yen reached its highest level against the dollar. Moreover, much of the Japanese wealth is rooted in land prices which are substantially higher than in the United States. Nonetheless, the figures indicate that Japan has come a long way since the end of WWII.

It is also noteworthy that as of May 1988, among the top ten "Global 1000" corporations, measured by sales volume, six were Japanese; of the top ten measured by market value, eight were Japanese, while the other two IBM and Exxon, were American.[3] These and other related measures show that Japan has indeed arrived as an economic power.

But the Japanese have not yet managed to decide how they should use this newly won power and, thus, what role they should play in the world. They are finding out that building a powerful economy was a simpler task than creating and defining a global role that is compatible with national interests and with the expectations of the world community. People everywhere speculate about what the Japanese intend to do, but much of this speculation is misdirected because it projects an economically strong Japan as a global menace. This is not only unsubstantiated but also misleading. The Japanese are searching for a role that is commensurate with their economic power, serves their national interests, and, at the same time, contributes to the wellbeing of the global community.

Japan is not seeking a role as a political superpower for the simple reason that it neither wants to be nor is it equipped to become one. Its economic strength is not bolstered by military force or an ideology that appeals to the rest of the world, prerequisites that a political superpower must be able to meet. In 1988 Japan has taken some foreign policy initiatives such as sending people and funds to the United Nations' peacekeeping operations in Iran and Afghanistan. It also spoke up at the Bangkok meeting of Asian nations about the peace process in Cambodia and, most of all, offered its own plan at the Toronto summit for solving the debt problem of developing nations. But these moves were not followed by others. Moreover, the initial debt plan was received with a mixture of scepticism and hostility because many people thoughout the world still see Japan as standing for no ideal other than the quest for self-enrichment. This is an image problem that the Japanese must resolve if they want to assume a new global role in the future. Several possible alternatives offer themselves to improve their image, including that of a promoter and financier of the worldwide peacekeeping and environmental protection efforts, that of a co-leader of the global economy together with the United States and the EC, and that of an economic leader of the developing Asian-Pacific region.

The eventual fulfillment of any of these possible international roles is likely to be influenced by historically conditioned national concerns. The Japanese, in spite of their new wealth, still feel vulnerable due to a lack of natural resources, the continued dependence on foreign markets, and the anxiety that another oil shock or some sort of embargo could destroy much of what they have worked so hard to achieve. Yet, the more they work to safeguard their vulnerable interests, the more they succeed, and the more they succeed, the more they seem to be vulnerable. Former Prime Minister Nakasone expressed this paradox by saying that what the country needs is "international nationalism" and urged his fellow citizens to become more international by becoming more Japanese in the best of traditions.

Although there is a sense of vulnerability in the country, the younger generation is less subject to it than those over 50. Spared the horrors of World War II and its painful aftermath, raised under continually improving living conditions and not burdened by the guilt complex of the war generation, the younger Japanese are going to be less influenced by it when dealing with the outside world. As a matter of fact, a more assertive Japan is already on the way. For example, some Japanese political leaders resent American suggestions that they must undertake greater "burden-sharing — if not directly in military expenditures, then in foreign aid. While increased burden-sharing through foreign aid is a legitimate U.S. expectation, the Japanese — who are already spending more on foreign aid in absolute dollar terms than any other nation, except America—do not want it if it means the validation of America's geo-political priorities. They want to provide assistance on their own terms, that is, by combining international needs with legitimate national interests.

However, no matter how assertive Japan's future leaders turn out to be, they cannot exert the kind of dominance over the world economy that some pundits predict. They will have to function as co-leaders together with the leaders of the United States and the European Community. America continues to be a major economic force, although the current global economic readjustment represents a shift from her absolute dominance during the post-World War II years to a relative superiority shared by others. The era of global interdependence which was managed by the United States within a clearly defined set of rules has disappeared, and in the new era of global indeterdependence economic affairs must be jointly managed by co-leaders residing in Washington, Tokyo, and Brussels. These co-leaders have to cooperate within the narrow confines of domestic politics and a modestly expanding global economy, a far more complex and difficult undertaking than America's task during the post-World War II years when the United States was the dominant force and the world economy grew at a rapid pace. Calling such an evolutionary trend "trading places with Japan" or "allowing the Japanese to take the lead" represents a shortsighted and ethnocentric view of the world that is devoid of any historical content. In the new era, America, Japan, and the EC must work together and compete against each other, and they must also create a new set of international trade rules; otherwise the new interdependence of the 1990s is going to be corroded and eventually destroyed by domestic political considerations. Such an outcome would be a tragedy for the entire world.

An area in which Japan is demonstrating an increasing readiness to become an influential co-leader is international finance.[4] Today, the Japanese control a large amount of dollars, but in recycling them they want to avoid the mistakes the American banks made in the 1970s when they aggressively lent petro-dollars to just about any country that wanted them. Japan's dollar recycling program is based on a more conservative approach and calls for a close working relationship with the International Monetary Fund (IMF) and the World Bank. For example, under the program announced in May 1987, Japan adds $20 billion to the previously committed sum of $10 billion earmarked for the developing nations. But, of the total $30 billion to be recycled, $27 billion is for additional subscriptions and co-financing arrangements with the various multilateral organizations. Japan designated its Export-Import Bank as its financing intermediary, a decision that the Americans and others fear could lead to export-promotion, a charge the Japanese deny. At the same time, they insist on influence that is commensurate with the financial contributions they are making to the multilateral organizations. The Japanese do not see their co-leader role the same way the Americans do, that is, they do not believe that only the United States should supply the leadership while they supply the funds. Thus, the issue of shared decision-making has to be resolved in a mutually satisfactory manner before too long.

Japan's role as a co-leader also requires a rearrangement of its bilateral economic relations with America. To the United States this means the reduction of the bilateral trade imbalances, but the real issues at hand are far more complicated. No doubt, continued Japanese trade surpluses in the $40 to $50 billion range are both economically and politically unsustainable. However, the simplistic notion that the placement of Japan on the Super-301 list of the Omnibus Trade and Competitiveness Act of 1988 could solve the trade imbalances must be laid to rest as quickly as possible by Washington. No amount of unilateral condemnation, however emotionally satisfying, can remove the underlying causes of the imbalances which were due to economic policies on both sides of the Pacific over a number of years. It would be a tragedy not only for U.S.–Japanese bilateral relations but for the entire global trading system if America's trade policy for the 1990s were based on aggressive use of the Super 301 section. America's trade policy toward Japan must be based on the fact that while the United States buys 36.5 percent of Japan's exports, Japan is the best consumer of American agricultural products. Furthermore, Japan is one of the major investors in the United States, and American firms are the largest direct investors in Japan. The resulting relationships transcend trade imbalance measures, although the political implications of the imbalances in terms of employment cannot be ignored by either side.

"Managed trade" is not a solution either because the idea of assigning fixed market shares to individual countries to balance trade is not only contradictory to the multilateral trade system but is also impractical. The know-how needed to simulate international competition in sophisticated technological products in the global markets is simply not available, particularly as technology and demand conditions change on short notice. Moreover, "managed trade" would force governments to supervise private-sector companies closely, an interference that neither the large Japanese *kaisha* nor the huge American multinational corporations with global rather than national interests would tolerate. Managed trade between two of the world's most important economies could also severely damage the developing nations which need new markets, suffer from a heavy external debt and experience slow growth. Furthermore, to demand that the Japanese import certain types and amounts of American manufactured products would require that the Japanese government play a major role in the domestic marketplace, a role that to some extent it played in the past and for which it was heavily criticized abroad. Finally, at the time when the United States is praising the benefits of the free market system not only to the developing nations but also to the reforming socialist countries of Eastern Europe and expresses concern about a possible "Fortress Europe" by 1993, a trade cartel with Japan would be the height of hypocrisy. America is still one of the bastions of free trade and must remain so not only for the benefit of the global economy but for her own sake no matter how appealing a notion such as "managed-trade" may appear in the short run.

While the idea of a United States–Japan free-trade agreement sounds inviting, such an agreement would probably create more problems than it could resolve. The combination of the world's two most powerful economies could deal a fatal blow to the multilateral trade system as it exists today. The world economy can put up with a post-1992 integrated EC market and a United States-Canada Free Trade Agreement as long as the nations involved do not overemphasize the bilateral relations at the expense of multilateral considerations. But a United States–Japan free trade agreement that would exclude the other Asian-Pacific nations is not in the interest of either Japan or America and could damage global economic interests. In contrast, an agreement to improve cooperation between the two nations would provide a more effective framework to explore economic issues of mutual interest because it could replace the currently used confrontational and haphazard approach that causes more problems than it resolves.

The much heralded structural impediments negotiations represent a new stage in U.S.–Japan trade relations. After the sectoral discussions and the devaluation of the dollar in 1985–1987, the structural impediments negotiations represent the third approach to reduce the bilateral trade imbalances. America expects the Japanese to change a number of domestic economic features such as the distribution system and practices as, for example, land tax and zoning laws. Other expectations include more infrastructure investments, the pass-through of the yen appreciation to consumers, the reduction of working hours and the dismantling of the "keiretsu" systems. In contrast, the Japanese emphasize the need to reduce America's fiscal deficit and consumer spending, to increase savings, to improve productivity, to export more aggressively, to change management's short-term orientation and to better educate the labor force.

Undoubtedly, the issues raised by both sides are important and changing them could lead to improvements in the trade imbalance in the long run. However, the expected adjustments are so complex and involve so many political and social considerations, let alone economic ones, that it is unrealistic to expect any short-or even medium-term results. Moreover, the features and practices questioned are domestic matters which do not violate any of the existing international trade laws or agreements. Thus, both sides are likely to pay lip-service to most issues and side-step changes hat could be politically inconvenient. While the United States wants to see concrete results or at least a "blue print" for action by the spring of 1990, the Japanese are more realistic and believe that, at best, only some preliminary under-standings can be achieved by that date. Thus, there is a real danger that these set of talks will also fail not because the two sides are unwilling to acknowl-edge the relevance of the issues raised, but because domestic political considerations necessitate quick results in America and only slow and gradual changes in Japan.

In the meanwhile, the United States and Japan must cooperate in the current GATT Uruguay Round talks. The two nations together account for about 70 percent of the GNP of the major industrialized nations and about 40 percent of global GNP; therefore, their close cooperation is essential. The resolution of the different issues, particularly of the agricultural subsidies problem, is going to be a severe test of Japan's commitment to free trade and the internationalization of its economy. While agreements can only be reached if the United States and the EC are also willing to make economic and political sacrifices, attention is going to be focused on Japan to see to what extent one of the world's dominant trading nations is willing to revise its agricultural import policies.

America must also get its own economic house in order through the reduction of the huge fiscal deficits and through significant improvements in the international competitiveness of its industries. There is no easy way to do all of this; therefore, Americans must realize that only through a painful policy restructuring process involving reduced consumption, better education, and a better coordinated international trade policy formulation process can the nation's economic vitality be restored.

The Asian-Pacific region is comprised of Japan, the People's Republic of China, the NICs (Republic of Korea, Taiwan, Singapore, and Hong Kong), and the ASEAN countries, including Brunei, Indonesia, Malaysia, the Philippines, and Thailand.[5] In addition to their rapid growth, these nations are also becoming more and more interdependent through trade, investments, finance, and technology transfers. In 1988, for example, Japanese exports to the ASEAN nations increased by close to 40 percent over the year before, and imports from the same region grew by over 20 percent. Japanese exports and imports with the NICs are also in the double-digits, while Japanese direct investment is soaring in the area, particulary in Thailand, Singapore, and Malaysia.

These trends imply that Japan's economic future is increasingly tied to the Asian-Pacific region rather than to North America and Western Europe. As long as the Asia-Pacific region nations keep growing, Japan can do more business with them and thereby reduce its own dependence on Western Europe in general and America in particular. By virtue of its economic power, Japan is also well suited to become the informal economic leader of the region, responsible for promoting greater economic cooperation among the nations and promoting their economic interests vis-a-vis the rest of the world. To test this idea, the Japanese government recently proposed annual conferences of regional trade ministers. According to MITI officials, such conferences could help regional economic policy coordination on a wide range of issues and enable the region to reduce its dependence on the increasingly more protectionist American and EC markets. The talks would also include the United States, Canada, and New Zealand, but to what extent the People's Republic of China and Taiwan would participate is a political question that cannot yet be answered.

Not all Asian-Pacific nations are enthusiastic about or even receptive to Japan's growing influence in the region. The idea of Japanese economic leadership arouses anxieties, particularly in the Republic of Korea and the People's Republic of China, both of which have suffered a great deal from past Japanese military ventures. The proposal for an annual trade conference reminds many Koreans, Chinese, and others of the Greater East Asia Co-Prosperity Sphere concept advocated by the Japanese during the 1930s and early 1940s. To counter the proposal, the Australians in early 1989 even recommended the creation of an Asian-Pacific version of the OECD to which in the region currently only Japan, the United States, Canada, Australia, and New Zealand belong. To promote the idea, Australia hosted the first exploratory meeting in Canberra in November 1989 which was attended by most nations in the region, including the United States and Canada. However, for political reasons neither the People's Republic of China nor Taiwan or Hong Kong were invited. The ASEAN group nations, understandably, expressed some reservations about the Australian plan because they did not want the influence of ASEAN to be compromised by a larger regional trade bloc.

While it is understandable that the memories of past Japanese military ventures are still painful in some countries and that other nations may have different views concerning the forms of cooperation, Japan's economic dominance of the region is a fact, and must therefore be recognized as the reality of the 1990s. To address the resulting issues, the LDP leadership established a parliamentary league in the fall of 1988 with the mission to study the nation's economic and cultural cooperation alternatives. A total of 206 LDP Diet members, 150 from the Lower House and 56 from the Upper House, belong to the league.

Because the United States is no longer able and willing to absorb more imports from the Asian-Pacific nations, Japan's economic cooperation with them must be based on increasing its own imports from the area. It could be argued that the future of global trade relations depends on Japan's ability and willingness to do so, because otherwise America may become very protectionist, a move that the world community cannot afford. Thus, only if, in addition to aid and technology, Japan can offer new markets to the region's nations can it become an effective representative of their economic interests and join America in the role of co-leader of the global economy.

In addition to these macro-level issues which will have to be addressed by Japan's policy-formulators, a number of developments are also taking place at the micro level or corporate level whose resolution is in the hands of corporate managers. The following section presents an overview of several such micro issues. It is important to keep in mind, however, that most of these changes are just getting underway and that their overall effect on the Japanese corporate world cannot yet be estimated.

Selected Corporate-Level Developments

Japan is changing from the "factory of the world," that is, the exporter of mass-produced goods, to the "banker of the world," or the largest global supplier of capital. Its net long-term capital exports in 1988, for example, totaled U.S. $130 billion and its return on investment was about U.S. $10 billion. Thus, it is not an exaggeration to say that Japan is taking over the role occupied earlier by Britain and then, later, by the United States as the major world creditor.

The new role as the world's banker calls for different corporate competitive strategies. As the yen's appreciation and the export-substitution effects of foreign direct investment are gradually taking their toll, Japanese companies are modifying their strategies. According to a recent study by the Industrial Bank of Japan (IBJ), the external demand for Japanese-manufactured products (exports and off-shore production) is likely to stay at a constant 16 percent of total demand. However, the study also predicts that the proportion of off-shore production would increase to nearly 10 percent by 1992, indicating a major shift from domestic to off-shore product sourcing. In FY 1988 overseas production represented 4.8 percent of total production, up from 4 percent in FY 1987, as reported by MITI.

This trend implies a diminishing role for industries supplying mass-produced, standardized goods such as automobiles and consumer electronics to the domestic market. Some economists even predict a merchandise trade deficit sometime in the late 1990s. At the same time, they also project a shift to higher value-added offerings, that is, better designed products, increased variety, higher technology content, as well as a shift to finance, consumption, and leisure services. As part of these shifts, corporate strategies are undergoing gradual changes.[6]

Corporate Objectives

The ongoing corporate strategy changes can best be illustrated by comparing Japanese corporate behavior with that of American companies. The 1986 "U.S.–Japan Comparative Survey of Corporate Behavior," for instance, found that several of the major objectives of Japanese corporations are now

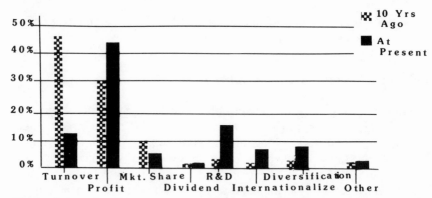

Figure 9-1. Japanese Corporate Objectives 10 Years Ago and at Present. *Source*: Based on data from "Management Strategy—A Japan–USA Comparative Study," (Tokyo: Japan Committee for Economic Development and Japan Productivity Center, 1986).

similar to those of American companies.[7] While ten years ago the *kaisha* managers considered a "higher turnover" most important, they now put "higher profits" on top of this list of goals. Figure 9–1 illustrates this trend over time.

Japanese corporate managers today are also placing less emphasis on the economies of scale as a means of maximizing profits than they did in the past. Moreover, many of them are now exploring new pricing strategies to cope with competitors, and they also place a great deal more emphasis on diversification which usually restricts short-term earnings. But unlike their American counterparts, who are reluctant to invest in new businesses unless profits can be obtained within the first three years, Japanese managers are still willing to diversify even if they obtain profits only over the medium to long run. At the same time, the survey found that "future market potential"' is the most important product development consideration in both U.S. and Japanese companies. However, U.S. corporate managers consider the size of the profit margin more important than the Japanese who rank immediate turnover ahead of profit margins. Furthermore, Japanese executives also place much emphasis on R&D spending—in particular, on basic research. The drive to diversify into new fields is enhanced through the updating and improvement of R&D capabilities.

The survey showed that Japanese managers continue to consider "company growth" and "company stability" to be very important, just like their stockholders who want to maintain long-term dividend performance. In contrast, as illustrated by figure 9–2, the priority of American

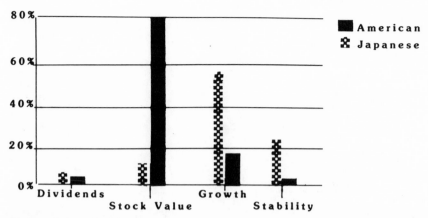

Figure 9-2.   American and Japanese Shareholder Expectations. *Source*:
"U.S.-Japan Corporate Survey," *Tokyo Business Today* (November 1988), p. 43.

shareholders is "increase in stock value," although managers believe that corporate growth and stability are also important.

For the most part, this difference in expectations can be explained by cross-shareholdings as Japanese financial institutions, parent companies, subsidiaries, and other affiliates are major shareholders in companies, whereas the major shareholders of American companies are "rate-of-return-countries" conscious institutional investors. Figure 9-3 and 9-4 provide comparisons of the distribution of stock ownership in the United States and Japan.

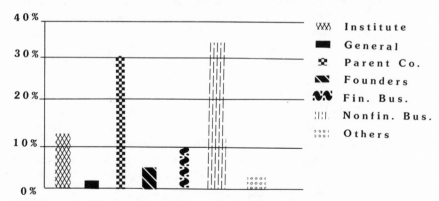

Figure 9-3.   Percentage Distribution of Stock Ownerships in Japanese Companies by Type of Investor. *Source*: Data from "U.S.-Japan Corporate Survey," *Tokyo Business Today* (November 1988), p. 43.

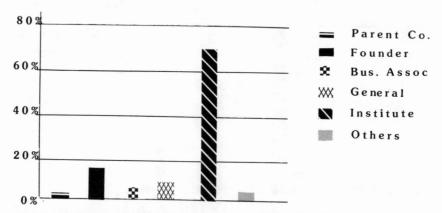

Figure 9-4. Percentage Distribution of Stock Ownerships in American Companies by Type of Investor. *Source*: Data from "U.S.-Japan Corporate Survey," *Tokyo Business Today* (November 1988), p. 43.

Mergers and Acquisitions

As expected, *endaka* or the "high yen" has had an enormous impact on the Japanese corporations. They were forced to recapture declining international competitiveness through, among others, reduced profits and efficiency improvements, such as the shifting of production to low labor-wage countries. As the yen appreciated, acquisitions became much less expensive, and so the *kaisha* began setting up subsidiaries abroad that led to the Japanese overseas mergers and acquisitions (M&A) boom. The growing danger of protectionism in America and the European Community's post-1992 market integration plan were additional reasons that caused the movement abroad during 1987–1989. Japanese managers quickly found out that M&As are more efficient and effective than the traditional start-up operations they preferred in the past.

According to a 1988 report by Japan's Fair Trade Commission (FTC), the number of domestic and international corporate mergers and acquisitions soared to a record 2,527 in 1988 with domestic mergers accounting for 1,215 and domestic acquisitions (buyouts) for 1,084 transactions. Foreign acquisitions (buyouts) accounted for 315 transactions in 1988 as opposed to 228 transactions in 1987 and 44 in 1984. Figure 9–5 illustrates the growing trend from 1984 through 1988.

The unprecedented Japanese drive to acquire overseas businesses is not entirely due to the yen appreciation. A 1988 survey conducted by Sumitomo Bank also ascribes overseas acquisitions to lower Japanese interest rates and easy access to funds. The real cost of capital in Japan is about one-third that

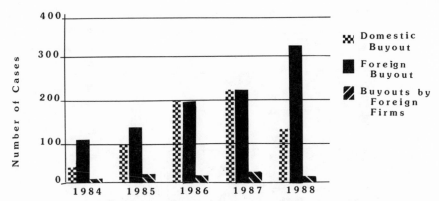

Figure 9-5. Japanese M&A Activities: 1984–1988. *Source: The Japan Economics Journal* (Tokyo: July 30, 1988), p. 1.

of the real cost in the United States. Furthermore, Japanese companies can take quick advantage of M&A opportunities because they are very liquid and can easily raise funds through the banks which are eager to lend.

Japanese managers believe that overseas investments through M&As coupled with similar domestic expansion strategies strengthen overall competitive positions. In undertaking overseas acquisitions, particularly in America, they also expect yen-term payments to drop significantly as the currency continues to appreciate. However, in developing and applying domestic and foreign corporate expansion strategies, corporate managers continue to be cautious and do not take undue risks.[8]

The recent increase in M&A activities is significant, as traditionally Japanese firms have long avoided mergers and acquisitions for they have considered corporate buyouts as an unacceptable business strategy. The word *nottori*, the Japanese term for corporate acquisitions, also means "hijacking." Although *nottori* is still used, it carries with it fewer negative connotations than it has in the past. As the merger and acquisition spree, particularly abroad, gathers more steam, it is gradually chipping away at the traditional anti-takeover corporate culture of the Japanese business community.

The increased interest in mergers and acquisitions is illustrated by a 1988 survey of 917 leading corporations.[9] The survey revealed that nearly two-thirds of the corporate managers believe that mergers and acquisitions are strategically necessary for both diversification and the acquisition of new technologies. At the same time, these managers are no longer as interested in assets such as land, inventories, or goodwill as they were in the past. Figure 9-6 shows the M&A objectives of Japanese corporate managers.

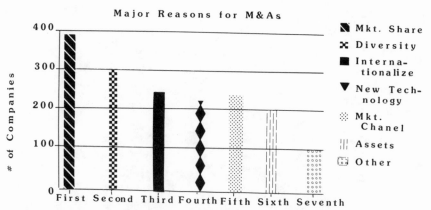

Figure 9-6.   M&A Objectives of Japanese Corporate Managers. *Source: The Japan Economic Journal* (Tokyo: October 15, 1988), p. 4.

Of the 917 firms surveyed, the managers of 171 companies (19 percent) have reported that they have already engaged in M&As or that they expect to increase their participation in both domestic and overseas mergers and acquisitions. More specifically, 596 companies (65 percent) replied that they were "interested in" M&A, while 74 firms (9 percent) said that they were "extremely interested." The managers of 601 companies (66 percent) stated that M&As had already, or would soon become, a "business necessity," while 201 (22 percent) thought it "necessary" and 362 (39 percent) thought it would be "necessary in the future." Figure 9–7 shows the M&A interest of the managers of the firms surveyed.

The recent surge in Japanese acquisitions of foreign companies is even more impressive if the value of these transactions is considered. They include such 1987–1988 mega-deals as Dainippon Ink & Chemicals' (DIC) U.S. $535 million purchase of Reichhold Chemicals Inc.; Aoki Corporation's $1.3 billion acquisition of Westin Hotels & Resorts; Sony's $2 billion buyout of CBS Records; and Bridgestone's $2.6 billion takeover of Firestone Tire and Rubber Co. Other acquisitions range from "The Talbots," a chain specializing in classic New England women's apparel, to French "Societe Leroy," which distributes Romanee-Conti, the world's most expensive red Burgundy wine. The costs for these foreign acquisitions in 1988 totaled Y1,938 billion ($15.5 billion at U.S. $1.00:Y125), twice as much as in 1987. Of all foreign corporate acquisitions made by Japanese companies in 1988, 67.8 percent were American companies, 8.5 percent Australian, 4 percent French, while British and Hong Kong businesses represented a 3.4 percent and a 2.8 percent share, respectively.

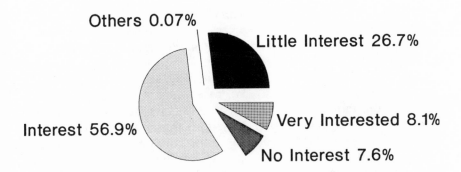

Figure 9-7.   Corporate Manager's Interest in M&As. *Source: The Japan Economic Journal* (Tokyo: October 15, 1988), p. 4.

Japanese managers are realizing that the efficient and effective use of M&As calls for new types of organizational structures. Thus, they are redesigning particularly the structures large firms to take better advantage of the M&A opportunities as they arise. The managers of 163 of the 917 firms surveyed (18 percent), for example, indicated that they are in the process of changing structures. While 111 of them are still at the elementary stage of adding M&A-related functions, 21 reported that they had already designed special M&A divisions. An example of such a company is Sumitomo Metal Mining Co., which created a Corporate Information Development Committee made up of 12 top executives to focus on M&As. Even companies that do not have special divisions for M&As claim that they can instantly take necessary measures if an opportunity arises; still others emphasize that they are prepared to form special project teams if there is a need to do so. It is noteworthy that the managers of more than 90 percent of the respondent firms chose a strong relationship with dependable shareholders as the best self-defense against possible takeover attempts.

M&A activities also call for changes in the traditional Japanese corporate decision-making process. The slow consensus-building approach is eroding and giving way to the top-down quick decision-making process, particularly in large corporations. It is not accidental that the most successful practitioners of M&As are the so-called "founder-dominated" firms, such as Minebea Co., Ryobi Ltd., Secom Co., Aoki Corp., and Misawa Homes Co. In these companies a small number of top executives can act promptly and without hesitation whenever an opportunity arises.

While Japanese corporate managers are following American and European executives in resorting to mergers and acquisitions to diversify and to be more competitive, there is still an important motivational difference. Non-Japanese executives often use mergers and acquisitions as part of a broader strategy to acquire still other companies. They buy firms or sell off parts of their own assets merely to obtain the cash to pay for future acquisitions and, as one M&A leads to another, the major goal is to reap short-term profits. In contrast, Japanese managers want to integrate acquired firms into their corporate systems because they want to provide them with growth opportunities. They do not sell parts of the acquired companies to generate funds to buy other firms, because M&As are considered part of a broader corporate strategy to strengthen international competitiveness. The case of Dainippon illustrates the point. Dainippon bought six foreign companies mainly to reinforce its business base overseas and has not resold any of the acquired firms for immediate profit.

Japanese managers, however, are beginning to find out that M&As may cause problems. Heavy write-off burdens and difficulties in managing newly acquired firms create unexpected difficulties. For instance, in the buyout of Firestone, Bridgestone paid over 3.5 times the amount of money it had initially planned to outbid a counteroffer by Italy's Pirelli. Furthermore, after Bridgestone won the bid, General Motors, a big client of Firestone, made an unexpected announcement that it would stop purchasing automobile tires from Firestone in two years. Such experiences and the poor performance of some of the acquired companies as, for instance, Heller International Corp., purchased by Fuji Bank, may eventually weaken the traditional view that acquired firms should not be sold off.[10]

A continuing Japanese M&A practice is the disclosure of post-purchase plans. Host corporate managers map out post-purchase plans when they engage in M&A activities to reduce misunderstandings. The executives of firms such as Toyo Sash Co., which has purchased 13 firms since 1984, claim that their success in the domestic M&A market is primarily due to the disclosure of post-purchase plans to the targeted firms, thus making the acquisition more friendly and acceptable. The Japanese M&A philosophy is that they key to a successful merger or acquisition is the understanding of the targeted firm's corporate culture and tradition. Of course, Japanese managers are well aware that such a philosophy is not applicable in the United States or other industrialized nations.

While Japanese acquisitions abroad are going to increase in the future, it is unlikely that acquisitions of Japanese businesses by foreign corporations will also grow. The reluctance of Japanese corporate managers and investors to sell to non-Japanese investors even parts of their organizations is demonstrated by the only 10 percent foreign participation in the domestic mergers and acquisitions market during 1988. Domestic M&A activities are not increasing at the same rapid pace as abroad, because not only are

Japanese managers reluctant to sell parts of their companies but, more important, because the price of Japanese firms is much higher than that of equivalent American or European concerns. The average price/earnings ratio of Japanese stocks listed on the TSE, for example, in 1989 stood at approximately 60, almost double that of the New York stock market. Furthermore, the traditional cross-shareholdings in Japanese companies provide a strong defense against unfriendly takeovers.[11] A rare exception in Japan's relatively peaceful domestic M&As market was the April 1989 acquisition of the largest single shareholding in Koito Manufacturing Co., an automotive parts maker closely aligned with Toyota Motor Co., by Boone Pickens, a well-known Texas corporate raider. This was one of the first major hostile investment attempts by a non-Japanese investor. The resistance to unfriendly takeovers and investments was apparent as Pickens did not manage to make a quick profit. In the days following the announcement, Koito's stock prices fell while the Nikkei index soared.[12] Additionally, Koito has repeatedly refused Pickens request to appoint 3 members to the company's board. Toyota and other Koito shareholders have pooled their votes to obtain a majority position to keep Pickens from intervening in management decisions. This incident clearly demonstrates traditional Japanese business practices as typically the majority shareholders of publicly owned corporations tend to be their principal customers. As a result, when a third party without close ties to the corporation purchases a large number of shares, it is viewed as an unwanted intruder. As expected this incident has brought about U.S. criticism of Japanese business practises as Japanese companies are free to pursue hostile takeover bids in the U.S. However, not all foreign acquisitions in Japan are unwelcomed or hostile. An example of this is the buyout of Sansui Electric Co. by Britain's Polly Peck International PLC in the fall of 1989. Sansui had contracted more than 20 firms in Japan, the U.S., Europe and South Korea in a quest for a buyer due to huge debts. Sansui could not keep up in the technology race (digital audio developments), which coupled with the yen appreciation resulted in a significant loss in market share.

Involvement of Financial Institutions

The M&A spree has given rise to new investment opportunities to large banks and securities companies. The involvement of financial institutions in M&As went through several successive stages. In the first stage which began in 1986, due to the rising yen, Japanese corporate managers became interested in acquiring American companies. In the second stage, major Japanese banks and securities houses, using their strong business ties with the client firms, began acting as advisors to Japanese corporate buyers. In stage three, the financial institutions started to enter into joint-ventures with foreign partners to acquire M&A know-how as well as information about companies for sale. The banks and securities houses nowadays are also becoming directly involved in overseas mergers and acquisition deals. According to Wall Street estimates, Japanese banks, for example, already finance between 30 percent to 40 percent of all U.S. leveraged buyouts.

To increase their participation in the future, banks such as the Industrial Bank of Japan, which advised Aoki in the Westin hotel chain buyout, are forming international M&A teams. Fuji Bank has joined James D. Wolfensohn to form Fuji Wolfensohn International and Yasuda Trust and Banking joined with M&A Strategy. Such M&A joint-ventures are modifying the roles of Japanese banks. In addition to providing financing, they now are also offering financial advisory services because corporate clients expect banks to analyze investment risks and to provide financial advise in all stages of the project. Thus, firms like Nomura Securities Co., the largest Japanese securities house, has invested $100 million in Wasserstein-Perella & Co., one of the most aggressive M&As firms on Wall Street; Nikko Securities Co. has joined with the Blackstone Group; Yamaichi Securities Co. has formed a joint-ventue with Lodestar Management Co., and Daiwa Securities has joined Ifil SpA. Table 9–1 shows a list of Japanese financial institutions in M&A partnerships with U.S. and European firms as of April 1989.

Despite the aggressive moves by the "Big Four," many banks are in a better position than securities houses to take advantage of the overseas M&A opportunities. Banks are more often chosen as intermediaries due to the clients' loyalty and because they have the necessary cash to lend. Moreover, most securities firms are inexperienced in M&A activities.[13] However, nowadays many Japanese firms planning foreign acquisition are turning to the M&A advisory teams of blue-chip financial firms, either Japanese or foreign. This is loosening the "cozy, long-held" relationships with lead or "main" banks. Japanese banks recognize that advising also involves other business, such as bankrolling funds for takeovers. An example is the Sony Corporation's buyout of Columbia Pictures Entertainment Inc. in September 1989. Sony asked the Blackstone Group, a New York-based M&A house to handle the acquisition and not Mitsui Bank, Sony's lead bank. Although Mitsui had offered to serve as the advisor for the deal and Sony refused, Sony asked Mitsui to extend loans for the takeover.

Leveraged Buyouts

The $25 billion buyout of RJR Nabisco Inc., by Kohlberg Kravis Roberts &

TABLE 9-1.   Japanese-American M&A partnerships

Japanese firm	Foreign partner	M&A Joint-venture
Securities Firms:		
Nomura Securities	Wasserstein Perella & Co. (U.S.)	Nomura Perella (Oct 1988)
Daiwa Securities	Ifil SpA (Italy)	Daiwa Europe (M&A) * (March 1989)
Nikko Securities	Blackstone Group (U.S.)	No venture planned (July 1988)
Yamaichi Securities	Lodestar Management (U.S.)	Lodestar Partners (Oct 1988)
Long-Term Credit Bank:		
Industrial Bank of Japan	IBJ Schroder Bank & Trust (U.S.)	** (Dec 1985)
Long-Term Credit Bank	Peers & Co. (U.S.)	*** (May 1985)
City Banks:		
Fuji Bank	James D. Wolfensohn (U.S.)	Fuji Wolfensohn Intl. (Spring 1989)
Turst Banks:		
Yasuda trust & Banking	M&A Strategy (U.S.)	Joint-venture set up in June 1989

Note: * —Wholly owned by Daiwa Europe, the London-based subsidiary of Daiwa
            Securities.
        ** —Acquired subsidiary.
       *** —LTCB has 1 percent stake in Peers.
Source: The *Japan Economic Journal* (Tokyo, March 25, 1989), p. 6.

Co. (KKR) in 1988, has placed a spotlight on the increased Japanese involvement in financing American leveraged buyouts (LBOs). This single largest corporate takeover in history left the 17 Japanese banks involved with a financial exposure of $6.1 billion which is the largest exposure of foreign banks participating in the $14 billion bank financial arrangement. This compares with the share of American banks of $5 billion and that of European banks of $1.4 billion. The Japanese loans range from $10 million to $600 million, and the lender group is comprised of 11 city, three long-term credit, and three trust banks. According to Wall Street sources, since April 1986, Japanese banks participated in the financing of the majority of major U.S. buyouts; their 1988 LBO loans were approximately double those of 1987.

The MOF, MITI, and BOJ keep a close watch on all M&As and LBO financing arrangements involving Japanese corporations and banks at home and abroad. They are particularly concerned about the billions of yen loaned by the Japanese banks to finance high-risk, high-return leveraged buyouts in the United States as exemplified by the RJR-KKR deal. However, in doing so, they face a dilemma because apart from offering guidance, they cannot control lending activities. Moreover, they want to avoid straining U.S.–Japanese relations. Nonetheless, in December 1988 the MOF and BOJ asked banks to keep them informed about their buyout involvements. In addition, they began to investigate commerical bank LBO loan services and are reviewing the banks' outstanding balances of such loans as well as their risk management practices. They encourage banks to avoid making too many loans to any specific industry and to check the business performances of borrowers as well as of the firms purchased by them.

The increased scrutiny by the MOF and BOJ has made many Japanese banks review their LBO financing strategies. They believe that the MOF, MITI and BOJ concern stems from the fact that Japanese banks have limited experience in financing LBOs. Currently, for example, about 40 regional and *sogo* (mutual) banks are participating in LBOs through secondary purchases of loans from major American and Japanese banks. The concern about the inexperience of many banks is reflected by the unwillingness of the major Japanese banks involved in the RJR-KKR deal to sell their loans to the smaller banks until KKR has sold at least part of the acquisition. Furthermore, to avoid a negative impact on the secondary market, the banks are planning to pool the loans before selling them.[14]

In conclusion, it can be argued that the overseas M&A activities of Japanese corporations are going to increase in the future as they have become an integral part of corporate strategies to maintain and improve international competitiveness. The managers of the large *kaisha* understand that if they want to continue as or become global competitors, they must establish manufacturing, marketing and research, and development bases throughout the world. As the economy becomes more internationalized, M&A activities are also going to grow domestically. The methods used, however, are going to reflect the Japanese ways of doing business for many years to come.

Additional Considerations

Concurrent with the overall corporate strategy modifications, other corporate practices are also beginning to undergo changes. One of the most interesting of these is the gradual decline of lifetime employment, once a hallmark of the Japanese corporate world. As discussed previously, motivated by several factors, Japanese corporations have rapidly expanded abroad in recent years. This is beginning to raise questions about the long-term costs of continually retraining and/or transferring employees whose jobs have been eliminated. Changing social values are also affecting lifetime employment, as younger workers are more ready nowadays to switch jobs to obtain higher pay or more satisfying working conditions. Many are also motivated by individualism as they seek to satisfy their personal needs and reject traditional employment practices. A number of studies, in fact, have found that workers in Japan consider their employment less satisfying than similar workers in the United States.[15]

Associated with the decline in lifetime employment is the growth of part-time or contract employment. Rather than hiring people as permanent employees, companies are now seeking individuals for temporary positions. This approach benefits corporations by providing them with more flexibility to reassign, retain, or dismiss workers depending on economic conditions, and reduces expenses for health care benefits, vacations, or pensions. These cost savings can be crucial for coping with intense domestic competition and the strong yen. But temporary employment also appeals to individuals who want to avoid the restrictions of a permanent job and to enjoy more freedom and leisure time. The extent of temporary employment is reflected by estimates that there are 400 job offers for every 100 people looking for part-time employment. The Ministry of Labor estimates that 12 percent of Japan's labor force, or 5.3 million people, work on a temporary basis.[16]

Top management is also no longer reluctant to look to other companies for mid-level managers. Traditionally, Japanese firms hired college graduates who were trained in the company's values and advanced up the corporate hierarchy over time. Recently, however, many firms have diversified into new types of businesses. To obtain the needed management expertise, they are approaching "head hunters" to identify and hire managers from other companies. At the shop level, many companies have turned to foreign workers to fill unskilled positions. The foreigners work for lower wages, though their presence may be distressing to many Japanese.

Union leadership is beginning to be concerned about the quality of life of its membership. *Rengo* (the Japanese Private Sector Trade Union Confederation), as part of the 1989 *shunto*, included demands for reduced working hours. However, it is uncertain how far such moves may go as some unions have opposed shorter work hours as a disguised pay cut, and even some younger workers, those thought to want more free time, seem to be continuing the work habits of their parents. In many cases, management also rejects the reduction of working hours because of concerns about productivity implications.

Women are entering the workforce in growing numbers. They now compose nearly 50 percent of all employees, and recently the employment of women grew faster than that of males. This may represent a change in the tradition that considered the man as the bread-winner and the woman as the homemaker.

There are a number of factors underlying the rise in female employment. In 1986 the government passed the Equal Employment Opportunity Law which mandated the equal treatment of women. More importantly, the increased educational levels motivate many women to have careers and, thus, to seek more satisfying employment and to delay getting married and having children. Economic pressures on the family are another reason, leading women to seek jobs to supplement their husbands' income. This may be a major consideration in the 1990s as nearly 60 percent of all female workers are married compared to 39 percent in 1965, and about one-third of the women employed in part-time positions work in the lower-paid service sector.[17]

The career and work commitment of women is still somewhat problematic as survey results reveal contradictory attitudes. In 1987 the Women's Affairs Office of the Prime Minister's Office released a report indicating that most Japanese women continue to put marriage and children ahead of a career. A 1987 Ministry of Labor survey of personnel department managers found that 70 percent of respondents believed that women's own lack of ambition was the greatest handicap in advancing up the corporate ladder. To overcome the obstacles to advancement in male-dominated corporations, young women are studying for an MBA (Masters of Business Administration) in the United States. On return, they often join foreign firms to avoid the discrimination they still face in Japanese companies.

Despite the difficulties that women face in Japanese companies, a number of firms recognize that they can be valuable employees with special needs. They have dropped the gender-biased promotional policies and devised several alternative career tracks that can accommodate women's special circumstances. One is the *sogo-shoku* track which is for women who aspire to management positions; this track requires that they accept transfers, including overseas assignments. The second path is *ippan-shoku* which entails routine clerical work and involves no transfers or promotions. This second path is attuned to women who are more interested in eventually having a family rather than a long-term career. Currently most women opt for an *ippan-shoku* position rather than the *sogo-shoku*. Recently, several companies have offered a variation of the *sogo-shoku* which provides advancement opportunities but does not require transfers.

The labor union movement is undergoing a reorganization. Traditionally, Japanese unions functioned as "enterprise unions," that is, they were affiliated with individual companies, and their memberships included both blue-collar and white-collar employees. As could be expected, the close relations between the companies and their unions generally led to cooperative labor relations. Unions usually accepted management's requests for lower wages or work condition changes to maintain the competitiveness of the firms. They often worked in partnership with management, looking after the welfare of the companies even ahead of the needs of the union members. This collaborative relationship was facilitated by the workers' commitment and readiness to sacrifice for the benefit of the companies. Outside observers considered such union-management partnerships as a major strength of Japanese business, enabling smooth adjustments in corporate strategies. Others, however, have noted that enterprise unions are similar to the American plant-level union locals which function independently of the national union.

While unions are organized at the company level, they are also members of national federations. In the late 1980s these federations went through major organizational changes. Three of them, *Domei, Churitsu Roren*, and *Shinsanbetsu*, disbanded in 1988 to form *Rengo*, the Japanese Private Sector Trade Union Confederation, as a more potent force to purse labor objectives. A fourth, *Sohyo*, with 4.2 million members, joined "Rengo" in late 1989.

The formation of *Rengo* was greeted with mixed reactions. Some believed that is would give labor a more powerful position to advocate change favorable to worker and union interests. Others, however, saw *Rengo* as a philosophically conservative organization that would not advocate significant political, social, or employment changes. In fact, *Rengo's* initial programs were aimed to increase union membership, and to induce more unified action among opposition political parties traditionally aligned with labor, the Japan Socialist Party, and the Democratic Socialist Party. But Rengo's leaders also spoke of more collaboration with the ruling LDP in order to advance labor's objectives such as improved living standards.

Japan's unions currently face several challenges that may affect their future survival. As in other industrialized countries, the unions experienced a decline in membership from 35 percent in 1970 to about 25 percent in 1988. The decline was due to a number of factors, including a shift from manufacturing to service industries and the economic restructuring that often caused firms to locate production in countries with lower labor costs. The loss of workers in both instances hurt union membership and also created new requirements for worker retraining and reassignment. Unions today must also deal with the aging of the workforce and the need to represent retirees. Additional developments are the increasing use of foreign workers to fill unskilled jobs and the rise in female employment. Furthermore, the increased entry of foreign firms in Japan creates new employment opportunities, but also introduces methods that disrupt traditional business and labor practices. The privatization of several government entities such as the former Japanese National Railroad also led to adjustment problems that sometimes became violent.

These developments may give unions new opportunities to increase their membership and national roles, but they are also departures from past conditions that will test unions' ability to adapt to new circumstances. Initial union responses to these changes have taken several forms. They have continued the past practice of close collaboration with management to work out industrial restructuring problems in a satisfactory manner. Leadership in wage negotiations — the annual *shunto* wage drive — has been passed from declining sectors such as steel and shipbuilding to high-growth industries. Wage settlements also have become more closely linked to the conditions in each industry as opposed to the overall national economy, and job security has become a more prominent objective in negotiations than wages.

Concluding Observation

Thus, just as at the macrolevel, the Japanese economy is undergoing a series of changes on the micro or corporate level as well. The interaction of these two sets of changes, which are partially externally imposed, self-induced, and a function of myriad economic and social interdependencies, is internationalizing the economy at a very rapid pace. However, it would be a mistake to assume that this internationalization process is the same as "Westernization," a term frequently used outside Japan to describe the current developments. Throughout their long history the Japanese have always readily adopted whatever the outside world could offer in the form of useful ideas, products, and technologies. But in the end, they have also always adapted such ideas, products, and technologies to their own special needs. While an internationalized Japan can no longer claim to be unique and, thus, expect special treatment from the rest of the world, it is going to carry on many of its traditions that non-Japanese may find difficult to understand and to accept. This, however, is not unique to Japan, other nations also continue to display characteristics which differentiate them from the rest of the world.

As far as the U.S.–Japan bilateral relationship is concerned, both nations need to lower their voices and refrain from fingerpointing. The widely reported 1989 survey finding according to which Americans view Japan's economic power as a greater threat than the military might of the Soviet Union is the result of the uncritical reporting in the American mass-media, the inflammatory speeches of politicians made for domestic consumption and the sensationalism of some authors. They have circulated ideas and arguments which serve only to inflame the bilateral relationship between the two highly interdependent nations. Conversely, the publication of a number of books in Japan excessively and unreasonably critical of America as well as the sensationalist mass media reporting on U.S.–Japan relations have hardened Japanese views of America. A December 1989 poll commissioned by *Business Week* found the Japanese not only more assertive than in the past (a finding to be expected) but also more resentful toward America, an outcome potentially harmful to both nations if not checked. Neither Americans nor the Japanese should allow the various economic disagreements to degenerate into resentment, distrust and perhaps even hostility. America and Japan are the world's two most important interdependent economies. They need each other and the rest of the world needs them. Competition and disagreements are part of the interdependence, but this competition and the disagreements must be managed in a mutually beneficial fashion. Anything less will produce not a winner and a loser but only losers involving not only the two countries but the rest of the world as well.

Notes

1. FY 1988 growth was estimated to be about 4.9 pecent in April 1989.
2. Balassa and Noland, *Japan in the World Economy*; *op. cit.*, p. 179.
3. *Business Week* (July 18, 1988), pp. 137–138.
4. For an insightful discussion of the issues surrounding Japan's global financial (co⁻) leadership see R. Taggart Murphy, "Power Without Purpose: The Crisis of Japan's Global Financial Dominance," *Harvard Business Review* (March-April 1989), pp. 71–82.
5. For a discussion of the evolution and potential future of the region, see *Economic Changes in the Asian Pacific Rim: Policy Prospectus* (Washington, D.C.: Congressional Research Service, August 1986).
6. *Tokyo Business Today* (August 1987), p. 6.
7. *Management Strategy — A Japan–U.S.A. Comparative Study*, Japan Committee for Economic Development, Japan Productivity Center, October 1986.
8. *JEI Economic Report*, Japan Economic Institute Washington, D.C., February 1989), p. 3; *Wall Street Journal* (March 14, 1988), p. 11; *The Journal of Commerce* (February 10, 1989), p. 7A; *Journal of Commerce* (November 1988), pp. 4, 5.
9. *The Japan Economic Journal* (October 15, 1988), p. 4.
10. *Journal of Commerce* (November 1988), pp. 4, 5. *Japan Economic Journal* (October 15, 1988), p. 4.; (October 29, 1988), p. 22; *Tokyo Business Today* (July 1987), p. 11.
11. *The Journal of Commerce* (February 10, 1989), p. 7A.
12. *Wall Street Journal* (April 27, 1989), p. A13.
13. *The Japan Economic Journal* (August 13, 1988), p. 21.
14. *The Japan Economic Journal* (February 11, 1989), p. 2.
15. "More Americans than Japanese Find Satisfaction On The Job," *The Japan Economic Journal* (February 11, 1989), p. 15; and "Study Finds Working Conditions in US Superior to Those in Japan," *The Journal of Commerce* (September 1, 1988).

16. Masayoshi Kanabayashi, "Japanese Workers Aren't All Workaholics," *The Wall Street Journal* (May 8, 1989) p. A12.

17. *Asahi Evening News*, March 28, 1989; and *The Japan Economic Journal* (March 5, 1988), pp. 1+.

Bibliography

Articles

"Advertising in Japan: Land of the Hardening Sell." *The Economist*, 10 September 1988, pp. 85–86.

"Advertising Outlays in Japan Rose 12% to $34.88 Billion in '88." *The Asian Wall Street Journal Weekly*, 6 March 1988, p. 6.

"After the Superconductivity Boom." *Tokyo Business Today* (April 1988): 48–49.

"Agreement Reached on Defence Patent Protection." *Japan Economic Institute Report*, No. 16B, 21 April, 1988, p. 8.

Ainlay, Thomas, Jr. "Direct Marketing Comes of Age." *The Journal of the ACCJ* (June 1988): 51–52.

Ainlay, Thomas, Jr. "Can Japan Go Direct?" *Tokyo Business Today* (October 1986): 26–31.

"Bank Backing of LBOs in U.S. Vexes Finance Ministry." *The Japan Economic Journal*, 11 February 1989, p. 2.

"Bank Expedites Reform for Freer Money Market." *The Japan Economic Journal*, 5 November, 1988, p. 3.

"Basic Research Adds to Japan–U.S. Friction." *The Japan Economic Journal*, 28 November 1987, p. 31.

Benson, Wes. "Japan's Distribution Systems a Barrier?" *The Japan Economic Journal*, 2 and 9 January 1988, p. 20.

Bergsten, C. Fred. "What to Do About the U.S.–Japan Economic Conflict." *Foreign Affairs* (Summer 1982): 1059–1075.

"Big-Lot Buyers Take Hostages on TSE." *The Japan Economic Journal*, 23 July 1988, p. 3.

"Bilateral Science and Technology Talks Continue: Outlook Unclear." *Japan Economic Institute Report*, No. 11B, 18 March 1988, p. 6.

"Blase Public Shrugs off Recruit Scandal." *The Japan Economic Journal*, 17 December 1988, p. 11.

"Bond Underwriting Still Unfair, U.S. Says." *The Japan Economic Journal*, 30 April 1988, p. 3.

Brooks, William L., and Orr, Robert M., Jr. "Japan's Foreign Economic Assistance." *Asian Survey* (March 1985): 322–340.

"Bringing Down Prices," editorial. *The Japan Economic Journal*, 17 September 1988, p. 34.

"Bureaucrats' Rebellion Against Nakasone." *The Oriental Economist* (July 1985): 12

"Business Fads: What's In and Out." *Business Week*, 20 January 1986, pp. 52–61.

"Business Move to Reorganize in Increased Stress on Profits." *Wall Street Journal*, 14 March 1988, 11.

"Can Japan Go Direct?" *Tokyo Business Today* (October 1986): 28.

"Cashing in on Singles." *Tokyo Business Today* (April 1989): 11.

"Chief Quits At Nippon Telegraph," *New York Times*, 15 December 1988, p. d1.

Chira, Susan. "Rich Man, Poor Man in Japan: Not an Economic Party for All." *The New York Times*, 26 December 1988, pp. 1+.

Choy, Jon. "Japan's Labor Unions Work to Meet New Challenges." *Japan Economic Institute Report*, No. 2A, 15 January 1988.

Choy, Jon. "Japan's Sogo Shosha: Back to the Future?" *Japan Economic Institute Report*, No. 34 A, 2 Sepember 1988.

Choy, Jon. "The Maekawa Reports: Reality or Rhetoric?" *Japan Economic Institute Report*, No. 39A, 14 October 1988.

"City Banks Move Loans into Investor Arena." *The Japan Economic Journal*, 10 December 1988, p. 2.

Clark, Gregory. "Share and Land Prices, and the Japanese Psychology." *The Japan Economic Journal*, 24 December 1988, p. 10.

Clarke, Rosy. "Women Starting to Come of Age in Society and the Workplace." *The Wall Street Journal*, 19 September 1988, p. 25.

Clarke, Rosy. "How 'Internationalization' Affects Japan's Consumers." *The Wall Street Journal*, 20 March 1989, p. B15.

Cline, John M. "Inter-MNC Arrangements: Shaping the Options for U.S. Trade Policy." *The Washington Quarterly* (Fall 1985): 57–71.

"COCOM Rules Confusing Firme." *The Japan Economic Journal*, 11 June 1988, p. 17.

"Corporate Acquisitions Hit a Record Last Year." *The Asian Wall Street Journal, Weekly*, 6 March 1989, p. 6.

"Credit Industry: Fight for Survival," *Tokyo Business Today* (December 1986): 56.

"A Critique of Pure Irrationality about Japan." *The Economist*, 12 December 1987, pp. 39–43.

"The Crumbling Walls of Lifetime Employment." *Tokyo Busines Today* (September 1988): 28–29.

Culbertson, John. "Free Trade in Improverishing the West." *The New York Times*, 28 July 1985, p. F3.

Culbertson, John. "Control Imports Through Bilateral Pacts." *The New York Times*, 11 August 1985, p. F3.

Cullison, A.E. "Study Finds Working Conditions in US Superior to Those in Japan." *The Journal of Commerce*, 1 September 1988.

Darlin, Damon. "Myth and Marketing in Japan." *The Wall Street Journal*, 6 April 1989, p. B1.

Darlin, Damon, and Graven, Kathryn. "In Japan, a Strong Yen Keeps Inflation Down and the Economy Up." *The Wall Street Journal*, 19 August 1988, pp. 1 + .

"Doing Business in Japan Gets No Easier." *Tokyo Business Today* (April 1989): 40–41.

"Engineer Brain Drain Saps Japan firms." *The Japan Economic Journal*, 23 July 1988, p. A1.

Fallows, James. "In Japan, Land is at the Heart of Life's Great Decisions." *Business Month* (July-August 1988): 22–26.

"Feeling Poor in Japan." *The Economist*, 11 June 1988, pp. 33–35.

Federal Reserve Board of New York. "Japan's Intangible Barriers to Trade in Manufactures." *Quarterly Review* (Winter 1985–86): 11–18.

Fields, George. "The Impact of Changing Cultural Values on the Japanese Market." *The Journal of the ACCJ* (February 1986): 48–60.

Fields, George. "The Year of the 'Shinjinrui' and 'Kokusaika.'" In *Dentsu JAPAN Marketing/Advertising Yearbook, 1988*. Tokyo: Dentsu Incorporated, 1987, pp. 64–68.

Fields, George. "Kakusa-A New Buzzword Triggers on Narrowing the Gap." *Tokyo Business Today* (January 1989): 25.

"Finance Ministry Brokers Futures Market." *Tokyo Business Today* (March 1988): 56–57.

"Financial Futures Trading Gets Green Light from Diet." *The Japan Economic Journal*, 4 June 1988, p. 3.

"For Japanese Women It's Still Family 1st, Government Study Shows." *The Japan Economic Journal*, 20 June 1987, p. 28.

"Foreign Brokers Flex Muscles Despite Market Shakeout." *Wall Street Journal*, 14 March, 1988, p. 12.

"Foreign Companies Raiding Japanese Research Centers." *The Japan Economic Journal*, 19 December 1987, p. 8.

"Foreign Investors Buying More Japanese Stocks." *The Japan Economic Journal*, 25 February 1988, p. 1.

"Free-Market Banking." *The Japan Economic Journal*, 26 November 1988, p. 10.

"From Blue Collar to Banker." *Tokyo Business Today* (August 1987): 6.

"The General Trading Companies of Japan." *Tokyo Business Today* (February 1989): 50–55.

"Gov't Allows Sogo Banks To Change." *Mainichi Daily News*, 14 February 1988.

"Gov't Proposes Plan to Deter Stock Speculators." *Asahi Evening News*, 28 November 1988.

Hiatt, Fred, and Shapiro, Margaret. "Is Enormous Wealth Corrupting Japan?" *The Washington Post*, 19 February 1989, pp. A1 + .

"A High-Yen Boom." *The Economist*, 16 January 1988, pp. 58–59.

"High Yen Hurts Competitiveness in High Technology." *Japan Economic Institute Report*, No. 7B, 19 February 1988, p. 3.

"The Hollow Corporation." *Business Week*, 3 March 1986, pp. 57–81.

Hosomi, Takashi. "The Ugly Japanese." *Tokyo Business Today* (March 1986): 8.

"How Japan Will Spend Its Cash." *Fortune*, 21 November 1988, pp. 195–201.

"How Nice To Be a Japanese, the Very Rich Can Always Please." *The Economist*, 29 October 1988, pp. 35–36.

"Importing a Lower Standard of Living." *Tokyo Business Today* (November 1986): 22–26.

"Industry Is Heavily Committed To Applied and Pure Research." *Wall Street Journal*, 14 March 1988, p. 8.

Inoue, Yuko. "Women Workers Force Changes in Co. Ethics." *The Japan Economic Journal*, 5 March 1988, p. 1 + .

Inoue, Yuko. "New 'Revolution' in Japan Retailing." *The Japan Economic Journal*, 24 December 1988, pp. 1 + .

Inoue, Yuko. "Soaring Corporate Profit Spurs Labor To Raise Ante in Pay Talks." *The Japan economic Journal*, 11 February 1989, pp. 1 + .

Inoue, Yuko. " 'Shunto' Raises Wages, Cuts Hours." *The Japan Economic Journal*, 15 April 1989, pp. 1 + .

"Insider Trading A Japan Tradition." *The New York Times*, 10 August 1988, p. D-1/5.

"Interim Agreement Reached on Bilateral Science and Technology Pact." *Japan Economic Institute Report*, No. 7B, 19 February 1987, p. 6.

"International Use of Yen Seen Increasing Steadily." *The Japan Economic Journal*, 14 May 1988, pp. 1&7.

"Internationalizing Science Here," editorial. *Asahi Evening News*, 25 December 1987.

"Interview: Promoting Greater Use of Yen." *Tokyo Business Today* (November 1988): 64.

"Intimate Links Within Japan's Corporate Groups." *Tokyo Business Today* (January 1989): 14–19.

"Is Japan Still a Developing Country?" *The Japan Economic Journal*, 28 November 1987, p. 17.

Ishikawa, Yoji. "Japanese Youth Today: Individualistic and Discriminating Lifestyles." *The Asahi Evening News*, 31 January 1989.

Ishikawa, Yoji. "Women on the Move." *The Asahi Evening News*, 28 March 1989.

Ishizuka, Masahiko. "New Self-Assertion, But Whither." *The Japan Economic Journal*, 11 October 1986, p. 6.

Ishizuka, Masahiko. "Rich Country, Poor People." *The Japan Economic Journal*, 14 June 1987.

Ishizuka, Masahiko. "Japanese Consumers Lack Group Indentity, Power." *The Japan Economic Journal*, 15 April 1989, p. 11.

"ITC Study Show Costs of Intellectual Property Rights Violations." *Japan Economic Institute Report*, No. 10B, 11 March 1988, pp. 7–8.

Iwamaru, Yoichi. "Foreign Advertisers Vying for Japan Market." *The Japan Economic Journal*, 13 February 1988, p. 16.

"Japan Becomes a Big Venture Capitalist." *Wall Street Journal*, 6 February 1989.

"Japan Firms Catching West's M&A Fever." *The Japan Economic Journal*, 29 October 1988, p. 22.

"Japan Is Employing Venture-Capital Tactics To Promote Research by Private Consortiums." *The Asian Wall Street Journal Weekly*, 13 February 1989, p. 10.

"Japan Leads in Optics, U.S. in Life Science." *The Japan Economic Journal*, 23 January 1988, p. 17.

"Japan Under Nakasone: Image of National Pride?" *The New York Times*, 26 September 1986, p. A13.

"Japan's About-Face on Mergers, Acquisitions." *The New York Times*, 1 August 1988.

"Japan's Ailing Health Care System." *Tokyo Business Today* (February 1988): 12–16.

"Japan's Clout in the U.S." *Business Week*, 11 July 1988.

"Japan's Different Stock Market." *The New York Times*, 7 December 1987, p. D-1/6.

"Japan's M&A Market." *Asahi Evening News*, December 1988.

"Japan's Merger Boom Reflects Strong Yen, Corporate Revamping." *The Journal of Commerce*, 10 February 1989, p. 7A.

"Japan's Retail Industry in Trouble." *Tokyo Business Today* (February 1986): 50–53.

"Japanese Finance." *The Economist*, 10 December 1988, pp. 1–34.

"Japanese Firm' Interest in M&A Is Growing." *The Japan Economic Journal*, 15 October 1988, p. 4.

"Japanese Firms: Coping with the High Yen." *Japan Economic Survey* (Washington, D.C.: Japan Economic Institute, February 1989), p. 3.

"Japanese Women Using U.S. MBAs To Boost Careers." *The Japan Economic Journal*, 20 August 1988, p. A1.

Jones, Randall S. "The Japanese Distribution System." *Japan Economic Institute Report*, No. 28A, 24 July 1987.

Jones, Randall S. "The Japanese Distribution System." *Japan Economic Institute Report*, No. 34A, 2 September 1988.

"Kabusaki 50—One Year Later." *Tokyo Business Today* (May 1988): 44–45.

Kanabayashi, Masayoshi. "Japanese Workers Aren't All Workaholics." *The Wall Street Journal*, 8 May 1989, p. A12.

Kato, Susumu. "Three Scenarios for Economic Policy." *Economic Eye* (September 1986): 19–22.

Kido, Sumio. "Getting Ready for Aging of Nation." *The Japan Economic Journal, 28 November 1987, pp. 1 +.*

Kido, Sumio. "Consumer Quest for Luxury Puts Economy on Easy Street." The Japan Economic Journal, 19 March 1988, pp. 1+.

Kilburn, David. "Challenge and Change in Japan's Ad Industry." The Journal of the ACCJ, June 1988, pp. 9-16.

Koike, Kazuo. "Japanese Labor—Really That Different?" Look Japan, 10 August 1986, pp. 4-5.

Komiya, Ryutaro. "Industrial Policy's Generation Gap." Economic Eye (March 1986): 22-24.

"Ladder of Success Too Short To Reach Land Prices." The Japanese Economic Journal, 3 December 1988, p. 9.

"The Last Stage of Financial Deregulation." Tokyo Business Today (October 1988): 44-45.

"Let Diet Examine Recruit Scam." Ashai Evening News, 27 July 1988.

Little, Jane Sneddon. "Intra-Firm Trade and U.S. Protectionism: Thoughts Based on a Small Survey." New England Economic Review (January/February 1986).

"Living Standards: A Self-Admiring Portrait." The Japan Times, 18 March 1986, p. 14.

"Losing Patience Over Patents." Asahi Evening News, 1988, p. 88.

Lukow, Stephen M. "Kodak Raises Profile To Lift Japan Profits." The Japan Economic Journal, 25 February) 1989, p. 6.

Lutfy, Carol. "Changing Expectations." Tokyo Business Today (June 1988): 14-17.

"M&A Competition Heating Up in Tokyo." The Japan Economic Journal, 9 April 1988, p. 7.

"M&A Game Played for Strategy, Not Quick Fix." The Japan Economic Journal, 13 August 1988, p. 21.

"M&A Tempts Japan Securities Firms." The Japan Economic Journal, 1 October 1988, p. 1.

MacKnight, Susan. "Japan's Distribution System: The Next Major Trade Confrontation?" Japan Economic Institute Report, No. 11A, 17 March 1989.

MacMaster, Norman A. "A Question of Relevance: Must Japanese Advertising Be Different to Be Successful?" Speaking of Japan (May 1985): 6-12.

Manoochehrix, G.H. "Suppliers and the Just-in-Time Concept." Journal of Purchasing and Materials Management (Winter 1984): 18.

Masuko, Takashi. "Small Shops Are Big Barrier to Deregulation." The Japan Economic Journal, 9 July 1988, p. 2.

Matsuzawa, Takuji. "Keidanren's Viewpoint on Government Spending and Future Administrative Reform." Keindanren Review (October 1985): 3.

"Mergers Increasing In Japan." Japan Economic Institute Report, 12 August 1988, pp. 3-5.

"MITI To Ease Paperwork on Exports to Eastern Bloc." The Japan Economic Journal, 10 September 1988, p. 10.

"Mitsubishi Motors Prepares for Stock Listing." The Japan Economic Journal, 12 November 1988, p. 3.

"MOF To Modernize Secondary Bond Market." The Japan Economic Journal, 30 April 1988, p. 4.

"More Americans than Japanese Find Satisfaction on the Job." *The Japan Economic Journal*, 11 February 1989, p. 15.

"More Foreign Researchers Working in Japan." *The Japan Economic Journal*, 10 September 1988, p. 21.

Morgan, Peter J., "Japan's Consumer Finance Industry." *The Journal of the ACCJU* (February 1985): 43.

"Most Japanese Don't Feel They Are Affluent: Survey." *Asahi Evening News*, 30 January 1989.

"Move Toward Basic Research Gains Momentum." *The Japan Economic Journal*, 16 January 1988, p. 24.

Murdo, Pat. "No Pension Until Age 65, Japanese Panel Recommends." *Japan Economic Institute Report*, No. 46B, 9 December 1988, pp. 5–6.

Murphy, R. Taggart. "Power Without Purpose: The Crisis of Japan's Global Financial Dominance." *Harvard Business Review* (March-April 1989): 71–82.

"The Myth of the Japanese Middle Class." *Business Week*, 12 September 1988, pp. 49–52.

Nakano, Takanobu. "Japanese Labor Gets Organized." *Asahi Evening News*, 1 December 1988, p. 6.

Nakata, Shinya. "Development of Store Management Systems Will Change Distribution." *Sumitomo Quarterly* (Winter 1988): 12–14.

Nakata, Shinya. "Retailing: Variety of Means and the Conglo-Merchants." *Japan Update* (Summer 1988): 18–20.

Nakata, Shinya. "Number of Wholesalers, Retailers Begins to Fall." *Sumitomo Quarterly* (Tokyo, Autumn 1988): 12–14.

Nakatani, Iwao. "High Consumer Prices in Japan Demand Examination To Find Cause." *The Japan Economic Journal*, 15 October 1988, p. 22.

"Negotiators Reach Basic Agreement on Science and Technology Pact." *The Japan Economic Journal*, 16 January 1988, p. 2.

"New Controversy in the Prepaid Card Business." *Tokyo Business Today* (April 1989): 30–32.

"New Face of Japanese Credit." *Tokyo Business Today* (April 1989): 34–35.

"The New Japan Goes Shopping." *The Economist*, 13 August 1988, pp. 55–56.

"A New Price Competitive Auction System." *Tokyo Business Today* (November 1988): 11.

"Nikko, Nomura: Why We like M&A." *The New York Times*, 10 February 1988, p. 4.

"1988: Japan Faces Choices for Economy." *Asahi Evening News*, 3 January 1988, p. 4.

"No Nottori, Buyouts Rise in New Japan." *World Paper/Journal of Commerce* (November 1988): 4–5.

"Now That 'Zaitach' Party Is Over, Foreign Trust Banks Face Crossroads." *The Japan Economic Journal*, 11 June 1988, p. 1.

"NTT Price Slump Hurts Investors." *The Japan Economic Journal*, 19 December 1987, p. 6.

Ohta, Moriaki. "Foreign Automakers Venturing Out of Japanese Nest." *The Japan Economic Journal*, 18 February 1989, p. 2.

Okawara, Yoshio. "Constructive Approaches Are What We Need." *Tokyo Business Today* (November 1986): 10.

Okawara, Yoshio. "The Dangers of Neonationalism." *Tokyo Business Today* (November 1986): 22–26.

Okita, Saburo. "Japan is Advised to Diversify Investments to Aid Developing Nations' Economic Growth." *The Japan Economic Journal*, 30 August 1986, p. 7.

"Open Door Is Tight Squeeze for Women Managers." *The Japan Economic Journal*, 31 December 1988 and 7 January 1989, p. 9.

"The Opening of Japan." *The Economist*, 17 December 1988, pp. 69–70.

"Osaka Due Financial Futures Exchange." *The Japan Economic Journal*, 16 July 1988, p. 3.

Oshima, Izumi. "Havoc Lurks at Threshold of Sales-Tax Maze." *The Japan Economic Journal*, 25 February 1989, p. 32.

Oshima, Izumi. "Shoppers' Pay-in-Advance Cards Challenge Cash." *The Japan Economic Journal*, 16 July 1988, p. 28.

Ostrom, Douglas. "The Changing Japanese Consumer." *Japan Economic Institute Report*, No. 45A, 2 December 1988.

"Overseas Research Yields Advantages." *The Japan Economic Journal*, 18 June 1988, p. 15.

"Panel Sets Steps To Streamline Distribution." *The Japan Economic Journal*, 9 July 1988, p. 2.

"Pity Those Poor Japanese." *The Economist*, 24 December 1988, pp. 48–50.

"Price No Barrier for '88 Consumer Favorites." *The Japan Economic Journal*, 28 January 1989, p. 8.

"Problems Experienced by Japanese Companies Investing in the EC: Keidanren Survey." *Keidanren Review* (February 1986): 8–11.

"Rapid Increase in Japanese Overseas M&A." *Tokyo Business Today* (January 1989): 20.

"Rapid Recovery in Foreign Bank Profits." *Tokyo Business Today* (October 1988): 26–29.

"Reagan and Takeshita Sign Accord on Scientific Research." *The Washington Post*, 21 June 1988, p. A15.

"Recruit." *Asahi Evening News*, 25 November 1988, p. 6.

"The Recruit Expose." *Tokyo Business Today* (October 1988): 22–24.

"Removing Barriers to Joint Studies." *Look Japan*, 10 August 1986, p. 14.

"Research and Development Stunted in Japan?" *Japan Economic Institute Report*, No. 17B, 21 April 1988, p. 11.

"The Rise and Rise of the Japanese Yuppie." *Business Week*, 16 February 1987, pp. 54–56.

"Rethinking Japan," *Business Week*, August 7, 1989, p. 44.

Sashida, Akio. "The Shock of the 'New.'" *The Japan Times*, 9 March 1986.

Sashida, Akio. "The 'Youthquake' and Business." *The Japan Times*, 10 March 1986, p. 6.

Sato, Seizaburo, and Matsuzaki, Tetsuhisa. "Policy Leadership by the Liberal Democrats." *Economic Eye* (December 1984): 25–32.

Saxonhouse, Gary R. "The Micro- and Macroeconomics of Foreign Sales to Japan." In *Trade Policy in the 1980s*. Edited by William R. Cline. Washington, D.C.: Insitute for International Economics, 1983, pp. 259–304.

Schofield, Michael J. "Japan's Distribution System: Manufacturers and Middlemen." *Tokyo Business Today* (May 1987): 20–22.

Schreffler, Roger. "Japan: Targeting a Tough Market." *Distribution* (October 1987): 44–45 +.

"Sci/Tech Diplomacy." *The Japan Economic Journal*, 2 March 1988, p. 26.

"Science and Technology Agreement." *Japan Economic Institute Report*, No. 14B, 8 April 1988, p. 10.

"Science and Technology Agreement May be Finalized at Toronto Summit." *Japan Economic Institute Report*, No. 23B, 17 June 1988, pp. 4–5.

Scott, Bruce R. "National Strategies: Key to International Competition." In *U.S. Competitiveness in the World Economy*. Edited by Bruce R. Scott and George C. Lodge. Boston: Harvard Business School Press, 1985.

"Selling in Japan Gets Less Befuddling." *Business Week*, 20 February 1989, pp. 122B–122F.

"Shakeout of Joint Ventures in Japan." *Tokyo Business Today* (July 1987): 11.

Shapiro, Margaret, and Hiatt, Fred. "Japan: From Pauper to Patron in 25 Years." *The Washington Post*, 22 February 1989, pp. A1 +.

Shibayama, Shigehisa. "Discount Stores Win Big Selling Cheap Imports." *The Japan Economic Journal*, 12 March 1988, p. 3.

"A Shopping Spree Starts Turning Japan Around." *Business Week*, 17 August 1987, pp. 50–51.

"Sogo Banks on the Way Out." *Tokyo Business Today* (November 1988): 8.

"Sogo Shosha Switch Emphasis to Domestic Market." *Tokyo Business Today* (February 1988): 26–30.

"Sogo Shosha: Sales Department of Japan, Inc." *Tokyo Business Today* (April 1986): 50–55.

"Steady Growth Due to Expanded Domestic Demand." *Tokyo Business Today* (November 1988): 8–9.

Sternberg, Ron. "Japanese and U.S. Ad Agencies: There is a Big Difference." *The Journal of the ACCJ* (June 1988): 18–20.

"Stock Scandals May Unravel Entwined Corporate Relations." *The Japan Economic Journal*, 6 August 1988, pp. 1 +.

"Struggle for Survival." *Tokyo Business Today* (March 1987): 38–42.

"Subsidiaries Reunite." *Tokyo Business Today* (January 1988): 46–48.

"Survey Japan: A Job for Life No More." *The Economist*, 5 December 1987, pp. 17–18+.

Takahashi, Noburo. "Success Awaits Savvy Foreign Firms in Japan." *The Japan Economic Journal*, 12 March 1988, p. 3.

Takahashi, Noburo. "Pension Officials Get the Gray-Folks Blues." *The Japan Economic Journal*, 3 December 1988, p. 32.

"Technological Innovation Drives Structural Changes in Corporations." *The Japan Economic Journal*, 4 June 1988, p. 26.

"Technology Flow No Longer One Way." *The Japan Economic Journal*, 16 July 1988, p. A1.

"Technology Friction." *Asahi Evening News*, 1 February 1988, p. 3.

Thayer, Nathaniel B. "Nakasone Is Not a Racist." *The Washington Post*, 30 September 1986, p. A15.

"Thoughts on August 15." *Asahi Shimbun*, 16 August 1986, p. 9.

"Tokyo Stock Exchange Names Members." *The Japan Economic Journal* (January 1988): 2.

"Tokyo Stock Exchange to Admit 16 Foreign Securities Firms." *Asahi Evening News*.

"Tokyo Stock Market Emerges as World Leader." *Tokyo Business Today* (May 1988): 46–47.

Tokyo Urgently Needs Finance Center Complex." *The Japan Economic Journal*, 27 February 1988, p. 3.

"Too Many Shopkeepers." *The Economist*, 28 January 1989, pp. 70–71.

"Trade Unions Realigning." *Tokyo Business Today* (April 1988): 54–55.

Tsuchhiya, Hideo. "Japan Cashing in on New Wealth." *The Japan Economic Journal*, Special Edition (February 1989): B1+.

"Tsukuba Net To Ease Technical Data Exchange." *The Japan Economic Journal*, 26 March 1988, p. 27.

Uchida, Masaru. "The Changing Japanese Market." *Journal of Japanese Trade & Industry* (No. 1, 1986): 36–37.

"U.S. Pressure Riles High-Tech Industry." *The Japan Economic Journal*, 20 February 1988, p. 3.

"Undervalued Assets Alter Stock Price Picture." *The Japan Economic Journal*, 23 July 1988, p. 4.

"University, Industry Seek Research Cooperation." *The Japan Economic Journal* (January 1988).

White, Theodore. "The Danger of Japan." *The New York Times Magazine*, 28 July 1985, pp. 18–22+.

"World Economy Survey: Consumers, Every One." *The Economist*, 24 September 1988, p. 51.

Yamamoto, Shuji. "The Characteristics of Japan's Distribution System." *Tokyo Business Today* (February 1986): 22–25.

Yoshikawa, Miho. "Spotty Quality Tarnishes Image of NIE Products." *The Japan Economic Journal*, 1 April 1989, p. 4.

Yoshikawa, Miho. "Visa, MasterCard Link-ups Spark New Credit Card Battle." *The Japan Economic Journal*, 5 November 1988, pp. 1 +.

Zengage, Thomas R. "New Media and New Directions in Advertising." *Tokyo Business Today* (August 1987): 36–40.

Asahi Evening News (Tokyo), 25 April 1986, p. 9; 20 May 1986; 2 August 1986; 20 December 1986, p. 7; 25 December 1987; 1 February 1988, p. 3; 21 July 1988, p. 5.

The Asian Wall Street Journal Weekly, 6 March 1988, p. 6.

Business Week, 8 April 1985; 5 May 1986; 14 July 1986; 24 November 1986; 11 July 1988, p. 72; 18 July 1988, pp. 137–138; September 19, 1988, pp. 100–135; 8 April 1984, p. 53.

The Daily Yomiuri (Tokyo), 28 March 1986, p. 5.

The Economist, 10 December 1988, pp. 1–36.

Japan Economic Institute Report (Washington, D.C.: Japan Economic Institute), No. 6A, 12 February 1988; No. 16B, 21 April 1988; No. 17B, 29 April 1988; No. 22A, 10 June 1988; No. 25B, 1 July 1988; No. 34A, 2 September 1988; No. 35B 16 September 1988; No. 36B, 25 September 1988; No. 42B, 4 November 1988; No. 43B, 11 November 1988; No. 45B, 2 December 1988; No. 47B, 16 December 1988.

The Japanese Economic Journal, 18 January 1986; 22, 29 March 1986; 12 April 1986; 3 May 1986; 7 June 1986, p. 1; 5 July 1986, p. 7; 9, 30 August 1986; 6, 13 September 1986; 11, 18, 12 October 1986; 1, 15 November 1986; 13 December 1986; 28 November 1987, p. 31; 19 December 1987, p. 6; 16 January 1988, p. 2; 11 February 1988, p. 10; 5 March 1988, p. 1, 26; 26 March 1988, p. 27; 30 April 1988, p.4; 7 May 1988, p. 22; 14 May 1988, pp. 1, 7; 4 June 1988 p. 26; 11 June 1988, p. 1; 16 July 1988, p. A1; 23 July 1988, p. 3, 4, A1; 13 August 1988, p. 21; 10 September 1988, p. 10, 21; 15 October 1988, p. 4; 22 October 1988, p. 23; 29 October 1988, p. 22; 24 December 1988, p. 25; 11 February 1989, p. 2; 25 February 1989, p. 19.

Japan Economic Survey, Washington, D.C.: Japan Economic Institute, February 1989.

The Japan Times, 7, 12, 16 March 1986; 24, 28 April 1986; 28 July 1986; 28 August 1986; 14 October 1986.

The Journal of Commerce (New York), 7 July 1986; 10 February 1989, p. 7A; November 1988, pp. 4, 5.

Look Japan, 10 August 1986, p. 14.

Mainichi Daily News, 14 February 1988.

The New York Times, 1 September 1985; 18 January 1986, p. 36; 3 May 1986; 17 January 1989, p. 27.

Tokyo Business Today, July 1987, p. 11; August 1987, p. 6; April 1988, pp. 48–49; May 1988, pp. 44–47; October 1988, p. 21, 44–45; November 1988, pp. 8, 64: January 1989, pp. 14–16.

The Wall Street Journal, 23 October 1985, p. 36; 13 December 1985; 29 August 1986, p. 20; 14 March 1988, p. 12; 27 April 1989, p. A13.

The Washington Post, 31 July 1985, p. F-1; 15 September 1986, p. A10; 14 March 1988, p. 11; 21 June 1988, p. A15; 28 March 1989.

Books

Abegglen, James C., and Stalk, George Jr. *Kaisha: The Japanese Corporation.* New York: Basic books, Inc., 1985.

Aho, Michael, and Aronson, Jonnathan Davis. *Trade Talks: America Better Listen.* New York: Council on Foreign Relations, 1986.

Balassa, Bela, and Noland, Marcus. *Japan In the World Economy.* Washington, D.C.: Institute for International Economics, 1988.

Bergsten, C. Fred, and Cline, William R. *The United States–Japan Economic Problem.* Washington, D.C.: Institute for International Economics, 1985 and 1987.

Burstein, Daniel. *Yen! Japan's New Financial Empire and Its Threat to America.* New York: Simon and Schuster, 1988.

Dentsu Japan Marketing/Advertising Yearbook, 1988. Tokyo: Dentsu Incorporated, 1987.

Destler, I.M.; Fukui, Haruhiro; and Sato, Hideo. *The Textile Wrangle: Conflicts in Japanese-American Relations 1969–1971.* Ithaca, N.Y.: Cornell University Press, 1979.

Destler, I.M., and Sato, Hideo. *Coping with U.S.–Japanese Economic Conflicts.* Lexington, Mass.: D.C. Heath, 1982.

Fields, George. *The Japanese Market Culture.* Tokyo: The Japan Times Limited, July 1988.

Higashi, Chikara. *Japanese Trade Policy Formulation.* New York: Praeger Publishers, 1983.

JETRO. *The Japanese Market: A Compendium of Information :For the Prospective Exporter.* Tokyo: Japan External Trade Organization, 1987.

Johnson, Chalmers. *MITI and the Japanese Miracle.* Stanford, Calif.: Stanford University Press, 1982.

Kennedy, Paul. *The Rise and Fall of Great Powers.* New York:. Random House, 1987.

Ogura, Kazuo. *U.S.–Japan Economic Conflict.* Tokyo: Nihon Keizai Shimbum, 1982.

Ohmae, Kenichi. *Triad Power: The Coming Shape of Global Competition.* New York: Free Press, 1985.

McCraw, Thomas K., ed. *America versus Japan: A Comparative Study.* Boston: Harvard Business School, 1986.

Mouer, Ross, and Sugimoto, Yoshio. *Images of Japanese Society.* London: KPI Limited, 1986.

Pepper, Thomas; Janow, Merit E.; and Wheeler, Jimmy W. *The Competition: Dealing With Japan.* New York: Praeger Publishers, 1985.

Porter, Michael E., ed. *Competition in Global Industries.* Boston: Harvard Business School Press, 1986.

Prestowitz, Clyde, Jr., *Trading Places: How We Allowed Japan To Take the Lead.* New York: Basic Books Inc., Publishers, 1988.

Rosecrance, Richard. *The Rise of the Trading State.* New York: Basic Book, Inc., 1986.

Tolchin, Martin and Susan, *Buying into America*. New York: Time Books, 1988.
Vogel, Ezra F. *Japan as Number One*. Cambridge: Harvard University Press , 1979.
Wolf, Marvin. *The Japanese Conspiracy*. New York: Empire Books, 1983.
Wolferen, van Karel, *The Enigma of Japanese Power*. New York: Alfred A. Knopf, 1989.

Studies

Columbia University Graduate School of Business. *the Performance of Foreign Affiliated Firms in America*. New York: Graduate School of Business, Columbia University, 1989.
Japan Committee for Economic Development (Keizai Doyukai). *Technological Innovation and the Changing Industrial Society*. Tokyo: Japan Committee for Economic Development, 1985.
———. *Management Strategy—A Japan–U.S.A. Comparative Study*. Tokyo: Japan Productivity Center, October 1986.
Japan External Trade Organization. *Japanese Manufacturing Companies Operating in Europe*. Tokyo: Japan External Trade Organization, 1986.
Organization for Economic Cooperation and Development. *Costs and Benefits of Protection*. Paris: organization for Economic Cooperation and Development, 1985.

Special Reports

Organization for Economic Cooperation and Development. *Japan*. Paris: Organization for Economic Cooperation and Development, 1985.
———. *Japan*. Paris: Organization for Economic Cooperation and Development, 1988.
———. *Urban Policies in Japan*. Paris: Organization for Economic Cooperation and Development, 1986.
U.S.–Japan Trade Study Group. *Progress Report: 1984*. Tokyo: U.S.–Japan Trade Study Group, 1984.
U.S.–Japan Trade Study Group. *TSG Progress Report 1986*. Tokyo: U.S.–Japan Trade Study Group, September 1986.
The Advisory Committee for External Economic Issues. *Report of the Advisory Committee for External Economic Issues*. Tokyo: 9 April 1985.
The Report on the Advisory Group on Economic Structural Adjustment for International Harmony. Tokyo: Advisory Group on Economic Structural Adjustment for International Harmony, 1986 and 1987.

Statistical Summaries

Japan Economic Alliance: 1988. Tokyo: Japan Economic Journal, 1988.
Keizai Koho Center. *Japan 1985: An International Comparison*. Tokyo: Keizai Koho Center, 1985.

———. *Japan 1986: An International Comparison.* Tokyo: Keizai Koho Center, 1986.

———. *Japan 1988: An International Comparison.* Tokyo: Keizai Koho Center, 1987.

Tokyo Chamber of Commerce and Industry. *Japan and the World in Statistics: 1986* Tokyo: Tokyo Chamber of Commerce and Industry, 1986.

World Bank, *1983 World Bank Atlas.* Washington, D.C.: The World Bank, 1983.

Statements

Keizai Koho Center. *How Can Japan Contribute to a Healthy World Economy.* Tokyo: Keizai Koho Center, March 1986.

———. "Needed: More Active Economic Cooperation." Tokyo: Keizai Koho Center, 28 June 1986.

Government Sources
United States

Congressional Budget Office. "The Effects of Targeted Import Surcharges." Staff Working Paper. Washington, D.C.: Congressional Budget Office, 1985.

Congressional Research Service. *Economic Changes in the Asian Pacific Rim: Policy Prospectus.* Washington, D.C.: Congressional Research Service, August, 1986.

General Accounting Office. *United States–Japan Trade: Issues and Problems.* Washington, D.C.: Government Accounting Office, 1979.

Office of the United States Trade Representative. *The Japanese Government, External Economic Measures: The U.S. Government's Assessment of Their Implementation and Impact.* Washington, D.C.: Office of the United States Trade Representative, 1984.

Office of the United States Trade Representative. *National Trade Estimate: 1986 Report on Foreign Trade Barriers.* Washington, D.C.: Office of the United States Trade Representative, 1986.

U.S. Congress. Joint Economic Committee. *Industrial Policy Movement in the United States: Is it the Answer?.* Washington, D.C.: U.S. Government Printing Office, 1984.

U.S. Congress. Joint Economic Committee. *The U.S. Trade Position in High Technology: 1980–1986.* Washington, D.C.: Joint Economic Committee, October 1986.

U.S. Department of Commerce. Office of Budget Analysis. *Trade Ripples Across U.S. Industries.* Working Paper. Washington, D.C.: U.S. Department of Commerce, 1986.

U.S. Department of State. *U.S.–Japan Joint Report on Sectoral Discussions*, by George Shultz and Shintaro Abe. Washington, D.C.: U.S. Department of State, 10 January 1986.

U.S. President. *Economic Report of the President.* Washington, D.C.: U.S. Government Printing Office, 1986.

U.S. President. *Economic Report of the President*. Washington, D.C.: U.S. Government Printing Office, 1987.

Vogt, Donna U. "Japanese Import Barriers to U.S. Agricultural Exports." Report No. 85–153 ENR. Washington, D.C.: Congressional Research Service, Library of Congress, 1986.

Japan

Economic Planning Agency. *Economic Survey of Japan (1984–1985)*. Tokyo: Economic Planning Agency, 1985.

———. *40 Years Since the End of World War II: On the Threshold of the Age of Maturity*. Tokyo: Economic Planning Agency, 1986.

———. Internal Working Papers. Tokyo: n.p., March 1986.

———. Internal Working Papers. Tokyo: n.p., May 1986.

———. *Outlook and Guidelines for the Economy and Society in the 1980s*. Tokyo: Economic Planning Agency, August 1983.

———. *White Paper on National Life: FY 1986*. Tokyo: Economic Planning Agency, 1986.

———. *White Paper on the Japanese Economy*. Tokyo: Economic Planning Agency, 1988.

Economic Planning Agency, Economic Council, Long Term Outlook Committee. *Japan in the Year 2000*. Tokyo: The Japan Times Ltd., 1983.

Fair Trade Commission. Internal Documents. Tokyo: n.p., March 1986.

Japanese Government-Ruling Parties Joint Headquarters for the Promotion of External Economic Measures. *The Action Program for Improved Market Access*. Tokyo: 1985.

Ministry of International Trade and Industry. *Japan in the Global Community: Its Role and Contributions on the Eve of the Twenty-First Century*. Report of Roundtable Discussions on "Japan in the Global Community." Tokyo: Ministry of International Trade and Industry, April 1986.

Ministry of International Trade and Industry. *White Paper on Small and Medium Enterprises in Japan, 1985*. Tokyo: Ministry of International Trade and Industry, 1985.

Ministry of International Trade and Industry, Industrial Structure Council. *The Vision of MITI Policies in the 1980s*. Tokyo: Ministry of International Trade and Industry, March 1980.

Ministry of International Trade and Industry, Industrial Structure Council, Coordination Committee, Planning Subcommittee. *An Outlook for Japan's Industrial Society Towards the 21st Century*. Interim Report Focusing on International Perspective. Tokyo: Ministry of International Trade and Industry, February 1986. Internal Documents. Tokyo: n.p., May 1986.

Ministry of Labor. Internal Dcouments. Tokyo: n.p., March 1986.

Office of the Prime Minister. *Survey on People's Life*. Tokyo: Office of the Prime Minister, 1985.

Office of the Prime Minister. *Survey on National Attitudes on Living Standards*. Tokyo: Office of the Prime Minister, 1986.

Appendix A
The Repetitive Pattern of
U.S.–Japan Trade Conflicts

While minor trade skirmishes went on most of the time, the first event in a major U.S.–Japan trade conflict usually involved the publication of trade data in the United States showing the nation's deteriorating global trade balance in general, and worsening bilateral trade balance with Japan in particular. Extensive treatment of these disputes by the mass media usually ignored the complex underlying causes, and this was normally accompanied by equally questionable statements and speeches by those members of Congress whose districts encompassed the most affected industries. The gradually more aggressive and protectionist rhetoric was eventually joined by those other members of Congress who found it politically expedient to do so. Since they all knew that any President would veto a strongly protectionist bill, they enjoyed what is known in Washington parlance as a "free ride"; members of Congress received the benefits of political posturing without the possibility of incurring any cost to themselves or to the nation. Simultaneously, the Administration was compelled to find ways to satisfy Congressional demands without relenting too much to the special interest groups; the Administration had to juggle its free trade stance and protect America's international trade obligations while maintaining good relations with its most important ally in the Far East. If Congressional elections were on the horizon, such maneuvers, difficult even under the best of circumstances, called for a great deal of political savvy and visible White House actions. One of the ways to achieve these ends was either to continue existing negotiations or to initiate a new round of talks with the Japanese, who at this point were usually relying on their Washington lobbyists for insights into unfolding events and cues on how to react. The narrowly defined American negotiation demands were usually accompanied by tough Administration statements issued partially to pressure the Japanese and partially to appease the Congressional critics who blamed the Administration for not doing enough for America's farmers and manufacturers.

Throughout all this, the Japanese mass media representatives in Washington fielded their exaggerated reports about the increasingly ugly mood in America and the Congressional activities shaping punitive legislation directed against Japan. They embellished the basic theme that the large, but now ineffient, America was again intimidating the small, but efficient, Japan with whatever illustrative stories they could find. Amid emotionally charged atmospheres, the negotiations, interspersed with Congressional hearings, disagreements along party lines, clashes among interest groups, and the usual give-and-take between Congress and the Administration, proceeded at a snail's pace. Delays were caused by the Japanese who had no proactive negotiation strategy and were usually engaged in consensus-building across several ministries, interest groups, and some key Liberal Democratic Party politicians who wanted to make the most of any difficulty the Prime Minister faced to strengthen their domestic political base for the time when their chance to take the government helm would arrive. The delayed Japanese responses to the forceful American demands were usually defensive and, more often than not, took the form of a "package" of market access measures. The Americans, exhausted by the long negotiations and irritated by what they saw as deceptive Japanese strategies, were additionally frustrated by the packages which could not possibly reduce the trade imbalances, no matter how unrealistic such expectations were in the first place, Americans regularly accused the Japanese of "doing too little, too late." The Japanese, upset by the outright rejection of what they considered to be their best efforts, were indignant, and felt misunderstood and unappreciated. To the Japanese the sentiments about the unreasonable and aggressive Americans were proved all over again.

Eventually some sort of accommodation was reached. More often than not, the accommodation involved Japanese concessions, and this usually enabled both sides to take a respite. However, it was just a matter of time before the entire major conflicts cycle repeated itself. The only difference might have been a change in the Administration, slightly realigned Congress, or maybe a new Prime Minister in Tokyo; regardless, attitudes and approaches remained the same.

Appendix B
Financial Deregulation Measures:
1985 to Mid-1989

- January 20, 1985:   The withholding tax on Euroyen instruments held by nonresidents was repealed.
- February 1985:   Direct brokering of yen-dollar exchange was started.
- March 1985:   Money Market Certificate (MMC) was created (minimum unit: Y50 million or $400,000).
- April 1, 1985:   A short-term government bond market was introduced.
- April 1985:   Middle-term and long-term Euro-yen loans were deregulated.
- June 1, 1985:   Securities houses were now allowed to trade in CDs (in March 1985, 13 banks were first permitted to trade in CDs).
- June 1985:   Yen-denominated banker's acceptance market was established.
                       Entry of non-Japanese banks to trust banking business was approved.
- October 15, 1985:   In order to support the newly introduced short-term government bills, a government bond futures market was established.
- January 1986:   Bank of Japan (BOJ) began spot operations in government short-term securities.
- February 1986:   The Tokyo stock Exchange (TSE) permitted membership of six non-Japanese security firms.
                       U.S.: Merrill Lynch Japan Inc., Goldman Sachs Japan Corp., and Morgan Stanley International Ltd.
                       U.K.: Vickers da Costa Ltd., Jardine Fleming (Securities) Ltd., and S.G. Warburg Securities (Japan) Inc.
                       Short-term government bond was issued in open bidding.

- March 1986:   Easing of operating rules for handling foreign securities by life and non-life insurance companies were eased.
- April 1986:   Minimum deposit unit for large-term deposit was lowered to Y500 million. Conditions on MMC were made more flexible.
  Restrictions on sale of government bonds were eased.
  Issuing conditions for CDs were made flexible.
- May 1986:   Spot trusts market permitted small and medium-size securities houses to manage investment trusts.
- July 1986:   Settlement period for bond transaction was shortened to maximum 20 days.
- By mid-1986:   The Euroyen market was all but completely liberalized.
- September 1986:   Minimum unit for large term deposit was reduced to Y300 million ($2.4 million) and MMC brought down to a minimum of Y30 million ($240,000).
- October 1986:   Variable life insurance was introduced into the market.
- November 26, 1986:   Regulations leading to stricter control on the investment consulting business were introduced due to the rapid increase in fraud brought on by the investment boom.
- December 1, 1986:   Tokyo's offshore market, Tokyo International Banking Facility, was opened.
- 1986:   New capital ratio rules were enforced mandating that a bank's net-worth-to-total-asset ratio had to be 4 percent by end of fiscal 1986. There was a tightening of the accounting methods for loans to subsidiaries and loan guarantees.
- February 1987:   Qualification standards for unsecured bonds were eased.
- April 1 1987:   Interest rate decontrol — the issue ceiling for CDs and MMCs was increased to 300 percent from 250 percent. Minimum unit for large-term deposit was reduced from Y300 million to Y100 million. MMC's minimum deposit unit reduced (Y30 million to Y20 million) and maximum term was extended (1 year to 2 years).

Issuing of convertible bonds by regular banks was approved.

Commissions of securities were reduced.

• May 11, 1987: The maximum settlement period on a banker's acceptance was increased to one year from a previous six months, and the minimum unit in this market was reduced from Y100 million ($800,000) to Y50 million ($400,000).

• June 3, 1987: The MOF "widened its unofficial policy" allowing foreign banks to enter the securities market. U.S. banks were now allowed to create joint-venture securities firms with nonfinancial institutions if their interests did not go beyond 50 percent.

• June 9, 1987: Osaka Stock Exchange (OSE) began futures trading with the Kabusaki 50, a futures contract based upon a basket of 50 issues traded on the TSE (rather than the Nikkei 225 Average).

• June 1987: In order to increase foreign involvement in the primary bond market, foreign members of the bond-buying consortium were no longer required to open a special account with the Bank of Japan to be able to bid directly at actions.

• July 13, 1987: Japanese government bond futures were introduced in the London International Financial Futures Exchange. The subsequent trading of these bonds in the Chicago market in November of the same year commenced the 24-hour trading of this instrument.

• October 5, 1987: Further interest rate decontrol—the issue ceiling for CDs and MMCs were abolished; the minimum MMC was lowered to Y10 million ($80,000) and the minimum term for large deposit was reduced to one month from three months.

• October 20, 1987: Twenty-one seats were added to the TSE. New members were announced on December 16, 1987. Six seats were assigned to Japanese firms while 16 seats were assigned to foreign firms: 6 American, 4 British, 2 each from France, W. Germany and Switzerland (an extra seat was available due to a merger). New members began trading in May 23, 1988.

• October 19, 1987: A special panel was introduced to examine insider trading problems after a major bond futures trading scandal erupted.

• November 1987: An open auction system for 20-year bonds was introduced.

• November 20, 1987: A commercial paper market was introduced into the Japanese financial system; 178 companies were eligible to float offers. By the end of the year approximately 30 companies had issued stock. Also in an effort to further the cause of the international use of the yen, foreign firms were permitted to issue yen-denominated commercial paper in Europe.

• December 1987: The MOF has allowed *sogo* banks (mutual banks) to change their status to commercial following a recommendation by the Financial System Research Council.

• December 10, 1987: Japan was part of a "landmark international agreement" on the issue of bank capital adequacy ratios. The Bank of International Settlements set up the following guidelines to be met by 1992 for the banks of the ten industrialized nations: core capital (equity and retained earnings) must equal at least 4 percent of total risk-weighted assets, and this ratio must reach 8 percent when secondary capital is included. In this agreement Japanese banks could place 45 percent of their unrealized stock gains in secondary capital.

• January 5, 1988: The Japanese government eased *Tokkin* (specified trust) accounting rules so that companies do not have to report *Tokkin* losses due to the 1987 October stock crash.

• January 14, 1988: In order to have better control over the money supply, BOJ has set up new loan guidelines. BOJ has raised almost 40 percent of its new funds from the open market and bill market rather than on call as these markets are most strongly influenced by the central bank.

• April 1, 1988: The postal savings system and life insurance companies were allowed to sell government bonds over the counter.

MOF reduced the period between registration of a bond issue and its flotation from 30 days to 15 days.

• April 1988:   Nontaxable savings systems were changed.

Minimum deposit for large-term deposits was reduced to Y50 million ($400,000).

• May 25, 1988:   The diet passed the "Revised Securities and Exchange Law" and the "Financial Futures Trading Law."

• July 2, 1988:   A 24-hour futures market opened in TSE and OSE. Trading in government bond futures will be based on a fictitious 100-yen standard 20-year bond with a coupon of 6 percent, a minimum face value unit of Y100 million ($800,000), and maturities of 3, 6, 9, 12 and 15 months. The TSE began the trading of the Tokyo Stock Exchange Price Index (TOPIX) and the OSE, the trading of the Tokyo Stock Exchange Stock Price Averages futures.

• August 23, 1988:   In response to the TSE insider trading scandals the MOF received stronger surveillance powers (Article 154 of the Securities and Exchange Law).

• September 3, 1988:   Futures trading based on stock price index began on the TSE and OSE.

• October 1, 1988:   Introduction of specific regulations governing insider trading (Article 188 and 189).

• December 24, 1988:   Takeshita's tax reform package passed the upper house after an all-night session and became law on December 24, 1988. It will be implemented in stages. (Capital Gains Tax was introduced.)

• February 7, 1989:   MOF expanded ceiling on trust banks' investment in non-Japanese securities. Trust banks were allowed to invest up to 5 percent of total assets from a previous 3 percent.

• February 9, 1989:   MOF, TSE, and securities houses agreed to set rules on the allocation of new shares to third parties by listed companies. Rules were to

	become effective in April 1989.
• March 10, 1989:	Japan precious metals futures market permitted foreign firms to trade on the Tokyo Commodity Exchange for Industry (TOCOM). However, these foreign firms are only associate members of the exchange and must still place their trade orders through Japanese traders and are only allowed to trade for there own accounts.
• April 1, 1989:	New insider trading laws.
• April 1989:	Introduction of over-the-counter (OTC) bond options. Establishment of bond-leasing market and permission for short sale of bonds. Introduction of a competitive bidding system for underwriting 10-year government bonds.
• June 1, 1989:	MOF announced plans to ease controls on overseas personal bank accounts. This would allow Japanese residents to hold overseas bank accounts denominated in foreign currencies up to a maximum equivalent to Y5 million beginning July 1, 1989. Accounts holding foreign currencies valued up between Y5 million and Y30 million would be permitted for a maximum period of two years with permission from the Bank of Japan. Introduction of new small-lot MMCs.
• June 5, 1989:	Money Market Certificates with a floating interest rate and minimum value of Y3 million is introduced by banks as "Super MMCs" and by post offices as "Posts."
• June 5, 1989:	The Japanese government allowed banks to trade 10- and 20-year government bonds on behalf of individuals, companies or other institutions.
• June 12, 1989:	Japan's first true stock index option was made available to institutional investors in the Osaka Stock Exchange. The Index is based on the Nikkei Stock Average of 225 selected stocks.
• June 30, 1989:	Opening of the Tokyo International Financial Futures Exchange (TIFFE). TIFFE has 96

clearing members including 11 foreign firms. Both banks and securities houses can trade freely on either exchange and, with a few exceptions, they can both deal in most instruments such as stocks, bonds, currencies, and interest futures. Non-Japanese firms dealing exclusively in futures would not be subject to any restrictions; and the new system would be reviewed by 1990.

- December 1, 1989:   The TSE began trading in U.S. Treasury bond futures.

Appendix C
Highlights of the 1989 Insider
Trading Regulations

1. Material information not allowed under new law.
   a The following decisions are considered insider trading material information: bankruptcy filing, issuance of new shares, dividend change, mergers and acquisitions, recapitalization, share split, dissolution, commercialization of new technology, stock delisting.
   b The following events are considered unlawful to disclose without the proper discloure guidelines: litigation involving property rights, request for injunction, business failure, loss of major clients, discovery of natural resources.
   c The following settlement information is considered unlawful under the new laws: business forecasts, changes in pretax profits, and net profits of 30 percent or more.
2. The list of people who would qualify as insider traders if they engage in improper disclosure of information.
   a Insider traders: company executives and employees, major shareholders with 10 percent or more stock holdings.
   b Semi-insider traders: executives and employees of client banks and securities companies, employees of government regulatory agencies, attorneys, certified public accountants.
   c Recipients: those who have received materials information directly from insider traders or semi-insider traders.
3. Disclosure.
   Material information has to be publically announced through disclosure

to at least two media organizations. The information is considered public 12 hours after it is disclosed.
4. Penalties.
   Prison term of six months or less, or a fine not exceeding Y500,000 ($4,000).

Source: Ministry of Finance (Tokyo, March 1989).

Appendix D
1989 Capital Gains Tax Law

1. Capital gains from securities transactions will be taxed in one of two ways at the taxpayer's discretion:
   a Actual gains (gains minus losses in one calander year) will be subject to a 20 percent central and a 6 percent local tax.
   b One percent of the total transaction value will be withheld by securities brokers.
2. Restraint of insider trading:
   a Gains from the public sale of stock within three years of its initial public offering will be subject to a 20 percent tax. This applies only to those who held the stock before the initial public sale.
   b After the three-year period, half of any capital gain will be tax-exempt.
   c Founders and officials of the company will be subject to an additional one percent tax if they profit from the public sale of their stock within one year of the initial public offering.

Source: Ministry of Finance (Tokyo, March 1989).

Appendix E
Non-Japanese TSE Members as of
January 1989

The first six non-Japanese firms to join the 99-member exchange, in Feburary 1986, were:

U.S.	Merrill Lynch Japan Inc., Goldman Sachs Japan Corp., and Morgan Stanley International Ltd.
U.K.	Vickers da Costa Ltd., Jardine Fleming (Securities) Ltd., and S.G. Warburg Securities (Japan) Inc.

Following these admissions, the TSE granted 16 more memberships to non-Japanese securities houses effective May 1988:

U.S.   First Boston (Asia) Ltd., Kidder Peabody International
                Corp., Prudential-Bache Securities (Japan) Ltd., Shearson
                Lehman Brothers Asia Inc., Smith Barney, Harris Upham
                International Inc., and Solomon Brothers Asia Ltd.

U.K.   Baring Securities Ltd., County NatWest Securities Japan
                Ltd., Kleinwort Benson International Inc., and Schroder
                Securities (Japan) Ltd.

W. Germany   DB Capital Markets (Asia) Ltd. and Dresdner-ABD
                Securities Ltd.

Switzerland   SBCI Securities (Asia) Ltd. and UBS Phillips & Drew
                International Ltd.

France   Sogen Securities (North Pacific) Ltd. and W.I. Carr
                (Overseas) Ltd.

Appendix F
Interest Rate Liberalization
Through 1988

Dates	Large Scale Time Deposits Dep. Units	Terms	MMCS Dep. Units	Terms	Int. Rate	CDs Dep. Units	Terms
May. 79	—	—	—	—	—	Y500 m.	3 mth-6 mths
Apr. 85	—	—	Y50 mil.	1–6 mth	CD rts +0.75%	Y100 m.	1 mth-6 mths
Oct. 85	Y1 bil.	3 mths-3 years	↓	↓	↓	↓	↓
Apr. 86	Y500 m.	→	→	1 mth-1 year	→	→	1 mth-1 year
Sep. 86	Y300 m.	→	Y30 m.	→	→	→	→

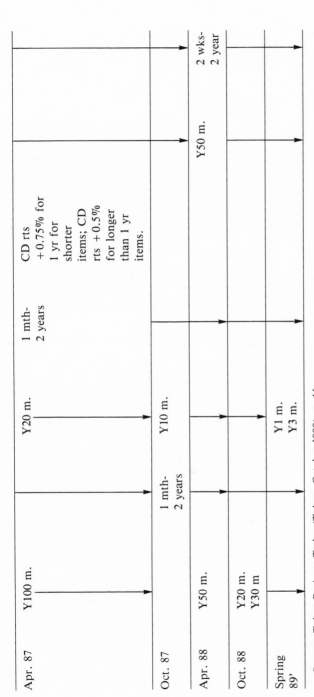

Apr. 87	Y100 m.	Y20 m.	1 mth-2 years	CD rts +0.75% for 1 yr for shorter items; CD rts +0.5% for longer than 1 yr items.		
Oct. 87		Y10 m.	1 mth-2 years			
Apr. 88	Y50 m.				Y50 m.	2 wks-2 year
Oct. 88	Y20 m. Y30 m					
Spring 89'		Y1 m. Y3 m.				

Source: *Tokyo Business Today (Tokyo, October 1988), p. 44.*

Appendix G
Bank of International Settlements
Guidelines

The December 1987 guidelines state that commercial banks in all member countries must raise their core capital (common equity capital and disclosed reserves) to 4 percent of total assets; total capital (core capital plus 45 percent of the current market value of stocks and bonds or other hidden reserves) must be 8 percent by 1992. Japanese bank's core capital ratios range from 2 percent to 3.5 percent; their total capital ratios are between 4 percent and 6 percent. Under the MOF rulings to ensure compliance with the BIS guidelines all Japanese banks engaged in international operations (currently 35 percent of all Japanese institutions) must raise their core capital ratios to a level between 5–6 percent and raise their overall capital-to-asset ratios to 7.25 percent by October 1, 1992 and then to the full BIS-mandated 8 percent by March 31, 1993.

Appendix H
The Key Points of the 1988
U.S.–Japan Science and
Technological Agreement

- Reciprocal access to scientist from both countries to each other's publicly funded research projects. The U.S-government-funded research is conducted primarily in universities, whereas, in Japan, government-sponsored or -supported programs are carried out behind closed doors in private companies.
- Overall theme to have public access to the research information, but specific steps were taken with dealing with the protection of the intellectual property rights issue.
- Neither country can disclose any discoveries that have military application; however, all other findings are for public use.

The other less controversial issues that Japan agreed to in principle were:
- Promoting not only joint research in nine areas (including super-conductors, biotechnology, information technology, and development of data bases) but also the promotion of major bilateral R&D projects in leading-edge technologies.
- Admitting U.S. researchers to projects jointly funded by the Japanese government and private sector.

- Transferring 30 government-sponsored R&D projects to new organizations which allows foreign researchers better access. For example: the basic technology development project and the fifth computer development project.
- Creating a senior-level governmental committee to discuss science and technology issues.
- Appropriating Y300 billion to accept 300 foreign researchers for fiscal 1988 through fellowships by MITI, the Ministry of Education, and the Science and Technology Agency; in addition, the formation of a Japanese language and cultural study center in Tsukuba for the foreign researchers.
- Including a provision stipulating that "ownership of patents and other intellectual property stemming from joint research projects will be granted to either the United States or Japan on a case-by-case basis, depending on the degree to which each country contributed to the research."
- Incorporating a measure clarifying that "national security considerations will be taken into account so that research does not fall into the hands of communist countries."

About the Authors

Dr. Chikara Higashi is a member of the Japanese Diet since 1983. He is also the Founding President of the Research and Exploration Center for International Affairs in Tokyo and the Chairman of the Board as well as the President of the Japanese branch of Temple University. Prior to entering politics, he was a career official in the Ministry of Finance where he advanced to the position of Special Adviser to the Minister. Dr. Higashi is a graduate of Tokyo University and received his doctorate from the School of Government and Business Administration of The George Washington University. He is the author of several books in Japanese on various domestic issues, of a number of English and Japanese articles, and, in English, *Japanese Trade Policy Formulation*, published by Praeger in 1983.

Dr. G. Peter Lauter is a professor of international business at the School of Government and Business Administration of The George Washington University in Washington, D.C. He is the author of three books and a number of scholarly articles on various aspects of international business. He served as a consultant to U.S. government agencies and to private business firms in the United States and abroad. Dr. Lauter is a senior associate of the Research and Exploration Center for International Affairs in Tokyo. He holds a Ph.D. from the Graduate School of Management of the University of California at Los Angeles.

INDEX